Mondrian and Cubism

Paris 1912–1914

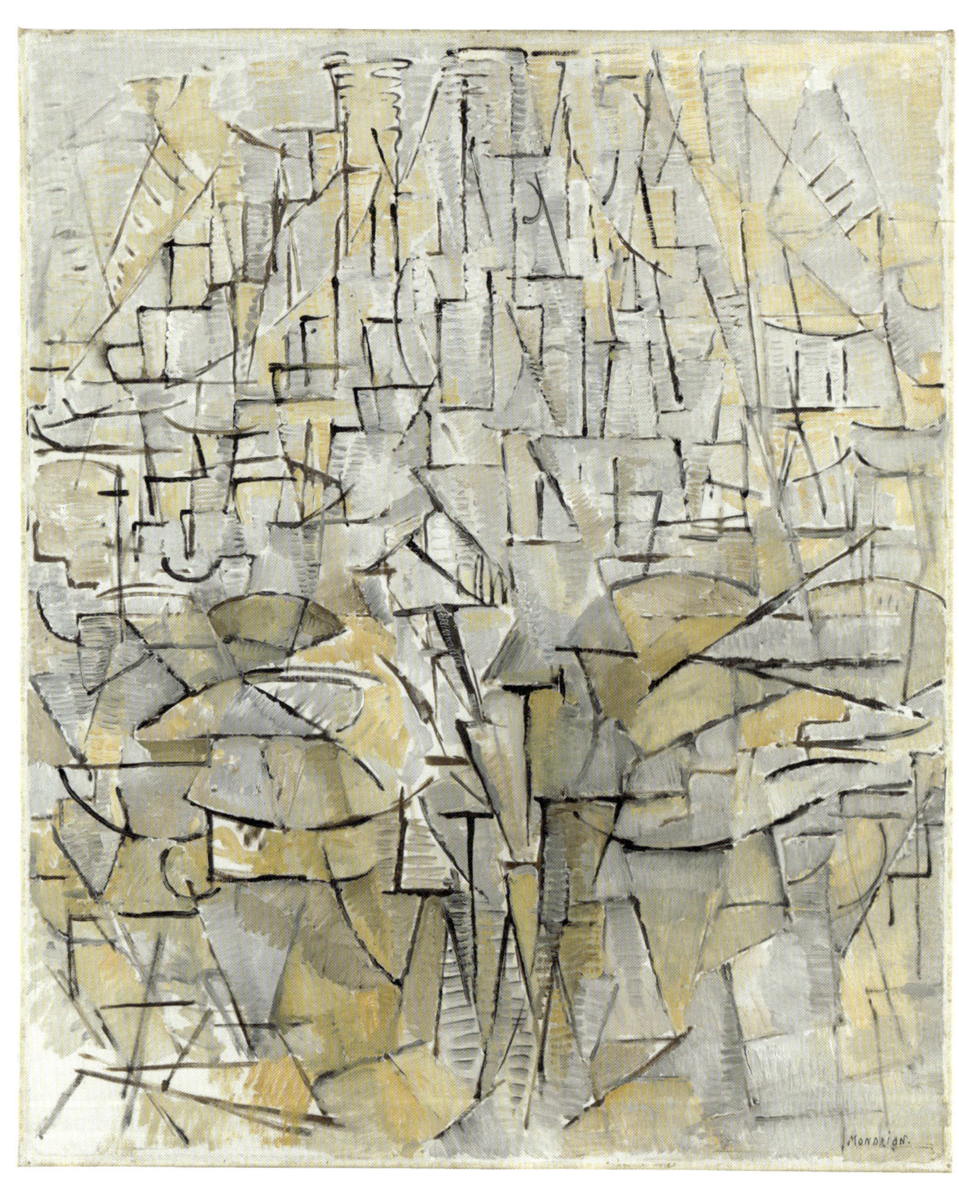

Composition NO. VIII 1913
(B27 – Tableau NO. 4 / Compositie NO. VIII / Compositie 3)
Oil on canvas, 95 x 80 cm
Gemeentemuseum Den Haag, The Hague

Mondrian and Cubism

Paris 1912–1914

Hans Janssen

Ridinghouse
Gemeentemuseum Den Haag

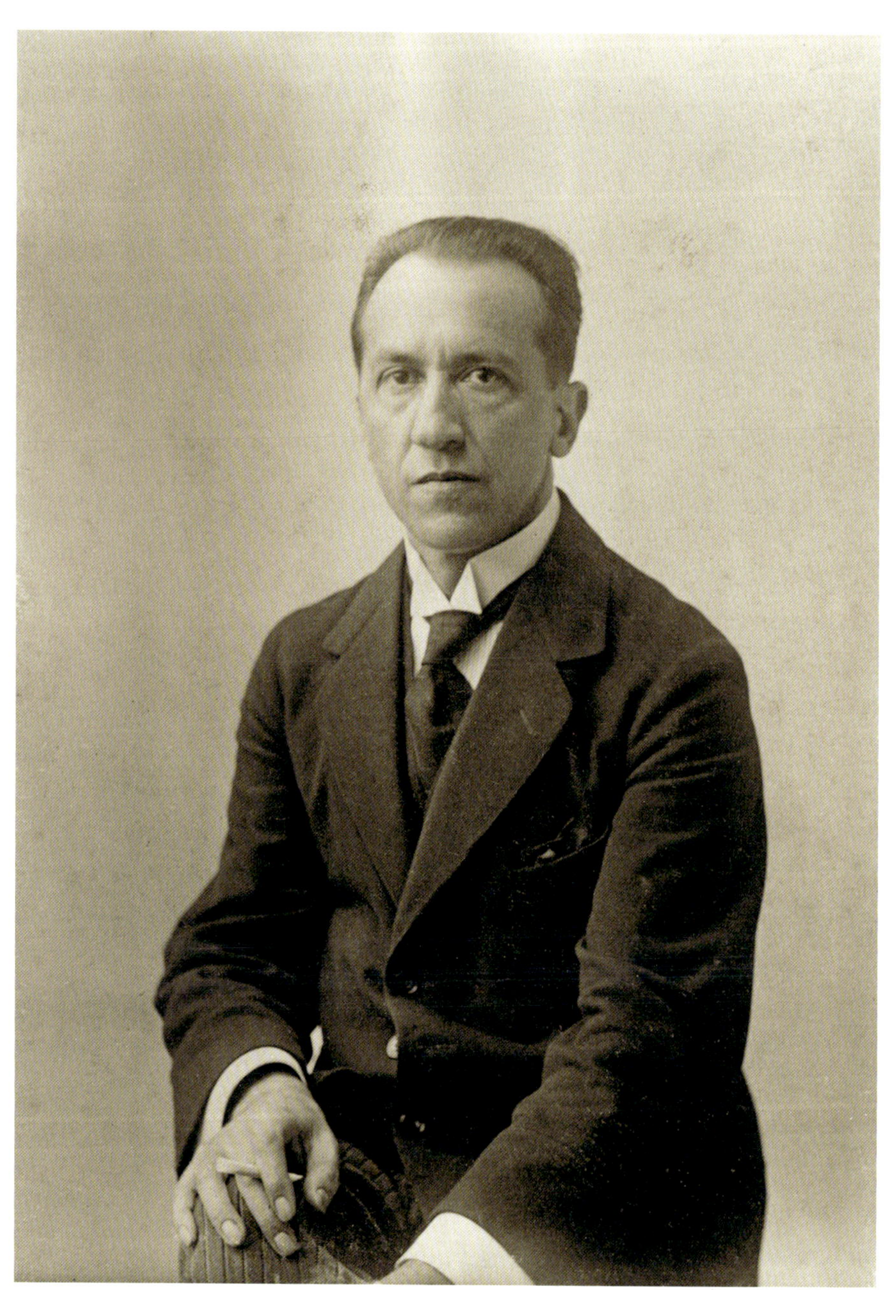

Piet Mondrian, 1917
Photographer unknown

Contents

Benno Tempel
Director of the Gemeentemuseum Den Haag

Preface

Looking back on the development of modern art more than a century later, we are unable to truly understand just how innovative Cubism was. Pablo Picasso and Georges Braque – the artists who produced the first Cubist paintings in Paris – dared to do something that no one else had thought of in all of the preceding centuries. A painting need not stick to reality but, released from the element of time, could show several sides of a person or an object at once. The image becomes fragmented. This idea unleashed an inconceivable flood of artistic innovation. Barely six years after the emergence of Cubism, the door to non-representational art stood wide open.

In the late autumn of 1911 Piet Mondrian decided to become involved in this new artistic development, and set off for Paris early the following year. Two-and-a-half years later he displayed the results of his quest at Kunsthandel Walrecht, The Hague: 17 paintings he had produced in Paris were shown to Dutch visitors and fellow artists. Exactly a hundred years later, in 2014, the Gemeentemuseum Den Haag marked the 70th anniversary of Mondrian's death by reconstructing that exhibition as precisely and comprehensively as possible. Strikingly, these works show us that Mondrian was already more daring than the Parisian Cubists. The fragmented image was confusing; to keep Cubism accessible, artists like Picasso and Braque would generally choose two main colours for their paintings, which often gave a tonal impression. To gain control of the edges of the painting Mondrian opted for the oval, giving the composition a calm and concentrated air.

In the paintings he produced between 1912 and 1914, there is a clear direction in the development of Mondrian's work. Sometimes the painting is top-heavy, with forms concentrated in the upper part (see *Composition No. VII*; p.104), and sometimes the reverse is true, with the emphasis on the bottom of the image (see *Composition No. I*; p.76). The titles alone – *Compositions* – indicate the free, musical role that line and colour were to play in these paintings. Mondrian quite deliberately pushed back some parts of the picture plane in order to emphasise the top or bottom of the picture. This often produced a pronounced horizontal (p.94) or vertical effect (p.84). Such observations clearly show that – more than in his earlier work – Mondrian was now letting himself be guided by colour and line, listening to what the composition wanted to become in his hand.

On studying the paintings in this important exhibition, one notices that they have an organic structure – for example the branches on a tree – and that the basis for the majority of the cubist paintings lay in the portfolio of naturalistic sketches that Mondrian took with him from Amsterdam to Paris in January 1912. When the artist then returned to Paris in 1919 after the First World War, he found his portfolio still intact. In this publication, the curator responsible for the Gemeentemuseum exhibition, Hans Janssen, links all 17 cubist paintings to specific sketches in Mondrian's portfolio for the first time.

But it is not only the interplay of colour and line that is so fascinating in these compositions, nor is it merely the way Mondrian transformed the basic image into something entirely unprecedented. In 1915, barely a year after the exhibition at Kunsthandel Walrecht, Mondrian wrote to art critic Augusta de Meester-Obreen, who at the time was writing a piece for the magazine *Elsevier's Geïllustreerd Maandschrift*:

> My idea is that an artwork should by plastic expression alone give a sensation of beauty and – in my work – one of the most general type. The rhythmic height and width expansion, or radiation, or whatever it is, is the very general image of the lovely commotion in the world. It is greater and more beautiful than anything a mere human can 'say' by individual depiction of the particular.

This quote clearly demonstrates Mondrian's intention in his cubist paintings. It was all about what the painting radiates, the thing that defines the beauty of every work of art and a matter of showing it in its purest form.

In 2009 the Gemeentemuseum Den Haag organised an exhibition entitled *Cézanne – Picasso – Mondrian: A New Perspective*, which centred around Mondrian's first encounter with the work of Picasso in 1911. Five years later the museum paid homage to Mondrian, the most important Dutch artist of the twentieth century. Since his death, the expressive power of his work has only increased.

We would like to thank all of the researchers and staff who helped make this project a success. Our colleagues in other countries were on hand to contribute when we asked, in what was often a time-consuming process. We are pleased that, thanks to the significant scholarship and publications coming from the Gemeentemuseum Den Haag in the past few years, so many of our international colleagues are eager to work together with the museum and our curator Hans Janssen. We are also grateful to Els Kerremans, who pushed the boundaries of design in order to make the results of the research accessible within this book. Above all, however, we would like to thank those who so generously loaned us the paintings – many of which are extremely fragile – for the reconstruction of the 1914 exhibition. The result is a worthy tribute to an extraordinary artist.

Hans Janssen

Foreword

In 2014 the Gemeentemuseum Den Haag presented an exhibition that reunited for the first time the 17 paintings that formed Mondrian's show at Kunsthandel Walrecht, The Hague, exactly a century ago, in 1914. The 1914 exhibition marked a huge watershed in Mondrian's career. The paintings in the exhibition – all made between his arrival in Paris in January 1912 and his temporary departure for The Hague in June 1914 – were carefully considered by the artist with the gallery space in mind. By closely examining the works with technological research and analysing the historical circumstances in which they were created, we have been able to learn not only about the intentions of the artist, but also the intricate details of the paintings' construction. Like his friend Albert van den Briel wrote in a letter to author JM Harthoorn on 3 December 1965, Mondrian himself always knew exactly what he tech-nically wanted to accomplish in a painting, although the experimental nature of his work did sometimes have startling, or even troubling, aspects at first.* Whilst eager to clarify technical issues to anyone interested, the artist was also convinced that it might not be very interesting, if at all understandable.*

Technological research is, in my opinion, only helpful up to a point. A macro photograph gives the impression we are penetrating a painting; an infrared photograph suggests looking into its bowels; an ultraviolet photograph glimpses at its construction in time. It must be remembered, however, that art history is a form of storytelling, and this particular adventure that Mondrian undertook between 1912 and 1914 was full of wonder. Although he was always convinced that the public should be informed of the reasons behind new artistic developments, Mondrian also disliked simplified statements. The reality of his practice can be regarded more closely to the act of searching for or stammering over words.* As long as we are conscious of the limitations of a purely scientific approach, I am convinced that it might bring us closer to Mondrian's search within this new art. Moreover, it allows the reader to follow the artist on his adventure by displaying all of the observations and showing them for what they are, rather than placing a thorough interpretation of the data on top of each painting and indeed the Walrecht exhibition as a whole. Interpretation of this important body of Mondrian's work can, and should, lay bare – not bury – what art reveals.

This project could not have been accomplished without the contributions of many individuals, above all the lenders to the exhibition. I would particularly like to thank Cynthia Albertson, conservator at the Museum of Modern Art, New York; Corey d'Augustine, conservator; Claire Barry, conservator at the Kimbell Art Museum, Fort Worth; Madeleine Bisschoff, conservator; Wietse Coppes at the Dutch Institute for Art History, The Hague; Sjoerd van Faassen, historian; Michael Gallagher, conservator at the Metropolitan Museum of Art, New York; Rik Klein Gotink, photographer; Keziah Goudsmit, art historian; Ruth Hoppe, conservator at the Gemeentemuseum Den Haag, The Hague; Guus Janssen, composer; Joop M Joosten, art historian; Margje Leeuwestein, conservator at the Kröller-Müller Museum, Otterlo; Jan Erik van Regteren Altena, violonist in the Mondrian Quartet, Amsterdam; Lidwien Speleers, conservator; Arnold Truyen at Stichting Restauratie Atelier Limburg; Katja van Wetten, conservator at the Staatsgalerie Stuttgart, Stuttgart; Louise Wijnberg, conservator at the Stedelijk Museum, Amsterdam.

We also wish to thank the following for their unstinting kindness and help at various stages during the preparations of exhibition and catalogue: Paloma Alarcó, Director at the Museo Thyssen-Bornemisza, Madrid; Henning Autzen, conservator at the Staatsgalerie Stuttgart, Stuttgart; Louis Baltussen at Van Abbemuseum, Eindhoven; Jim Coddington, Chief of Conservation at the Museum of Modern Art, New York; Brenna Cothran at ESKart LLC, New York; Leah Dickerman, curator at the Museum of Modern Art, New York; Gillian McMillan, Associate Chief of Conservation at the Solomon R. Guggenheim Museum, New York; and Lisette Pelsers, Director at the Kröller-Müller Museum, Otterlo.

An English edition of our catalogue was suggested to us by Karsten Schubert at Ridinghouse. I am grateful to him and his team for embracing this project so enthusiastically and for working so hard on its realisation. Special thanks are due to Louisa Green and Diana Perry Schnelle who supervised the project from its inception.

In particular, however, I would like to thank Bridget Riley. She was deeply intrigued by the first, Dutch edition of this book that accompanied an exhibition at the Gemeentemuseum, and her enthusiasm for this important project has driven the publication of this English edition. I would therefore like to dedicate this book to her.

* Albert van den Briel, letter to JM Harthoorn, 3 December 1965. Reproduced in *Herbert Henkels, 't Is alles een groote eenheid, Bert', Piet Mondriaan, Albert van den Briel en hun vriendschap aan de hand van brieven, documenten en fragmenten bezorgd en van een nawoord voorzien door Herbert Henkels,* Joh. Enschedé, Haarlem, 1988, pp.107-09.

Editor's note: All of Mondrian's paintings mentioned in this publication are referred to by the titles the artist gave them for the exhibition at the Kunsthandel Walrecht, The Hague, in 1914. All other titles that Mondrian gave the paintings in earlier and later exhibitions are given in accordance with Joop M Joosten and Robert P Welsh, *Piet Mondrian: Catalogue Raisonné of the Work of 1911–1944*, vol.2, Prestel, Munich, 1998. Where reference is made to these paintings in the captions they are listed in parenthesis and their number in the catalogue raisonné is given.

Hans Janssen

Chronology 1911–1914

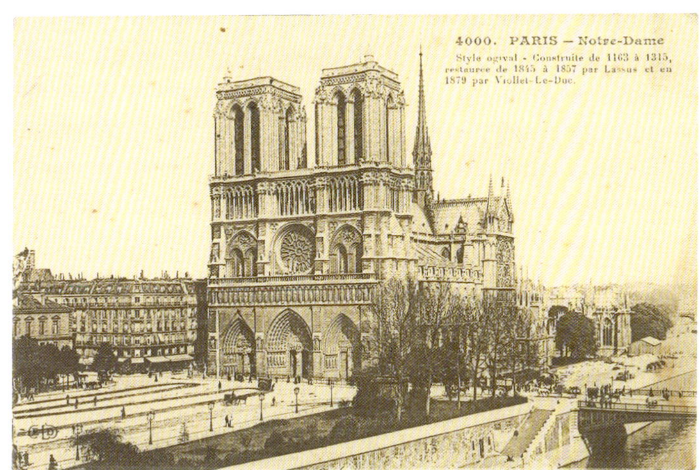

A postcard sent from Mondrian in Paris to Simon Maris in Amsterdam, 19 May 1911.

Mondrian

› Piet Mondrian (1872–1944) visits Paris from 13–23 May as a member of the board of the newly established art society Moderne Kunst Kring (Modern Art Circle). 'I get a lot out of being here', he writes to his friend Simon Maris, 'everything is so big and grand'.[1] He was invited to Paris by art critic and painter Conrad Kickert (1882–1965) to see the latest art.[2] Mondrian takes part in the Salon des Indépendants along with Kickert and their friend, painter Lodewijk Schelfhout (1881–1943), who is well acquainted with Pablo Picasso (1881–1973). Schelfhout knows important collectors and dealers of cubist art, such as Wilhelm Uhde (1874–1947) and Daniel-Henry Kahnweiler (1884–1979). It is quite possible that Mondrian sees work by Picasso or Georges Braque (1882–1963) at Uhde's gallery on rue Notre-Dame-des-Champs, or at Kahnweiler's recently opened gallery on rue Vignon. However, prior to 1911 they mainly had older work by Picasso and Braque from around 1906. Mondrian shows a painting called *Soleil*. It is not known which work this was.

› Mondrian's contribution to the first exhibition staged by the Moderne Kunst Kring, which opens in Amsterdam on 6 October, does not show any clear influence of the Cubism of Picasso and Braque. It is in fact his own interpretation of the Cubism of the Groupe Montparnasse, which can be described as a facetted and more geometrical version of the contours in the image. Paintings like *Dune Landscape* and *Evolution* (p.15) show the direct influence of Jan Toorop (1858–1928), who works in a figurative ornamental style that evokes a kind

Paris

› Shortly before the Salon des Indépendants opens, a group of young artists take over the 'commission de placement', which until now has been populated by sedate neo-Impressionists. The coup is staged by Henri Le Fauconnier (1881–1946), Albert Gleizes (1881–1953), Jean Metzinger (1883–1956), Fernand Léger (1881–1955) and Robert Delaunay (1885–1941), who have formed the Groupe Montparnasse. They are now in a position to assemble their work in a single gallery, allowing them to attract attention with their paintings that seem strongly oriented towards the Cubism of Picasso and Braque.[3] They sell well to *dénicheurs* (bargain hunters). This term was coined by André Level (1880–1954), who in 1904 had established La Peau de l'Ours, a group of investors who speculated on rising prices by buying the work of newcomers, mostly young artists.

› After the Salon d'Automne opens on 1 October, Guillaume Apollinaire (1880–1918) manages to persuade Picasso to go for a drink with him. Picasso takes the entire group (Le Fauconnier, Léger and Gleizes) along to Kahnweiler's gallery to show them his own work. Gleizes later summarises his own criticisms and those of his companions: Picasso's work is illegible, it is an 'Impressionism of form', depicting trivial subjects.[6] Picasso is

The Netherlands

› The annual exhibition at the Guild of St Luke opens in Amsterdam on 30 April with a special entry by Kees van Dongen (1877–1968) consisting of 21 paintings from 1907–11.[4] The corner room where the portraits and nudes hang soon becomes known as the 'chamber of horrors'. In Paris, Van Dongen is regarded as one of the *jeunes maîtres* (young masters), but things are not as easy in Amsterdam. Prince Hendrik exclaims, 'Well, I could do that!', and the mayor and councillors of Amsterdam have four indecent paintings removed, which only attracts more publicity and prompts members of St Luke's – particularly Jan Sluijters (1881–1957) – to fiercely defend this latest art. A special evening event is even arranged at Café Americain. Mondrian stays away, both from the exhibition and from all the commotion. It is not long before he cancels his St Luke's membership.

› Jan Toorop gives the opening address at the Moderne Kunst Kring exhibition in Amsterdam on 6 October: 'Let us turn our fine thoughts to Cézanne, to faithful, spiritual Cézanne ... There is certainly in [this artist] a spiritual element, a deep spiritual element, a psyche, yet one must understand and penetrate it through long contemplation of his work and by recognising his spiritual beauty through the beauty of his paintings. [Without]

Pablo Picasso
La Femme au pot de moutarde
(Woman with Mustard Pot), 1910
Oil on canvas, 73 x 60 cm
Gemeentemuseum Den Haag, The Hague

Henri Le Fauconnier
L'Abondance (Abundance), 1911
Oil on canvas, 191.5 x 123 cm
Gemeentemuseum Den Haag, The Hague

Jan Toorop
Bartholomeus (Bartholomew), 1912
Chalk on paper, oak frame, 100 x 100 cm
Gemeentemuseum Den Haag, The Hague

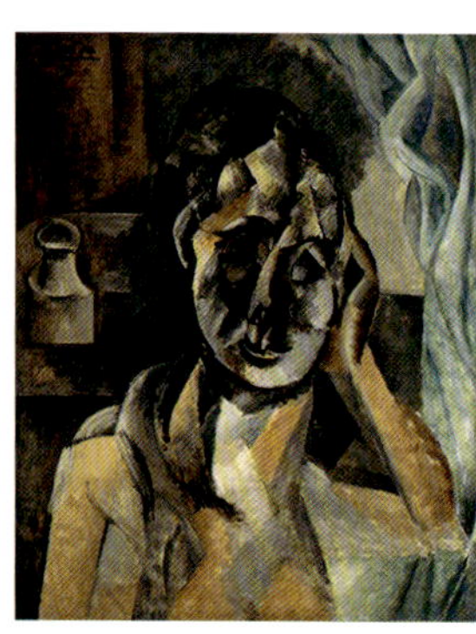

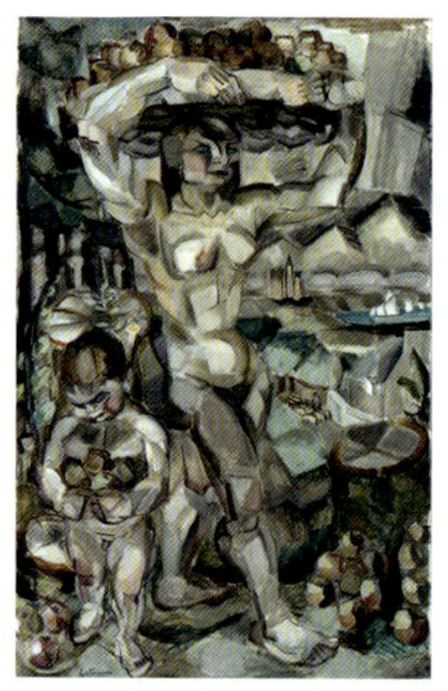

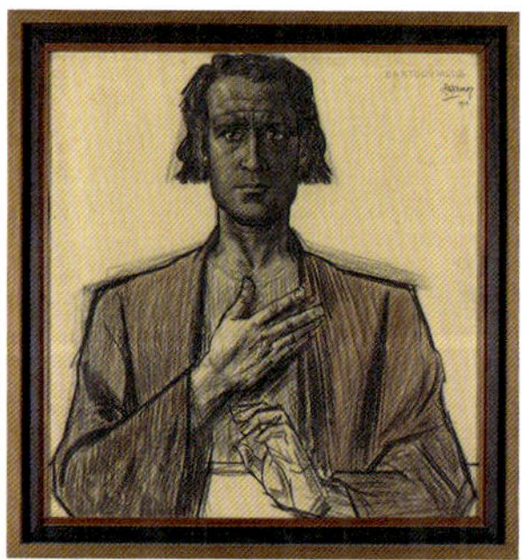

of suggestive symbolism. Mondrian himself is working towards a flat, decorative style that is also informed by the work of Henri Matisse (1869–1954) and Kees van Dongen. 'It is impossible to imitate or abstract a representation of nature', Mondrian later admits, 'but it is possible to create a valid equivalent which is the true pictorial reality'.[5]

› Having studied the foreign, especially French, art at the Moderne Kunst Kring exhibition, Mondrian realises – as he would put it in 1918 – that the new art alienates and irritates by using form and colour autonomously and free of representation of what Mondrian calls the 'natural appearance of things'; he feels that this alienation is a good thing.[9] Colour and form have a spiritual effect on perception and create an imaginary space in which the viewer is consciously interacting with the painting.[10] It is as if the sense of sight, on perceiving pure colour and form, turns inward. It seems Mondrian approaches the new art as analytically as possible.

unperturbed. It distinguishes him and Braque from the rest, which is necessary if they are to play a leading role in the Paris art market, where many collectors are in search of suitable candidates to take the place of the Impressionists.[7]

› Gino Severini (1883–1966) writes in his memoirs that there is an extreme sense of dynamism among artists in Paris in 1911. 'There was a frenzied desire for freedom in the air, an inexpressible appetite for innovation and adventure, and a profound need to re-establish contact with a reality not distorted by the academies.'[11]

On 11 October, Apollinaire notes in his journal that all artists currently tend towards a *style du mobilier*, a style that goes well with the furniture.[12] He believes the public at the Salon d'Automne is being challenged to consider how nice it would be to have their dining room or study decorated by contemporary artists like Marie Laurencin (1885–1956), Raymond Duchamp-Villon (1876–1918) or Fernand Léger.

the calm, beautiful austerity and strict discipline of sacred emotion there can be no true depth; in other words, no great monumental art can be wrought to quench man's pure, I say pure spiritual thirst.'[8]

› Daily newspaper *Het Nieuws van den Dag* describes how laughter and indignation can give way to admiration if one gradually becomes acquainted with the latest art. The newspaper gives an account of British writer Lewis Hind's (1862–1927) gradual familiarisation with the new art, first in Germany, then in Amsterdam (Cézanne at the Rijksmuseum) and then in France. 'The desire of the new school is to see, to draw, to paint with an unspoilt view of things; to observe things in the original way, as they were observed by natural primitive people ...'[13] There are more desperate ways of approaching the new art.

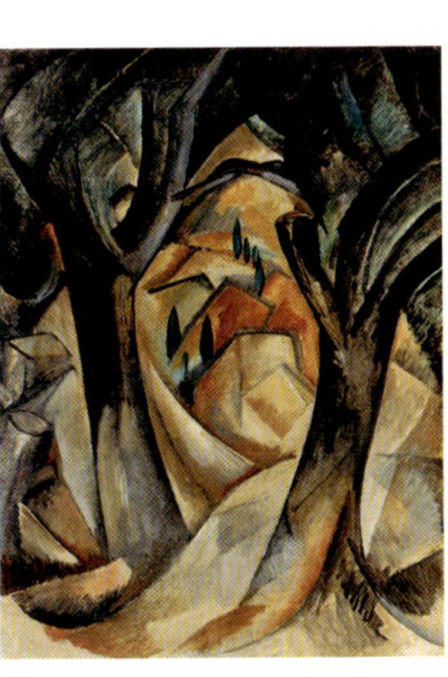

Georges Braque
Arbres à *L'Estaque*
(Trees at L'Estaque), 1908
Oil on canvas, 79 x 60 cm
Metropolitan Museum of Art, New York
Leonard A Lauder Cubist Collection

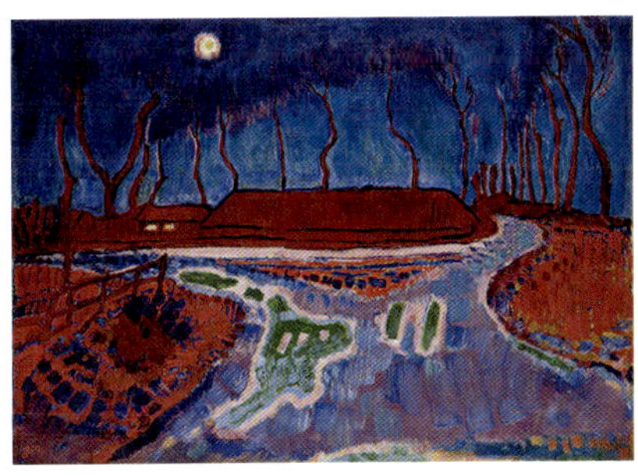

Jan Sluijters
Maannacht (Moonlit Night), 1911
Oil on canvas, 52 x 73.4 cm
Gemeentemuseum Den Haag, The Hague

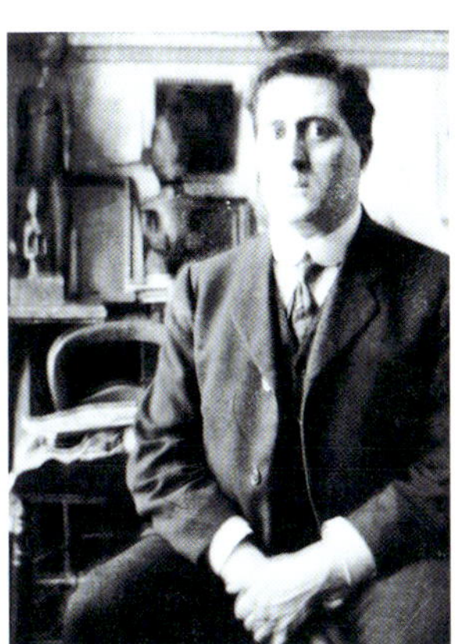

Guillaume Apollinaire at Pablo Picasso's studio, 11 boulevard de Clichy, Paris, November 1910.

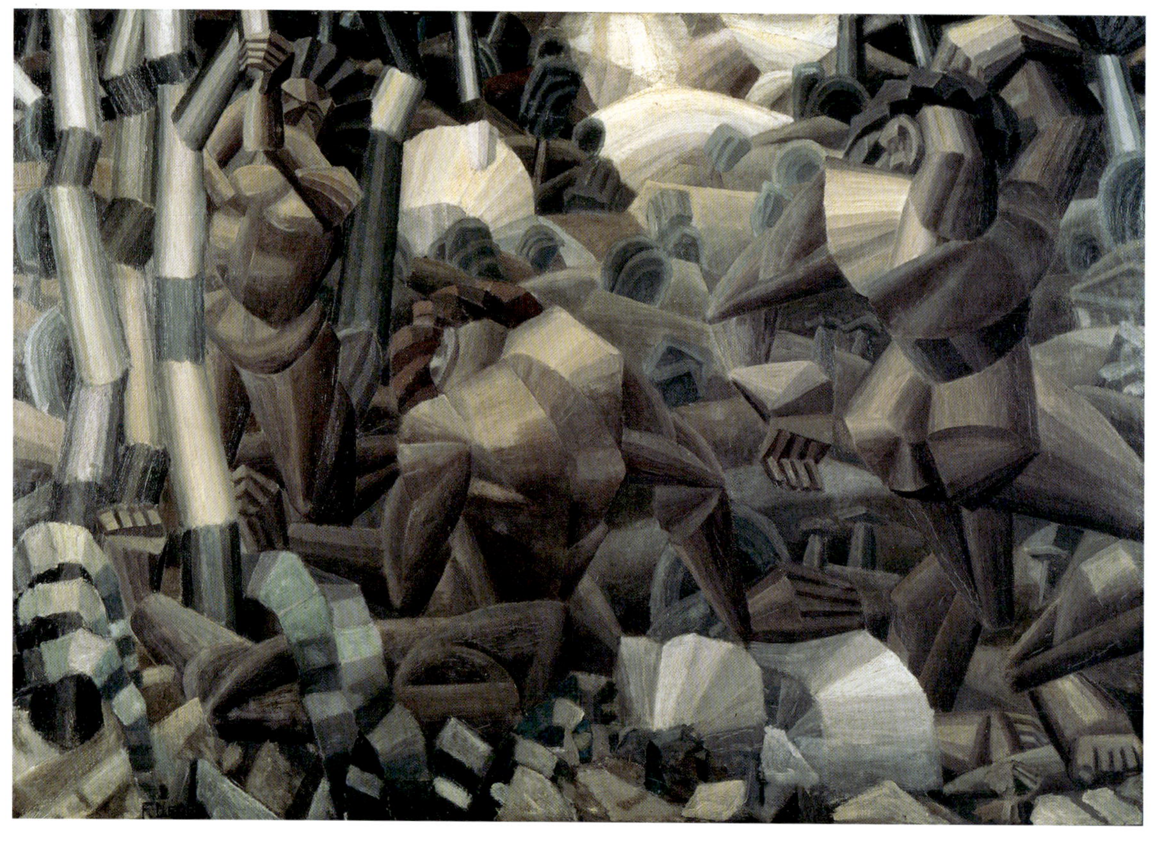

Fernand Léger
Nus dans la fôret (Nudes in the Forest), 1911
Oil on canvas, 120 x 170.5 cm
Kröller-Müller Museum, Otterlo

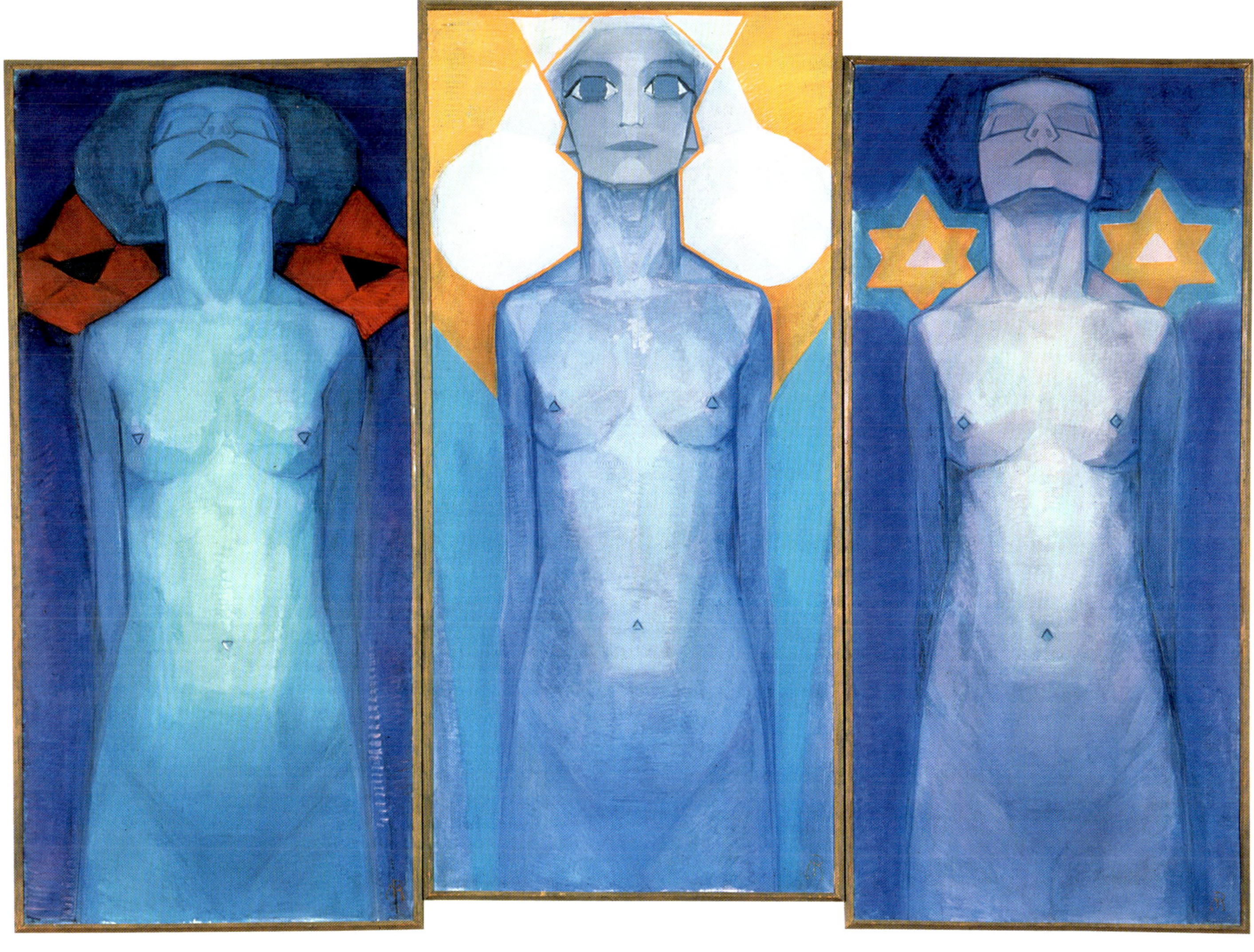

Piet Mondrian
Evolutie (Evolution), 1911
Oil on canvas
Triptych: 178 x 85 cm, 183 x 87.5 cm, 178 x 85 cm
Gemeentemuseum Den Haag, The Hague

Mondrian

› Mondrian decides to go to Paris. He gives notice on his studio at Sarphatipark and terminates his registration with Amsterdam City Council on 20 December, giving his destination as Paris. He also breaks off his engagement: 'Although I have always lived for art, the beautiful in life also attracts me greatly, and so I sometimes do things that seem strange', he apologetically writes to his fiancé, the violinist Aletta de Jongh (1887–1975).[14] He does not take much of his old work with him to Paris. He sells some of it and the rest he leaves with friends for safekeeping. He takes only a few paintings and otherwise mainly drawings and sketches: views of the Gein river, a portrait and a nude study of his former girlfriend Eva de Beneditty (1888–1970), tree studies and oil sketches.[15] We cannot rule out the possibility that Mondrian was already making plans and sketches for compositions that he did not complete until 1913.[16]

› Mondrian arrives in Paris by train. According to Mary Simon, a friend in Amsterdam, for the first few days he stays in the guest room at the headquarters of the French Theosophical Society. We do not know this for certain, however.[20] Mondrian finds accommodation with Kickert and Schelfhout at 33 avenue du Maine. It cannot have taken long before he noticed that he was unable to go along with Schelfhout's restless inclination to associate Cubism unthinkingly with the concept of the 'spiritual', as Toorop did.

Paris

› Gallery owner Kahnweiler erects a *cordon sanitaire* around Picasso and Braque, holding onto their work, seeking buyers abroad and leaving the public in Paris and the Groupe Montparnasse wondering how the two artists' work is developing. This strengthens the impression that the Groupe Montparnasse is more official, more serious, more classical and spiritual, and that Braque and Picasso are mainly out to defy painting and to cause irritation. Their prices rise. But their isolation also has another effect. Their work becomes stylistically concentrated and elaborate, with secret references and messages that the uninitiated can only guess at. This entrenches the gap between artist and public, in a manner that will become typical of the voluntary isolation of the avant garde.[17]

› Art critic Louis Vauxcelles (1870–1943), who coined the term Cubism in 1908, estimates that every year some 17,000 new paintings are shown at the official Salons. This does not include the 10,000 works shown at the alternative Salons in the hope of finding an audience. Only a small proportion of them are sold, and the rest are painted over or destroyed. Only about 50 artists attract the attention of the press.[21] The other artists also need to earn a living, and most of them end up in the *Cités d'Artistes* – dilapidated

The Netherlands

› Frans Vermeulen, an influential art critic with the magazine *Elsevier's Geïllustreerd Maandschrift*, writes in *De Ploeg* that where democracy gains influence, social bonds also become clearer. Purer understanding brings forth a new form of artistic expression, in which the monumental plays an important role. Artists are on a quest for the 'clearly expressed, in terms of pure form, for the permanent portrayal of pure intellect', until they arrive 'at the lasting, most tightly delineated synthesis'.[18]

At the Moderne Kunst Kring exhibition, Conrad Kickert buys a painting by Braque, *Trees at L'Estaque* (1908; p.13), and an unidentified drawing by Picasso, presenting them to the Rijksmuseum as a permanent loan on behalf of the board of the Moderne Kunst Kring.[19]

› A scandal begins when the organisers of the Quadrennial, due to open on 13 April, choose a mechanical enlargement of a drawing by Rembrandt for the poster illustration. The Guild of St Luke protests. When it is found in February that the foreign artists invited to exhibit are mainly Impressionists and Luminists, and that modern art is conspicuously absent, the scandal erupts. Meanwhile, Jan Sluijters experiments with colour-

Le Café de la Paix, boulevard des Capucines, Paris, 1911.

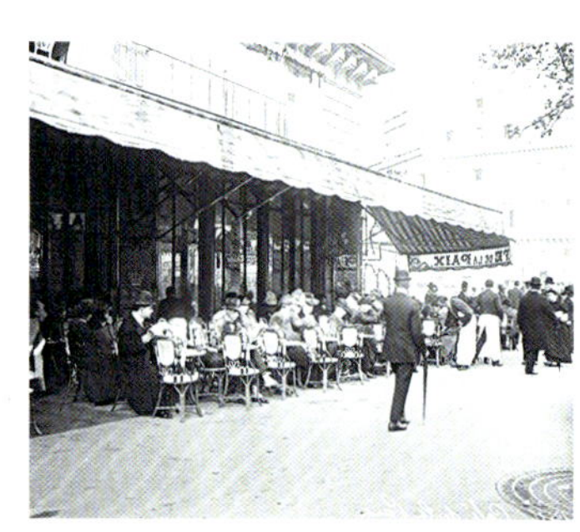

Marie Laurencin
Les jeunes filles (Young Girls), 1910–11
Oil on canvas, 115 x 146 cm
Moderna Museet, Stockholm

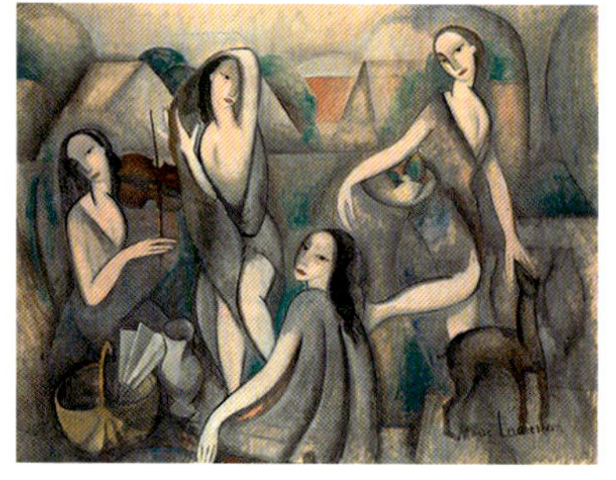

The painter Auguste Herbin visiting Picasso's studio at 11 boulevard de Clichy in Paris, late 1911, photographed by Picasso.

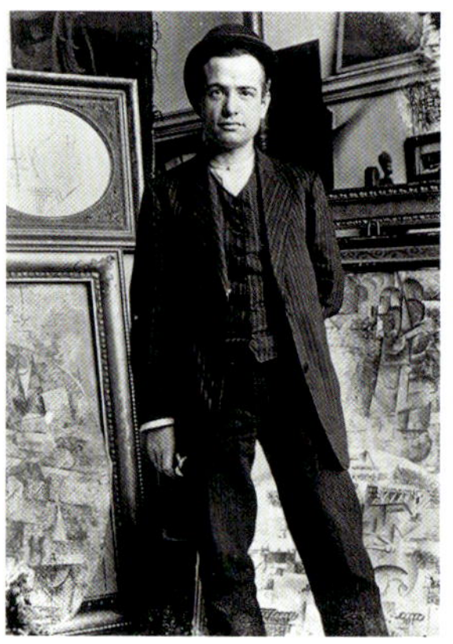

complexes where, for a modest rent, they can share something that resembles a studio with pests and vermin. There are many such complexes in Montparnasse.

ful, two-dimensional geometric images, and Leo Gestel (1881–1941) produces futuristic flower paintings in Bergen.

› Mondrian writes to Aletta de Jongh that it was difficult in the beginning, 'with all the unfamiliarity and setting up the studio…I have only a small room, but the studio is just as big. And it is no more expensive for me than in Amsterdam, though much more instructive, you understand. You can be yourself so marvellously in such a big cosmopolitan city!'.[22] He is working on his entry to the Salon des Indépendants in March. He meets Fernand Léger, but is reluctant to establish contact with Picasso, for fear of being outdone.[23]

› The first issue of the influential new literary and art magazine *Les Soirées de Paris* features an article by founder and editor Guillaume Apollinaire. He acknowledges that the subject is disappearing from the work of young artists like Picasso and Braque, making way for a *peinture pure*. In the course of writing this article, Apollinaire explained his views in a letter to a friend, surmising that for 'the artistic concept to be able to impose itself, it is necessary for mediocre things to appear at the same time as sublime ones. In this way one may measure the extent of the new beauty.'[24]

› Leo Gestel retreats to Bergen with his wife in order to paint the landscape of the North Holland province. He becomes addicted to working outdoors. The huge skies above the polders, woods and dunes do not, however, preclude any desire for more abstraction, though they do ensure that everything remains within the bounds of reason. Jan Sluijters also focuses on family life, his work expressing the systematic nature of Cubism mainly in a decorative manner.

› Based on later reports, we can assume that from the start of his stay in Paris Mondrian remained well abreast of what was happening in the art world. In the early period, at any rate, he dines with Kees van Dongen on a weekly basis, where he meets the influential critic Félix Fénéon (1861–1944), who showed Van Dongen at the Galerie Bernheim-Jeune.[25] Kickert and Schelfhout will have taken Mondrian to the café La Closerie des Lilas, introduced him at the weekly soirées at Le Fauconnier's – who at that time was working

› An exhibition of Futurist work is organised by Félix Fénéon at Galerie Bernheim-Jeune featuring 35 paintings by Luigi Russolo (1885–1947), Carlo Carrà (1881–1966), Umberto Boccioni (1882–1916) and Gino Severini. They produce vivid paintings with an instantly recognisable, caricatural imagery that is confusing and fragmented, using a visual language that reflects the dynamism of modern life. Galerie Barbazanges, at 109 rue du Faubourg Saint-Honoré, stages an exhibition of the latest work by Robert Delaunay and Marie Laurencin. The gallery is financed by fashion designer Paul

› The non-representational visual idiom of artists like Gestel and Sluijters gradually comes to be regarded in the Netherlands as a 'programme'. What had previously been attributed to a need for the 'spiritualisation of things' is interpreted by leading critics, like JH de Bois, and NH Wolf of *De Kunst*, as 'a reflection of the sensation experienced by the artist on seeing things'.[27] This strictly personal interpretation of the artistic process becomes common currency in the

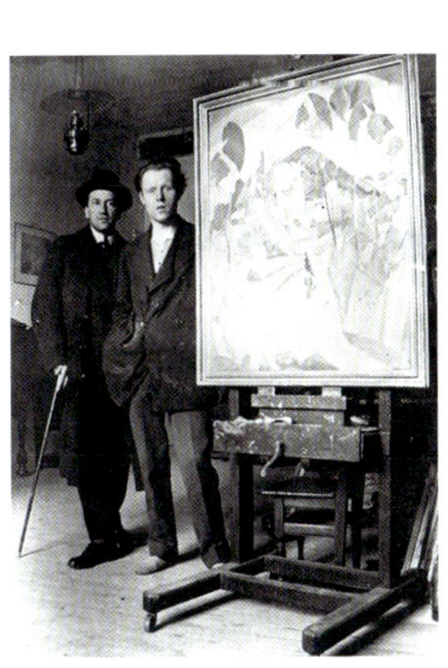

Lodewijk Schelfhout and Piet Mondrian at Schelfhout's studio, rue du Départ, Paris, spring 1912. On the easel stands Schelfhout's 1912 painting *Country Road Near Villeneuve-les-Avignon.*

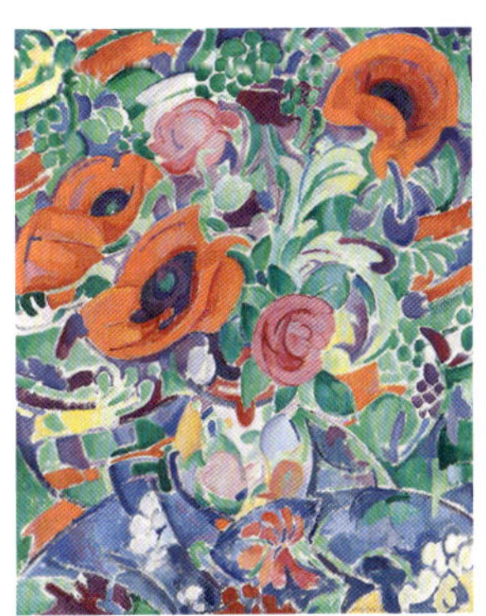

Leo Gestel
Bloemstuk met papavers
(Flower Arrangement with Poppies), 1912
Oil on canvas, 102.5 x 87 cm
Gemeentemuseum Den Haag, The Hague

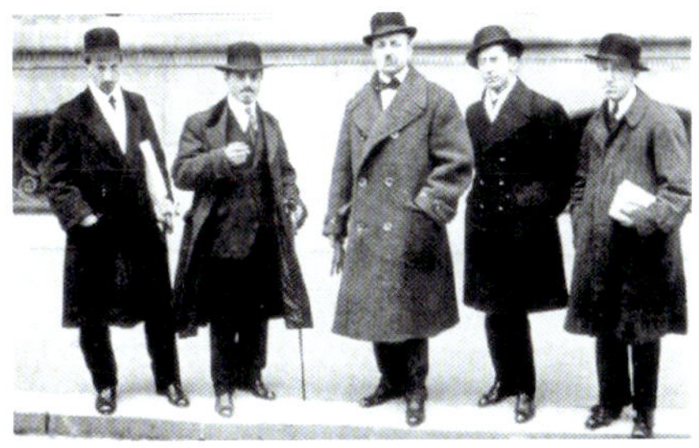

From left to right: Luigi Russolo, Carlo Carrà, Filippo Tommaso Marinetti, Umberto Boccioni and Gino Severini in front of Galerie Bernheim-Jeune, Paris, 24 February 1912.

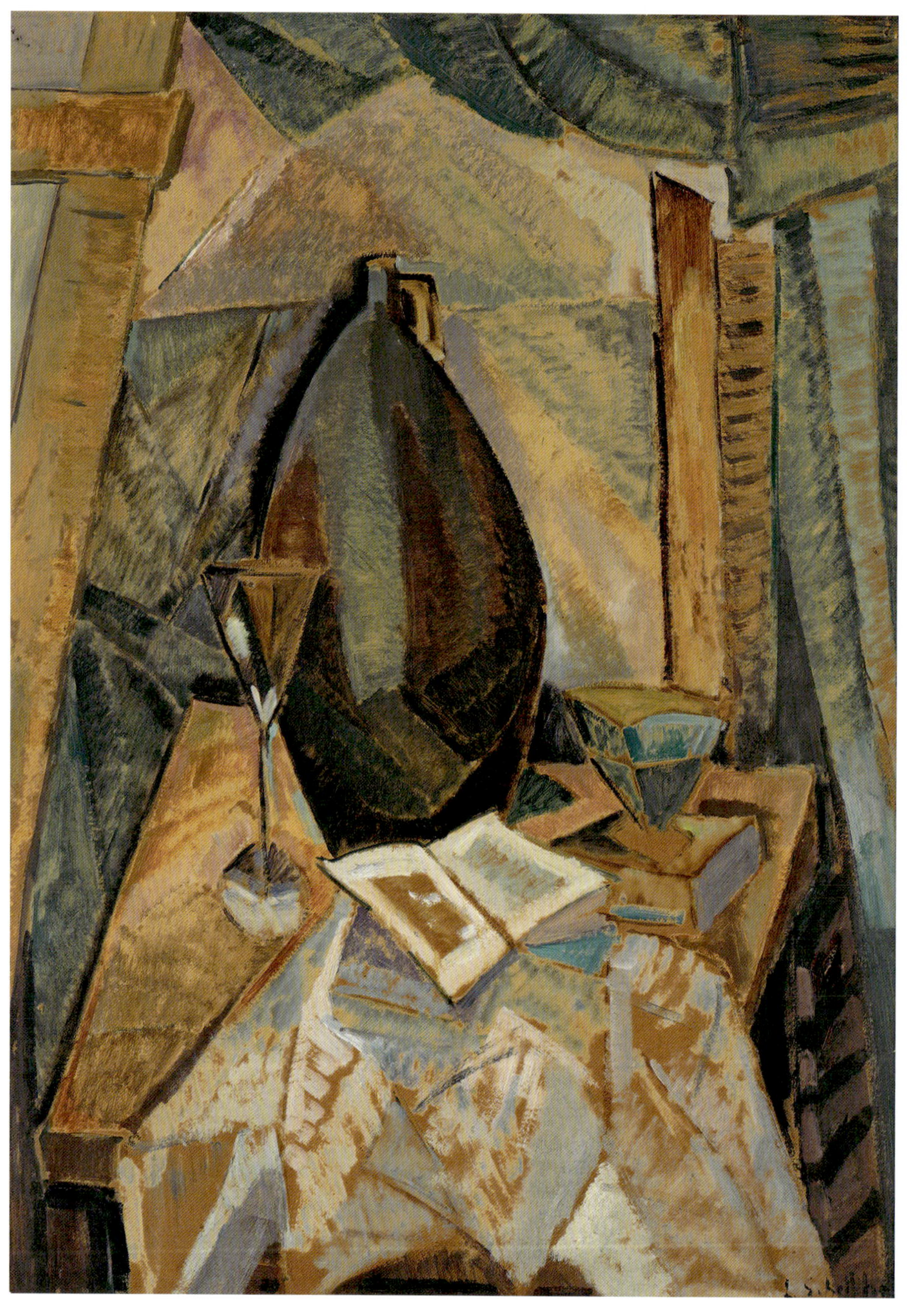

Lodewijk Schelfhout
Stilleven (Still Life), 1912
Oil on card, 81 x 61 cm
Gemeentemuseum Den Haag, The Hague

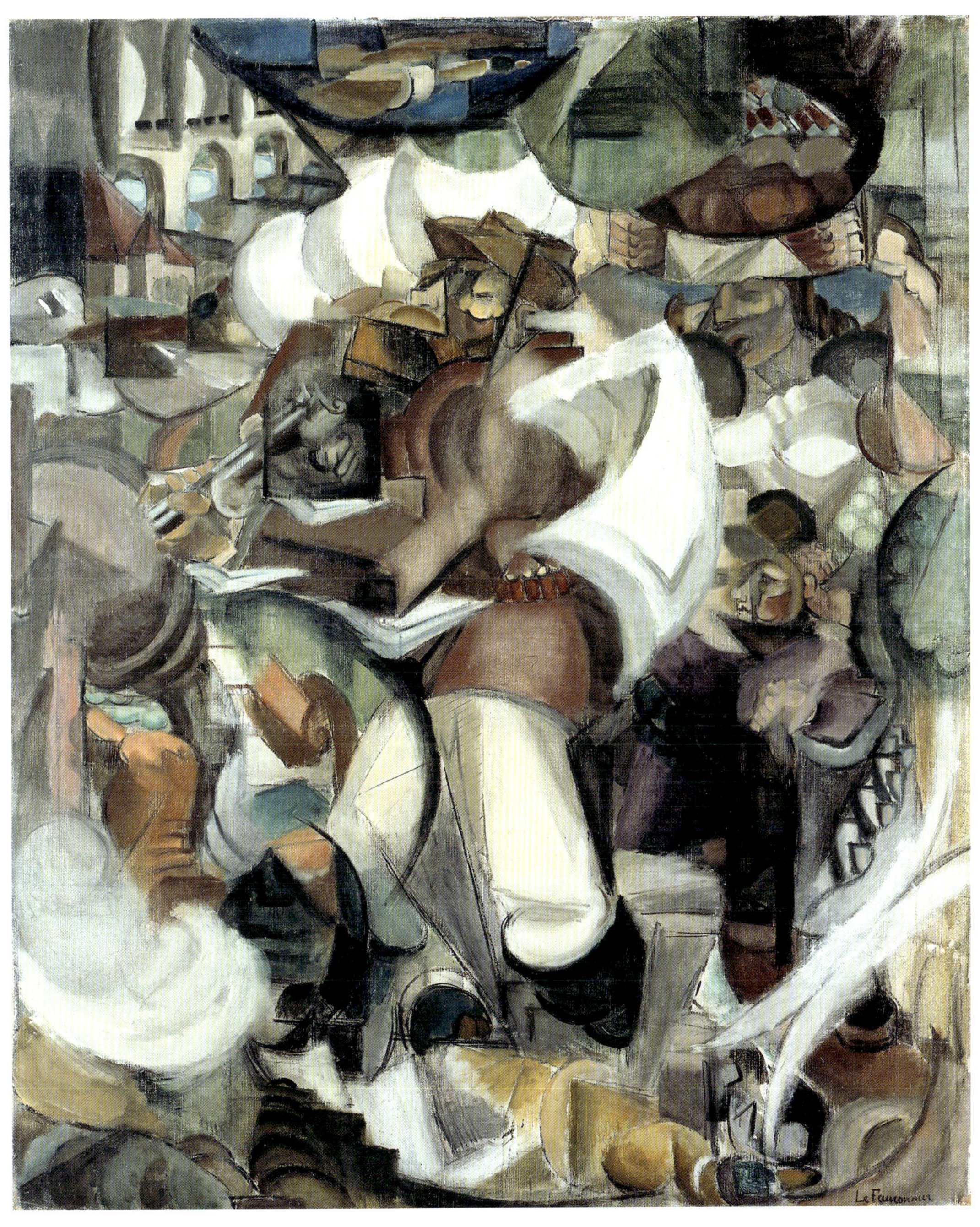

Henri Le Fauconnier
Le Chasseur (The Hunter), 1912
Oil on canvas, 221 x 185.5 cm
Gemeentemuseum Den Haag, The Hague

Mondrian

on *The Hunter* (p.19) – and he met Wilhelm Uhde at Café du Dôme. Uhde might have made him aware that some artists had been allowed to see photographs of recent work by Picasso at Kahnweiler's, and that they could see works that had not been submitted to exhibitions abroad or were as yet unsold.[26] Mondrian gets to know Fernand Léger better through Dutch painter Peter Alma (1886–1969), who also takes him to the *jours* of poet Paul Fort (1872–1960) at La Closerie des Lilas, where *tout Paris* can be found every Tuesday evening.

› Mondrian enters two paintings of female figures and a painting of a woodland view to the Salon des Indépendants.[29] His work is hung in Salle 20, a room at the Salon where artists like Gleizes, Metzinger, Le Fauconnier and Léger are showing decorative works – in a Cubist style! – for a psychiatric clinic. This placement at least guarantees that Mondrian's work will stand out and be discussed, rather than being overwhelmed by the 4,700 other artworks by 1,000 artists. Apollinaire does not mention him in his review of the Salon, and other critics, like Louis Vauxcelles, mention only his name.[30] But the young poet André Salmon (1881–1969) describes *le royaume des cubistes* (the kingdom of the Cubists) in Salle 20 in a review. He remarks that Mondrian 'blindly produces a kind of Cubism, in total ignorance of the law of volumes, taking his inspiration from Van Dongen'.[31] Mondrian must have told Salmon this himself.

Paris

Poiret (1879–1944). Here the dynamism of modern life shows itself in images fractured by unexpected form shifts and with chequered fields in dazzling colours: art can be attractive and glamorous.

› The most important and radical painting at the Salon des Indépendants is *The Hunter* by Le Fauconnier. It is Le Fauconnier's response to the representation of simultaneity and the dynamic depiction of reality by artists like Boccioni, and an attempt to anticipate developments in the work of Braque and Picasso, at which he can only guess. This gives *The Hunter* the air of a caricature, confining it within the safe boundaries of tradition. The tumultuous visual language, with clouds and landscape features that displace or overlap each other, ultimately remains classical and conformist.

The Netherlands

Netherlands. The term '*Expressionisme*' is coined for this purpose, in imitation of the Germans who called the work of Van Dongen, André Derain (1880–1954), Maurice de Vlaminck (1876–1958) and Picasso '*Expressionismus*' at an exhibition organised by the Berliner Secession.[28]

› An exhibition of the work of Jan Sluijters is presented at the Kunstzaal Meylink gallery in Rotterdam. The *Algemeen Handelsblad* newspaper comments that the ultra-Modernists have copied their technique from Vincent van Gogh (1853–1890) in order to mask their own lack of talent, as demonstrated by *Moonlit Night* (1911; p.13), which most people seem to find hard to appreciate. Sluijters is an exception, however, the critic thinks. His delicate touch and fine skills are unmistakable, and the reviewer has every confidence that the artist will know which lines should not be crossed.[32]

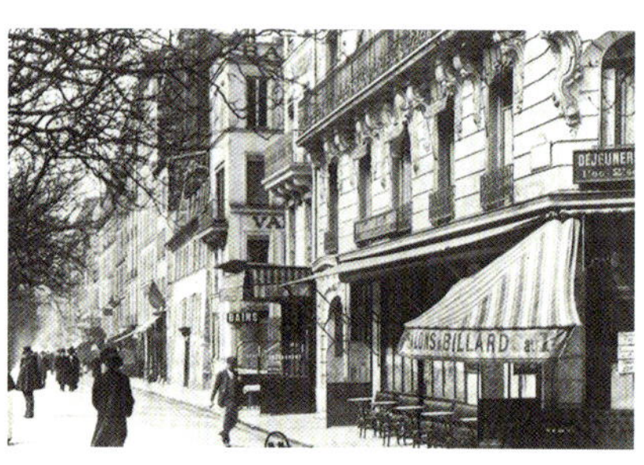

La Closerie des Lilas, boulevard du Montparnasse, the centre of artistic life in Montparnasse, c.1910.

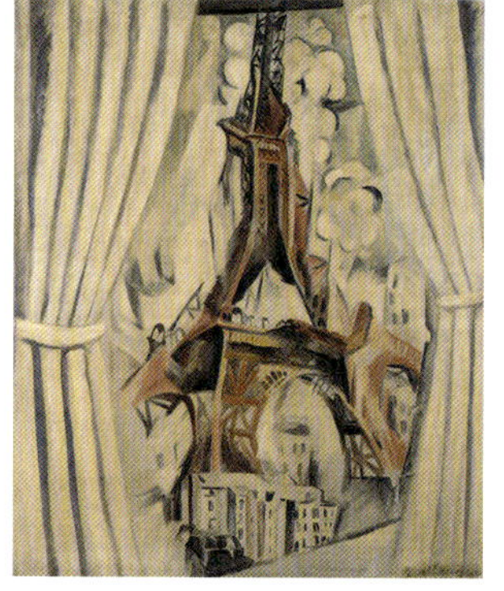

Robert Delaunay
La Tour au Rideaux
(Tower with Curtains), 1910
Oil on canvas, 116 x 96.5 cm
Kunstsammlung Nordrhein-Westfalen, Dusseldorf

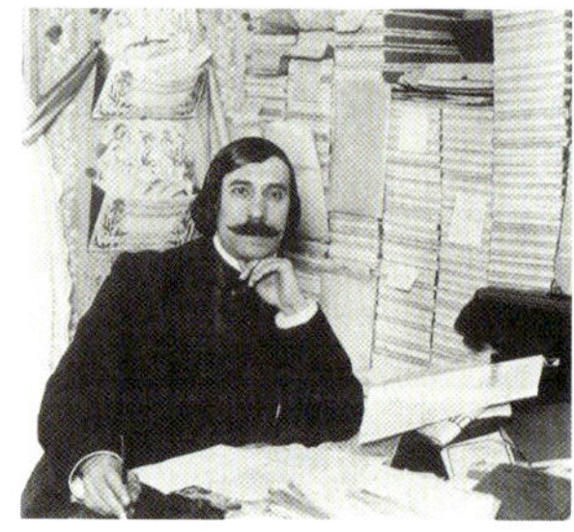

Paul Fort, 'Prince of Poets', in his apartment at 24 rue Boissonade with unsold copies of his literary journal *Vers et Prose* stacked against the wall, c.1910.

› Mondrian relocates to the newly built studio complex at 26 rue du Départ, along with Schelfhout, Kickert, Rudolf Lévy (1881–1944) and Diego Rivera (1886–1957). He moves into the studio on the top floor and immediately begins work on his entries to the second exhibition of the Moderne Kunst Kring in Amsterdam: cubist interpretations of a tree, based on drawings from 1908–10 referring back to *Evening: The Red Tree* (p.112), a *Seascape* and *Dunes*, as well as landscapes he previously painted in Domburg, on the north-west coast of the Netherlands.[33] He sketches and draws a lot in preparation for compositions that were probably not committed to canvas until the autumn. He is working on a still life with which he has had problems for some time.[34] It is based on an earlier still life, which depicts a ginger pot in a style that attempted to understand and address works by Paul Cézanne (1839–1906) that Mondrian had seen in 1911 in an exhibition at the Rijksmuseum of the Hoogendijk collection. Mondrian never sacrifices the handling of the paint to appearance, and brushstrokes are given the opportunity to become quite structural. But the translation of all of this into a cubist idiom causes serious troubles, if only because representation is constantly getting in the way.

› The Paris correspondent of a Dutch newspaper describes an evening at the café La Closerie des Lilas on boulevard du Montparnasse: 'One hears all languages spoken there: Poles, Danes, Italians, Germans, Swedes, English, Norwegians, Greeks, even Dutch. In the corner of the room, which has gradually become very crowded, are the Cubists: Le Fauconnier, Metzinger, Gleizes etc., sitting quietly and squarely together! Not far away Marinetti the Futurist is blathering on, while at a nearby table some young people are discussing setting up a magazine.'[35]

The popular magazine *Je sais tout* publishes an interview with Kahnweiler by critic Jacques des Gachons (1868–1945), illustrated with a work by Braque, *The Guéridon*, from the early months of 1912, reproduced beside Picasso's *Man with a Clarinet* (p.22) from the same period.

› Conrad Kickert manages to place work by Mondrian, Otto van Rees (1884–1957) and Adya van Rees (1876–1959), Lodewijk Schelfhout and Peter Alma at the exhibition presented by the Sonderbund Westdeutscher Kunstfreunde und Künstler in Cologne, which is to open on 25 May. The Dutch press pays little attention to the exhibition, which causes something of a stir internationally as Germany intends it to bridge the gap between modernity and society. Helene Kröller-Müller (1869–1939), wife of one of the wealthiest businessmen in the Netherlands, and HP Bremmer (1871–1956), art critic, art dealer and adviser, go to Paris for a few days where they buy work by Georges Seurat (1859–1891), Paul Signac (1863–1935) and Van Gogh for a total of 60,000 guilders. The pieces are intended for the museum of modern art that Kröller-Müller plans to establish in Holland.

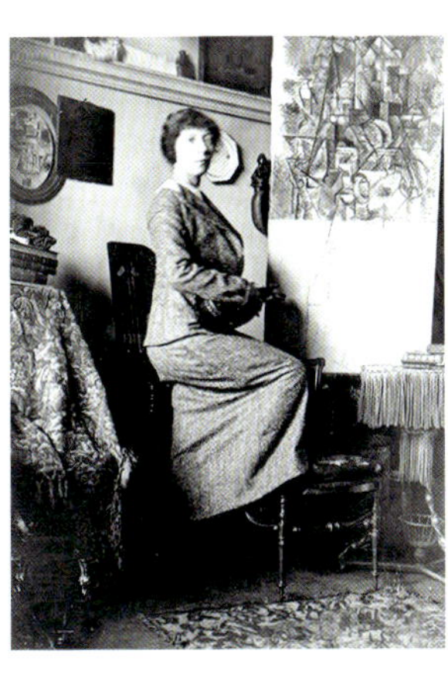

Marie Laurencin visiting Picasso at his studio at 11 boulevard de Clichy in autumn 1911, photographed by Picasso.

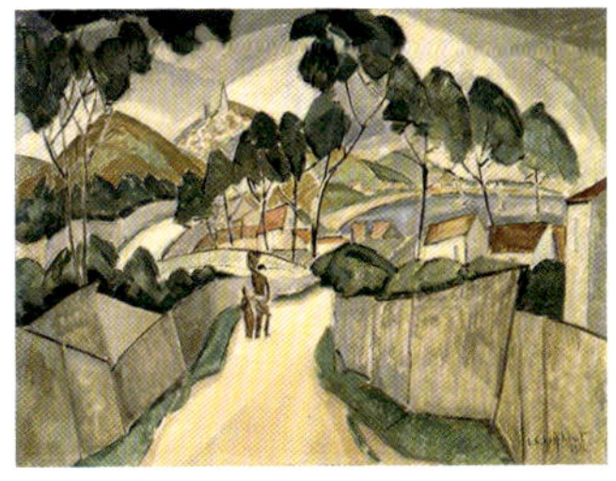

Lodewijk Schelfhout
Country Road Near Villeneuve-les-Avignon, 1912
Oil on canvas, 46 x 55 cm
Gemeentemuseum Den Haag, The Hague

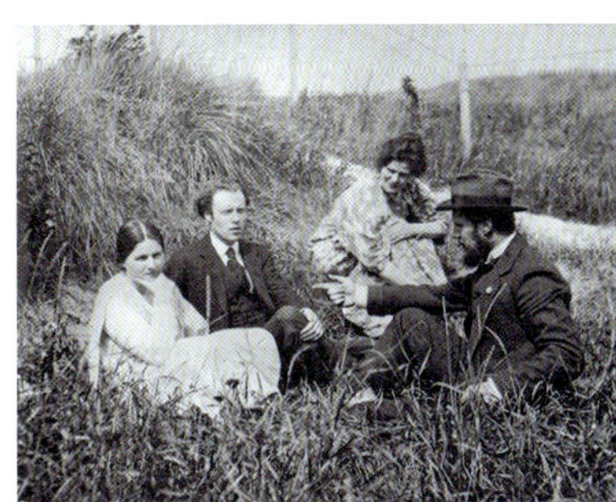

Lodewijk Schelfhout, Conrad Kickert and two women in the dunes at Zandvoort, adopting a pose from Édouard Manet's *Déjeuner sur l'herbe* (1862–63), autumn 1912.

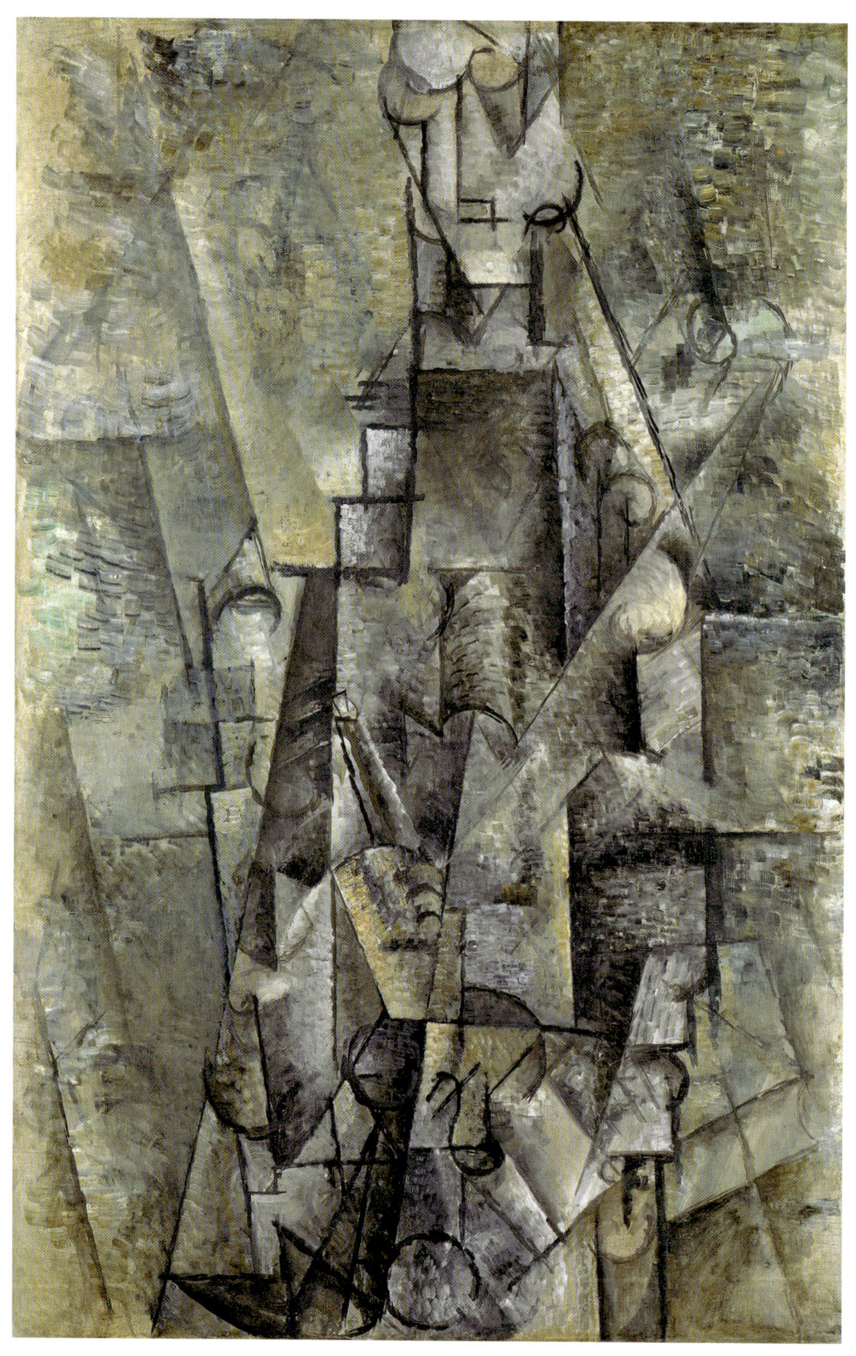

Pablo Picasso
Homme à la clarinette
(Man with a Clarinet), 1911–12
Oil on canvas, 106 x 69 cm
Museo Thyssen-Bornemisza, Madrid

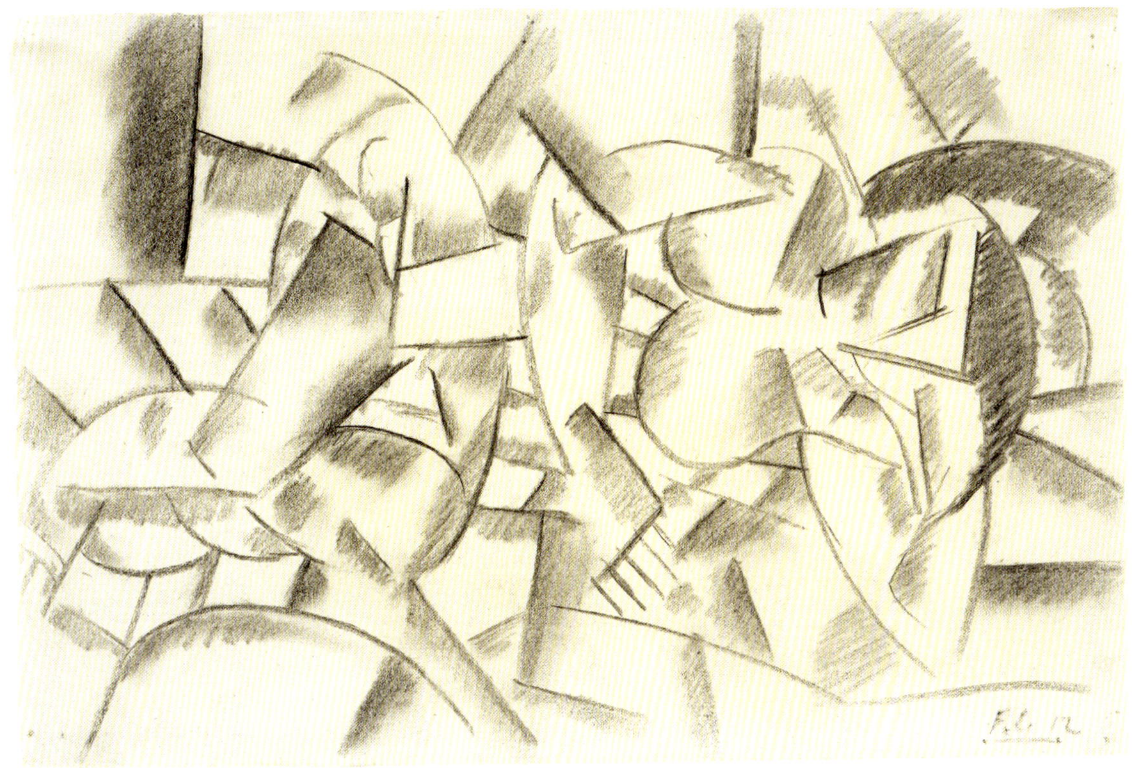

Fernand Léger
Femme nue couchée
(Reclining Nude), 1912
Charcoal on paper, 32 x 48.2 cm
Triton Collection Foundation, Rotterdam

Mondrian

› Mondrian registers with the Préfecture de Police in Paris, giving his address as 26 rue du Départ, and is issued a residence permit. The still life continues to occupy him, but he is also producing sketches for cubist compositions based on earlier sketches of trees and woodland views. The natural themes serve as a starting point, but in the final work nature has to be 'overcome'. Mondrian continues to produce work that is an extension of the realism that can be associated with Impressionists like Claude Monet (1840–1926).[36] At the same time, however, he tries to find new ways of creating an 'inwardly deepened image', as he calls it.[37]

› The Dutch painter Jacoba van Heemskerck (1876–1923) and her wealthy friend Marie Tak van Poortvliet (1871–1936) visit Paris. Van Heemskerck submits three paintings to the Salon des Indépendants. Otto van Rees later recalls meeting Van Heemskerck at Mondrian's studio.[39] The women buy paintings by Le Fauconnier, Lévy and Schelfhout, and try to acquire a Braque from Uhde.[40] It is unlikely they buy work from Mondrian because he has nothing finished to sell, but he agrees to visit them in the summer.[41]

Paris

› Picasso begins to work with enamel. He produces his first collage, *Still Life with Chair Caning*. Braque is experimenting with unmixed blue, red, purple and violet in order to escape the ochre, grey and white colour range. None of these works are publicly visible before October 1913, though they are intensely discussed in cafés and studios.

› Apollinaire will remark later, in 1914, that the heyday of Montmartre, with its fake artists, eccentric industrialists and imprudent opium smokers, was over, and that the real artists were now to be found in Montparnasse, dressed in the American style. Some were still snorting the white powder, but that did not matter, says Apollinaire, because most artists were against indulging in artificial paradises of any kind.[42] The police turn a blind eye to unconventional behaviour but take firm action against criminal activities.[43]

The Netherlands

› 'The Hague is still ignorant of the Amsterdam Modernists', one critic bemoaned in January.[38] On 8 May, however, an exhibition opens at the Biesing gallery in the Hague, composed of artworks by members of St Luke's in Amsterdam that had been rejected from the Quadrennial. The board of St Luke's hurriedly releases a statement to the press pointing out that it did not organise the exhibition. The *Modern Amsterdam School* exhibition makes a great impression in The Hague.

› A growing number of Dutch collectors are beginning to focus on the very latest international art. Willem Beffie (1880–1950) focuses on German Expressionists, as does the Reverend Hendrick van Assendelft (1875–1928) of Gouda, who also collects work by Gino Severini and Mondrian. Kröller-Müller starts buying Mondrian, Bart van der Leck (1876–1958) and Schelfhout, in addition to Van Gogh, Signac and Théo Van Rysselberghe (1862–1926). Dr JFS Esser (1877–1946) and Piet Boendermaker (1877–1947) also collect art, mainly by contemporary Dutch artists.

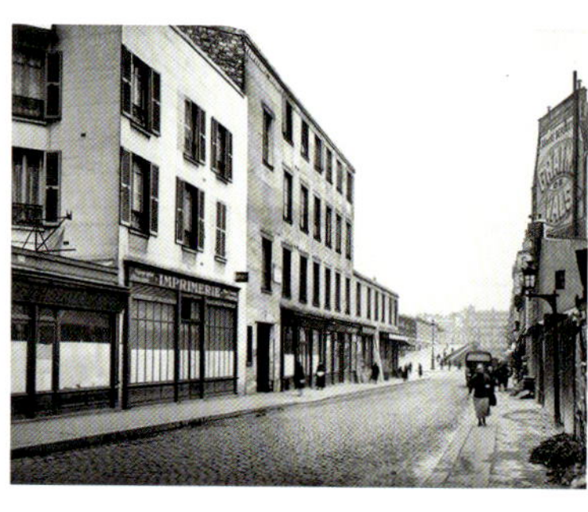

Rue du Départ, looking towards Gare Montparnasse, c.1922. The top window above the entrance to the alleyway through the grey apartment building was Mondrian's studio.

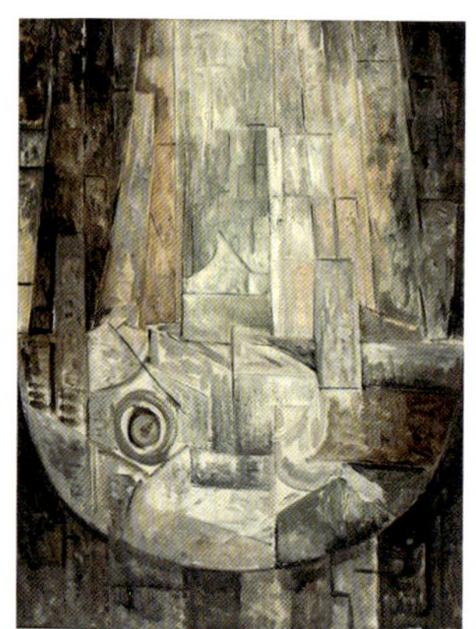

Jacoba van Heemskerck
Compositie No. 2
(Composition No. 2), 1912–13
Oil on canvas, 83 x 62.9 cm
Gemeentemuseum Den Haag, The Hague

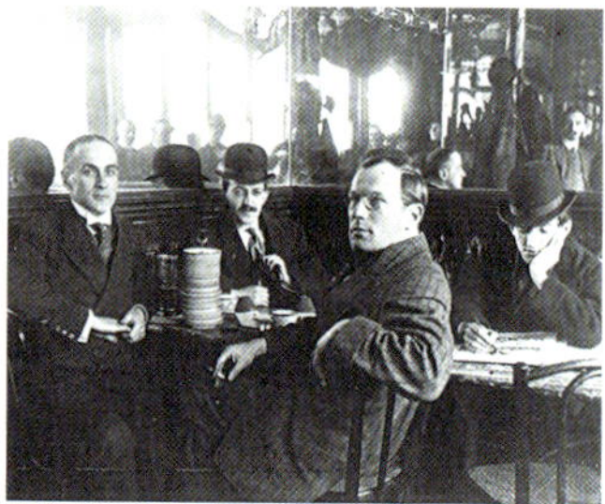

From left to right: Wilhelm Uhde, Walter Bondy, Rudolf Lévy and Jules Pascin at Café du Dôme, Paris, 1912.

› Mondrian takes part in a Sonderbund exhibition in Cologne, showing a drawing identified as *Hyacinths*, which, given its title, subject and style, could be part of a group of three similar drawings now known as *Cat's Tails* (c.1909).[44]

Artist Jan van Deene (1886–1977) recalls Mondrian in Paris as 'a simple, charming man without pretention. He was keen to be noticed however, and therefore attended all openings. [Jacob] Bendien called him "Here-I-am-again Piet" because of this habit'.[45]

A remark in a letter to Lodewijk Schelfhout of 7 June 1914 suggests that at first Conrad Kickert paid the rent on Mondrian's studio, and that Mondrian promised him artworks in exchange.[46]

› Claude Monet exhibits his views of San Giorgio Maggiore in Venice at dusk at Galerie Bernheim-Jeune. The paintings have a luminous palette featuring strong, vibrant reds, yellows and violets, which makes the rainbow look bleached. Each painting features a different atmosphere and tone, and a different depth and light. Although the Cubists, with their restrained palette, are generally seen as reacting against this type of Impressionism, it must be said that all of these painters, not only Mondrian but also Braque, Delaunay and Severini, see painting in terms of the effect of light. In Paris, Monet is a kind of 'flipside of the same'.[47]

Mondrian later remarks, in 1942, that just as the Cubists responded with their restrained palette, his ochres and greys were a response to the pure, saturated colours he was using when he left the Netherlands. He concludes that, in their intensity, those pure colours still express too much individual emotion. The greys and ochres borrowed from the work of the Cubists allowed him to gain more control of the line. Nevertheless, for a long time – until 1916–17 – he continues to feel that he was working as an Impressionist.[48]

› Carel Lodewijk Dake (1857–1920), previously a professor at the Academy of Fine Arts in Amsterdam when Mondrian was a student there and now also a highly conservative critic with *De Telegraaf*, writes an article entitled 'Where are we going?', in which he describes how artists and audiences have lost the way and decay is taking the place of development. There is no longer any 'powerful directional principle'. The subject in painting has disappeared, and technically most artists are simply letting things run their course. Dake cites the work of Floris Verster (1861–1927) as an example of how it should be.[49] On the same page of *De Telegraaf*, one column to the left, there is a report on the auction of artworks that had belonged to the eccentric collector Cornelis Hoogendijk (1866–1911), who had lent works by Cézanne and Van Gogh to Willem Steenhoff (1863–1932), director of the Rijksmuseum, in 1909.[50] On the morning of 21 May, German and French dealers bid against each other for the Van Goghs, Cézannes, Renoirs, Manets and Daumiers. In their wake, even Matthijs Maris (1839–1917) and Jan Toorop achieve record prices.

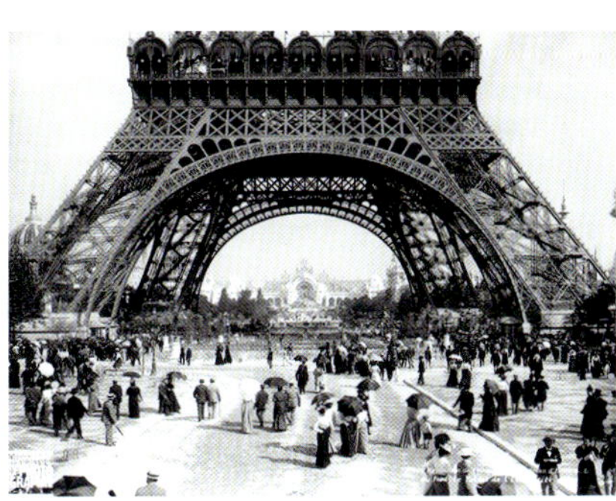

Strolling along the Pont d'Iena, Paris, c.1912.

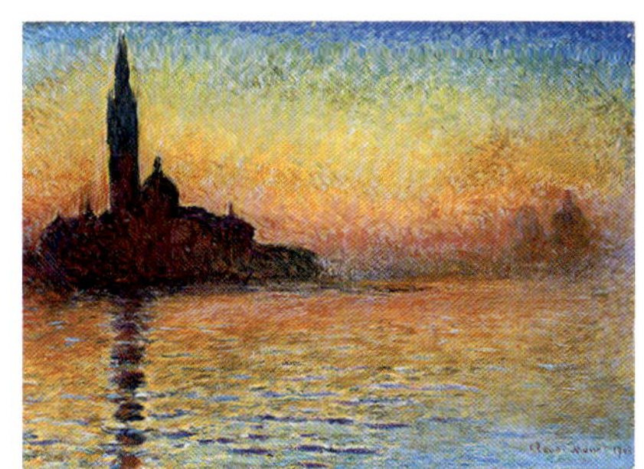

Claude Monet
Saint-Georges majeur au crépuscule
(San Giorgio Maggiore at Dusk), 1908
Oil on canvas, 65 x 92 cm
National Museum of Wales, Cardiff

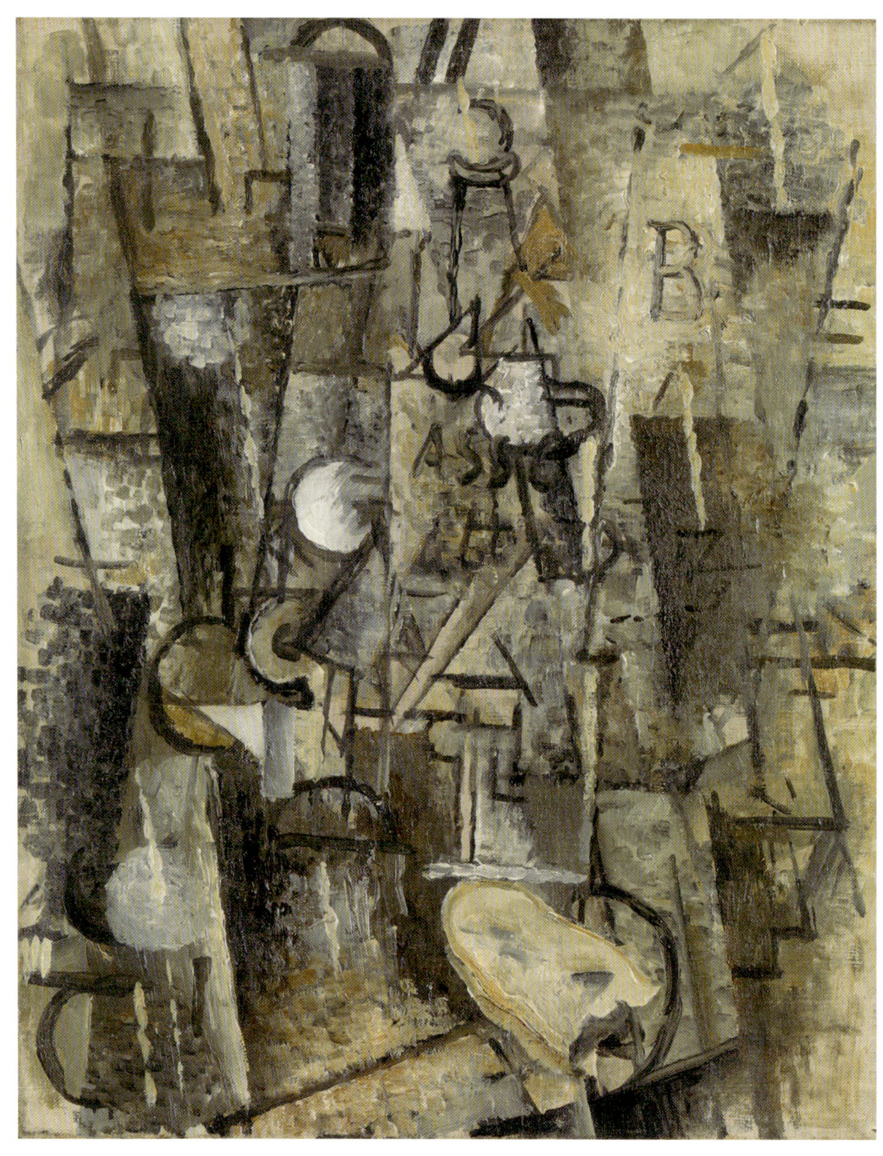

Georges Braque
La Bouteille de Bass (Bottle of Bass), c.1911–12
Oil on canvas, 41.5 x 35 cm
Triton Collection Foundation, Rotterdam

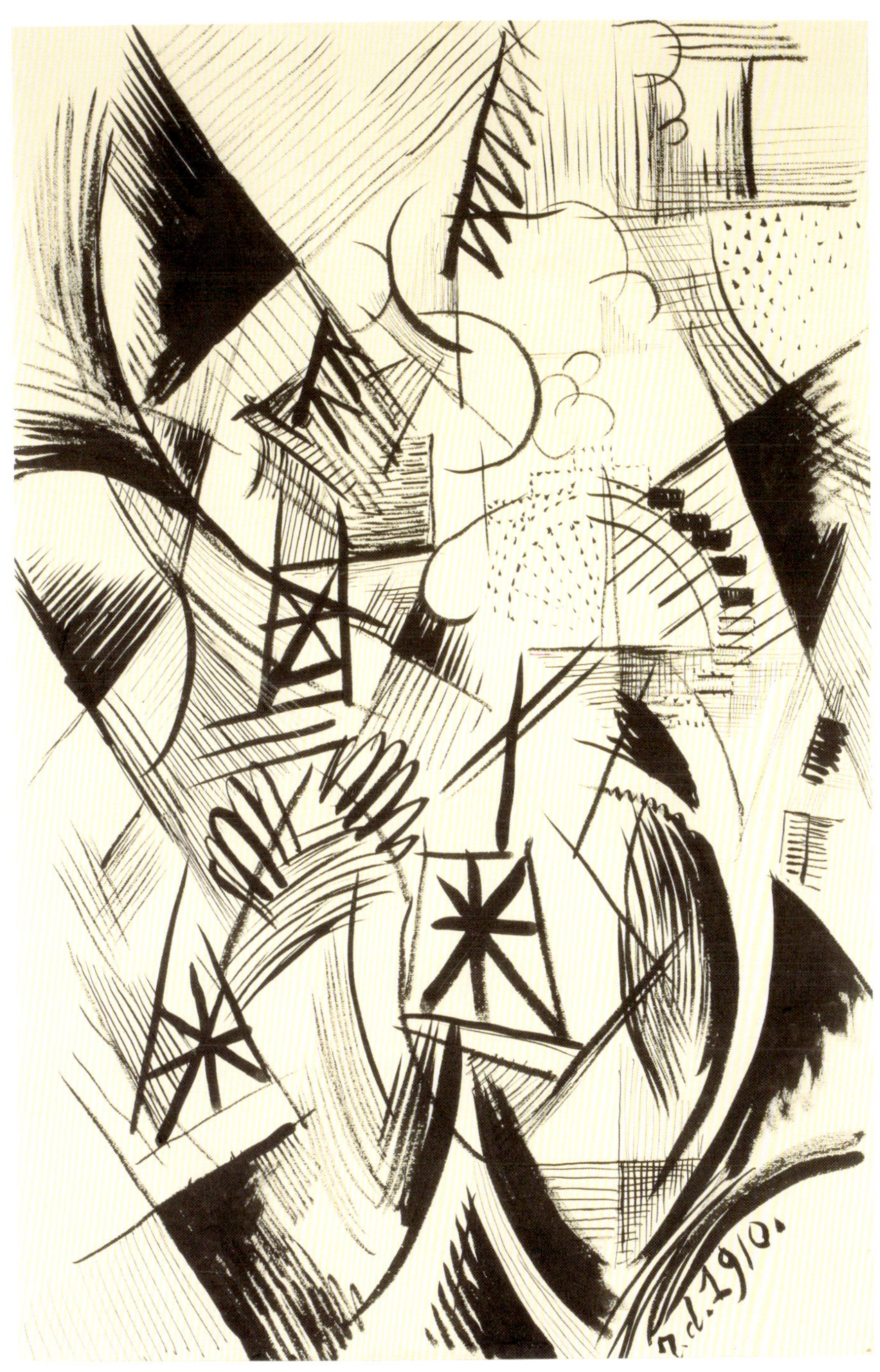

Robert Delaunay
La Tour Eiffel et la Roue
(The Eiffel Tower and the Ferris Wheel), 1910
Pen and ink on paper, 49.5 x 31.7 cm
Triton Collection Foundation, Rotterdam

Mondrian

› The management of the Musée du Louvre give Mondrian permission to make copies in its galleries. It is not known what he copied, but it seems likely he would have worked on the much copied *Pietà of Villeneuve-lès-Avignon* by Enguerrand Quarton (c.1410–1466), commissioned by Marie Tak van Poortvliet, to be included in her growing collection of contemporary art because of its spiritual similarities to the new art (pp.31, 32).

Mondrian replies to a letter from Lodewijk Schelfhout in which he referred to him as a hermit, pointing out that this is a distortion of the truth. '[An] illusory life would be no life at all to me, and so I preferred nothing. I was also having great difficulties at the time, as I was seeking my own way of expressing myself, and I was greatly troubled to hear in a letter from Kickert that you had suggested I might not be working etc. – while I was in fact seriously in search of something but had little to show'.[51] It seems likely that work that was completed in the spring of 1913 was already underway by then.[52]

From June, Mondrian is in contact with the poet Dop Bles (1883–1940), who works at the publishing house Hachette in Paris and is a close acquaintance of Severini and Van Dongen. Bles has already had contact with Reverend Hendrick van Assendelft in Gouda thanks to his activities as a poet, writer, theatre critic and bookseller at Hector & Bazendijk in Rotterdam.[53] Bles believes Dutch theatre can become modern if it is purely realistic and clearly objective, depicting for example psychological reactions in an unemotional way.[54]

Paris

› As Picasso and Braque are incorporating many readymade literal quotes from popular culture into their work (in the years prior to this they had largely used fragmentary references in words and images), Apollinaire begins to refer in his notes and critical writings to the modern style so clearly emerging in wrought iron, sheet steel and in the aesthetics of technology.

The Netherlands

› In an open letter, painters, writers, sculptors, architects, journalists, critics, doctors, lawyers and 'ordinary people' inform Amsterdam city council of their lack of confidence in Carel Dake's chairmanship of the Quadrennial, because he has failed to do justice to 'that important movement of our day, which seeks closer connection with a purer relationship between the visual arts' and because of his failure to take account of 'the important spiritual movements of our time'.[55]

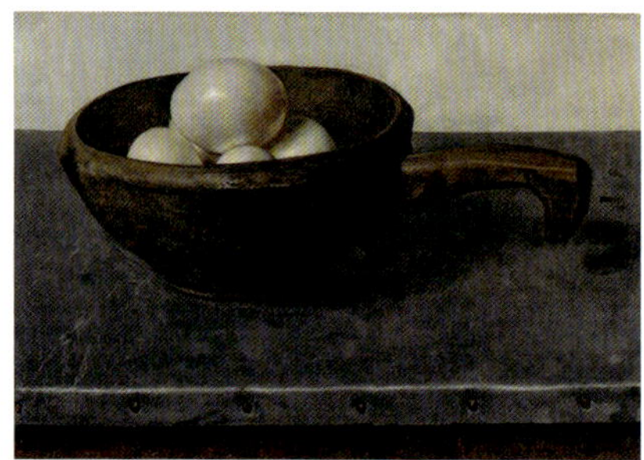

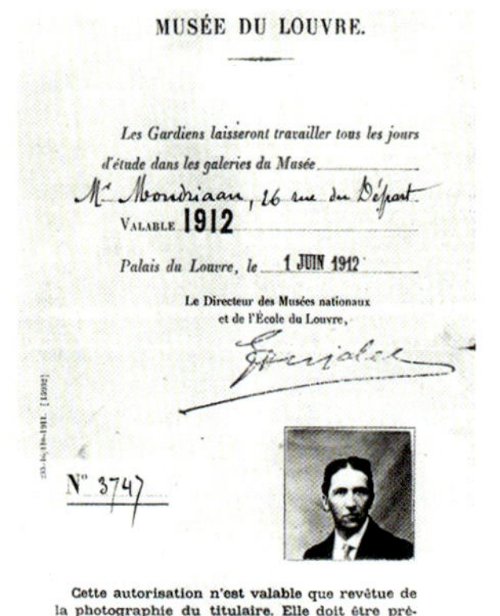

MUSÉE DU LOUVRE.

Les Gardiens laisseront travailler tous les jours d'étude dans les galeries du Musée

Mr Mondriaan, 26 rue du Départ.

Valable 1912

Palais du Louvre, le 1 JUIN 1912

Le Directeur des Musées nationaux et de l'École du Louvre,

N° 3747

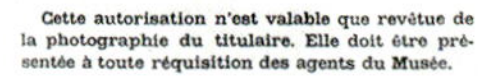

Cette autorisation n'est valable que revêtue de la photographie du titulaire. Elle doit être présentée à toute réquisition des agents du Musée.

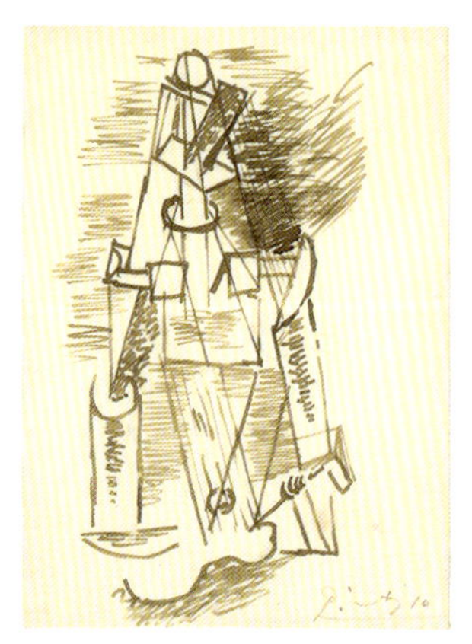

Floris Verster
Napje met eieren (Bowl of Eggs), 1906
Oil on panel, 24 x 37 cm
Gemeentemuseum Den Haag, The Hague

Official ticket from the Louvre giving Mondrian permission to work on a copy from the museum's collection, June 1912.

Pablo Picasso
Femme avec une Guitare, étude pour une sculpture (Women with Guitar, study for a sculpture), 1912
Ink on paper, 17.1 x 12.4 cm
Triton Collection Foundation, Rotterdam

› Jan van Deene reports that he has been to a fair on France's national holiday with Jacob Bendien (1890–1933) and Mondrian. 'Mondrian, by no means a hermit, gaily danced with the girls at the neighbourhood street ball on "quatorze juillet".' Van Deene also emphasises that Mondrian is taken with the often much younger artists around him, and that he takes their work seriously, always eager for new insights, and happy to debate with them.[56]

Mondrian enters a cubist painting in an exhibition in Nijmegen, the Netherlands, organised by Jan Toorop, and Toorop refers to Mondrian's work in his opening address.[57]

› Mondrian writes a postcard to Willem Steenhoff, director of the Rijksmuseum, telling him that he will 'have the copy finished tomorrow' and that he will then come to the Netherlands.[61] When he arrives in the Netherlands on 28 July he goes first to Arnhem to visit his father and sister, and then goes to Amsterdam. At the end of July he is in Domburg to deliver his copy of the *Pietà of Villeneuve-lès-Avignon* to Marie Tak van Poortvliet, and to enjoy a summer holiday as her guest.

› Umberto Boccioni writes from Milan to Severini in Paris, asking him to go as quickly as possible to Kahnweiler and obtain photographs of the latest works by Picasso and Braque. If possible, Severini should buy one or two photographs and send them immediately.[58] In preparing his new paintings, Boccioni probably wants to know what he has to take into account.

› Braque writes to Picasso, who has rented a house in Sorgues near Avignon in order to work in peace, telling him that he has seen recent paintings at Kahnweiler's gallery, which impressed Braque. These are works from spring 1912 in which brighter colours – red, blue and violet – play a more pronounced and more autonomous role.

› Mondrian shows one painting, *In the Garden*, at an exhibition in Nijmegen organised by Toorop, which opens on 1 July (this was possibly *The Grey Tree*, 1911, p.30). A review of the exhibition examines Mondrian's work, revealing again that he discussed his painting, because 'while the painters of this movement depicted things in a cubist manner, geometricising, synthesising their forms, they did not rob them of all form. Mondrian tried this. One believes one discerns a tree and a few roofs, though without being certain that one really sees them properly. Toorop spoke of spiritualisation. That must be it, though we are probably looking at a means more comprehensible to the initiated (Theosophists perhaps?) that they conventionally use to make themselves understood'.[59]

Jacob Bendien returns to the Netherlands from Paris in the second half of 1912, and works on a number of large, completely abstract paintings. He exhibits them in Amsterdam in November 1913 at De Onafhankelijken, an artists' society. Although Bendien explicitly states that these works represent the inner life expressed in the form of absolute painting, the public interprets them as decoration, as 'soap bubbles' or 'oscillations'.[60]

› German art dealer and trendsetter Herwarth Walden (1878–1941) opens the first Futurist exhibition in the Netherlands at the Kunstzaal Biesing in The Hague, on 7 July.[62] The exhibition later moves to Amsterdam where it is met with fierce criticism. In Rotterdam, artists respond more phlegmatically, as they did in The Hague. Walden owns a gallery, Der Sturm, in Berlin, where he displays Futurist works as part of a more general German Expressionist trend. In his opening address, Walden emphasises that the young artists are bent not on evolution but on revolution. Both past *and* nature will make way for the future.

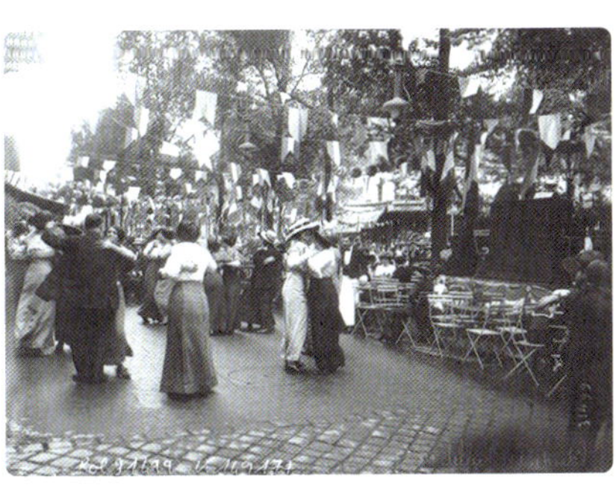

People dancing at a street party in Paris to celebrate Bastille Day, 14 July 1912.

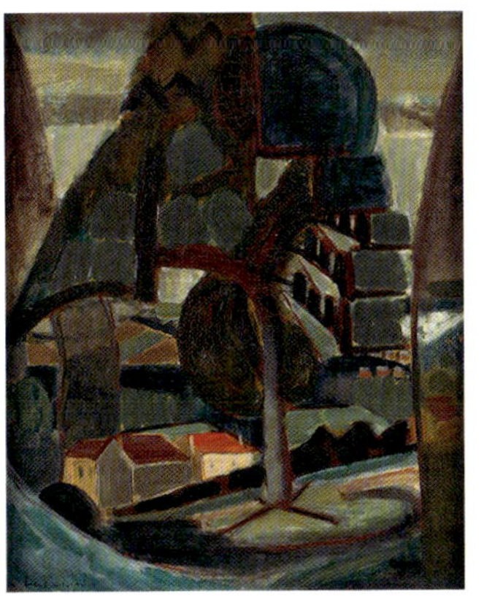

Henri Le Fauconnier
Paysage de Meulan-Hardricourt
(Landscape at Meulan-Hardricourt), 1912
Oil on canvas, 53.5 x 45.5 cm
Gemeentemuseum Den Haag, The Hague

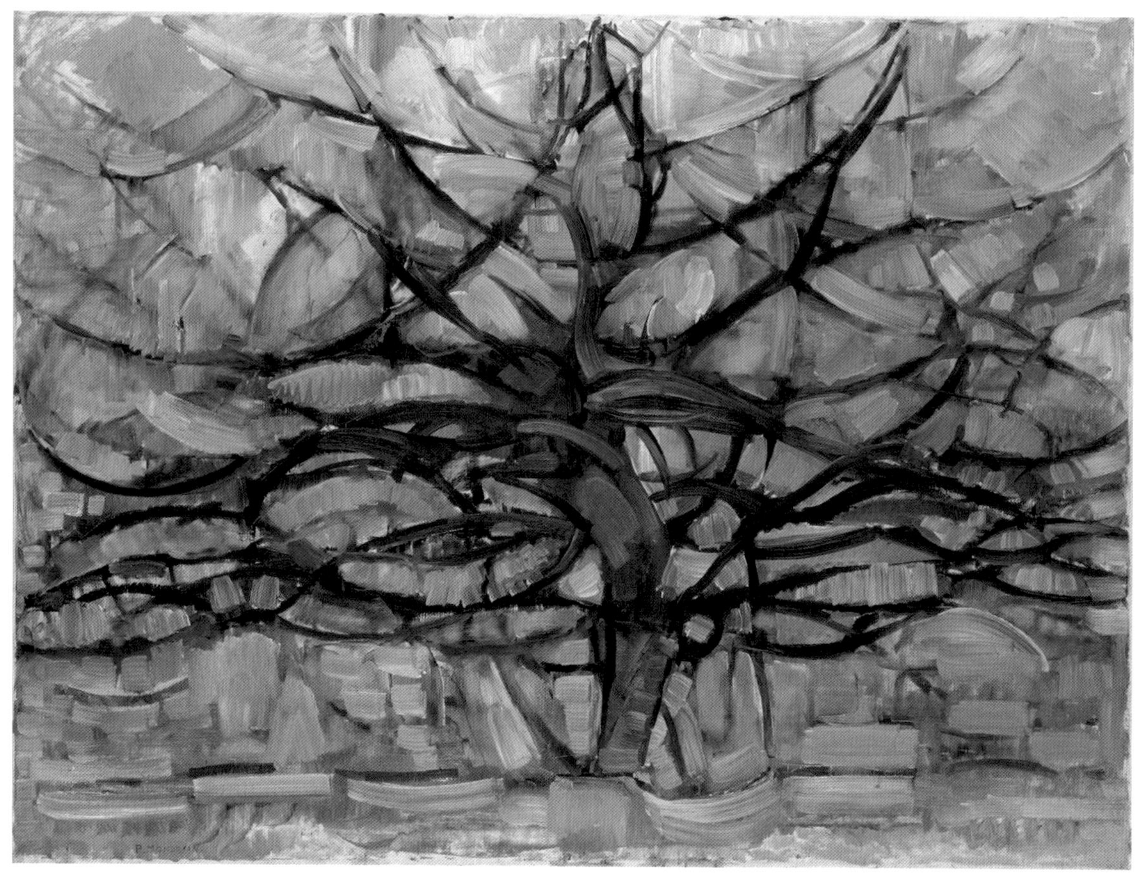

Piet Mondrian
De grijze boom (The Grey Tree), 1911
Oil on canvas, 79.7 x 109.1 cm
Gemeentemuseum Den Haag, The Hague

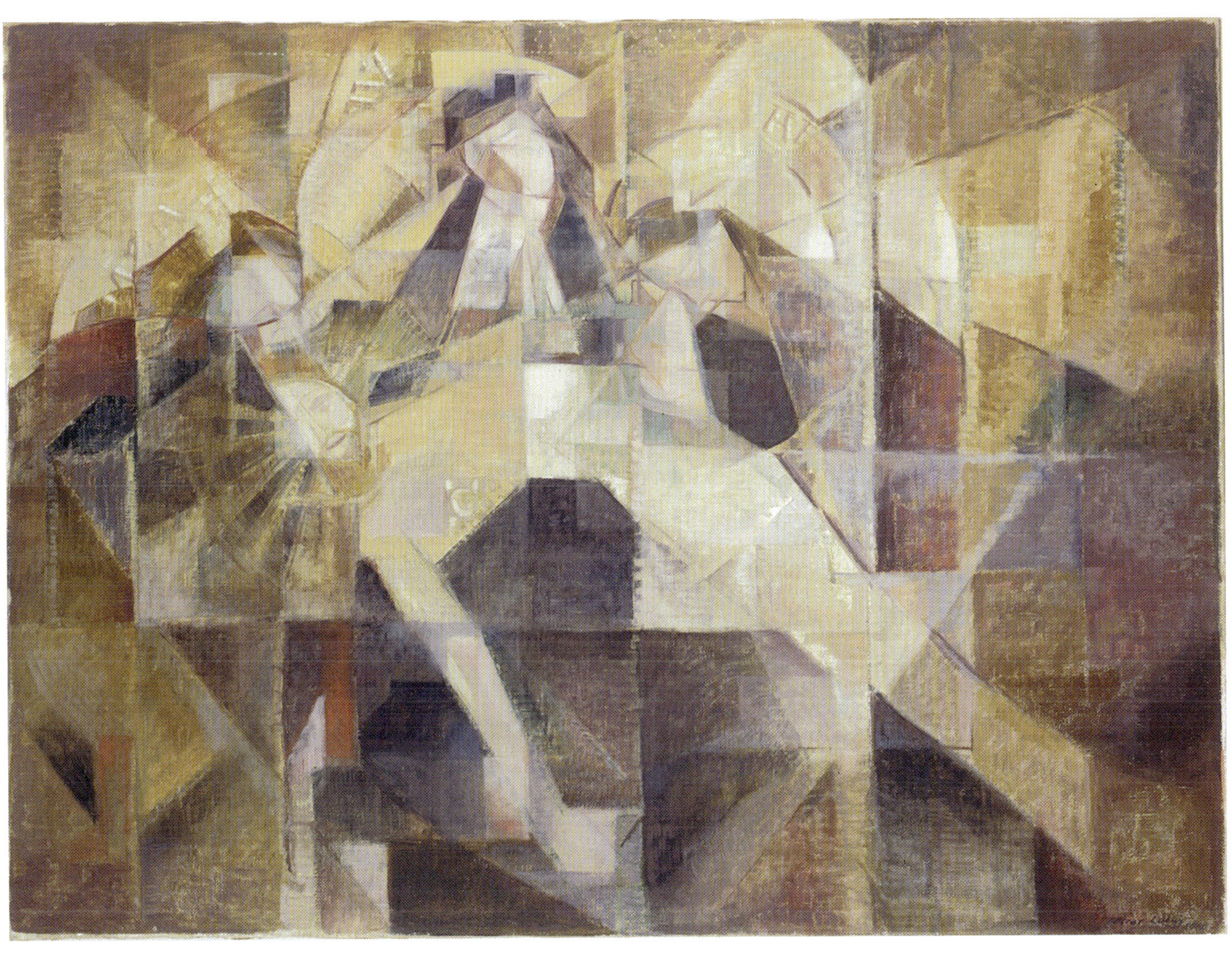

Oskar Lüthy
Variation zur Pietà von Avignon (Enguerrand Quarton, um 1450),
(Variation on the Pietà of Avignon by Enguerrand Quarton, 1450), 1913–14
Oil on canvas, 110 x 150 cm
Hermann and Margrit Rupf-Stiftung, Kunstmuseum Bern

Mondrian

› In Domburg Mondrian exhibits seven earlier works depicting landscapes and flowers.[63] He sells two drawings. He stays in Domburg until 13 August, as a guest of Marie Tak van Poortvliet, developing a number of sketches into compositions. One of these is *Trees, Sketch*, a piece that still features many elements also found in Schelfhout's work.[64] He also paints two new pieces there.[65] These are the first new paintings to 'succeed'.[66] He probably leaves them behind in Domburg, from where they are taken to Amsterdam for the Moderne Kunst Kring exhibition in October.[67] He draws a lot and makes notes on painting: 'About beauty in the appearance of things (Things as a whole and every piece of them – The surface beautiful.)'; 'Impossible to ~~imitate~~ depict. Representation more likely. Inner representation. Represent. Representation of idea of expansion.'[68] Though hesitant, his words try to make clear that substance lies not *within* the artwork, like a message in a basket, but on the surface, in the image.

› After returning to Paris, Mondrian spends the entire month working on four paintings.[72] On 25 August he reports, 'the still life will (I think) be good'.[73] On 20 September he writes to a friend that, 'thank God', his paintings are eventually on their way to Amsterdam. 'I am not dissatisfied with my work, particularly the trees. The still life is still not as I want it. If I do not dislike it when I hang it in Amsterdam, it will be the first time that I am "a little" satisfied.'[74]

Paris

› Braque goes to Sorgues to stay with Picasso. Together they visit Marseille to buy African mask sculptures. When Braque rents accommodation nearby, a competitive burst of creativity erupts between the two artists, as it previously had in Céret, resulting in the *papiers collés*. Kahnweiler writes that Apollinaire plans to write an article with illustrations of Braque's latest work.[69]

› One of the main attractions – the *Cubist House* (p.36) – is not complete when the Salon d'Automne opens on 1 October. The installation, a fully furnished house, has yet to open because the designers keep coming up with new things. Sensational paintings, by Albert Gleizes, Jean Metzinger, František Kupka (1871–1957) and Francis Picabia (1879–1953), cannot hide the fact that the key concern in *The Cubist House* is Cubism in the applied arts. Apollinaire takes a tour on

The Netherlands

› Jan Toorop gives the opening address at the summer exhibition in Domburg, in which he calls Mondrian a serious striver who 'is currently seeking more and more spiritualisation, outside natural forms'. He also praises the 'dramatic rhythmic movement of complementary colours and contrasting lines' in the cubist work that Lodewijk Schelfhout is showing.[70] A critic for *De Kunst* writes: 'Anyone who knows how cleverly [Jacoba van Heemskerck] used to produce "ordinary" drawings and paintings will follow her current progress in a new direction with all the more interest. Whether one agrees with Cubism or not, there is indisputably a big idea in this style, this aspiration: to express the sensitive emotions of the artist in lines and planes, forming a harmonious whole of colour and line; a quest for a composition that comes from the artist himself and not, as previously, from the objects he regards; that thus arouses feeling in the painter, but from the sensitive, self-encountered perception of a thing in nature – a person, a tree, the sea – that the painter orders in his emotions and lays down in colours and tones, in lines and planes, in rhythmic relativity, thus forming a whole.'[71]

› On 29 August Herwarth Walden opens the exhibition of Futurists in the large gallery at the company premises of De Roos in Amsterdam, in the presence of the mayor of Amsterdam and the curator of the Stedelijk Museum. His speech is full of derisive remarks: he is angry because no artists' society had agreed to house the exhibition. The weekly magazine *De Kunst* has paid for the exhibition. Similar to reactions abroad, there are few serious responses to the 24 paintings, despite the fact that these are artists following in the footsteps of Cézanne and Van Gogh, who are held in high regard in the Netherlands. There was only

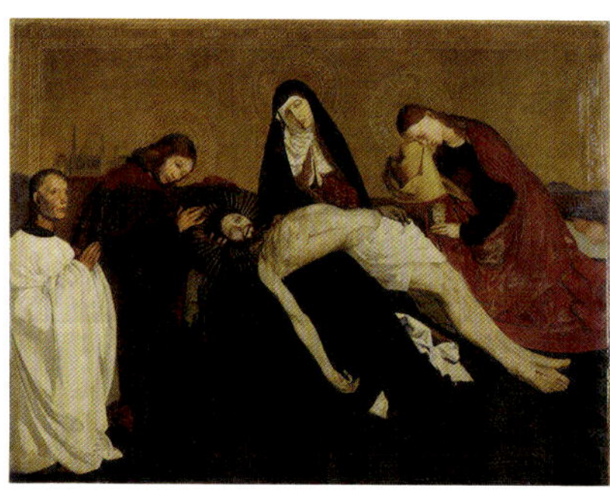

Piet Mondrian
Kopie naar de Pieta van Villeneuve-Les-Avignon door Enguerrand Quarton
(Copy after Enguerrand Quarton, Pietà of Villeneuve-lès-Avignon), 1912
Oil on canvas, 105 x 140 cm
Gemeentemuseum Den Haag, The Hague

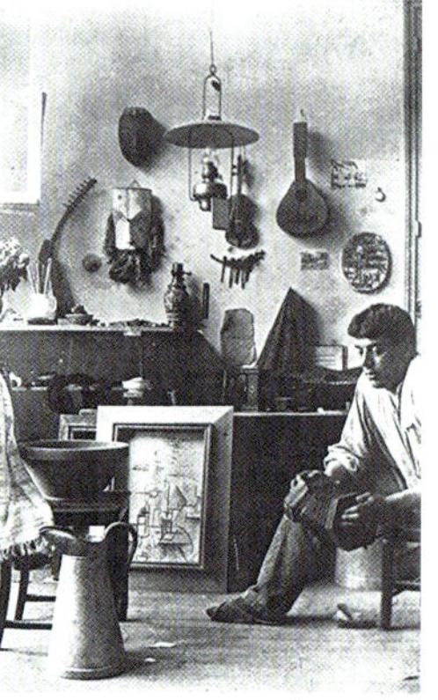

Georges Braque in his studio in Montmartre at 5 impasse de Guelma, Paris, 1911.

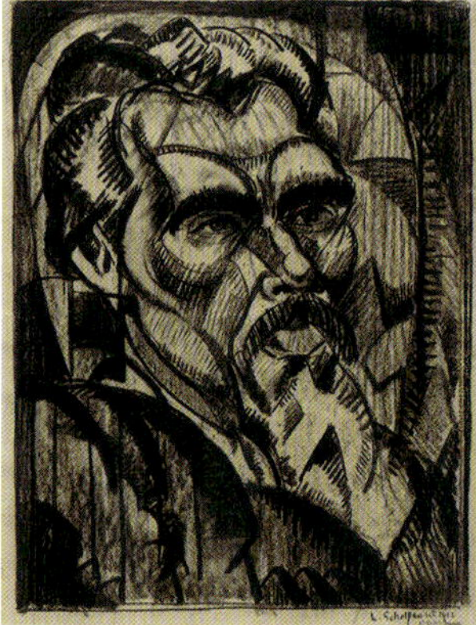

Lodewijk Schelfhout
Portret van Jan Toorop
(Portrait of Jan Toorop), 1912
Chalk on paper, 58.7 x 45.2 cm
Gemeentemuseum Den Haag, The Hague

› Mondrian participates in the Moderne Kunst Kring exhibition under the name P Mondrian.[78] He is in Amsterdam on Wednesday 2 October, as a member of the selection committee.[79] He is also present at the hanging of his work, *Hyacinths*, which can be identified as the triptych shown in Cologne at the Sonderbund exhibition that has just closed.[80] The exhibition features a broad sample of French Cubism: Le Fauconnier shows 33 pieces, and Kickert has managed to obtain six works from Braque, seven from Derain, four each from Gleizes, Metzinger and Auguste Herbin (1882–1960), 14 from Léger, and 12 from Picasso.

Mondrian dines with an old friend in Amsterdam, singer Katinka Hannaert (1868–1946). She brings along an acquaintance from her time in Berlin, Dutch pianist and composer Jakob van Domselaer (1890–1960). The conversation is somewhat stilted.

30 September and, even without seeing the whole thing, calls it 'elegant, simple and a testimony to good taste'.[75] Cubism is becoming fashionable. There are even calls for industry to be compelled to work with the artists.[76]

› Le Fauconnier demonstrates his independence from the mainstream Cubists, not only by showing just one painting at the Salon d'Automne (all his other work is in Amsterdam!), but also by his conspicuous absence from the Salon de la Section d'Or which opens on 11 October. Picabia, a man of independent financial means, sponsors 30 Cubists who show their work at the Salon, standing up to attempts to subsume Cubism into the *arts decoratifs* – the official salon that refused to take them seriously – and to the 'gallery Cubists', as artists from the Kahnweiler stable are known. Fernand Léger looks around the Salon d'Automne and, as he takes in the 'endlessly dull, grey paintings in neat frames', he hears from the neighbouring Salon d'Aviation the clanking and purring of engines and he sees beautiful, shiny machinery, 'plain steel in a thousand shapes against bright blue and pure vermillion, everything determined by the power of geometrical shapes'.[81]

one critic, according to Walden, who discussed the Futurists seriously in response to the exhibition in The Hague, and not in a positive light incidentally.[77]

› In a snarling review of the opening of the Moderne Kunst Kring, Carel Drake lashes out at Mondrian in *De Telegraaf*: 'His paintings feature grey patches transected by random ("rhythmic", if you will) lines, but there is no one in the world who can work out what the painter means by them and he probably does not know himself...He says he is in search of style. As if a style can be sought. Style always emerges of its own accord and as a result of an artist's endeavours to deliver the best possible and most complete work...And "style" was a "pillar" supporting the idea of the work because it stood on the firm base of conviction, study and objective observation. The "moderns", the "ultra-moderns", have no such firm base. How can a style, supporting an idea, be built on that?!'[82]

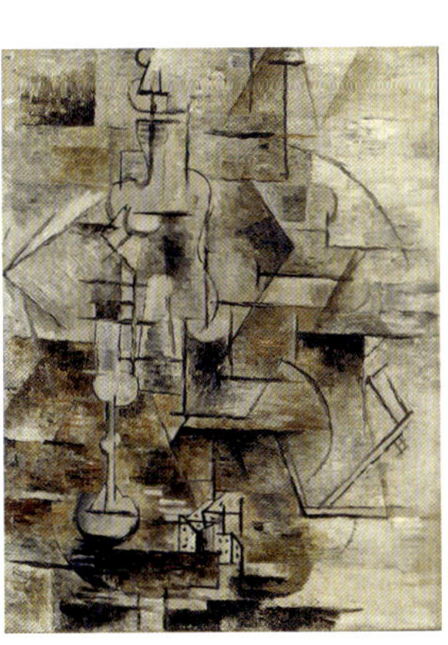

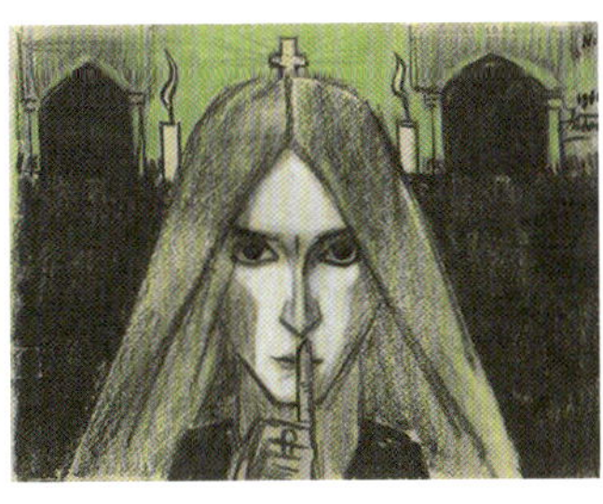

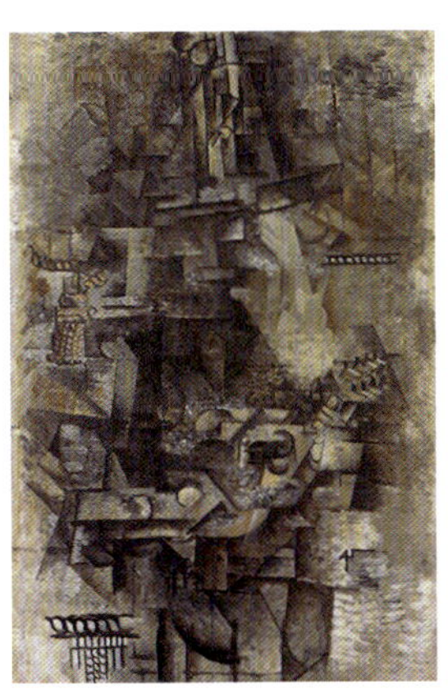

Georges Braque
Verre, bouteille et dés
(Glass, bottle and dice), 1911
Oil on canvas, 60 x 46 cm
Private Collection

Jan Toorop
De heilige vrouw (Holy Woman), 1914
Chalk on paper, 22.1 x 28 cm
Gemeentemuseum Den Haag, The Hague

Pablo Picasso
Le Mandoliniste (Mandolin Player), 1911
Oil on canvas, 100 x 65 cm
Beyeler Foundation, Riehen

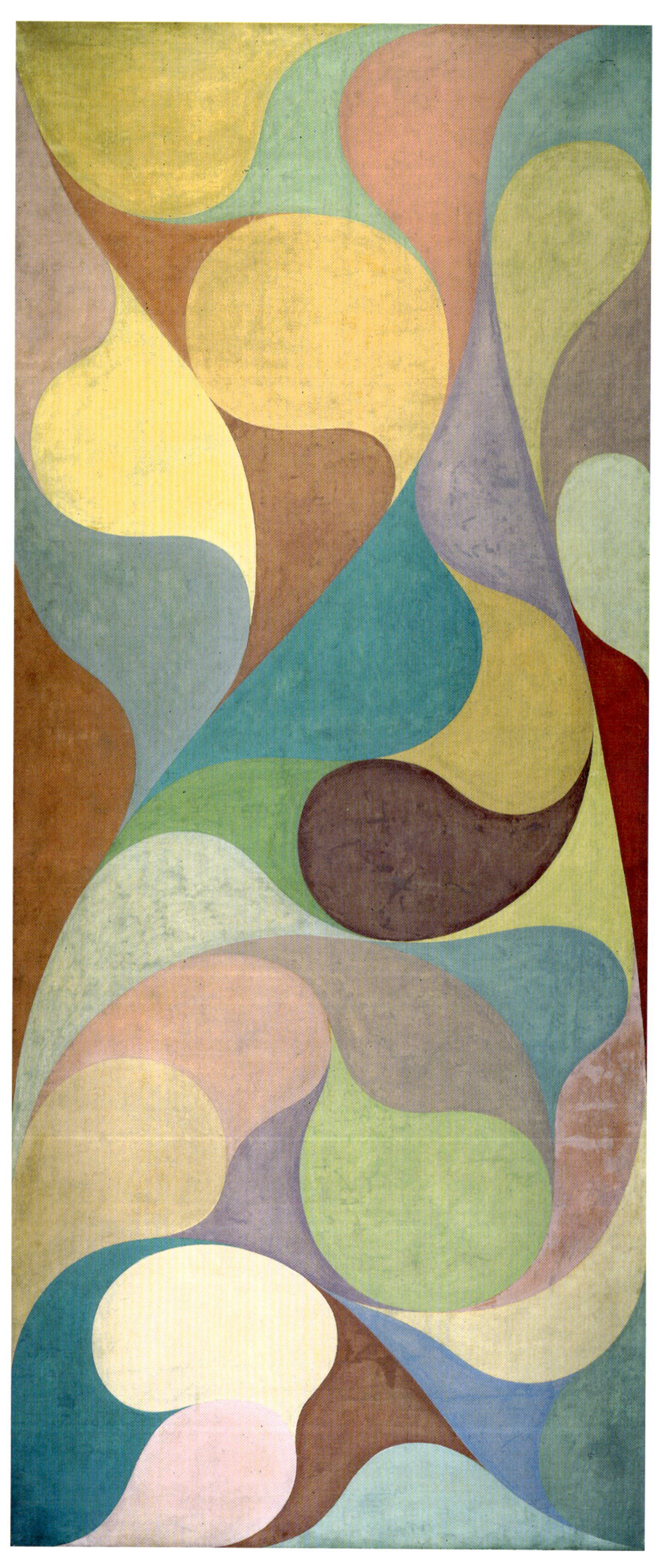

Jacob Bendien
Abstracte compositie
(Abstract Composition), 1912
Oil on canvas, 345 x 150 cm
Gemeentemuseum Den Haag,
The Hague

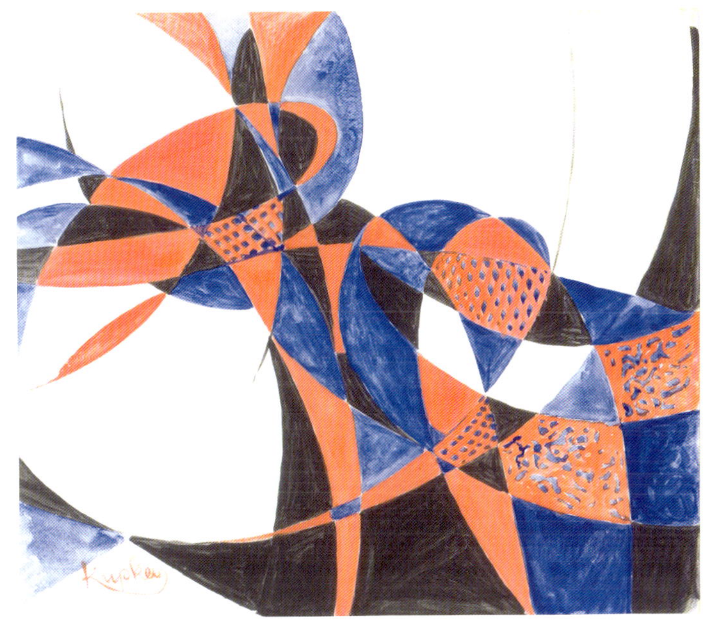

František Kupka
Study for Amorpha, 1912
Pencil over water-based paint on paper, 27.6 x 32 cm
Triton Collection Foundation, Rotterdam

Mondrian

› Mondrian sells three pieces at the Moderne Kunst Kring: one to Willem Beffie, one to Marie Tak van Poortvliet and one to Fritz Meyer-Fierz (1847–1917), a collector from Zurich. Kickert takes possession of one painting under his arrangement with Mondrian.[83]

Given this commercial success, it seems likely that Mondrian is in a position to buy a number of canvases for new work upon his return to Paris.

Paris

› The conservative Parisian newspaper *Le Temps* asks Apollinaire to explain whether Cubism actually means anything. Apollinaire describes the encounters between the artists and their passion for primitive masks. This has engendered in them a desire to paint the reality they perceive, rather than the reality they observe, an inner reality whose meaning is derived from concepts.[84]

The Netherlands

› In his review of the Moderne Kunst Kring exhibition in *De Amsterdammer*, Willem Steenhoff concludes that Le Fauconnier is not an artist of any particular merit, and Picasso and Mondrian are the most consistent moderns. When it comes to Cubism, 'they literally battle through thick and thin in this wilful repudiation of nature. Their abstract depiction of reality is absolute, yet highly varied. Picasso, the wily one, works with business-like purpose on the basis of a geometrically structured combination of lines of an unmistakably angular character... Though very vague, Mondrian is more decipherable. One outward difference from Picasso is that his form system is not rectilinear and angular, but presented in the form of curved lines and arabesques. It is much richer in illusion. I see in Mondrian a faithful devotee to a system, by which he thought he could proceed straight to a spiritualised art, as is his goal. But the artist in him seems in reality to be confined by this. It will be a temporary setback, I hope, and beneficial to the further, broader expansion of his aspirations. His great error would appear to me to be that he confuses the beauty of the rudimentary with the final goal. Though he is more abstract than last year, his work is purer and more internalised.'[85]

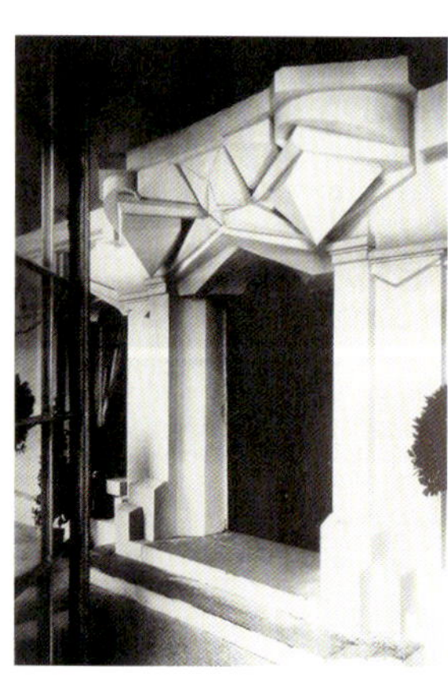

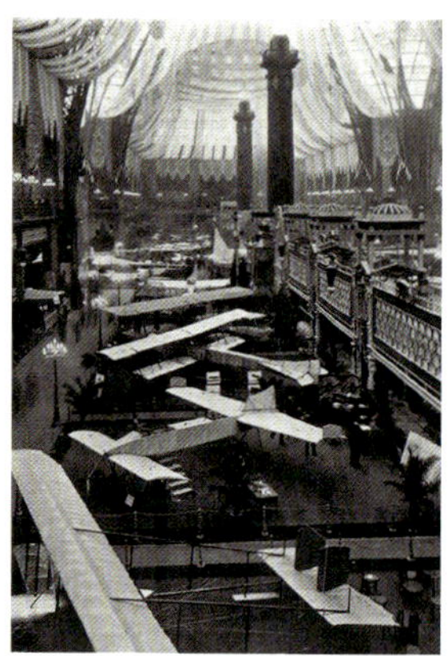

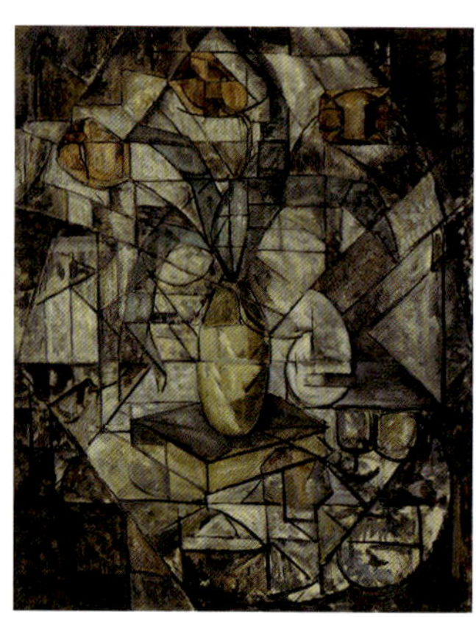

Entrance to *La Maison Cubiste* (Cubist House), designed by Raymond Duchamp-Villon, at the Salon d'Automne, Paris, 1912.

Exhibition hall, Salon d'Aviation, Paris, October 1912.

Jacoba van Heemskerck
Compositie No. 1 (Composition No. 1), 1912–13
Oil on canvas, 100.3 x 80.8 cm
Gemeentemuseum Den Haag, The Hague

› Jakob van Domselaer writes to Mondrian informing him that he is coming to Paris, with little expectation of receiving a reply. To his surprise, Mondrian is waiting for him at Gare du Nord, and has booked a nice little hotel for him on rue Jacob. They dine together and a friendship develops. Later in the year this friendship will lead to an intense exchange of ideas about the future of art and music.

Under the influence of the 1912 paintings by Braque and Picasso, exhibited at the Moderne Kunst Kring, Mondrian begins two or three paintings on his return to Paris in which he abandons the smooth and flat colour fill within a line structure, and starts to handle colour, line, stroke, light, shadow and tone independently, using brushstrokes stacked like brickwork. This produces frothy, silvery effects in white and ochre in which form, line, colour and, above all, composition appear to dissolve the subjects (the portrait of Eva de Beneditty he brought with him from the Netherlands (p.122) and a large study of trees) into rhythmic sparkling light and movement. He also begins an oval composition in the style of Picasso's *Man with a Pipe* (1911), which he had seen in Amsterdam.

› Picasso and Braque turn to *papiers collés*, using sand and Ripolin, a brand of enamel paint, in defiance of painting. On 26 October critic Max Goth (1893–1977) announces in response to an article by Louis Vauxcelles that Picasso has renounced Cubism in order to devote himself to 'higher speculations'.[86]

› Conrad Kickert persuades Henri Le Fauconnier to write an essay entitled '*La sensibilité moderne et le tableau*' (Modern Sensibility and the Picture) for the catalogue of the second Moderne Kunst Kring exhibition. Le Fauconnier argues that nowadays the superficial viewer believes a work of art to be the coincidental product of the human mind. Nothing could be further from the truth. Transport, machines, scientific discoveries, philosophical constructs and urban developments have all had an impact in the early twentieth century. The artist senses a new order, based on laws derived from art history. The complexity of modern life coincides with the complexity of contemporary composition. The artist can capture the vitality of his emotions in colour, form, and tonality, and allow the complexity to crystallise. The subject is merely a pretext to start painting; theories are secondary. The painting resists any attempt at subversion, ridicule or abuse by lesser talents. Young artists are concerned about this, but the artwork itself possesses a power that can resolve any confusion.[87]

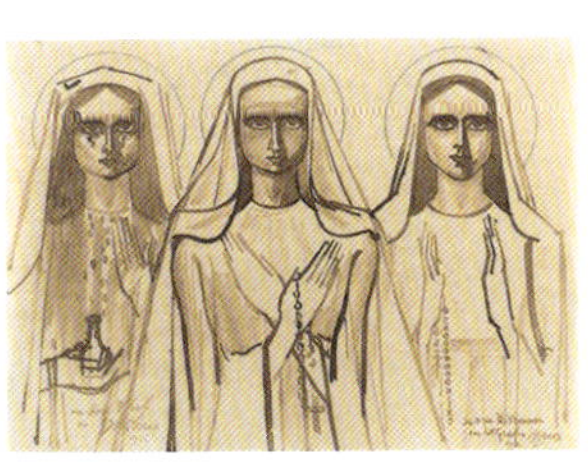

Jan Toorop
De drie Heilige Vrouwen aan het graf
(Three Holy Women at the Grave), 1912
Sepia on paper, 19 x 26.5 cm
Gemeentemuseum Den Haag, The Hague

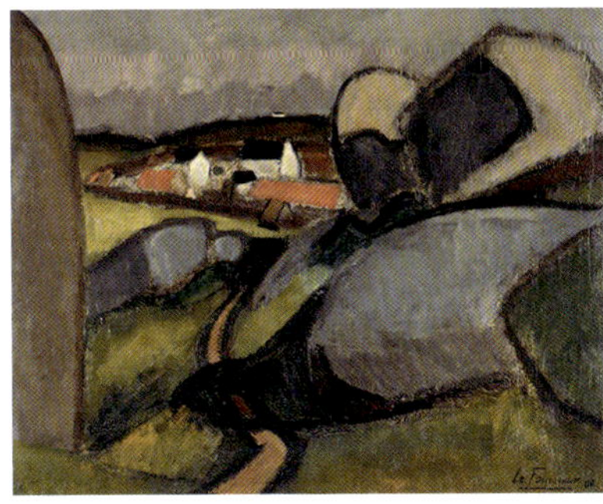

Henri Le Fauconnier
Le Village dans les rochers (Ploumanac'h)
(Village Among the Rocks (Ploumanac'h)), 1908
Oil on canvas, 93.2 x 75 cm
Gemeentemuseum Den Haag, The Hague

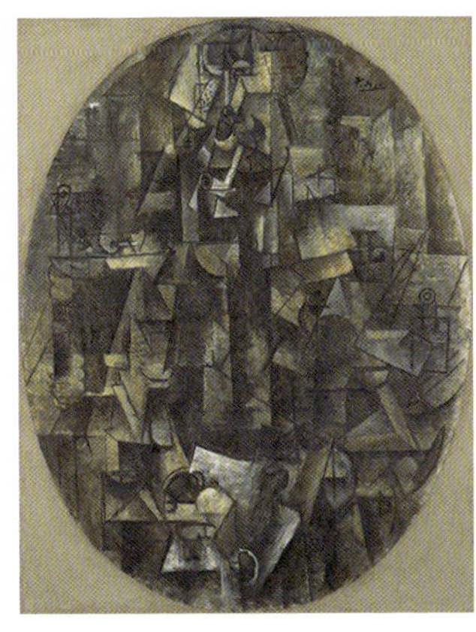

Pablo Picasso
Homme à la pipe (Man with a Pipe), 1911
Oil on canvas, 90.7 x 71 cm
Kimbell Art Museum, Fort Worth

Mondrian

› Mondrian continues to work on cubist compositions based on trees. 'I want to get as close as possible to the truth and am therefore abstracting everything until I get to the foundation (albeit still an outward foundation!) of things.'[88] In practical terms this means that Mondrian breaks the line more radically and gives free rein to intuitively applied brushwork and to a palette which, following the example of Picasso and Braque, he has reduced to ochre and white. He also produces a painting with no ochre at all, in which everything is casually constructed, as in a sketch, in black, white and grey, the black intersected here and there with red highlights.[89] At the end of November 1912, Conrad Kickert moves from 26 rue du Départ to 110 rue Denfert-Rochereau, where he remains until he leaves France in January 1914; Lodewijk Schelfhout returns to the Netherlands to get married in the spring of 1913. Mondrian's relationships with both men have cooled by this time.

› Jakob van Domselaer's wife, Maaike Middelkoop (1892–1979), recalls that Mondrian spent the entire winter working on trees. 'Although Mondrian lived very reclusively, Piet and Jakob saw each other several times a week. They would generally eat at a "Bouillon" and then spend the evening together. On Sundays they would sometimes take a long walk. They also occasionally called on Peter Alma or Otto van Rees in the evening. But solitude was vital for Mondrian. He found unexpected inter-

Paris

› Although its publication had been announced some time earlier, Albert Gleizes's and Jean Metzinger's book *Du Cubisme* is ultimately published in November. In the book, they attempt to position Cubism, and their own work, within a long tradition extending back to Rembrandt and Michelangelo. At the same time, they also defend the right of an artist to pursue his own ideal and to develop a language that the masses will only be able to understand in the future (to legitimise themselves in relation to the 'gallery Cubists').

› Questions are asked in the Assemblée Nationale about the unwholesome influence of Cubism and Futurism on French society. The member for Bourges observes that three of the 700 entries in the catalogue of the Salon d'Automne are by foreigners, and that no fewer than nine of the 16 jury members are foreigners. He wonders, should the government continue to make its public buildings available for such foreign activities that undermine

The Netherlands

› The *Algemeen Handelsblad* critic reports that he had barely recovered from the shock of the Futurists when another new event came along: an exhibition of Wassily Kandinsky's (1866–1944) work from 1901–12 at Kunsthandel Oldenzeel in Rotterdam. Kandinsky is presented as 'the leader of the German Expressionists'.[90] His latest work, in particular, is even harder to grasp than the work of the most obscure Futurists, the reporter laments. It sometimes reminds one of shells or coral or anemones, and the colours are elegant and not unpleasant, but titles like *Improvisationen* and *Kompositionen* leave the unsuspecting viewer stranded. After studying the exhibition at length, the reporter finally concludes that this is no charlatan at work, nor is Kandinsky an artist who has succumbed to the advertising craze: the work is robust and contains lines and colours that are invigorating and endlessly fascinating, despite being irrational.[91]

› The firm of Schüller and Eissenloeffel in The Hague decides to exhibit the work of progressive young Dutch artists. Leo Gestel is the first, with a major retrospective of his work from 1906 to 1913. The *Algemeen Handelsblad* reviewer concludes that it is all quite simple: while Divisionism dissected colour, so Cubism dissects line and form, all in order to reveal not the 'typical outward appearance', but the 'inner characteristic'.[95] Artist Erich Wichman (1890–1929) gives talks on the developments in art, predicting they will move in

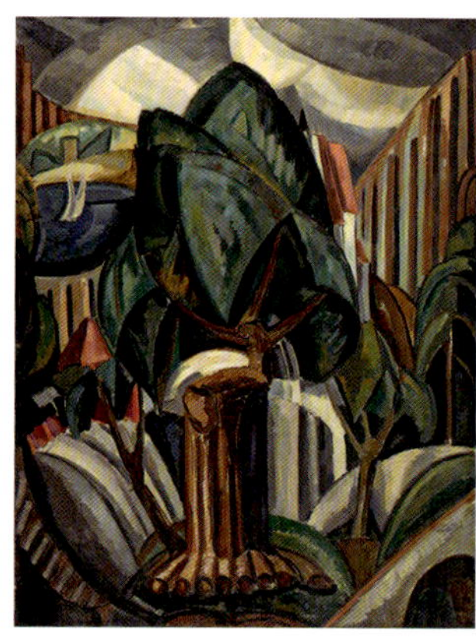

Lodewijk Schelfhout
Landschap met Bomen
(Landscape with Trees), 1912
Oil on canvas, 137.5 x 108.5 cm
Gemeentemuseum Den Haag, The Hague

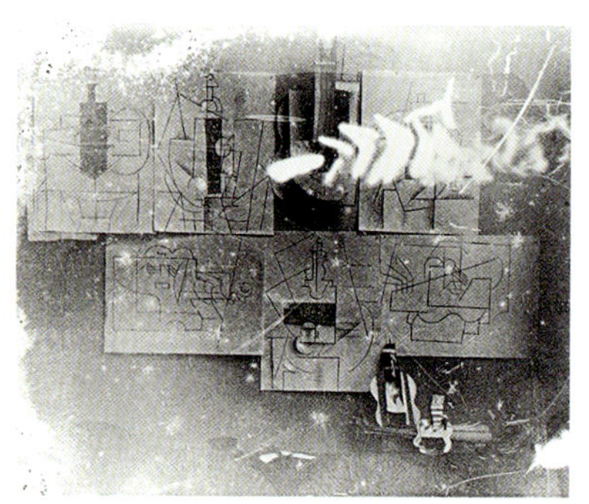

Picasso's studio on boulevard Raspail, Paris, November 1912.

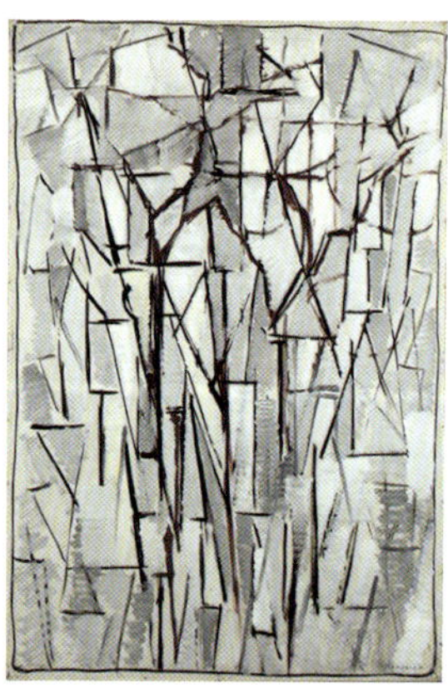

Piet Mondrian
Compositie bomen 2
(Tree Composition 2), 1912–13
Oil on canvas, 98 x 65 cm
Gemeentemuseum Den Haag, The Hague

ruptions highly unpleasant (and generally let it be known in no uncertain terms), and everyone spared him.'[92] An acquaintance from Laren, the Netherlands, of around 1917 recalled, incidentally, that Van Domselaer was also very fond of dancing. 'Van Domselaer was very good at it. A pleasure to watch.'[93]

› In the week of 10 March Mondrian sends three paintings to the Salon des Indépendants: *Tree*, *Flowering Trees*, and *Woman*.[98] Kickert ensures that all Mondrian's work hangs in the same hall – La Salle hollandaise, Salle XLIII – alongside work by Peter Alma, Otto van Rees, Lodewijk Schelfhout and Jacoba van Heemskerck.

› In his announcement of the Salon des Indépendants in *L'Intransigeant-Journal de Paris*, Apollinaire mentions 'Mondrian's *Trees*' as the second of six notable entries.[100] The same day he writes a militant piece for the biweekly illustrated journal *Montjoie!*, asserting that Mondrian produces 'a very abstract Cubism...Although he takes his inspiration from Cubism, he does not imitate them. It seems to me that he is influenced by Picasso, and yet his personality remains entirely his own. That form of Cubism appears to me to

the state? There should, at any rate, be guarantees that no 'scum' will be admitted.[94] Other members attempt to calm things down, reminding members that in the past artists who were initially scorned later received high praise. But the state should exercise its right of control over the decisions of the jury.

› Swiss painter Oskar Lüthy (1882–1945), a friend of Jean (Hans) Arp (1886–1966), spends the winter in Paris, where he meets the artists who frequent La Closerie des Lilas. They reconfirm his conviction that stylised geometrical painting is also suitable for religious painting. He sees the *Pietà of Villeneuve-lès-Avignon* at the Louvre and paints a Cubist version of it, *Variation zur Pietà von Avignon* (p.31).

› Apollinaire begins his discussion of the Salon des Indépendants in *Montjoie!* with a passage on light in painting: 'Light is not a process. It arrives at us by means of sensitivity (of the eye). Without that sensitivity there is no movement. Our eyes have an essential sensitivity that mediates between nature and our soul. The soul loves harmony. Harmony is generated the moment the soul perceives the degree and proportion of

two directions: a realistic direction that sticks to the comprehensible, and a decorative direction that seeks to free itself of any material subject.[96] Slowly but surely, artists are becoming convinced that 'subjectless' artworks based on colour and form guarantee concentration on the 'inward', as it becomes known.[97] To what extent this was influenced by the publication in the Netherlands of Kandinsky's *Über das Geistige in der Kunst* (Concerning the Spiritual in Art) is difficult to ascertain as its impact was not really felt until after 1915.

› Van Heemskerck writes to Lodewijk Schelfhout: 'Nothing unusual is happening in the painting world here, everything is as it was. I have been working very hard and now desire a little rest. I sent three paintings to the Indépendants.'[99]

› Sinologist and essayist Henri Borel (1869–1933) gives a lecture at the Kunstzaal Kleykamp in The Hague, in which he argues that, unlike Oriental art, Western art has no depth. Borel believes that Western art is interested only in 'the beautiful thing' while Chinese art is the 'art of the soul' and reflects inner beauty. Borel gives an example of a painter of the Emperor's horses who focused so much on the animals that, when he painted them, he transferred part of their souls to the work of art, after which the actual horses began to decline.

Leo Gestel
Vrouw tussen bloemen
(Woman among Flowers), 1913
Oil on canvas, 118.4 x 103.5 cm
Gemeentemuseum Den Haag, The Hague

Robert Delaunay
Fenêtre (Window), 1912–13
Oil on canvas, 64.5 x 52.5 cm
Kunstsammlung Nordrhein-Westfalen, Dusseldorf

Piet Mondrian
Eucalyptus, 1912
Charcoal on card, 47 x 39.5 cm
Gemeentemuseum Den Haag, The Hague

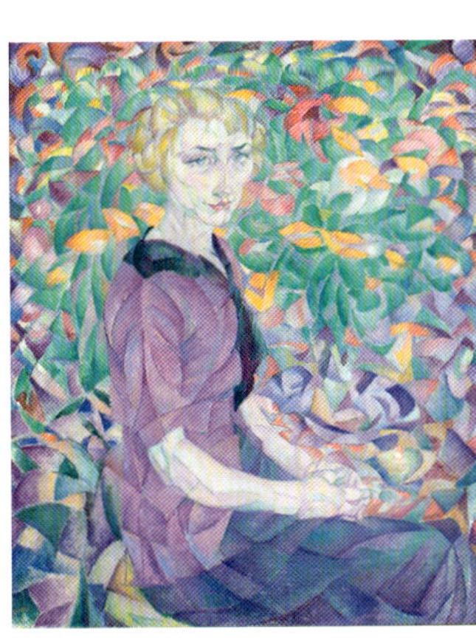

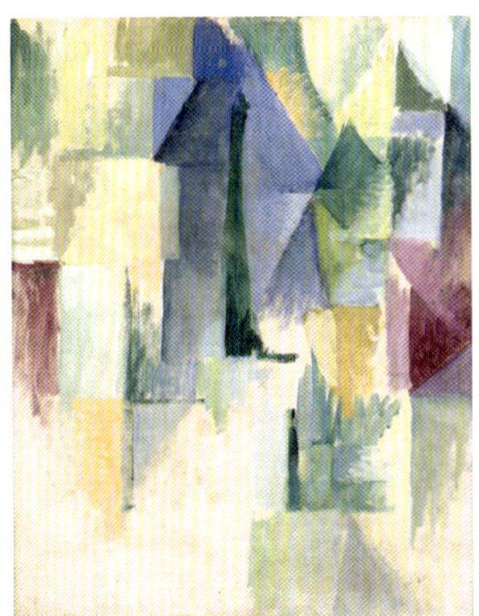

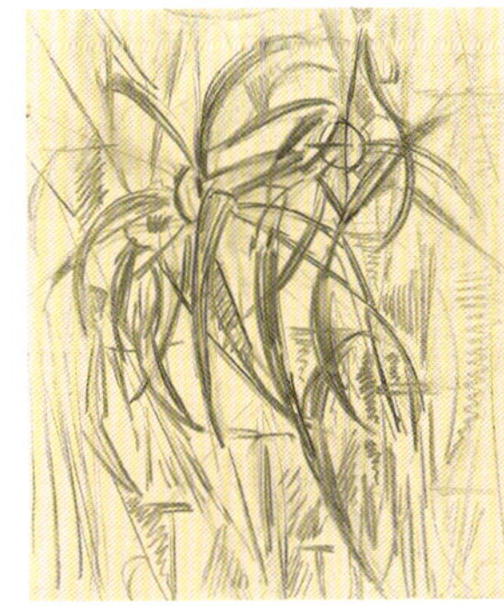

Mondrian

take a different direction from that of Braque and Picasso, who are currently devoting much attention to exploring the material'.[101] In another piece for *L'Intransigeant* four days later, Apollinaire again praises Mondrian.

Around this time Mondrian must have been a frequent visitor to a dance hall in his neighbourhood, where he could pursue his greatest passion in all seriousness, as evidenced by a remark in a letter written to the collector Salomon Slijper (1884–1971) six years later: 'That nice dance hall in my quartier has now gone too: soldiers are billeted there. It was much more convivial in Laren [where Mondrian frequently went out dancing between 1916 and 1919], but you know that the serious is more my thing'.[102]

› Mondrian does not sell anything at the Salon des Indépendants, but he learns something important as a result of entering his work: disrupting the form gives the picture a rhythm. 'Cubism disrupts the form, gradually omits it, and introduces other forms or lines; it even introduces straight lines where they are not immediately apparent in what one sees'.[105] Mondrian starts work on four other canvases which he bought at Blanchet, 38 rue Bonaparte, a shop selling artists' materials near the École des Beaux Arts. He is keen to put what

Paris

light, that extreme sensitivity of our eyes'. It seems likely that Apollinaire had spoken at length with Mondrian.[103]

Kickert's group, which Mondrian no longer really regarded himself a part of, is very pleased with the attention generated by Apollinaire's review in *Montjoie!*, as well as the fact that Cézanne and the Cubists can be seen by everyone in the Netherlands at the Rijksmuseum and Stedelijk Museum in Amsterdam, and that Braque and Picasso are displayed alongside Rembrandt. This solidifies the new art as part of a venerable tradition, making work that had been perceived as wayward and revolutionary suddenly appear quite the reverse.

› Fernand Léger gives a lecture at the Académie Vassiliev on 'The Origin of Painting and its Representational Power'. He makes it clear that the actual quality of a painting is entirely independent of the imitative. This truth is dogma to him. The value of a painting depends on three factors: lines, forms and colours and how they appear. The current developments in art are not a rebellion against Impressionism, but in fact a continuation of it. Today's way of life, fragmenting and accelerating compared to the past, requires a dynamic art.[108]

The Netherlands

The soul resides in symbolism, Borel concludes. The *Algemeen Handelsblad* critic who reports on Borel's lecture writes that this conclusion is premature: spiritualisation, in fact, emerges from the *use* of material means. Rembrandt taught us that emotion, and therefore also spiritualisation, lay in the form and in the material. As evidence that Western art certainly does have a spiritual dimension, the critic mentions the work of Jan Sluijters. It is currently on display at Schüller and Eissenloeffel in The Hague, as well as Fauvist work influenced by Kandinsky, works by the Symbolist painter Odilon Redon (1840–1916), and Futurist artworks.[104]

› Towards the end of February 1913, a lively exchange of correspondence begins between Reverend Hendrick van Assendelft and Wassily Kandinsky on the possible purchase of an artwork. It is not clear how the two first came into contact. The most likely scenario is that Van Assendelft visited Kandinsky's exhibition in Rotterdam, where he was struck by the spiritualised nature of Kandinsky's work, a spiritual power he himself was searching for in his ideas and his appreciation

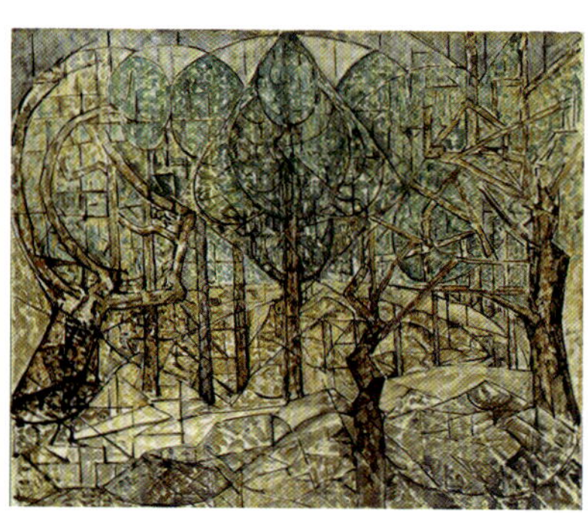

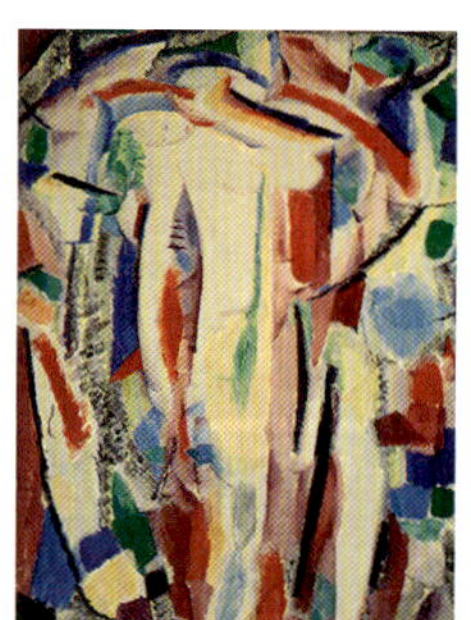

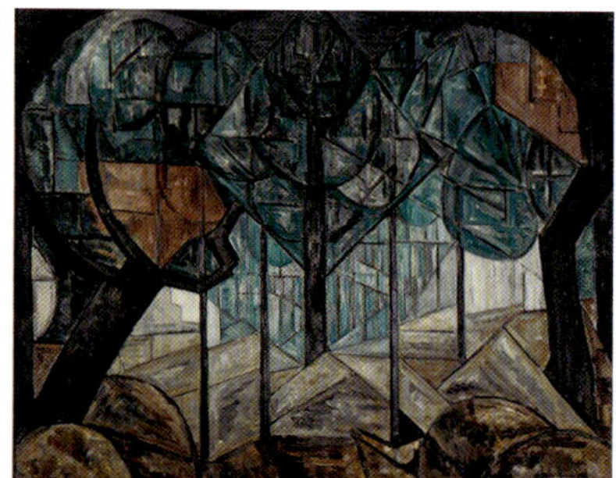

Jacoba van Heemskerck
Bos I (Forest I), 1913
Oil on canvas, 81 x 102 cm
Gemeentemuseum Den Haag, The Hague

Jan Sluijters
Adam en Eva (Adam and Eve), 1913
Oil on canvas, 126 x 96 cm
Singer Laren, permanent loan from Nardinc Collection, Laren

Jacoba van Heemskerck
Bos II (Forest II), 1913
Oil on canvas, 80.5 x 100.4 cm
Gemeentemuseum Den Haag, The Hague

he has learned into practice.[106] He also completes work on the canvases he began in spring 1912, which he had repeatedly returned to previously without arriving at any resolution.[107]

Jakob van Domselaer returns to Amsterdam, bringing a temporary end to the creative exchange between the artist and the composer. Mondrian has by then learned an important lesson from his discussions with Van Domselaer, which will be useful to him. Music is composed on the basis of previously defined elements: a rhythm that may change only if this is functional, repeating melodic patterns, a structure that can develop, and variation that can arise only out of order. This could be referred to as notation of musical elements. The idea of notation does not play any significant role in the paintings Mondrian has been working on since spring 1912. But working on the new canvases he has purchased at Blanchet, he makes increasing use of pre-defined 'notational elements': a curve, a diagonal line, a horizontal or vertical line. And, not insignificantly in relation to music, he works with combinations of these elements: right angles, acute angles, 'gallows', rectangles, circle segments and squares. It will be a long time, however, before he is satisfied with the combinations he achieves.

Sergei Diaghilev (1872–1929), founder of the Ballets Russes, is so encouraged by the scandalous success of his dance company's performance of *Afternoon of a Faun* by Claude Debussy (1862–1918), with Vaslav Nijinsky (1889–1950) as its lead, that he rents the modern new Théâtre des Champs-Elysées for a production of *The Rite of Spring* by Igor Stravinsky (1882–1971). Although neither the choreography nor the music has any direct association with Cubism, the premiere on 29 May 1913 is such a great success that even the popular press and the tabloids link the strange and primitive performance with Cubism. The scandalous becomes an indispensable ingredient of Cubism and even influences fashion. In artist circles, plans are made to take Cubism into the theatre, with music and dance, a plan that comes to fruition in 1917 with Diaghilev's ballet *Parade*.[109]

Gino Severini fears his chance of a solo exhibition at the Marlborough Gallery in London is in jeopardy. He does not have the money to pay to transport the work, and in fact, the contents of his studio have been seized. His friend Dop Bles pays off his debt, so Severini is able to continue with his plans. In exchange, Bles probably receives a watercolour of the *Eiffel Tower* with the dedication 'Souvenir très amical à Dop Bles / Severini 1913'.[110]

of art. Shortly afterwards, Van Assendelft sends Kandinsky several dishes by Dutch potter and designer Chris Lanooy (1881–1948), an artist well known at the time for the beautiful, spiritual patterns he achieved in his decorative glazing, such as *Wandbord 'Herfstblad'* (1910–13; p.42).

On 4 May the *Nieuwe Rotterdamsche Courant* reports that the St Luke's exhibition, due to open the next day at the Stedelijk Museum, Amsterdam, is a success, and that thanks to 'less lenience' and 'more stringent selection' a 'refreshed and more civilised palette' can be discerned.[111] The incredible quantity of work submitted leads the jury to decide that only a small proportion – of the 'more civilised' sort – can be shown. The 'rejected' artists stage an alternative exhibition, featuring lots of abstract work, and establish an association that they will call De Onafhankelijken (The Independents). The response is not long in coming. In *De Telegraaf*, Carel Dake criticises the conservatism of those in Amsterdam, but argues that, in the end, they simply want to climb the ladder of history one rung at a time, rather than omitting whole sections for convenience's sake, to impress or because it seems amusing, as they do in Paris.[112]

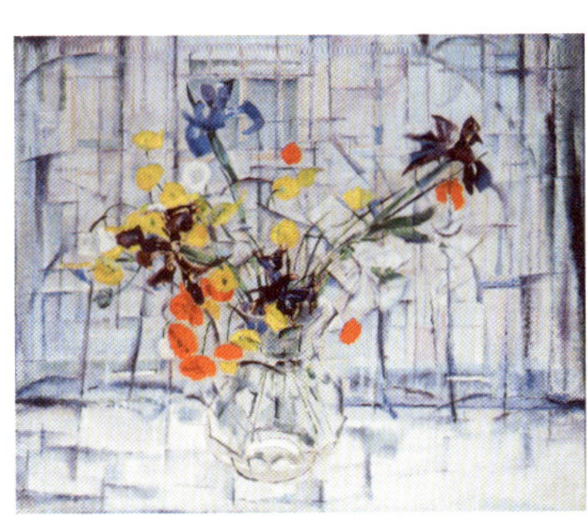

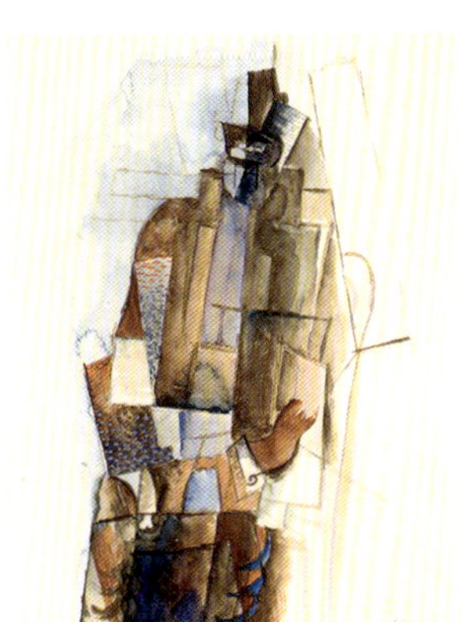

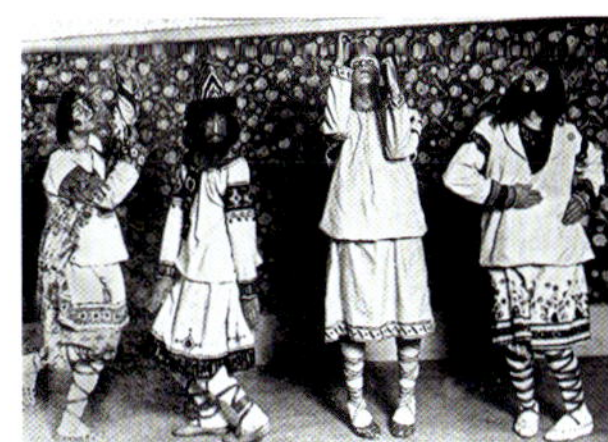

Jan Sluijters
Bloemen in een vensterbank
(Flowers on a Window Sill), 1913
Oil on canvas, 130 x 80 cm
Foundation Hannema-de Stuers Fundatie, Heino/Wijhe and Zwolle

Pablo Picasso
Personnage, homme assis (Seated Man), 1915
Watercolour on paper, 31.7 x 24 cm
Triton Collection Foundation, Rotterdam

Original performance of *Le Sacre du printemps* (The Rite of Spring), Théâtre des Champs-Elysées, Paris, 29 May 1913.

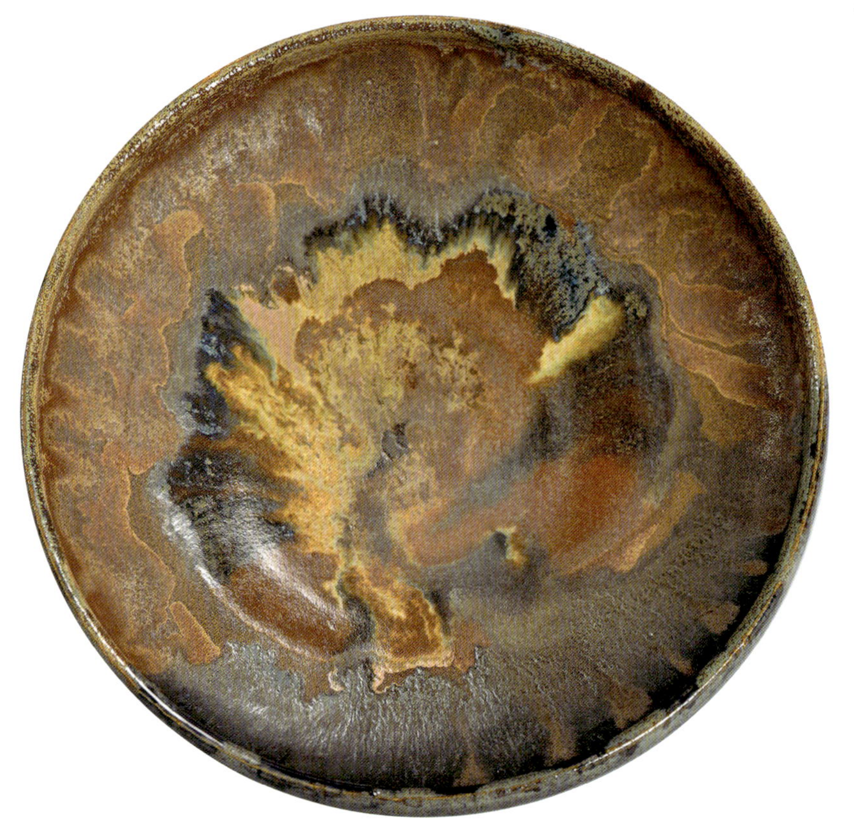

Chris Lanooy
Wandbord 'Herfstblad'
('Autumn Leaf' wall plate), 1910–13
Glazed earthenware, diameter: 19.2 cm
Gemeentemuseum Den Haag, The Hague

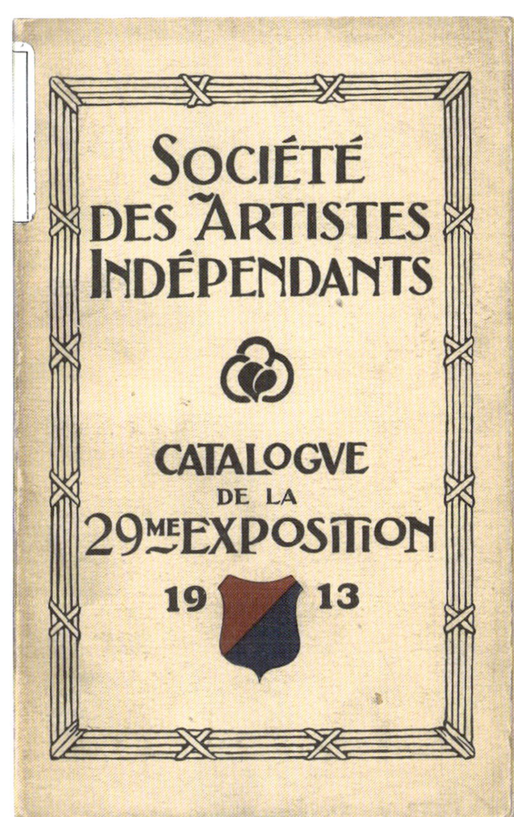

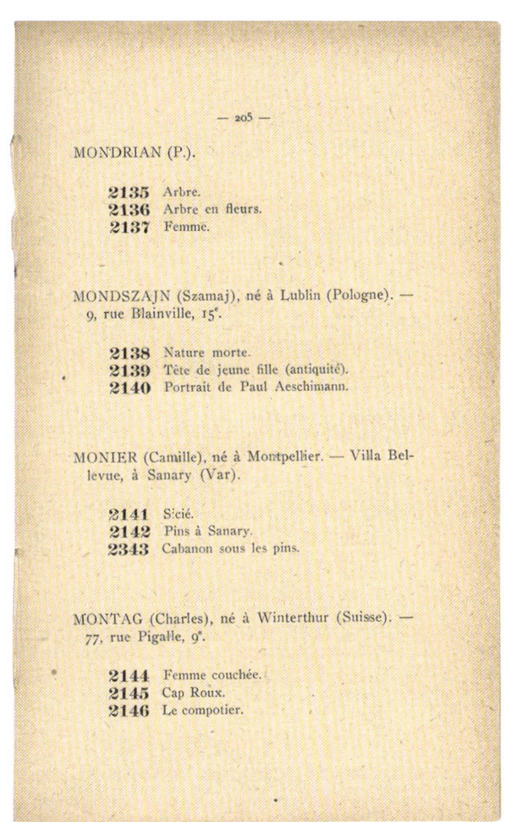

— 205 —

MONDRIAN (P.).

2135 Arbre.
2136 Arbre en fleurs.
2137 Femme.

MONDSZAJN (Szamaj), né à Lublin (Pologne). — 9, rue Blainville, 15e.

2138 Nature morte.
2139 Tête de jeune fille (antiquité).
2140 Portrait de Paul Aeschimann.

MONIER (Camille), né à Montpellier. — Villa Bellevue, à Sanary (Var).

2141 Scié.
2142 Pins à Sanary.
2343 Cabanon sous les pins.

MONTAG (Charles), né à Winterthur (Suisse). — 77, rue Pigalle, 9e.

2144 Femme couchée.
2145 Cap Roux.
2146 Le compotier.

Cover and inside of the Salon des Indépendants 1913 catalogue.

Mondrian

› Two Mondrian paintings are sent by collectors to the *Toorop, Schelfhout und die Niederländer* exhibition at the Neue Kunst – Hans Goltz Gallery in Munich, which has been promoting the latest art since October 1912. Reports in the press suggest that the paintings are *Trees* (owned by Willem Beffie) and *Landscape* (owned by Marie Tak van Poortvliet). Mondrian was apparently unable to send suitable work himself. Beffie is in Munich to visit Franz Marc (1880–1916), Wassily Kandinsky and Alexei Jawlensky (1864–1941).[113]

From 29 April to 13 June, Mondrian works on a copy of a painting by Abel Faivre (1867–1945), *Woman with Fan* (1901), at the Musée du Luxembourg. The painting is so popular that there are many postcards of it.

› Mondrian indicates in a letter to Lodewijk Schelfhout that he plans 'to stay in Domburg for a few weeks in the summer, like last year'.[115] His plans, however, come to nothing. Firstly, because he has little money: at the end of July he goes to the Netherlands for a few days to make a copy of an early nineteenth-century portrait. He has to, 'otherwise I will be short of cash again!'. Secondly, he must had his hands full with new developments in his work, as pieces he has been working on for a long time suddenly start to progress and he

Paris

› The first solo exhibition by Italian sculptor and painter Umberto Boccioni opens at Galerie La Boétie on 21 June. Apollinaire draws attention to the fact that Boccioni *décompose la matière* (breaks his motifs) using various materials – eyes made of glass, real hair, plasterwork, railing – and he feels that Boccioni thus effectively raises the issue of dynamism in sculpture. Picasso did so previously, says Apollinaire, in his glass of absinthe cast in bronze. But he also adds some 'news just in': 'The rumour says that muscles in velocity run wild with Boccioni. They can no longer be retrieved.'[114] Life is not only accelerating art, art is also accelerating life.

› Robert Delaunay and his wife Sonia Delaunay-Terk (1885–1979) continue with their plan to develop another type of painting alongside the cubist works they paint for a small, exclusive market of collectors. These will be large canvases featuring recognisable subjects from the world of popular entertainment – dancing, flying, football – that will allow them to reach a wider audience. Their cubist works are suitable for the exclusive

The Netherlands

› An exhibition at the Museum of Arts and Crafts in Haarlem of stained glass by Johan Thorn Prikker (1868–1932) for the Holy Three Kings Church in Neuss, Germany, attracts unexpectedly large numbers of visitors. The stylised windows (1910; p.46) in a 'modern style' highly reminiscent of Cubism is popular with the public, and several newspapers express their surprise at the fact. It seems the 'ultra-modern' and the decorative can be combined to great effect.

› In response to an exhibition of drawings and graphic art by Lodewijk Schelfhout at the new art gallery De Protector in Rotterdam, the 7 June edition of the *Nieuwe Rotterdamsche Courant* once again enumerates the problems with Cubism. What about this spiritualisation, which was said to be engendered by the fragmentation of form? 'The Cubists strive for style. The same desire for a fixed basis for life currently exercising the masses, sending them searching towards Buddhism, Theosophy, spiritualism, Steinerism, that same

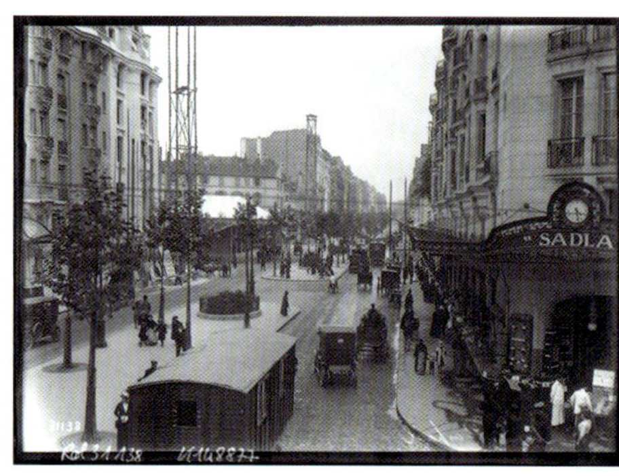

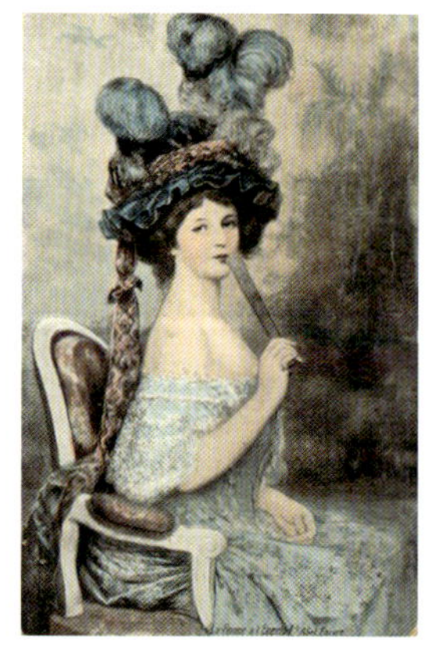

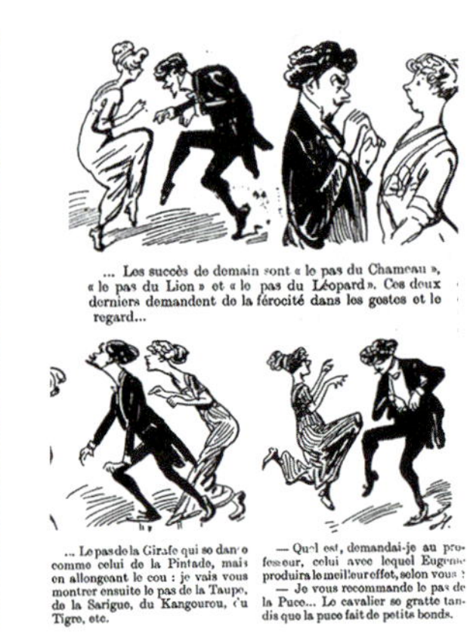

... Les succès de demain sont « le pas du Chameau », « le pas du Lion » et « le pas du Léopard ». Ces deux derniers demandent de la férocité dans les gestes et le regard...

... Le pas de la Girafe qui se danse comme celui de la Pintade, mais en allongeant le cou : je vais vous montrer ensuite le pas de la Taupe, de la Sarigue, du Kangourou, du Tigre, etc.

— Quel est, demandai-je au professeur, celui avec lequel Eugène produira le meilleur effet, selon vous ?

— Je vous recommande le pas de la Puce... Le cavalier se gratte tandis que la puce fait de petits bonds.

View onto boulevard Raspail, Paris in 1913, from the boulevard Saint-Germain.

Abel Faivre
La Femme à l'Éventail
(Woman with Fan), 1901
Oil on canvas, 80 x 114 cm
Musée Petiet, Limoux

Ménagerie de la danse, illustration from *Tango* magazine, Paris 1913.

produces four new works that he will submit to the Moderne Kunst Kring exhibition in the autumn.[116] Furthermore, it is not a hot summer, Jacoba van Heemskerck and Marie Tak van Poortvliet have relatives visiting, his relations with them are not as good as they had been, and Mondrian is not participating in the summer exhibition in Domburg. Peter Alma and Wilhelm Uhde do, however, visit Domburg.[117]

› Mondrian begins filling sketchbooks with quick, scribble-like sketches, of facades, roofs and architectural motifs in Paris. The city inspires him. It is 'abstract life given form' and it moves the artist, 'for in the metropolis nature is already tensed, ordered by the human spirit. The relationships and the rhythm of plane and line in architecture will move man more directly than the capriciousness of nature. In the metropolis, beauty is expressed mathematically'.[120] The motifs are curiously unique, and appear perfectly suited for the

market controlled by Kahnweiler, where Picasso and Braque are examples for all other artists, but this new work is destined for the Salon des Indépendants, where it attracts the attention of a large audience and does much to promote the works on the exclusive market. The reverse is also true: the exclusive market is a good vehicle for accessing the popular market.[118]

› Picasso returns to Paris, ill after a stay in Figueras, Spain. His lover, Eva Gouel (1885–1915), writes in a letter to Gertrude Stein (1874–1946) that he has typhoid fever. It could also be that Picasso is shocked by Eva's recent cancer diagnosis; she will die two years later.[122] But he is eventually gripped by the fever, a story that makes all the newspapers. On 15 July the magazine *Gil Blas* reports that 'our friend Pablo Picasso is confined to his bed by

longing fills the twentieth-century artist, who is no longer a materialist, no longer a nature-lover or Spinozaist (as the Barbizons were), but wants again to be a spiritual creature, a human being, in the image of God. Does that not also mean that a human being is a reflection of the visionary in life, of the mystical and the supernatural?'[119]

Willem Walrecht (1865–1927) registers as a resident at Smidsplein 4 in The Hague, next to Café De Posthoorn. He has moved from Rotterdam, where he worked as a caretaker at the Rotterdamse Kunstkring. He is socially awkward, and so often argued with visitors, mainly because he tried whenever possible to sell them works of art. In May 1913 Walrecht opens an art gallery at Smidsplein 4 with financial support from rich female friends of HP Bremmer and with advice from the man himself. Walrecht lives upstairs with his wife and four children. The gallery occupies the two or three interconnecting rooms on the ground floor. The first exhibition there features the work of Floris Verster.

› In his review of the Moderne Kunst Kring exhibition in the monthly journal *Elsevier's Geïllustreerd Maandschrift*, critic Cornelis Veth (1880–1962) compares Mondrian to Kandinsky. The latter, too, rejects the notion of a subject. 'What we have here, I suspect, is an extreme form of individualism that entirely rejects observation or recollection, and even believes it can dispense with the form of reality in depicting an inner vision. A nihilism that is the end of everything, or the beginning, as you will. Mondrian has also

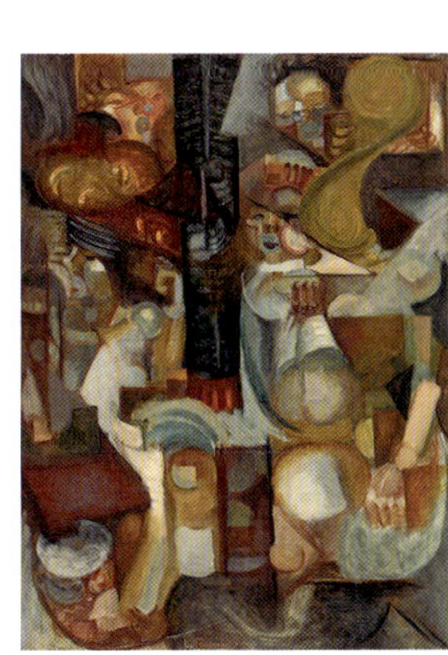

Henri Le Fauconnier
Zeeuwse boerinnen
(Zeeland Farmers' Wives), 1913
Oil on canvas, 161.1 x 120 cm
Gemeentemuseum Den Haag, The Hague

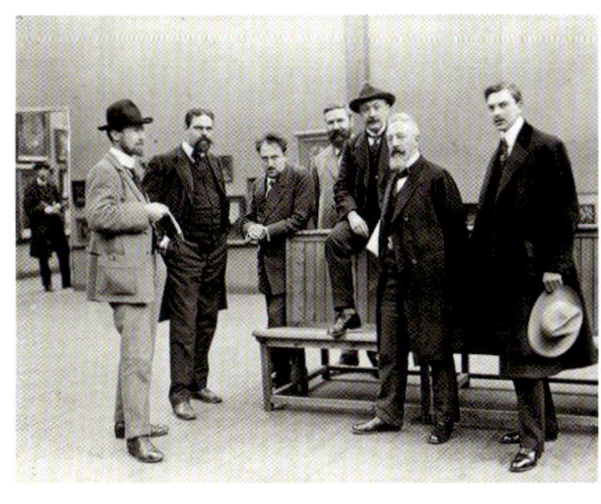

Board of De Onafhankelijken
(The Independents) at the opening
of the exhibition in 1913.

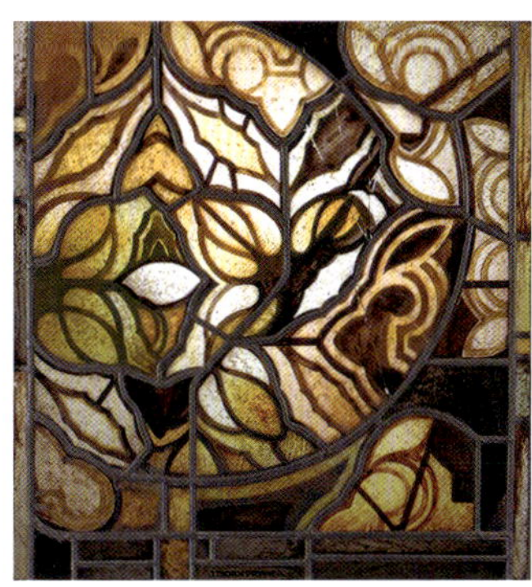

Johan Thorn Prikker
Glas in lood raam
(Stained glass window), c.1910
Produced by the Werkstätten für
Glasmalerei und Mosaïk, Berlin
Stained glass, lead, 58 x 58 cm
Gemeentemuseum Den Haag, The Hague

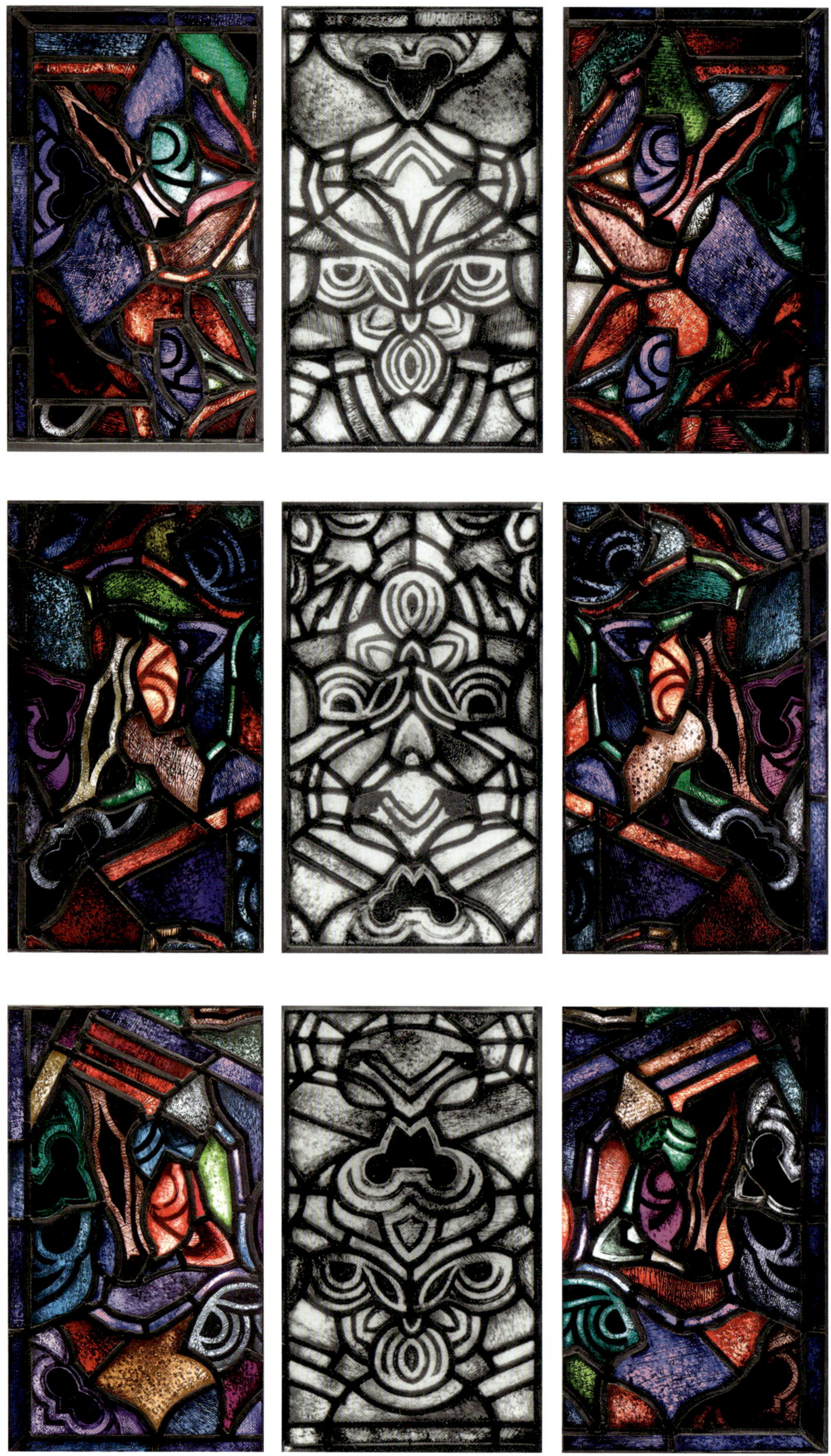

Johan Thorn Prikker
Glas in lood raam (Stained glass window), c. 1910
Produced by the Werkstätten für Glasmalerei und Mosaïk, Berlin

Stained glass, lead
Nine parts, three of which have been lost
97 x 65 cm (each)
Gemeentemuseum Den Haag, The Hague

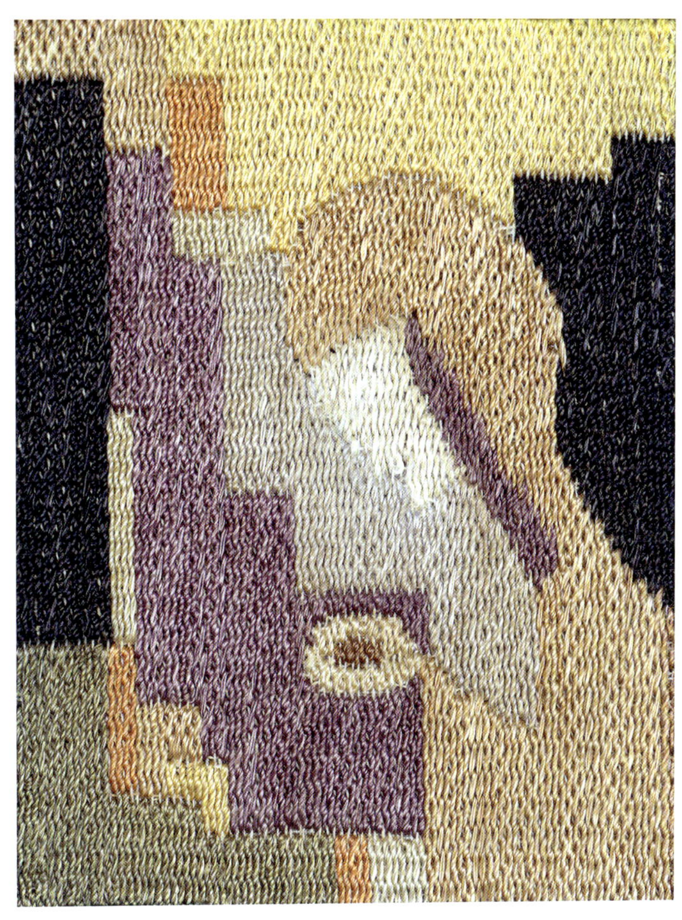

Adya van Rees
Madonna, 1914 or 1915–17
Silk embroidery, 22.2 x 19 cm
Gemeentemuseum Den Haag, The Hague

Mondrian

purpose, to distance his visual language even further from any obvious reference to reality: 'The plastic of Cubism is no longer naturalistic: it seeks the plastic, the plastic above all, but in an entirely new way. Cubism still represents particular things but no longer in their traditional perspectival appearance. Cubism breaks forms, omits parts, and interjects other lines and forms; it even introduces the straight line where it is not directly seen in the object...Cubism broke the closed line, the contour that delimits individual form; but because it also presents this breaking, it falls short of pure unity. While it achieves greater unity than the old art because its composition has strong plastic expression, Cubism loses unity due to the fragmented character of the natural appearance of things. For objects remain objects, despite their fragmentation'.[121]

› Mondrian sends two paintings to the *Erster Deutscher Herbstsalon* (First German Autumn Salon), which opens in Berlin on 20 September, though it is not entirely clear which two. The first possibility is a painting entitled *Painting I*, which was based on a large, detailed drawing of a wood, while *Painting II* would have been a composition based on the roofscape seen from the studio, across the railway lines behind Gare Montparnasse.[126] However, he may have sent two other paintings with the same titles, which

Paris

serious illness'.[123] His eternal rival Henri Matisse honours him with a visit and returns frequently in the weeks that follow. A day later *L'Homme libre* reports that Picasso's condition is improving, and on 9 August *Le Figaro* carries a report of the euphoria in the small southern town of Céret at the fact that the 'Master of Cubism' is back to enjoy a well-earned rest.[124] He gathers around him an entourage of artist friends and acquaintances, including Auguste Herbin, Georges Braque, Richard Kissling (1848–1919), Juan Gris (1887–1927), Ramon Pichot (1872–1925) and Jo Davidson (1883–1952).

› Pondering the manifesto *The Art of Noise* he has set out in an open letter to a friend – which has been discussed in all the newspapers[130] – the Italian Futurist Luigi Russolo becomes gradually more convinced that, thanks to the new life in an urban environment, the human ear has grown accustomed to sounds entirely different from those produced by traditional musical instruments with their harmonic sounds. He distinguishes six

The Netherlands

embarked on this path. Nevertheless, besides the fine and noble colours in these tableaux, one also discerns here a certain understanding of line expression, which at least bears witness to the talents of this curiously errant painter. If only those little squares and lines do not have some deep theoretical background or other. I fear it greatly.'[125]

Jacoba van Heemskerck, Charley Toorop (1891–1955) and Lodewijk Schelfhout exhibit cubist works in Domburg: Van Heemskerck exhibits a *Woodland View*, Toorop exhibits a *Farmer's Wife*, and Lodewijk Schelfhout exhibits landscapes in drypoint. All three are engaged in their own form of spiritualisation: Van Heemskerck in a gloomy tightening of Cubism, Toorop in a free religious stylisation and Schelfhout in a religious 'Rembrandtesque' manner.

› Van Heemskerck's work in the exhibition in Domburg catches the attention of a reviewer: 'Miss Van Heemskerck in particular...is not content with a depiction of reality that is true to nature. Though she acknowledges that she could certainly not do without nature, the painter wishes to show the spirit, the essence of what she sees and admires, which of course ultimately reflects the essence of the one who paints it. This reduces the subject to a side issue. And so this painter cannot

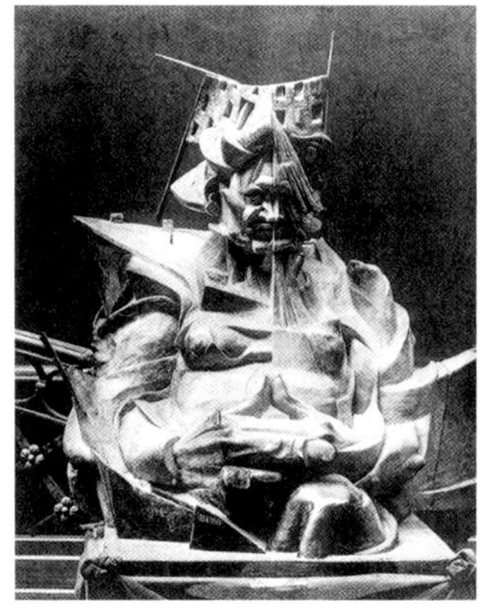

Umberto Boccioni
Testa + casa + luce
(Head + House + Light), 1912
Plaster
Exhibited at Galerie La Boétie, Paris, June 1913

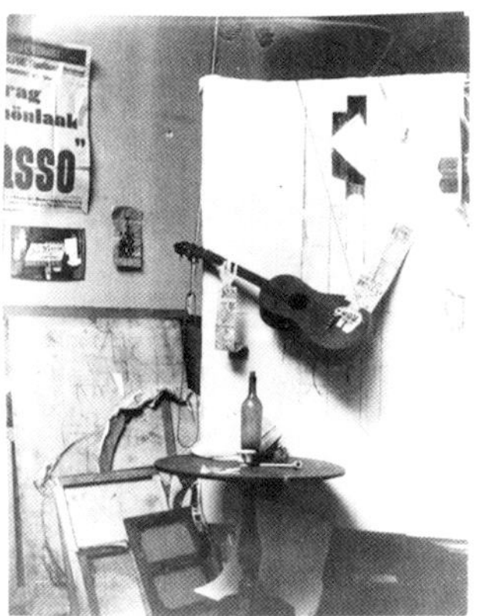

Picasso's studio at 242, boulevard Raspail, Paris, with a cubist composition developing in three dimensions, spring or summer 1913.

though based on a motif in the real world (facades and a roofscape), contain no recognisable trace of the motif in the end result.[127] These would be Mondrian's first completely non-representational paintings. The exhibition runs until December and the paintings are returned to Mondrian unsold. It could also be that Mondrian exhibited the two other paintings entitled *Painting I* and *Painting II* elsewhere in Germany in 1913, because he writes in a letter to Schelfhout in 1914 that he exhibited 'on several occasions' in Germany.[128] It is also possible that Mondrian picked the first pair of paintings for Berlin but then changed his mind and decided to submit less radical work.[129] The titles on the back of the canvases have been partially rubbed out and partially scored through.

› Relations between Mondrian and Schelfhout, Kickert and Le Fauconnier cool down, mainly because of Kickert's gossiping, which puts the friendship between Mondrian and Schelfhout under strain. The two now merely greet each other in passing. Kickert is not at all keen on Mondrian's new work. 'The fact that he does not appreciate it leaves me cold, he who even dares to run down Picasso.'[134] Though Mondrian does regard Le Fauconnier as an entertaining type, he does not really rate him as an artist.

groups of urban noises that can be used in a new music: thunderous explosions; whistling and puffing; gurgling and rumbling; blows on metal and wood; human voices; crackling and rustling. Russolo is a good friend of Severini's and a familiar figure on the Parisian cultural scene. It becomes known that Russolo is developing new musical instruments, which he calls *Intonarumori*, that can bring these sounds to life in contemporary compositions. He stages the first experimental presentation of the scoppiatore – the instrument that produced the whistling and puffing – at the Teatro Storchi in Modena on 2 June 1913. It causes an uproar.[131]

› Fernand Léger signs a three-year contract with Kahnweiler, giving the dealer exclusive rights to sell his work. Léger moves to a larger studio at 86 rue Notre-Dame-des-Champs, near Wilhelm Uhde's gallery.

reconcile herself with those who regard this and similar work as largely decorative art. She is in search of something higher than merely the harmonising of greens or reds or yellows.'[132]

Herwarth Walden organises the *Erster Deutscher Herbstsalon* in Berlin, a grand exhibition with 366 works by 80 artists from France, Italy, Germany, Russia, Spain, Switzerland, America and the Netherlands. The opening is in Berlin on 20 September and the show runs until December. The participating artists are invited by letter.[133] The Dutch participants are Leo Gestel, Van Heemskerck, Adriaan Korteweg (1890–1917), Mondrian, Albert Plasschaert (1874–1941), Otto van Rees, Adya van Rees, Schelfhout, Jan Sluijters and Erich Wichman.

› From September 1913, the public are able to visit the museum set up in the downstairs rooms at the offices of Müller & Co. on Lange Voorhout in The Hague by prior written arrangement, to view works by Van Gogh, Paul Gabriël (1828–1903), Seurat, Floris Verster, Henri van Daalhoff (1867–1953) and Joseph Mendes da Costa (1863–1939).

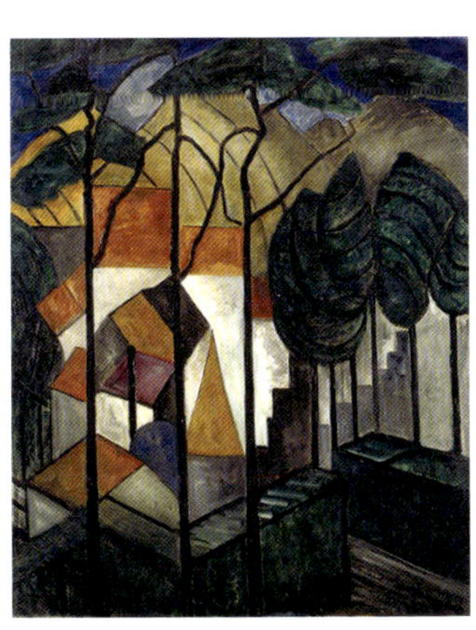

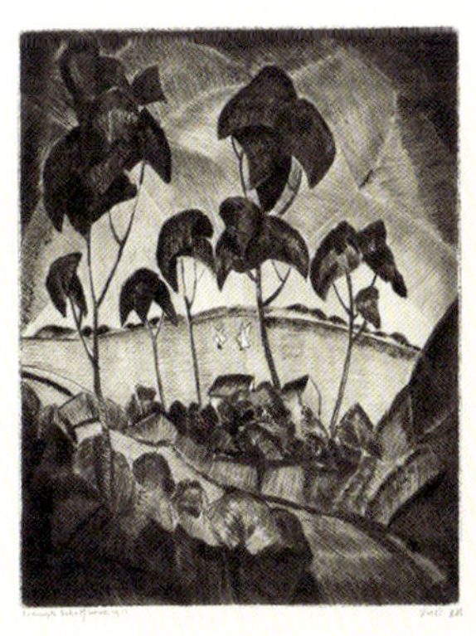

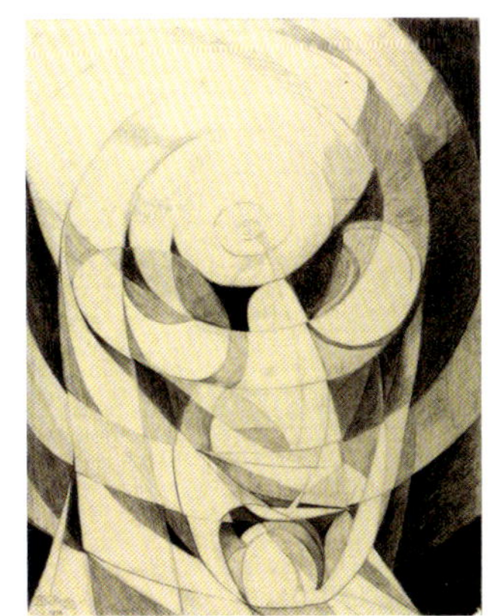

Jacoba van Heemskerck
Landschap No. 6 (Landscape No. 6), 1913
Oil on canvas, 100 x 80.4 cm
Gemeentemuseum Den Haag, The Hague

Lodewijk Schelfhout
Le lac (The Lake), 1912
Drypoint etching, 18.8 x 14.8 cm
Gemeentemuseum Den Haag, The Hague

Adya van Rees
Der Freie Geist (The Free Mind), 1913
Conté on paper on card, 41.5 x 32.7 cm
Gemeentemuseum Den Haag, The Hague

Mondrian

› Mondrian has taken his four paintings for the Moderne Kunst Kring exhibition, due to open on 7 November, to the French shipping agent. His entry also includes a painting coming from Berlin and another from Munich.[135] Kickert is disappointed that they are not recent works. The three most recent were completed in late summer 1913.[136] All of the works are based on tree motifs, although this can no longer be discerned in the last two. Helene Kröller-Müller's adviser, HP Bremmer, buys two paintings.[137] He keeps one for himself for the time being, selling the other painting to Kröller-Müller. This is an important success for Mondrian. He does not, however, go to Amsterdam, is not on the exhibition jury, and does not attend the opening. His absence is reflected in the reviews, which are suddenly uninformed as to the artist's thoughts and therefore less positive. One example is the generally amenable critic J Kalff, writing in the *Algemeen Dagblad* on 14 November: 'Mondrian has not titled his works, which consist of small squares defined by largely straight lines. What they depict is now a complete mystery. Some do however have a delicate tone. A nicely coloured rag would however say more to me. I hear this work is highly theosophical.'[138]

Paris

› The Salon d'Automne of 1913, which opens on 14 November, is full of influences from Cubism, Orphism and 'simultaneous contrasts', as Futurism is also known. The applied arts exhibition does not open until 16 November, when the entire exhibition is opened to the public. The colourful works of Matisse, Gleizes and Picabia steal the show, but Apollinaire believes that the applied arts section shows that French artists will turn their energies to the *art décoratifs* over the coming years, and that the most progressive artists will begin doing the work of the craftsman.[139]

The Netherlands

› The exhibition at the Moderne Kunst Kring is critically acclaimed. It seems all kinds of international movements are firmly leaning on none other than Dutch artists Van Gogh and Van Dongen. The exhibition is divided by country, but the Dutch are also well represented in the international competition. The participants are arranged in three separate spaces and the layout of the exhibition reveals the fact that things are changing in the art world in the Netherlands. Van Dongen, Charley Toorop, Sluijters, Gestel, Jaap Weyand (1886–1960) and Henri Ten Holt (1884–1968) are shown together in one space. As a 'Franco-Dutch' artist, Mondrian has been combined with Kickert and Peter Alma in a second space. Schelfhout shares the third space with his friend Le Fauconnier. 'There are painters – one hardly dare call them painters any longer – whose work is entirely removed from earthly matter. What they reveal to us on their canvases provides absolutely no footing for our imagination... Mondrian seems to us to have progressed furthest with the modern. His images no longer have anything in common with drawing or painting. I just don't know how to define his work. It appears to me a kind of cobbling, devoid of context. But *à la bonne heure*! I will accept this if necessary. I do not understand it. But it also completely eludes me. People like Mondrian are of a different fabric. They have cut through the cloth between themselves and the world that is visible and... conceivable to us.'[140]

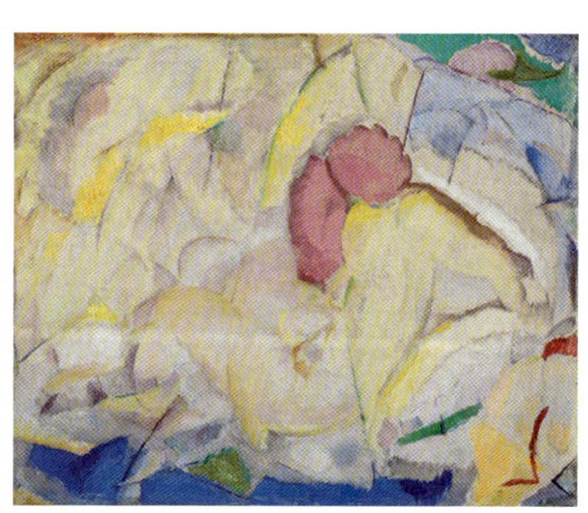

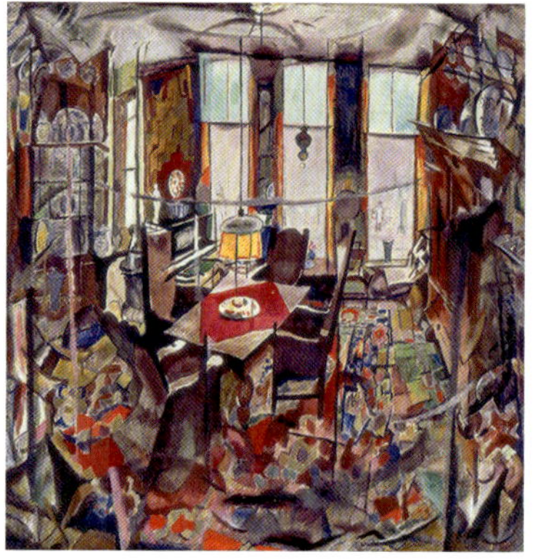

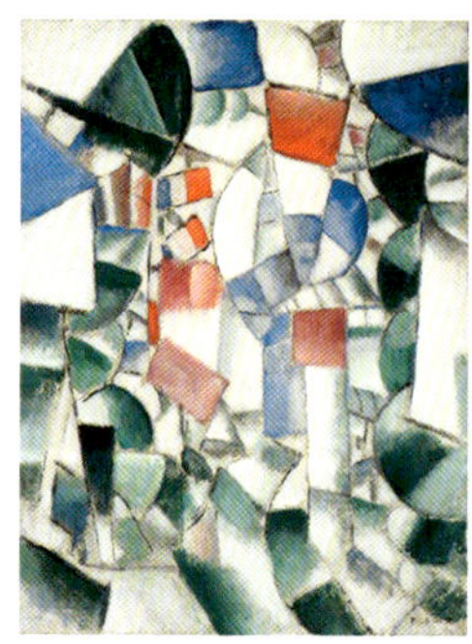

Jan Sluijters
Het ontwaken (Awakening), 1913
Oil on canvas, 85 x 106 cm
Singer Laren, permanent loan from a private collection, Laren

Jan Sluijters
Interieur (Interior), 1913
Oil on canvas, 185 x 178 cm
Stedelijk Museum, Amsterdam

Fernand Léger
Quatorze Juillet
(The Fourteenth of July), c.1912–13
Oil on canvas, 61 x 46 cm
Triton Collection Foundation, Rotterdam

› Mondrian is ill for three months ('catarrh of the stomach', as he reports in a letter to Schelfhout) and is unable to work much.[141]

He is asked by the Dutch journal *Theosophia* to write a piece about the latest art and its spiritual aspects. His notes in sketchbooks from 1912 provide the basis for an article that will keep him occupied from autumn 1913–spring 1914, and will help him hone his ideas about his work. It is known that later in his career Mondrian did not paint when he wrote and vice versa, as he was completely absorbed by his work and could think of nothing else. It is therefore likely that he barely painted during this period.

› Mondrian writes to Bremmer thanking him for sending a copy of *Beeldende Kunst* and takes the opportunity to explain his beliefs. The content of the letter is probably a summary of the article he was working on at the time (pp.54–55).

Mondrian sends four paintings to Kunstsalon Wolfsberg in Zurich, naming them in ascending order *Tableau* A, B, C and D. At the same time, he has to send work to Prague, where he has been invited to exhibit recent work. It is not clear which works he sends to Zurich, though in practical terms it

› The prestigious journal *Les Soirées de Paris* reappears, fully illustrated, in November, after a break of five months. Four spatial constructions of wallpaper, wood, card, paper and newsprint demonstrate further developments in Picasso's work. The editors have their offices on boulevard Raspail in Montparnasse, so the journal soon becomes one of the best-informed sources on developments in art and culture. Poet Max Jacob (1876–1944) even calls it *notre organe officiel* (our official organ).[142]

› Poet and art critic Alexandre Mercereau (1884–1945) was one of the first to join the Abbaye de Créteil, a utopian community based southeast of Paris, where poets and artists went to live beginning in 1906 in order to rediscover the deep spiritual origins of art. In 1913 Mercereau began organising a major exhibition that opens in Prague in 1914, at a similar community of artists and poets.

› The first issue of *Beeldende Kunst*, produced entirely by HP Bremmer appears in November. He discusses at length reproductions and copper intaglio prints of Chinese statuettes, a painting by Paul Gabriël, a seventeenth-century still life and a pastel by Odilon Redon. Finally, Bremmer turns to a small painting by the young artist Bart van der Leck. He points out that achieving the one-dimensional flatness of the image was the artist's goal, not to be different, but because, by withering away with form, as Bremmer calls it, he can reveal an enfolding symbol.[143] To illustrate the article, he included an image of *Need* by Van der Leck (p.52).

› Gestel and his wife, along with painters Else Berg (1877–1942) and Mommie Schwarz (1876–1942) and collector Piet Boendermaker, head for Mallorca, Spain, where they will remain until May. Gestel produces a large number of pastels and paintings there – small in size but bursting with colour and energy, based on a cubist visual language, but also moving away from it, as the forms and patterns lose their structure and tension and become colourful, with everything based on reality.

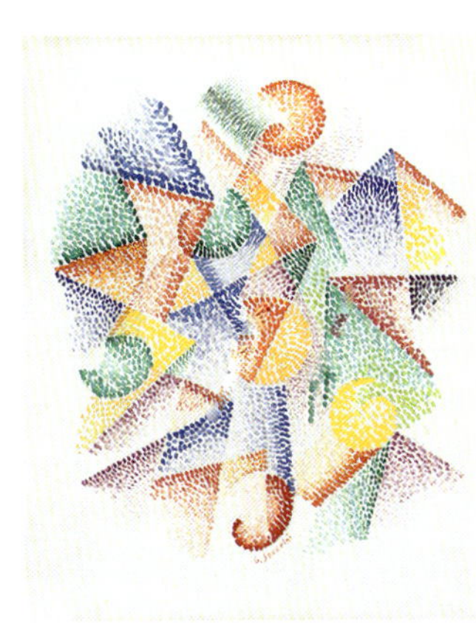

Gino Severini
Expansion of Forms – Light, 1912–14
Pencil, water-based paint and watercolour on paper, 29 x 23.5 cm
Triton Collection Foundation, Rotterdam

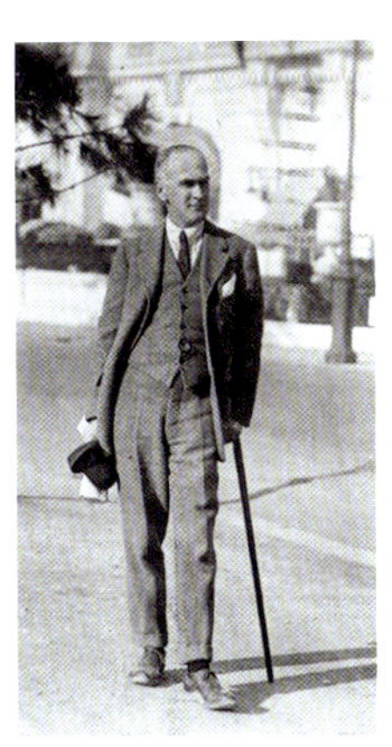

Wilhelm Uhde in the south of France, 1913.

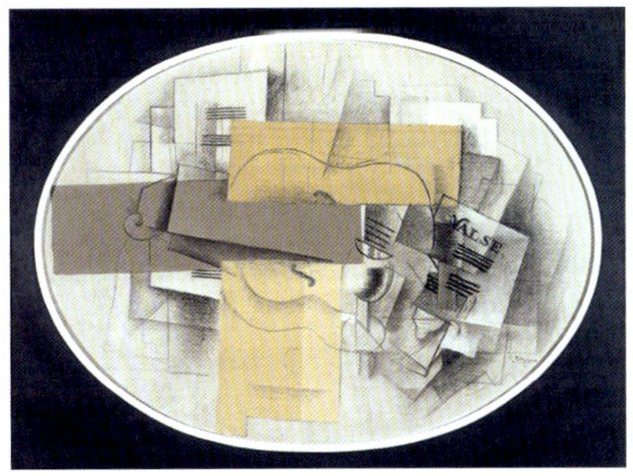

Georges Braque
Verre, Violon et papier à musique
(Glass, Violin and Sheet Music), 1912
Oil and charcoal on canvas, 64.5 x 91.5 cm
Museum Ludwig, Cologne

Mondrian

seems likely they will have been the four paintings he had not sold at the Moderne Kunst Kring exhibition in Amsterdam.[144] This might mean that the Zurich exhibition receives a kind of meandering journey through the developments of the last two years, and that Mondrian chooses to show the strongest possible group of works in Prague and Berlin.[145] It seems likely that he shows his recent work in Prague, in which subject and inspiration are no longer relevant, having made way for an interest in strict colour-line relationships. There is no hard evidence in support of this theory, however.[146]

› Mondrian has two paintings ready for the Salon des Indépendants, which is due to open on 1 March.[150] His entries, both titled *Tableau*, go mostly unnoticed this time. Though André Salmon and Apollinaire mention his work, they do not feel it necessary to examine it in depth.[151] Mondrian himself is not entirely happy with his entry, as suggested by letters he writes to Bremmer and Schelfhout two months later. The only critic who devotes any attention to Mondrian's work is journalist Leo Faust (1878–1974) who, in the Dutch

Paris

Moderní Uméni features the work of 29 artists from Montparnasse. Mercereau writes an introduction to the catalogue in which he argues that the era of electricity, dynamism and intensity, of large factories, cars and new inventions, has introduced new dimensions to the way people see. 'Today's art has a specific realism. Our artist is no mystery, as the painters of the 13th and 14th century were; they desire passionately to discover a comprehensive truth that can withstand the new reality. Entirely in accordance with the innovations in science, art wants to discover ultimate laws that go further than yesterday's.'[147]

The January issue of *Montjoie!* is devoted entirely to dance and popular culture. This is remarkable, as the magazine has hitherto largely championed the distinctive aesthetic of the avant garde over the decorative and fashion-oriented. Sergei Diaghilev's Ballets Russes is largely responsible for the popularisation of Cubism.[148]

› Matisse and Picasso develop a friendship that is not only close but also highly stimulating for both artists' creativity. In winter 1913–14 a rivalry emerges that will spur them both on to great creative heights. Picasso often goes to Matisse's house in Issy-le-Moulineaux, ten minutes by train from Gare Montparnasse, and the two artists go horse riding. News of the rapprochement spreads fast, and from early 1914 the two come to be regarded both in artists' circles and in the

The Netherlands

In late 1913 Jacoba van Heemskerck travels to Berlin where she stays with the Waldens.[149] Relations between them are apparently already good by then, and can only have been improved by the warm reception her art received in the Berlin press. From spring 1914 Herwarth Walden organises travelling exhibitions, *Sturm-Wanderausstellungen*, throughout Germany, and as a result Van Heemskerck becomes associated more with German modernism than with Dutch modern art, which leans more towards France or is strangely on its own, as in the work of Bart van der Leck.

› In *Beeldende Kunst*, Bremmer writes a complimentary article about Mondrian's *Tableau No. 3* (1913), which he dubs *Line Fantasy*, and in which he perceives a quality of 'the asymmetrical, the weighing of quantities left and right', that suggests an orderly mind. Anyone who looks closely can see that there is also liveliness, passion and action in the picture. He recognises 'emotion' in the abstract lines of

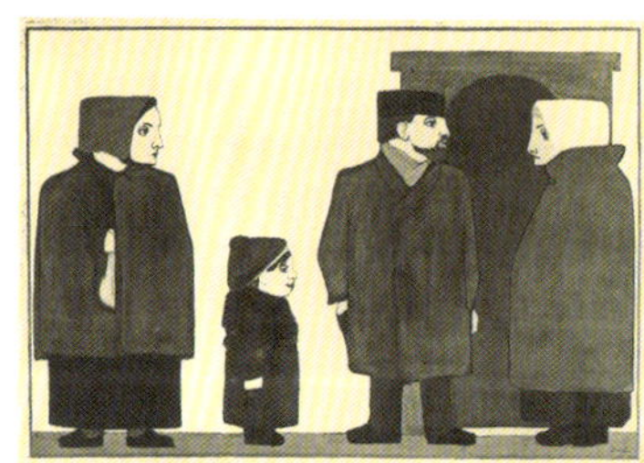

Bart van der Leck,
De Nood (Need), 1913
Reproduction in *Beeldene Kunst*,
November 1913

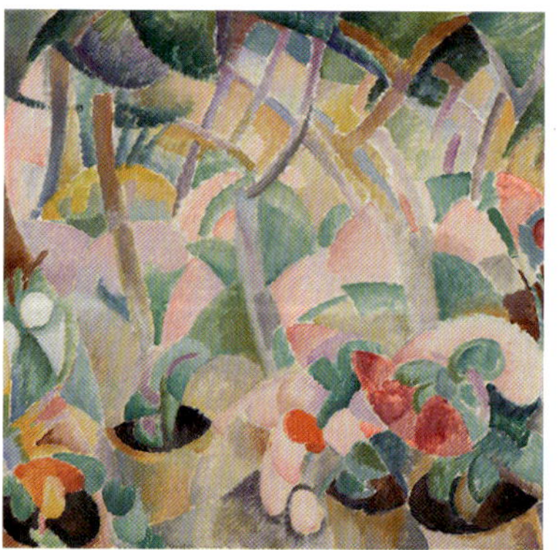

Leo Gestel
Tuintje, Mallorca (Garden, Mallorca), 1914
Oil on canvas, 78 x 81 cm
Gemeentemuseum Den Haag, The Hague

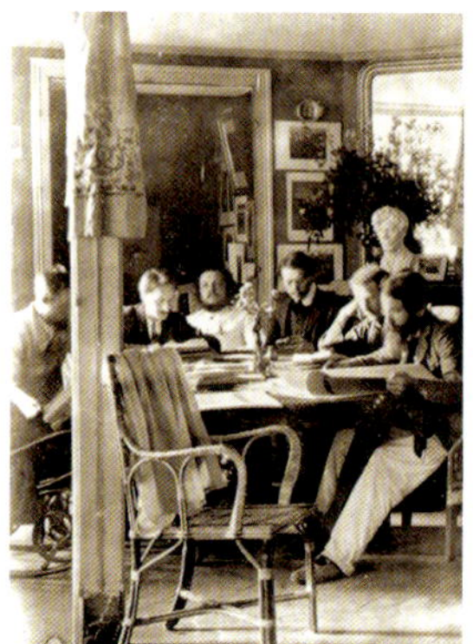

The poets, critics and artists of the utopian artists' community Abbaye de Créteil meeting in the sitting room. Alexandre Mercereau is seated second from left.

journal *De Kunst*, describes the paintings as 'original schemes' which 'at first glance look like maps of a maze. On a grey background, the painter has drawn horizontal and vertical lines along a ruler from one edge of the canvas to the other using dark-green paint, leaving only a small square open here and there, and the horizontal lines in two or three places as close together as the vertical. Furthermore, the straight line – this should in all honesty be pointed out – once or twice becomes a hesitant segment of a circle. Et c'est tout!...One might compare the whole thing to a profile drawing of a baker's oven with the grout between the bricks missing here and there. Mondrian apparently sees a difference between one painting produced by this procedure and another, for he submitted two. *Tableau*, he calls them, and asks 1000 francs apiece.'[152]

› Mondrian asks Bremmer to help him find some 'copying work' because he is not having much success selling his paintings. 'And here in Paris it does not yet seem to be the right time for me to attempt to exhibit in galleries.'[155] Bremmer likely responds by proposing an exhibition at Kunst-handel Walrecht in The Hague. Mondrian will be able to decide which works are shown.

Mondrian may have seen a curious painting at the Salon des Indépendants by a Russian painter, Kazimir Malevich (1878–1935), entitled

press as the tandem leaders of the avant garde, rather than as leaders of rival factions.[153]

› On 2 March 1914 the auction house Drouot holds a major auction of the collection amassed by La Peau de l'Ours, the group of 13 collectors who have collected Fauvist and Cubist works since 1904. Many important art dealers are present from Paris (Kahnweiler and Uhde) and abroad, particularly Germany – Alfred Flechtheim (1878–1937) and Heinrich Thannhauser (1858–1935) – as well as many artists (with the notable absence of Matisse and Picasso) and critics. The auctioned

the image. And that brings him to the subject of music, in which a similar thing occurs. 'An artist who wishes to express himself thus, rather than any other way, has the right to do so. Mondrian chose this means of expression because this is the purest form of expression in art.'[154]

› Van Heemskerck shows 21 paintings and drawings at the 23rd Sturm exhibition in Berlin, which opens in March 1914. They display the first signs of a change in her work, as she drifts away from ordered compositions with taut lines in restrained browns and greens. She moves towards more relaxed designs, with an unprecedented bright palette and a whimsical visual idiom. This was almost certainly due to the encouragement

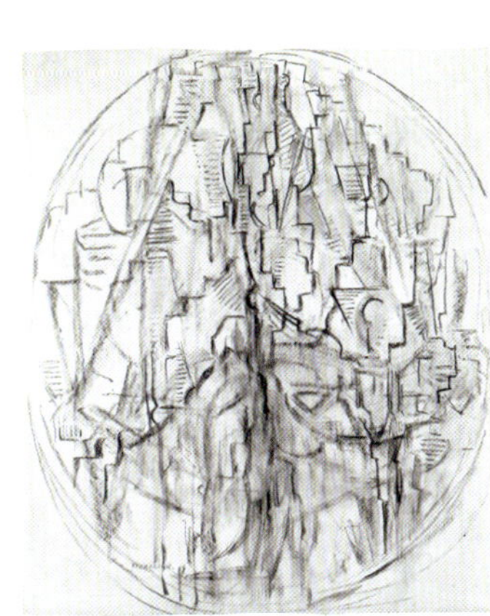

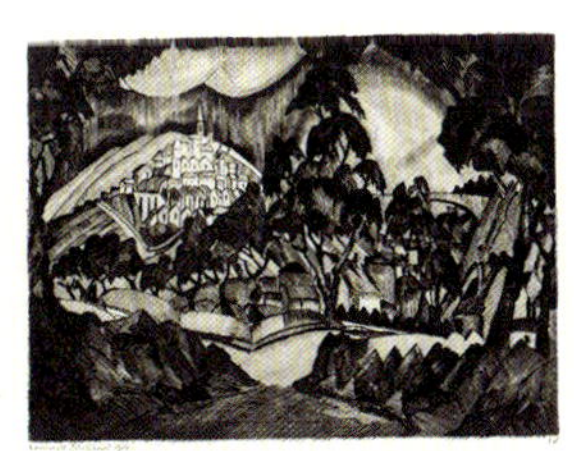

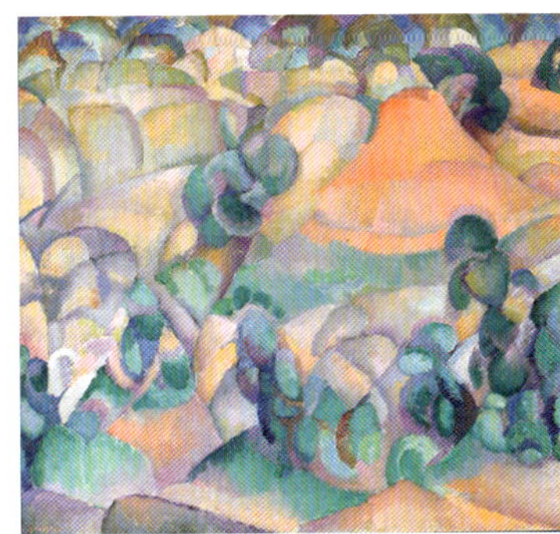

Piet Mondrian
Compositie in ovaal: studie voor Tableau no. 3
(Oval Composition, study for Tableau no. 3), 1913
Charcoal on paper, 85 x 70 cm
Gemeentemuseum Den Haag, The Hague

Lodewijk Schelfhout
Le Soir (Evening), 1914
Drypoint etching, 14.9 x 20.1 cm
Gemeentemuseum Den Haag, The Hague

Leo Gestel
Olijfbomen, Mallorca
(Olive Trees, Mallorca), 1914
Oil on canvas, 69 x 73.7 cm
Gemeentemuseum Den Haag, The Hague

26 rue du Départ, Paris, 29 January 1914

Dear Sir,

In reply to your letter I hasten to report that I greatly appreciate your estimation of my work and have no objection to you reproducing those two things. Now I have the opportunity of writing to you, perhaps you would like to hear briefly how I view my work. The masses find my work somewhat vague: at best it is said that it is reminiscent of music. Now, I have no objections to this, but I do if one then goes on to reason that my work does not belong to the realm of visual art. For I construct on a flat surface lines and colour combinations with the aim of, as deliberately as possible, depicting general beauty. Nature (or that which I see) inspires me, gives me, just as it does any painter, the emotion that prompts the urge to make something, but I want to get as close as possible to the truth and am therefore abstracting everything until I get to the foundation (albeit still an outward foundation!) of things. To me it seems true that by wishing to say nothing in particular, one actually says the most particular, the truth (which is all-embracing). To me, the architecture of the Ancients was the greatest art. I believe that it is possible, using horizontal and vertical lines, constructed deliberately but not in a calculating way and guided by deep intuition, and brought to harmony and rhythm, I believe using these basic elements of beauty – with the addition of other straight lines or curved lines, if necessary – to produce a work of art that is as strong as it is true. For those with deeper vision this is not therefore vague; it is vague only to the superficial observer of nature. And coincidence must be just as far removed as calculation. And it also seems necessary to me to constantly interrupt a horizontal or vertical line, for if these lines are not opposed by others, they also say something 'particular', something human. And my view is precisely that one should not wish to present anything human in art.

By not wishing to say anything human, by completely ignoring oneself, the artwork that emerges becomes a monument to Beauty: transcending the human; and yet human in its depth and generality! To me it is certain that this is the art of the future. Futurism, though it has gone a step beyond naturalism, is too concerned with human sensations. Cubism (whose substance is still too closely based on earlier products of beauty, and is thus less of its time than Futurism), Cubism has taken the great step towards abstraction and is therefore of the present and of a future time: modern therefore not in its substance but in its effect – I for my part regard myself as neither, but feel the spirit of the times in both and in myself.

Should you wish to see my work from a previous period, one of my acquaintances will be pleased to show it to you. During that period I was in search of the monumental as I am now, and sought to achieve abstraction by transforming the natural colours into several heightened colours. Later, however, I became convinced that this work was too outward and, although perhaps good for its kind, still not sufficiently 'structured'.

Finally, I should tell you that I was influenced by the work of Picasso, whom I admire greatly. I am not embarrassed to speak of this influence for I believe it better to be open to improvement than to remain always satisfied with an imperfection once found, and to believe that one is thus being more original! As many painters think – And furthermore I am sure I am entirely different from Picasso, as is generally said.

That acquaintance is Miss De Bruin of Van Beuningenstraat 112, The Hague. When I left for Paris this lady was so good as to agree to store several large canvases for me, and has already sold some for me. Should you wish to take the trouble to go and look, could you perhaps also recommend me to someone who might wish to buy? Forgive me this practical impertinence: the matter of living expenses is of course a major concern!!!

Thanking you for your consideration,
I remain with the greatest respect.
Yours faithfully,
Piet Mondrian

Letter from Piet Mondrian to HP Bremmer.

Mondrian

Samovar (1913). Malevich uses strange pink tones in the painting, which have a very strong effect in relation to the greys and the yellows. It might well be that Mondrian is reminded of the possibilities contained in the use of colour in this painting two months later, at a lecture by Léger on harmony and contrast in colour.

Mondrian is working on three paintings, all on canvases bought at Blanchet.[156]

› Mondrian finishes the article he has been asked to write for *Theosophia*. 'Although it is outside my field, I felt that it was something more "academic" and so I did it and set out my ideas. My idea of Evolution in art is entirely in line with Theosophical ideas. The article was difficult to write, even though I had been writing down my thoughts for years.'[159] He sends it to the editors, hoping it will be accepted. The article remains unpublished, however, and Mondrian continues to hone it until 1917, when it forms the basis of his first articles in *De Stijl*, the Dutch periodical founded by Theo van Doesburg (1883–1931). In April his paintings are returned from Prague and Zurich. He starts reworking two of them.[160] This in turn has implications for the work that returns from the Indépendants in early May. He distances himself more and more from the other Cubists, including those who live and work in the same building, such as Diego Rivera.

Paris

works eventually make four times the sum originally invested. Picasso's work sells for 12 times the purchase price. Cubism is no longer considered an undesirable element of modern art.[157]

The March issue of *Montjoie!* is devoted to modern applied arts: theatre sets, wallpaper, public art and fashion. Cubism is becoming tangible everywhere, including as an applied design element in interiors.[158]

› Filippo Tommaso Marinetti (1876–1944) and Russolo give their first experimental concert with the *Intonarumori*, as Russolo calls the instruments he has been developing since the autumn of 1913. The programme is in four parts: Awakening of a City; Meeting of Cars and Aeroplanes; Dining on the Terrace of the Casino; and Skirmish in the Oasis.

The Netherlands

of her ever-closer contact with Herwarth Walden. But she also begins to display a preference for the more Wagnerian aspects of German Expressionism, particularly as practised by Wassily Kandinsky and Franz Marc, with an emphasis on deeply felt inner truth and originality. Van Heemskerck enjoys huge – still often underestimated – success with this new work in Germany.

› Work by new young artists like Theo van Doesburg and Erich Wichman is shown at the Salon des Indépendants in Paris.

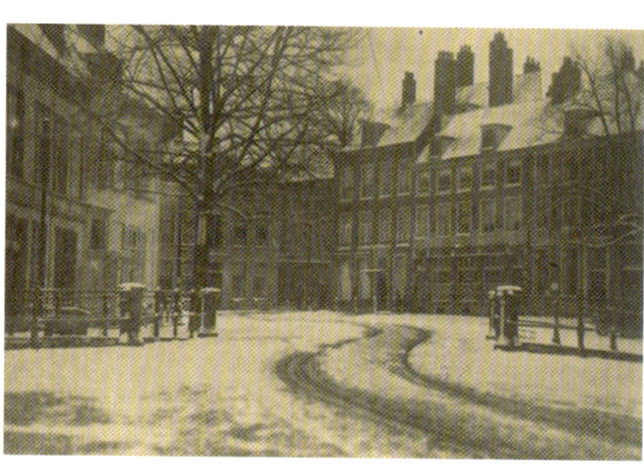

Smidsplein, The Hague in winter, n.d. Number 4, on the right next to Café De Posthoorn, was the home of Kunsthandel Walrecht from spring 1913 onwards.

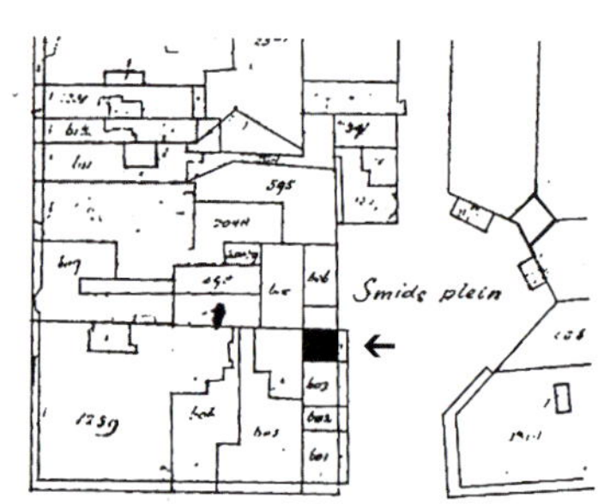

Land registry map of The Hague, The Hague city council, n.d.

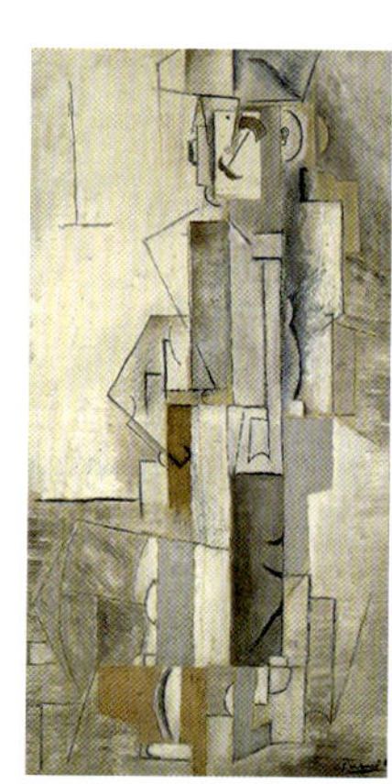

Pablo Picasso
Harlequin, Céret, 1913
Oil, sand and dust on canvas, 120.1 x 77.9 cm
Gemeentemuseum Den Haag, The Hague

› Mondrian reports to Bremmer that he has 'his work back from the exhibitions' and that he 'could exhibit 15 canvases in The Hague, if you think that time is not too short to go ahead. But in June people might still be in the city. Would there be enough time if the pieces were to arrive in The Hague at the end of the month? Perhaps the 24th or 25th of May? This is because I wanted to work on those from the Indépendants. I have several like the one exhibited in A'dam [Amsterdam] and one from later, but I cannot send the most recent ones because they are not ready. Perhaps that is good because then the small exhibition will be a more cohesive whole.'[161]

› Fernand Léger gives a lecture at the Académie Vassiliev entitled '*Les réalisations picturales actuelles*', on current developments in painting. He points out that there are two chromatic systems, one tonal and one exploiting relative brightness. He sees grey as a boundary between the two, the place where they merge. He also points out that yellow, purple or pink, and blue are colours which can be used either to achieve balance in a composition (the consonant) or to emphasise contrast (the dissonant). The lecture will be published a month later in the June issue of *Les Soirées de Paris*.[162] It seems highly likely that Mondrian attended this interesting lecture and that the changes he made to his paintings over the following weeks reflected his understanding of what he heard and learned from Léger that evening.

› De Onafhankelijken – a society of artists – opens its third international, juryless exhibition on 16 May at its premises on Amstelveenseweg in Amsterdam. Just after the opening ceremony, as the visitors spread out into the galleries to view the 400 exhibited works, a scuffle breaks out by a large abstract painting by Erich Wichman hung above the door. Art critic NH Wolf of *De Kunst* receives several 'wallops' from the painter, who also answers to the nickname 'The Flame'. Wolf's pince-nez falls off and members of the board of De Onafhankelijken are forced to intervene. Wichman declares that he had asked Wolf to refrain from expressing for the third time his critical opinion that Wichman is taking everyone for a ride, to which Wolf had responded: 'You are mad, are you not?'[163]

› Mondrian reports that he is busy working on a commissioned copy: 'otherwise I shall be on the rocks!'[164] He is also working on new pieces, one of which will go to The Hague for the exhibition at Kunsthandel Walrecht, 'a recent sketch', Mondrian writes in a letter to Schelfhout.[165] This is probably one of two paintings, one of which goes to Kunsthandel Walrecht as *Composition* NO. VI (p.100) on 24 or 25 May. The consignment of paintings is picked up around that date and transported to The Hague in three cases. Mondrian

› Apollinaire, writing in the cultural newspaper *Paris-Journal*, says of Braque: 'Mr Braque has his studio on the top floor of Hôtel Roma on rue Caulaincourt. A Czech painter, Mr Filla, recently visited the French innovator at his studio; he turns out to be an interesting painter. The visit was brief and polite, but Mr Braque was astounded to find Mr Filla in front of the hotel again the following day, and he saw him again two or three times

› After a largely unnoticed exhibition at Kunsthandel Walrecht in 1913, the work of Bart van der Leck gradually begins to display a stronger tendency towards taut, powerful, absolute forms. He has had enough of 'petty representations', as he calls them, and wants to present a formal, fixed reality. He visits Algeria in May, where the light has a 'particular clarity'.[168] At that time, independent

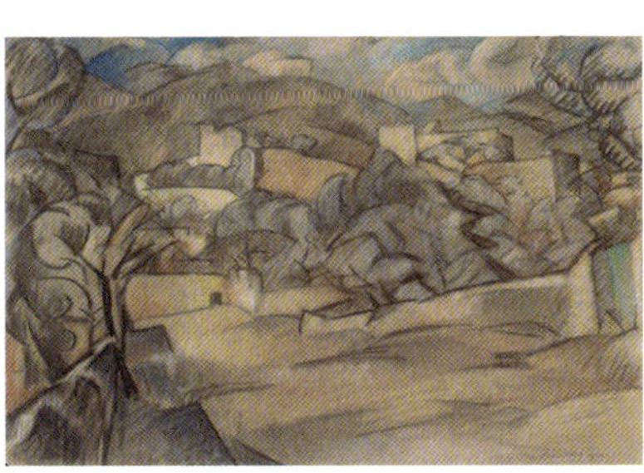

Leo Gestel
Landschap te Mallorça
(Landscape in Mallorca), 1914
Pastel on paper, 41 x 46.8 cm
Gemeentemuseum Den Haag, The Hague

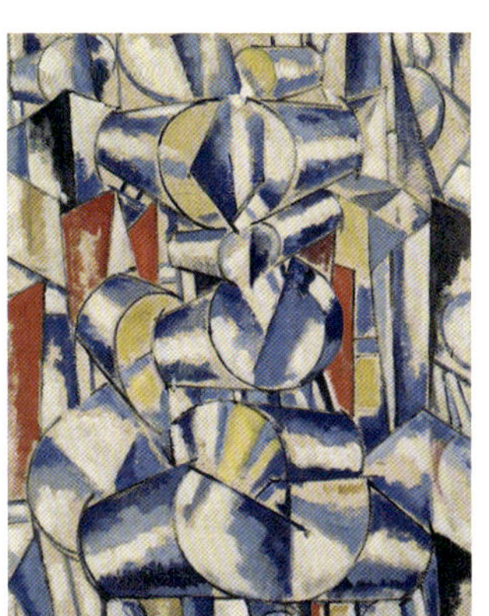

Fernand Léger
Contraste de formes (Contrast of Forms), 1914
Oil on canvas, 82.5 cm x 65.5 cm
Kunstsammlung Nordrhein-Westfalen, Dusseldorf

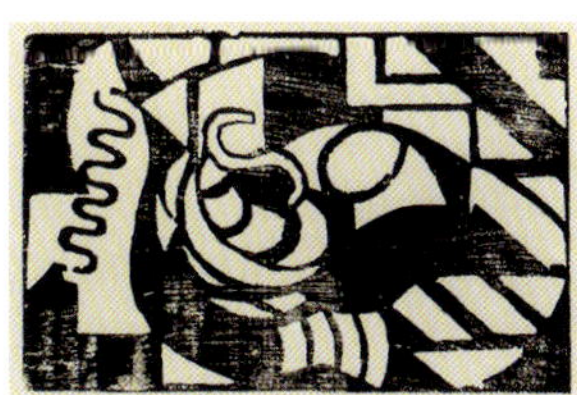

Jacoba van Heemskerck
Compositie (Stilleven)
(Composition (Still Life)), 1914
Woodcut on paper, 9.7 x 15.1 cm
Gemeentemuseum Den Haag, The Hague

Mondrian

readies the paintings he has selected for transportation by signing them and giving them all the same title on the back of the stretcher: the French word 'Composition' followed by a Roman numeral, all in blue paint. The numbering is not chronological. Numbers I to VI are the most recent paintings, with coloured patterns of rectangles in which representational functions can no longer be discerned. Some are also dated. Mondrian writes 'HAUT' (top) on the back of the paintings, suggesting it would be useful to bear this in mind when hanging them. Then there is a group of five works, *Composition NO. VII* to *Composition NO. XI*, from 1912–13 (pp.104–23), in ochre, grey and white, in which trees, a bouquet and a portrait remain recognisable in the structure, which consists of short line fragments and subdued colours. At the heart of this group – the centre of the exhibition – is *Composition NO. IX*, an entirely non-representational composition, which has the characteristic colours of the surrounding works. Finally, *Composition NO. XII* to *Composition NO. XVI* (pp.124–41) show Mondrian's transition from working with individual line fragments to working with blocks of colour. It seems logical to interpret the division of the paintings into three groups as a programmatic concept in the exhibition. But it might also have to do with the exhibition space at Kunsthandel Walrecht, which was spread over three rooms.

One more 'recent sketch' is omitted from the shipment to The Hague, as it will have been too wet to be transported.[166]

Paris

that day. He congratulated himself on having so aroused the curiosity of the Czech painter, until he found out that Mr Filla had been so unable to withstand the charms of Hôtel Roma, with its Cubist studios, that he had moved in, and that all Czech painters would soon come and live there. Georges Braque suggested to the proprietor that he hang an enamelled sign above the entrance bearing the inscription "Cubists on every floor".'[167]

The Netherlands

from any prevailing contemporary movement or style, Van der Leck chooses a position similar to that of Mondrian and Van Heemskerck. In his quest for absolute, abstract expression he compares his work to the latest art from abroad, breaking free of his own Dutch past. He too is balancing on a tightrope between symbolism and decoration, in search of a completely new way of making an abstract yet utterly real image.

Emil Filla
Stilleven (Still Life), 1915
Chalk and gouache on paper, 47 x 39 cm
Gemeentemuseum Den Haag, The Hague

Jacoba van Heemskerck
Bild no. 10 (Picture no. 10), 1914
Oil on canvas, 56 x 48.4 cm
Gemeentemuseum Den Haag, The Hague

Bart van der Leck
Bedelvolk (Beggars), 1914
Casein paint on Eternit, 64.6 x 48 cm
Gemeentemuseum Den Haag, The Hague

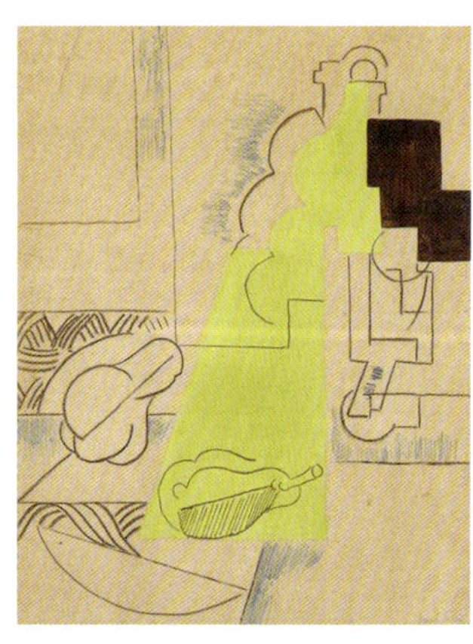

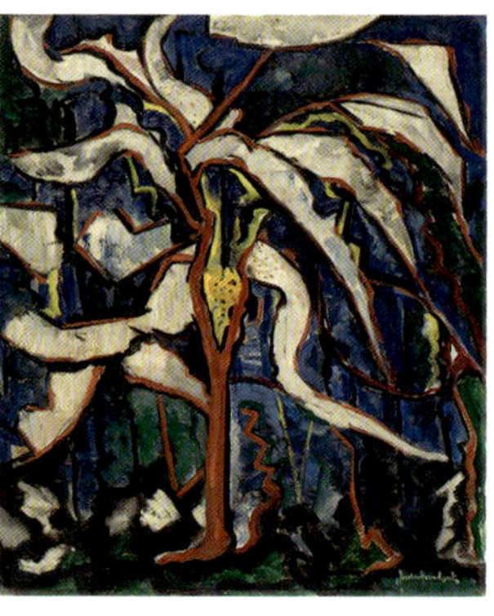

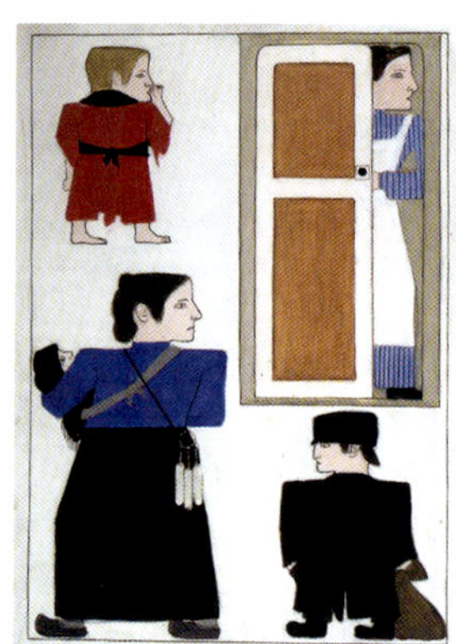

› Mondrian writes a letter to Schelfhout on 7 June. He says that he appreciates that 'you guys thought my work at the M.K.K. [Moderne Kunst Kring] had progressed. I was not very happy at the Indép. here, but after that I suddenly managed to make a good shot again'.[169] Upon receiving works back from Prague, Berlin, Zurich and the Indépendants, he frantically started to make radical changes.[170] Then he made smaller changes to three others.[171] Only three paintings remained untouched by radical revision, it seems.[172]

› After viewing the Salon des Indépendants and the Moderne Kunst Kring exhibitions Van Heemskerck declares them 'passé'.[173] She wants to distance herself and focuses exclusively on Herwarth Walden who visits her in Domburg together with his wife in July. Attempts to organise more Sturm exhibitions in the Netherlands come to nothing.

› On 25 July Mondrian arrives in the Netherlands with a recent 'sketch' in his luggage that he intends to add to the exhibition at Kunsthandel Walrecht. It is not known whether paintings had already been sold at that point. Van Assendelft was to buy three works, Kröller-Müller one and Bremmer two. It may well be that Mondrian brings the recent sketch along because buyers had withdrawn their purchases from the exhibition.

On 28 July Mondrian writes a letter to Van Assendelft from Arnhem, telling him that he is staying with his father and sister, and that he will be in Amsterdam around 10 August. He will visit Van Assendelft in mid-August. By then it is clear that the war will prevent him from returning to Paris. Van Assendelft will store the three cases of unsold paintings for the time being.

› On 28 July the Austro-Hungarian empire declares war on Serbia. Four days later, on 1 August, Germany declares war on Russia. France becomes involved in the conflict on 3 August. The Netherlands remains neutral, though it closes all its borders in the hope of staying out of the conflict.

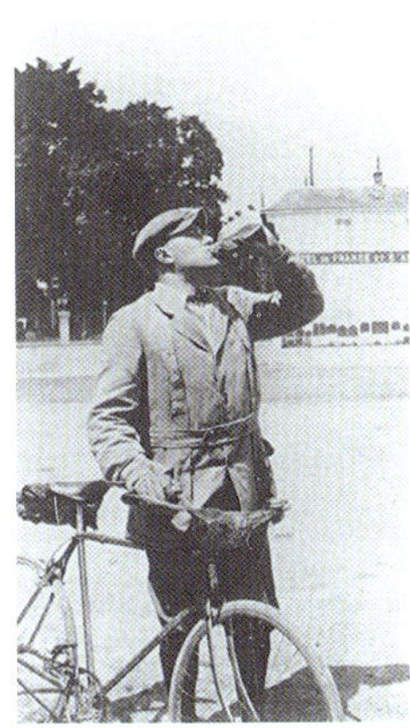

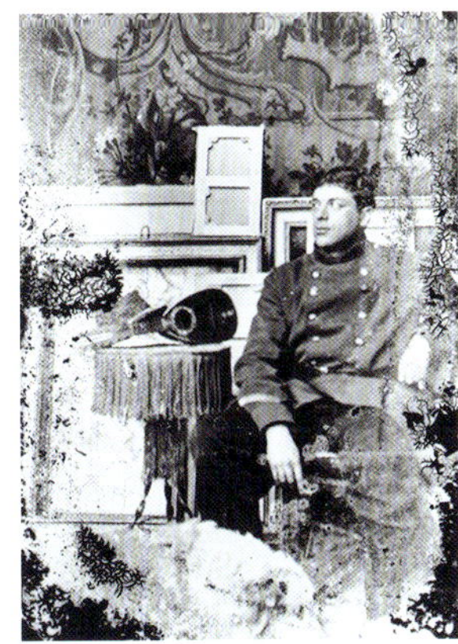

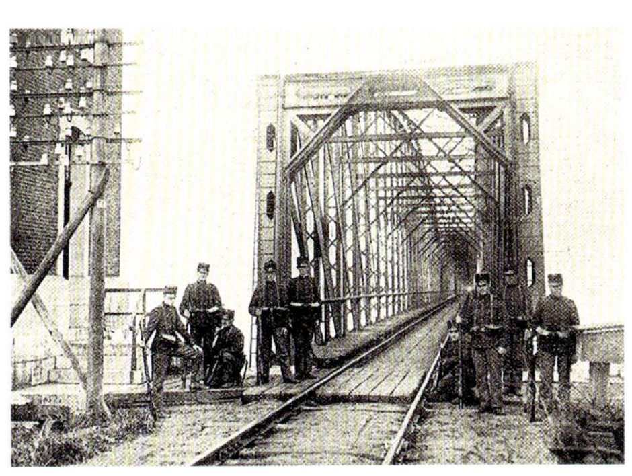

Braque on his way from Paris to Sorgues, in the south of France, where he visited Picasso, summer 1914.

Braque, in uniform, visiting Picasso at his studio, on his way to Le Havre where he had been mobilised, early August 1914.

Mobilisation in the Netherlands, on the south side of the bridge at Moerdijk in Brabant, which was barricaded by soldiers, July 1914.

Piet Mondrian
Toward the True Vision of Reality,
1942

'The problem was clarified for me when I realised two things: (a) in plastic art, reality can be expressed only through the equilibrium of *dynamic movement* of form and colour; (b) pure means afford the most effective way of attaining this.'

Keziah Goudsmit

Finding Balance in Art and Music
Piet Mondrian and Jakob van Domselaer's First Compositions

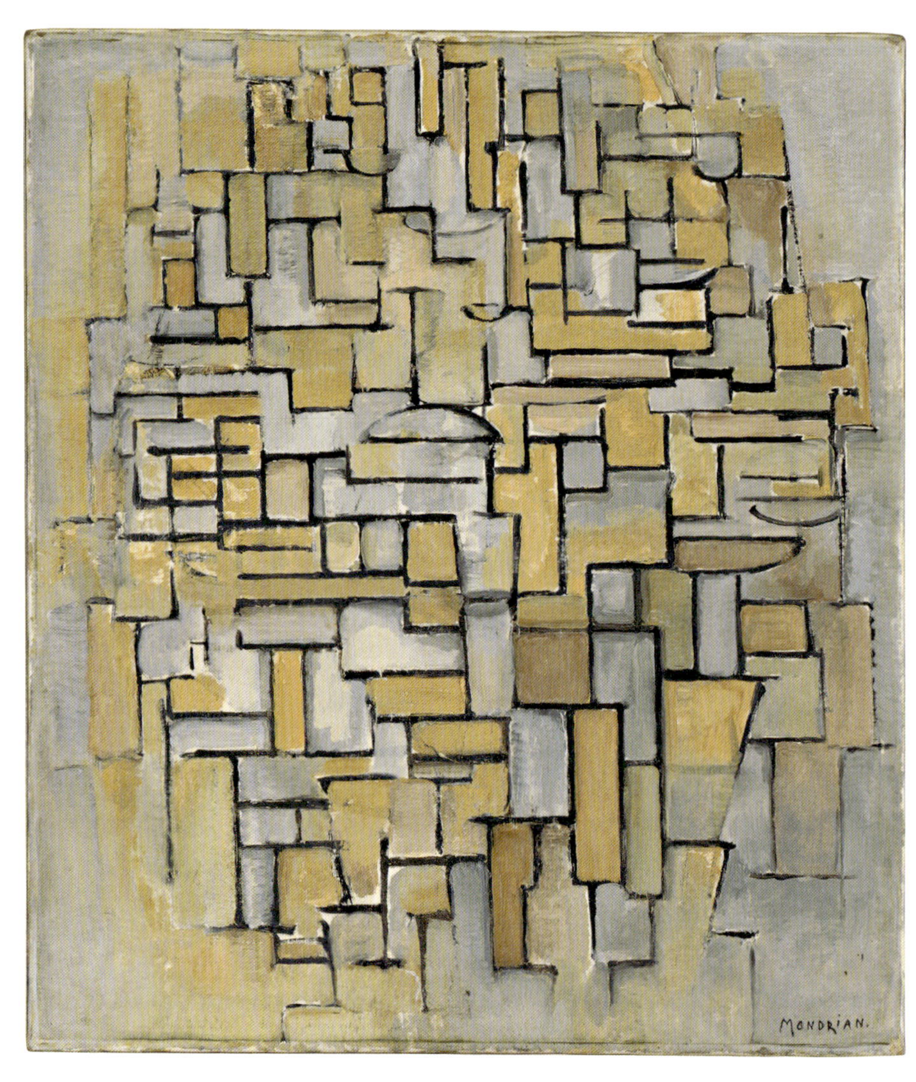

Composition NO. IX 1913
Oil on canvas, 85.7 x 75.6 cm
Museum of Modern Art, New York

In his first solo exhibition at Kunsthandel Walrecht, The Hague, Piet Mondrian presented 16 paintings, including *Composition No. IX* (1913). This painting remained unsold but came into the possession of musician and composer Jakob van Domselaer and his wife Maaike Middelkoop after October 1915. Whether Mondrian sold or gave them the painting is not clear. Mondrian and Middelkoop lived in the same guesthouse in Laren, in the Netherlands, which was in close proximity to Van Domselaer's home, and from July 1915 onwards the three friends lived together in a house on the Pijlsteeg in Laren. In October 1916 the couple married after an engagement that had lasted over a year, and sometime during that period Van Domselaer became the owner of *Composition No. IX*.

The painting is a layered composition of short horizontal, vertical and diagonal lines positioned at right angles. At first glance, it appears as if all the planes of grey and yellow are of the same colour, however each plane is slightly different: lighter, darker, larger, narrower or wider. Mondrian creates the perception of recurring forms, but does not use any actual repetition. The eye is drawn to the grey semi-circle, positioned almost in the centre, which differs in shape from the rest. Slightly lower and to the right is a similar form in ochre, the other colour that dominates the painting. This shape is horizontally mirrored, giving the impression that the entire work is a mirror image. Mondrian tricks the eye into thinking that he is reflecting and repeating, but after a long look the complexity of the work reveals itself. The diagonal lines recur or mirror each other, and the more horizontally oriented planes even appear to echo the vertical ones. Through layering the various elements, Mondrian creates rhythm and movement. Moreover, the blurred corners and lines at the edges of the work add depth and a sense of endlessness to the painting. When Van Domselaer wrote his first musical composition, he used a method similar to Mondrian's, which allowed the composer to add more depth and innovation to his piece than the listener initially recognises.

Mondrian is known to have appreciated the art of music. Surprisingly, however, little has been written about his relationship with Jakob van Domselaer, nor about the effect Van Domselaer's music had on Mondrian's painting. Music played a major role in Mondrian's life, both classical – performed by the Concertgebouw Orchestra in Amsterdam – and modern, which he encountered through his love of dancing. His friendship with Van Domselaer heightened Mondrian's focus on rhythm and composition.

From 1910 to 1912 Van Domselaer studied in Berlin with Beethoven expert Frederic Lamond, and there he met Catharina Hannaert (known as Katinka), who was taking singing lessons. Hannaert knew Mondrian from Amsterdam, and she introduced the two men in autumn 1912 because Van Domselaer wanted to move to Paris temporarily. Middelkoop recollected that during a dinner organised by Hannaert the conversation 'just wouldn't flow':

> Later Mrs. Hannaert had to visit someone briefly somewhere on the Keizersgracht, so she proposed that Mondrian and J. accompany her and wait outside so that they could go for coffee afterwards. Mondrian and J. walked back and forth along a dark, quiet canal; since one said nothing, the other also remained silent. The short visit took rather a long time... as not a word was exchanged.[1]

Van Domselaer hesitated to contact Mondrian when he was planning to travel to Paris in 1912. Nonetheless, he decided to write and announce his arrival and was pleasantly surprised to find Mondrian awaiting him at the Gare du Nord. Mondrian had arranged a hotel room for Van Domselaer at Hôtel L'Angleterre in rue Jacob, merely a 20-minute walk from his home. The composer and the painter met each other frequently for dinner and French lessons – they even diligently did their homework together. The future of art and music was a popular subject during their encounters.

Van Domselaer had become well acquainted with the music of international avant-garde composers, such as Ferruccio Busoni and Arnold Schönberg, during his studies in Berlin, and shared his insight with Mondrian. His friend, in turn, introduced Van Domselaer to contemporary visual art. The relationship between the composer and the painter blossomed through their conversations focused on finding what was 'new' in the arts. This exchange of ideas would have great significance for Mondrian's art and Van Domselaer's compositions.

Upon his return to Amsterdam in spring 1913, Van Domselaer – who still aspired to become a pianist – held a series of concerts, followed by his debut performance in London the following year. Around the same time he also started to compose, which he had not done since his university years, using a Bach choral work as a basis for a new composition, like Busoni had done a few years previously. For his part, Mondrian used the work of Pablo Picasso and Georges Braque as the foundation of his work during this period. More importantly, the two artists began to highlight rhythm as a significant element of their compositions in the summer of 1913.

Composition No. IX illustrates rhythm through dynamic interplay between planes and lines. Mondrian expresses this sense of rhythm independently of any representation or image – simply as a characteristic of the composition itself. Prior to this painting he had not used this method, and his discussions with Van Domselaer certainly played a part in its inception. The creation of rhythm through the use of layered elements – such as in *Composition No. IX* – can also be observed in Van Domselaer's *Proeven van Stijlkunst* (Experiments in Artistic Style, c.1912). The individual movements of this seven-part piano piece are composed over a long period of time. The title of the piece is significant: in the first movement, Van Domselaer experimented with a new style, just as Mondrian did in his painting. In their quest for something new, they both strove to find a balance between verticals and horizontals; between a melody (horizontal) and a harmony (vertical); between structure and depth. If these were in balance, the resulting works radiate a sense of rest to viewers and listeners. In the extremely innovative *Proeven van Stijlkunst,* Van Domselaer uses harmonies and minimalist repetitive elements to find this balance, and the piece emanates rest and silence.

In *Proeven van Stijlkunst* Van Domselaer incorporates a Bach choral work – a Protestant hymn with a strophic form – into the first movement and provides very few instructions for the performance of his piece, such as tempo or dynamics. He does, however, mention *Wer nur den lieben Gott lässt walten* (1724) at the end, which is the title of the hymn set to music by Bach. The similarity between Bach's piece and the first movement of *Proeven van Stijlkunst* can be recognised through the use of emphatic musical expression of triplets (three notes per beat). In Bach's work this is played by an oboe. The first movement of Van Domselaer's piece is in 4/4 time, and the repeating groups of triplets are emphasised through notes played on the first of each triplet. The piece has sequences, and once in a while there is a long four-quarter note, which marks the end of a

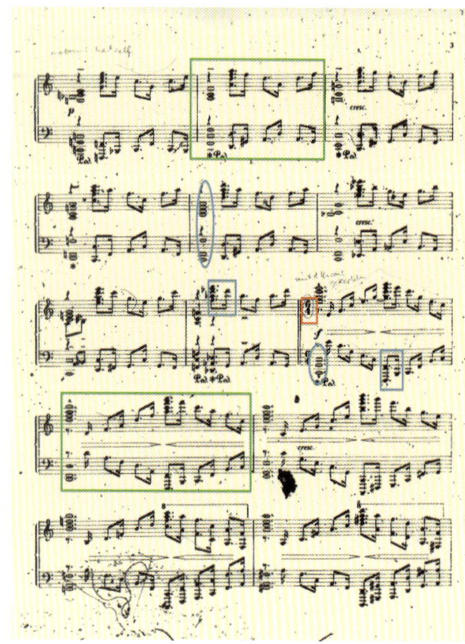

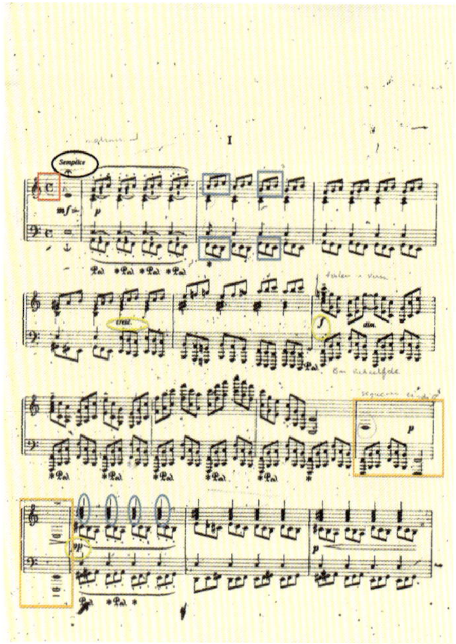

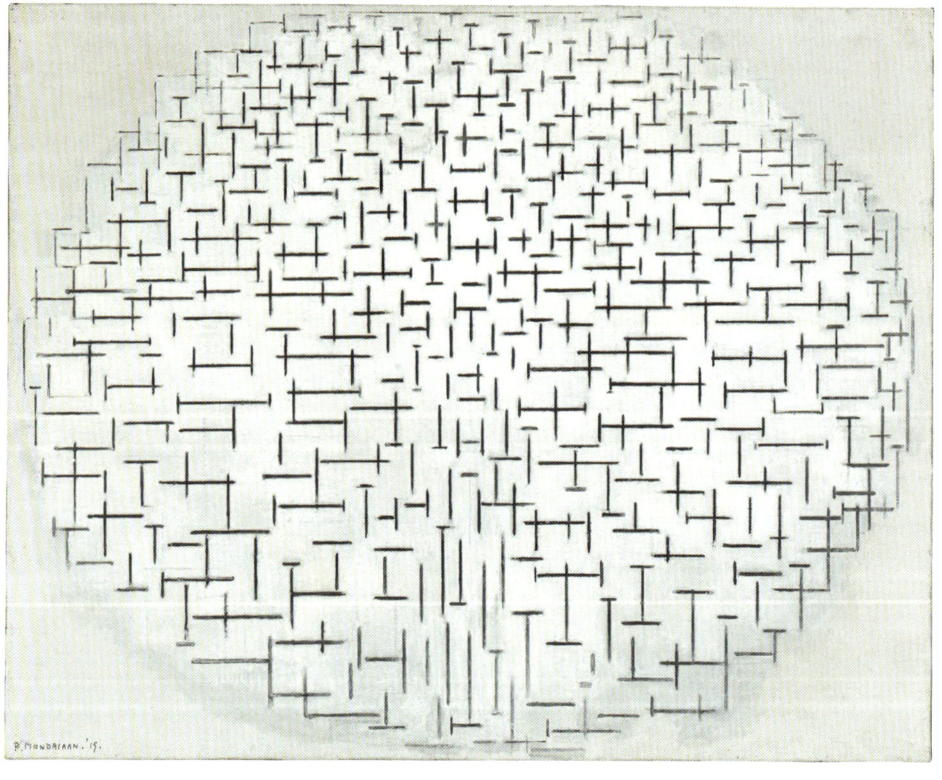

01 Jakob van Domselaer
Music sheet for *Proeven van Stijlkunst*, c. 1912

02 Jakob van Domselaer
Music sheet for *Proeven van Stijlkunst*, c. 1912

03 *Compositie 10 in Zwart en Wit*
(Composition 10 in Black and White), 1915
Oil on canvas, 85 x 108 cm
Kröller-Müller Museum, Otterlo

section (ill. 01). The chords remain parallel, or mirrored, in both hands.

The volume variations Van Domselaer does mention serve mainly to highlight the different textures throughout the piece. Later in the movement, the piece intensifies through the use of additional notes. The change from four to six beats per measure broadens the underlying sense of time, while the rhythmic cadence remains the same (see red, blue and green marking in ill.02). The horizontal and vertical elements of the piece can be heard in the slightly developing, yet constantly repeating, motif. In this respect, the first part is similar to Mondrian's painting from 1913: the repeating planes, the colours that seem similar but are in fact different, and the sense that the painting is mirrored. *Composition No. IX* is an experiment in finding rhythm between planes and lines, using a reduced starting point. The work is not completely abstract, however. Just as Van Domselaer retains the Bach element as a basis for creating something new, Mondrian's inspiration from the work of the French Cubists is also visible. The work of both artists is founded on that of others, yet their parallel search for the 'new' is apparent, and even critics refer to the early work of these two creatives in similar ways. Entirely independent of each other, music and art critics described the compositions of Mondrian and Van Domselaer as the inception of something new, something not yet defined, and not yet completely crystallised. One critic wrote of Van Domselaer's work in the Dutch newspaper *Algemeen Handelsblad*:

> Centuries of art lie behind us: every concept has taken beautiful form, every sentiment has been expressed, every passion captured in moving rhythm. This era suffers like no other from the pressure of a rich past and this explains how a composer like Van Domselaer can retain his composure in the face of that past and of his own production. He seems to me a man who stands among life in art, to whom reality has not yet been revealed in its totality, and who seeks in art what he has not found in life.[2]

In Mondrian's later works – produced during the period when war confined him to the Netherlands – his connection with Van Domselaer is more apparent, and a reinforced rhythm shines through his recursive play of taut lines. This is clear in *Composition 10 in Black and White* (1915), because the motif of the pier and ocean is almost reduced to complete abstraction through the rhythm and contrast of horizontal and vertical lines in the piece. Van Domselaer's influence on Mondrian is only gradually revealed in the early paintings, but after their close friendship developed his influence is almost impossible to overlook.

Mondrian lived with Van Domselaer and Middelkoop during his stay in the Netherlands, after returning from Paris in 1914. In searching for the new, the abstract, the eternal, they found rest and balance through achieving a true equilibrium between the vertical and the horizontal. Without this balance a work would not radiate rest to the audience. *Composition No. IX* proved to be only the beginning of this flourishing, fascinating friendship, and helped both creative forces find a completely new style in their respective fields.

The Exhibition at Kunsthandel Walrecht, The Hague

Kunsthandel W. Walrecht,
SMIDSPLEIN 4 (bij het Korte Voorhout)
's-GRAVENHAGE.

16 Juni—16 Juli 1914
TENTOONSTELLING
van 'n 16 tal composities van
P. MONDRIAN te Parijs.
In portefeuille: 26095.12
ETSEN van Ed. Manet en W. B. Tholen
Toegang vrij. Dagelijks geopend van 9—5 uur

An advertisement for the exhibition at Kunsthandel Walrecht, The Hague in *Nieuwe Rotterdamsche Courant*, 26 June 1914.

Composition Nos. I-IV

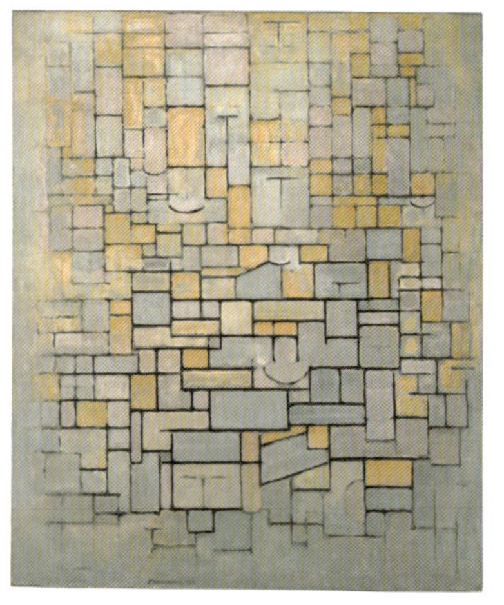
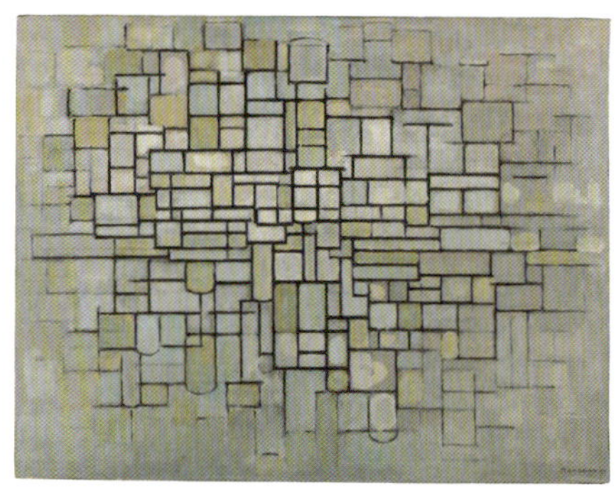
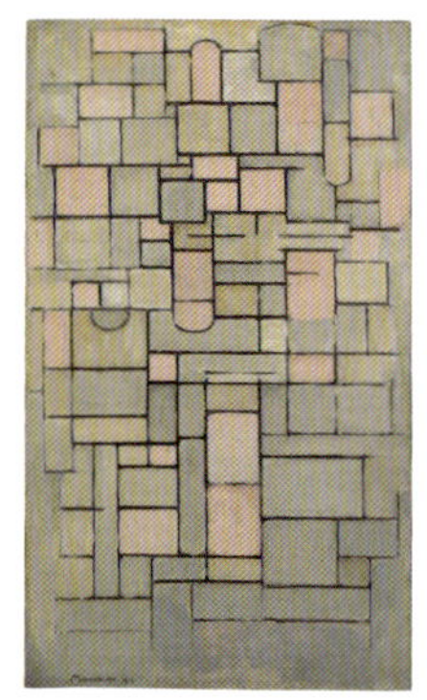
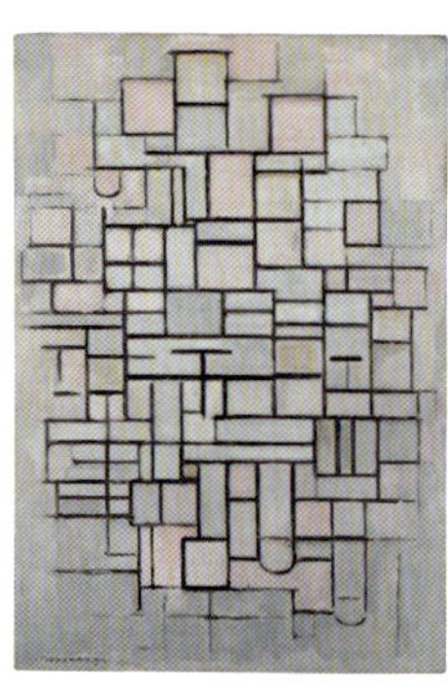

Composition Nos. IX-XII

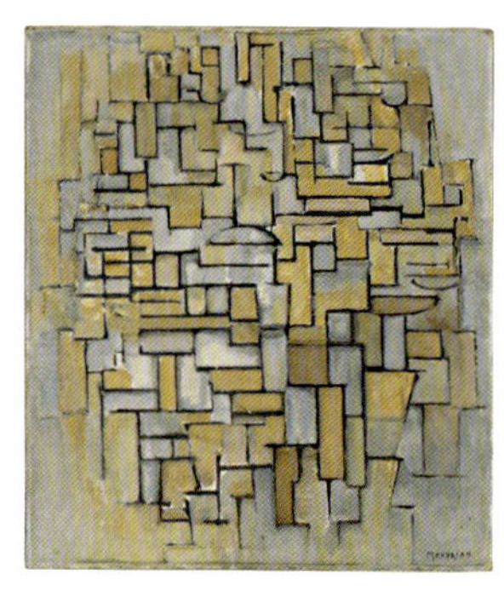
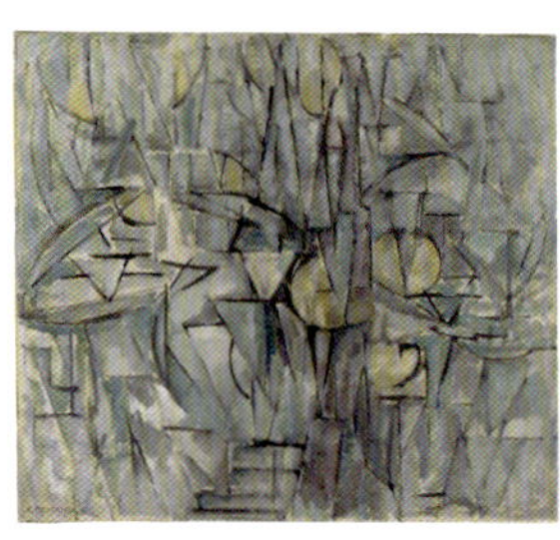
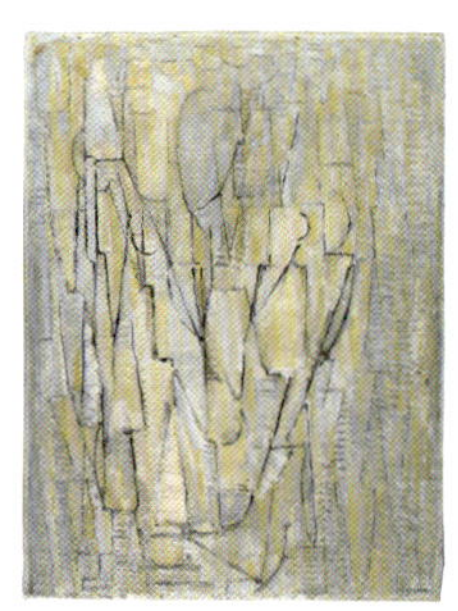
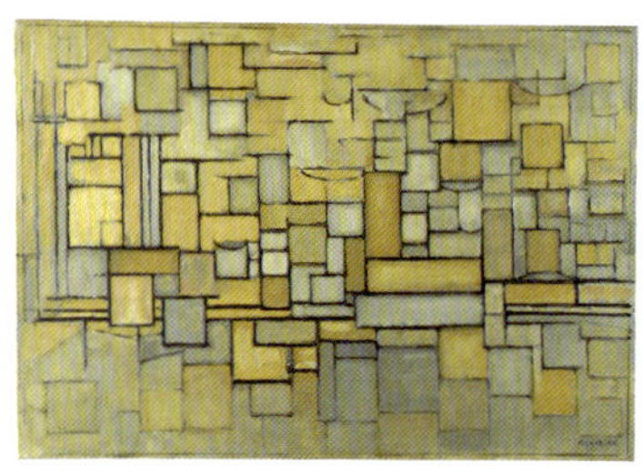

Piet Mondrian showed 17 Compositions at Kunsthandel Walrecht in The Hague, indicating the French origins of these abstract paintings in the use of the French word for the title.

It is not possible to recreate a plan of the exhibition space at Smidsplein 4, but based on the classification into three groups we have assumed the works were divided among three spaces: a front room, a double room divided by sliding doors, and a room at the rear.

Composition Nos. V-VIII

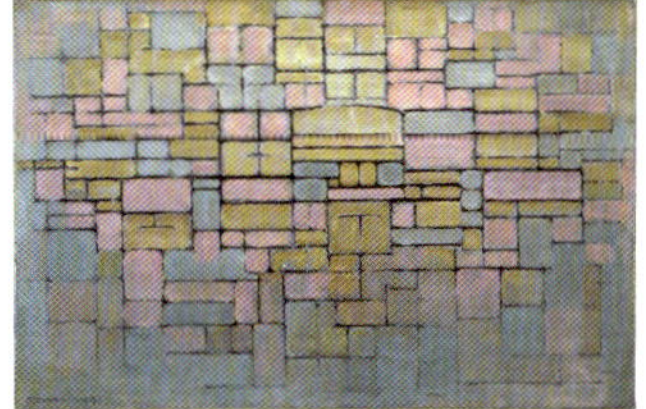
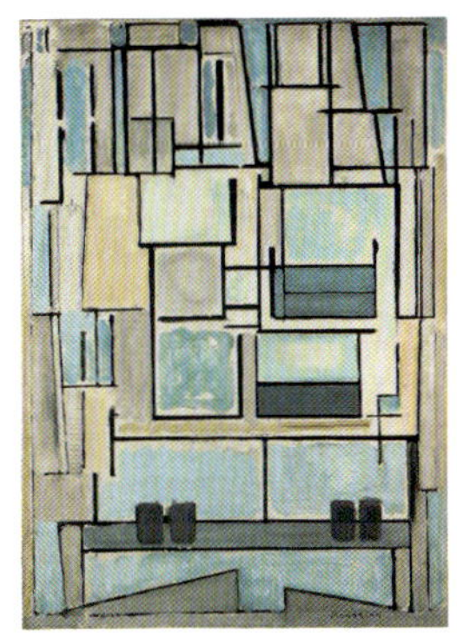
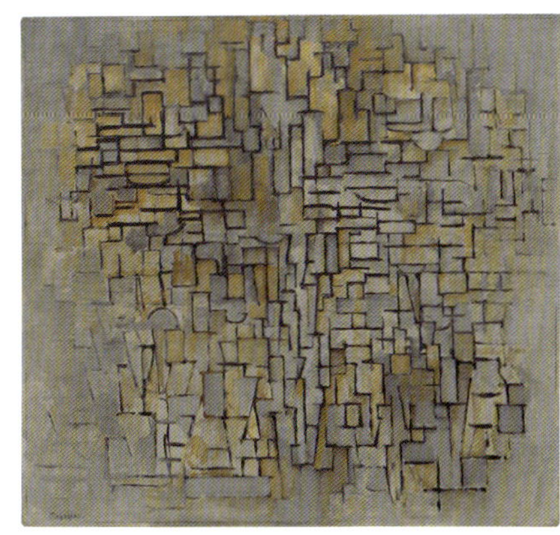
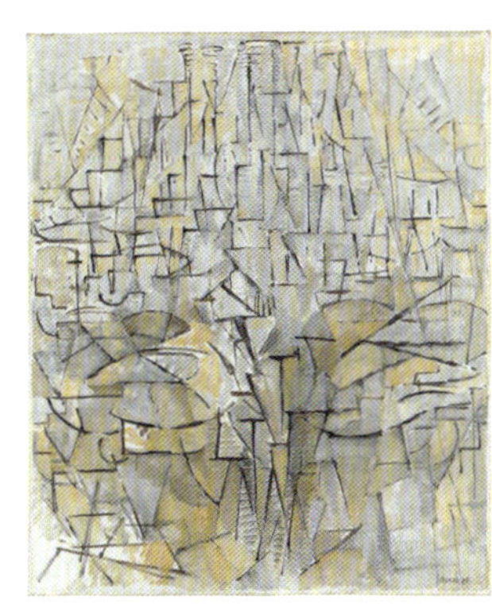

Composition Nos. XIII-XVI

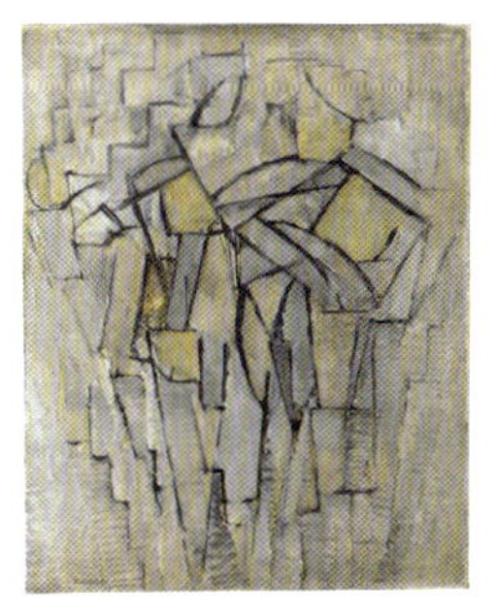
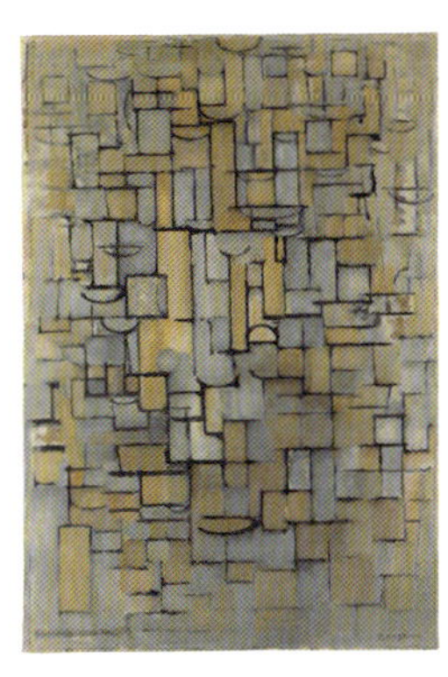
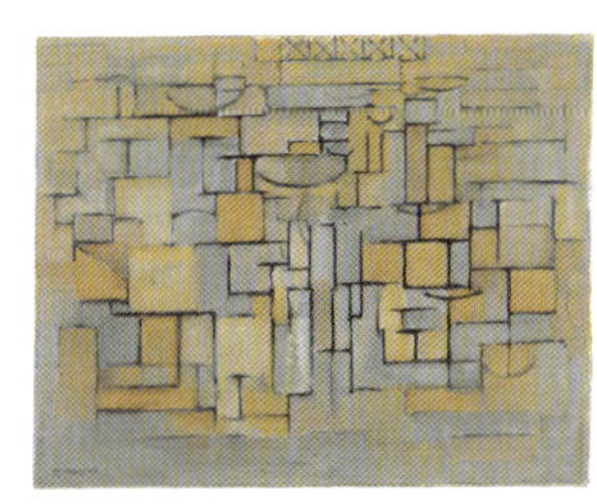
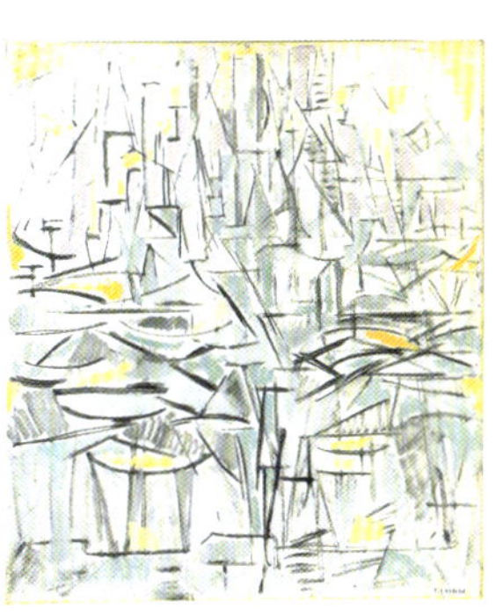

Composition with Colour Planes: Facade

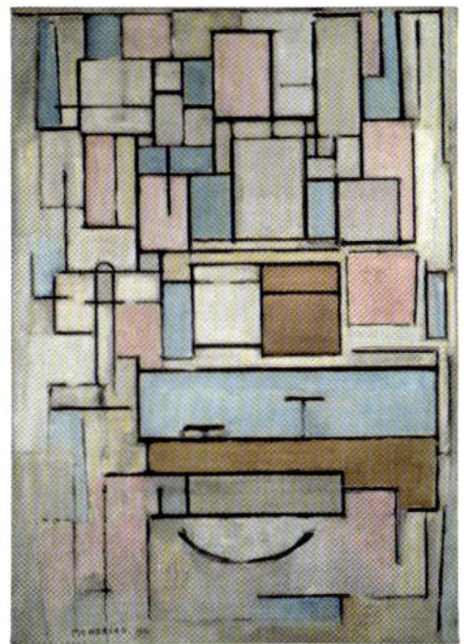

Composition NOS. I-IV

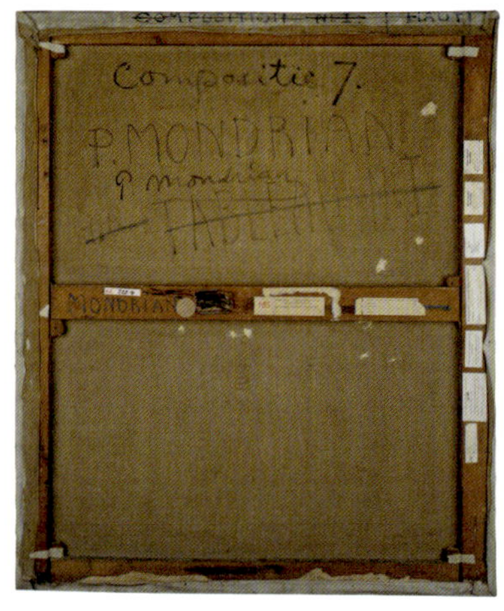

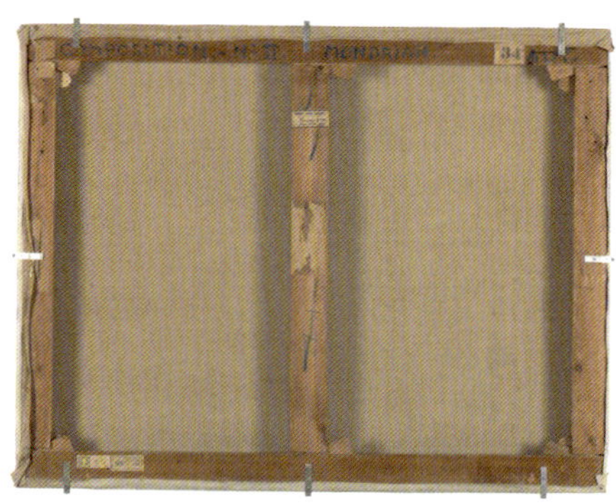

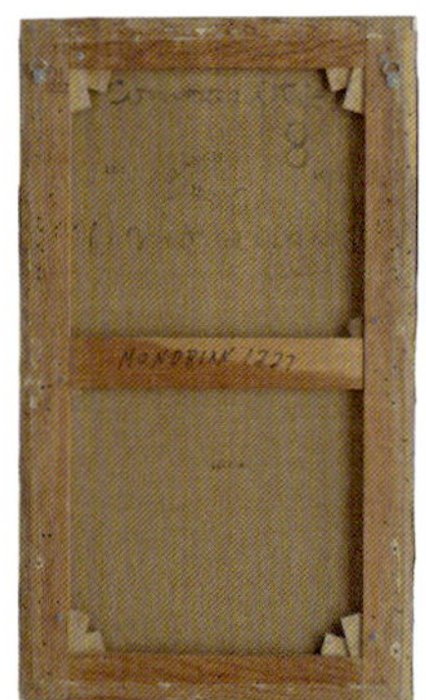

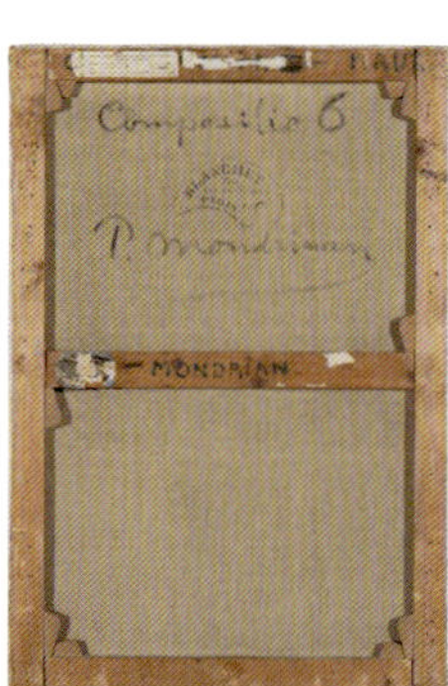

Composition NOS. IX-XII

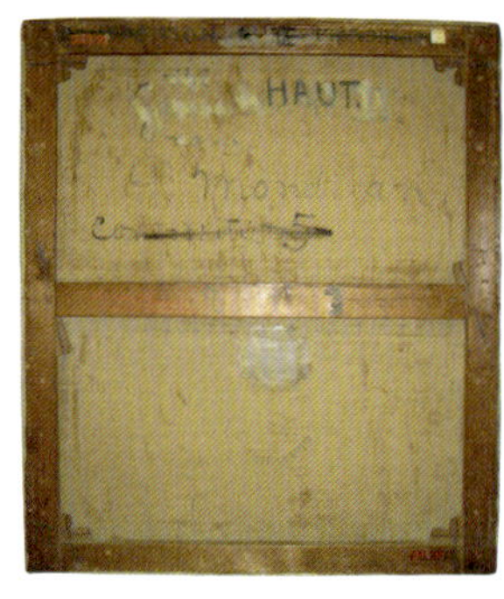

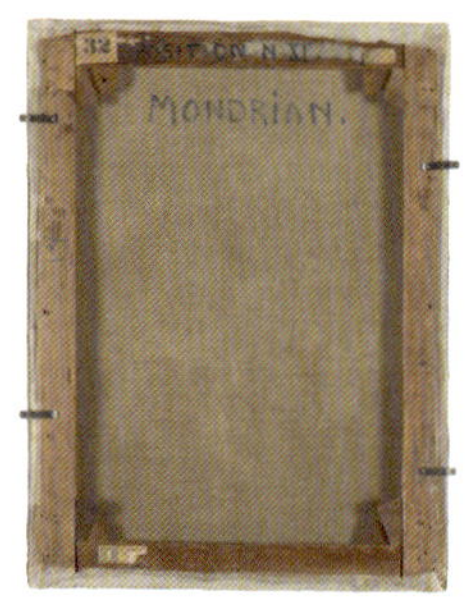

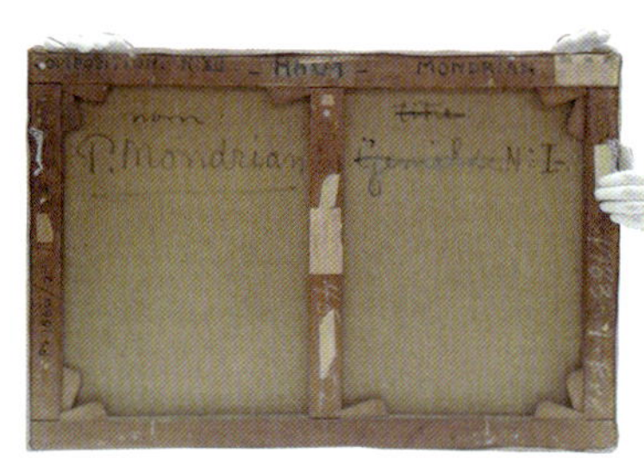

Composition Nos. V–VIII

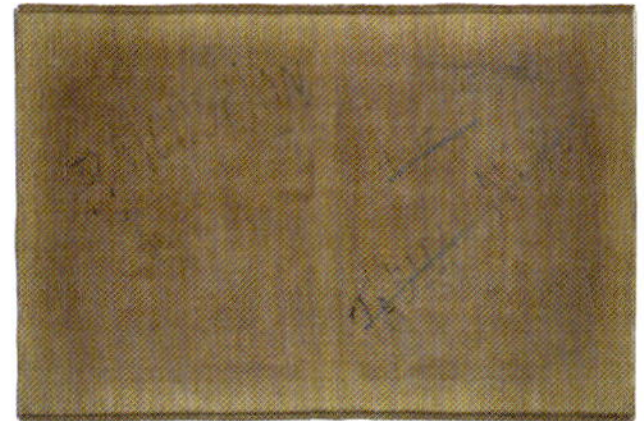

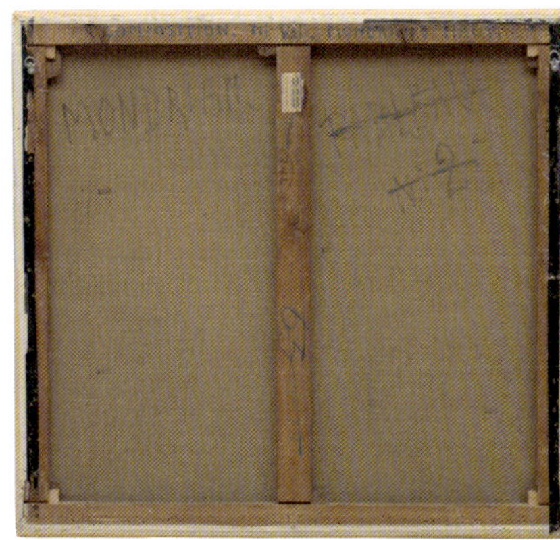

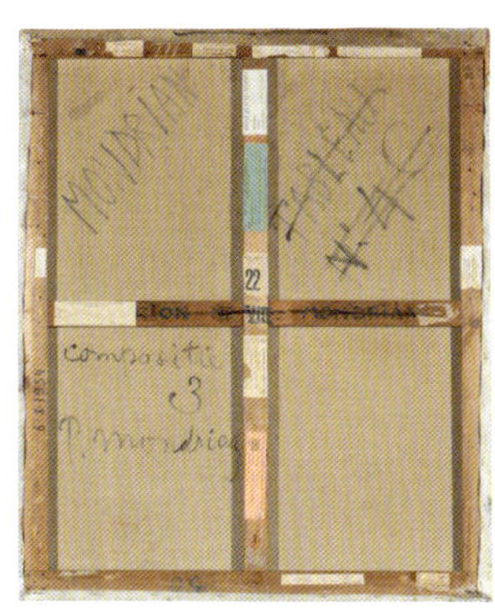

Composition Nos. XIII–XVI

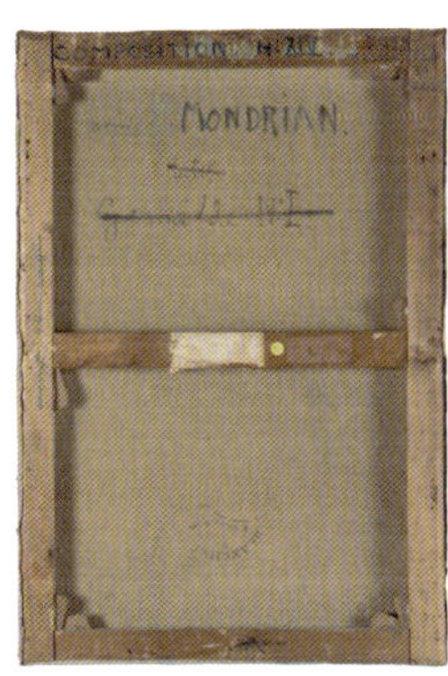

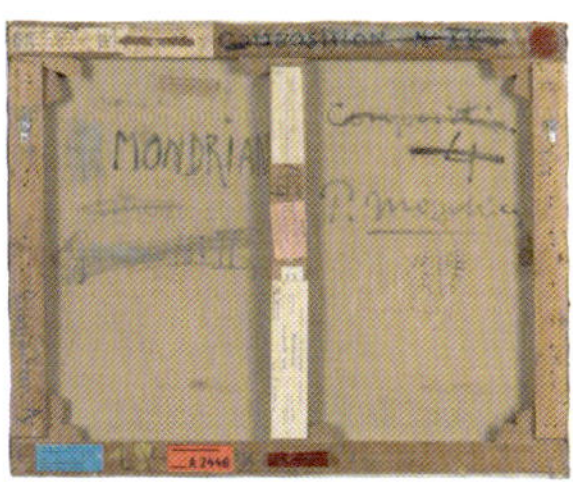

Composition with Colour Planes: Facade

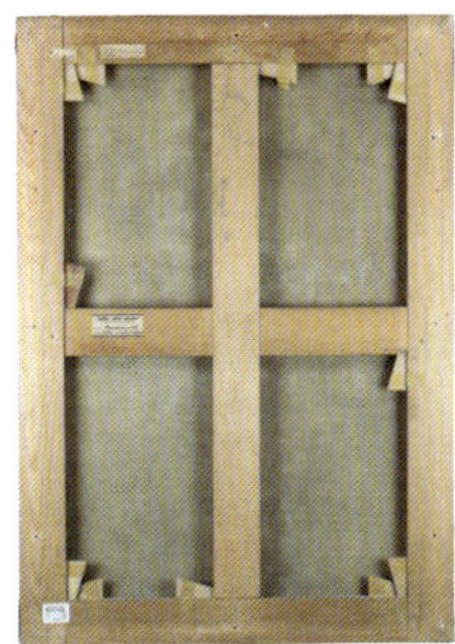

Editor's note: This section is composed of in-depth analyses of Mondrian's 17 Compositions from the 1914 Kunsthandel Walrecht exhibition. These technical analyses provide a great amount of detail about each painting, derived through examining the materials and the painted surfaces intensively, both with the naked eye and also with technical means, and by studying technical reports. The resulting analyses reflect vast amounts of research carried out by conservators and art historians from various institutions and were compiled in preparation for the *Mondrian and Cubism* exhibition at the Gemeentemuseum Den Haag in 2014. The gathering of all of this information was used - in conjunction with art historical research - to date the Compositions and place them in chronological order.

Raking light photography
When a painted surface is lit with a strong light source from a low angle – almost parallel to the plane of the canvas – tiny features in the relief of the paint surface can become visible as a result of the dark shadows that are cast. Any deformation of the canvas and the direction of brushstrokes become apparent, along with changes to the composition that cannot be seen in normal light.

x-ray images
When x-rays pass through a painted surface, pigments with a higher atomic mass (such as lead white) block them while other pigments (such as ochre) let them through. Since the x-rays are directed at the entire surface, they reveal all of the layers on a painted surface simultaneously. This also reveals essential information about the internal structure of and changes to the composition.

Ultraviolet fluorescence
Pigments and binders absorb ultraviolet (UV) light and re-transmit it at a different wavelength, in a slightly different colour if the blend of pigments is different, or if it was applied at a different time. The colours in a UV image therefore tell us how a painting came about, the material used and the order in which the paint was applied.

x-ray fluorescence spectroscopy (XRF)
x-rays cause molecules to enter a different energy state, emitting spectra under ultraviolet light that reveal many elements. This technique is highly suitable for determining which pigments an artist used. The problem is that, as well as the elements on the painting's surface, this also reveals deeper paint layers that may have different compositions.

Transmitted light photography
When a strong light source is positioned behind the painted canvas and a camera in front, the resulting photograph shows the light shining through thinly painted layers, or through places where the paint has been removed, or where the canvas was not painted. The image is darker in places where the paint layers are thicker, thus highlighting variations in thickness. Changes in the composition can also be seen on transmitted light photographs.

Infrared photography
An infrared filter can be used to filter out the visible light in photographic images. If a light-sensitive chip that is extra sensitive to infrared light is used it can reveal where the infrared light shines through the painted surface, and where it is absorbed or reflected by it.

Transmitted infrared photography
A combination of transmitted light photography and infrared photography can reveal peculiarities beneath the surface of a painting. Materials containing carbon – such as charcoal, pencil and bone black – absorb infrared light and therefore appear black on an infrared photograph.

Fourier transform infrared spectroscopy (FTIR)
This is a method particularly suited to the analysis of the organic components of materials. It uses molecular spectroscopy, a method that allows the vibration of molecules (or parts of molecules) to be detected. Fourier transform – a mathematical transformation – can be used to analyse the results and determine the components of a given material.

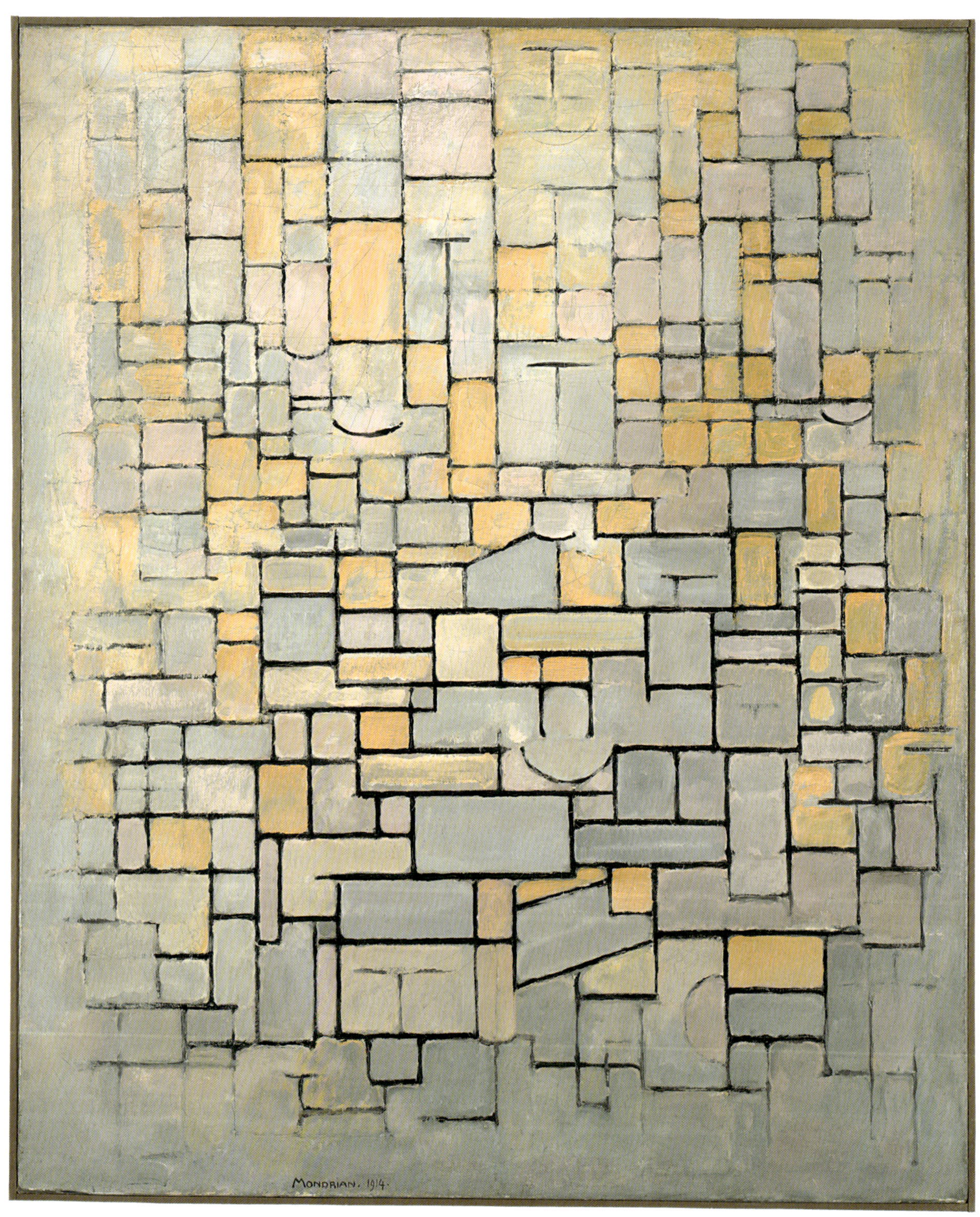

Composition No. 1 1913
(B44 – Tableau No. 1 / Compositie No. 1 / Compositie 7)
Oil on canvas, 120.6 x 101.3 cm
Kimbell Art Museum, Fort Worth

This text is based on the 'Technical Report, May 31, 1994' by Michael Gallagher, in the archives of the restoration department of the Kimbell Art Museum, Fort Worth.

Inscriptions
Front: signed and dated bottom centre in black paint: MONDRiAN. 1914.

Back: on the top half of the canvas, in black paint, using a narrow brush, in cursive script: *Compositie 7*. [A reference to the title at the exhibition in the Stedelijk Museum, Amsterdam in 1915]; beneath this, in large block capitals, in black paint and using a thin brush: P. MONDRiAN; beneath this, in cursive script, in black paint using a thin brush, underlined by the artist: *P. Mondrian*; below this, in block capitals, in black paint using a thin brush: titre: TABLEAU N: I. [crossed out in blue paint using a wide brush, when the work was given another title at Walrecht in 1914]; on the canvas turnover, along the top edge, in blue paint with a wide brush: COMPOSITION N:. I. [a reference to the title at Walrecht], and further to the right, framed by a line on either side: HAUT. [this inscription was crossed out using black paint and a narrow brush, probably when Mondrian changed the title to *Composition 7* in 1915]; on the wood of the left stretcher bar a German customs stamp consisting of the word *Zoll* and the figures 1–10; immediately beside this, a larger stamp of unclear origin; on the middle stretcher bar a number of inscriptions crossed out with black paint, beneath several later labels that indicate previous use of the stretcher; also a label decorated with a blue edge bearing the inscription: 61 Compositie H | P. Mondriaan | terug Mevr. Hannaert, Laren [this inscription has been crudely struck out with black paint]; next to this, in blue paint with a wide brush: MONDRiAN; on the bottom stretcher bar in pencil, in cursive script: *Mondrian*, and a number of inscriptions crossed out in black paint that indicate previous use of the stretcher for other compositions.

Stretcher
The canvas is probably cut from a larger stretcher. It has been hastily mounted and the drawing pins Mondrian customarily used to pull and affix the canvas provisionally round the back of the stretcher are still visible here and there. Along the top and the left side a selvedge can be seen where a thickened ridge of the ground marks the boundary between bare canvas and ground; such a ridge is generally created along the turnover edge when the stretched canvas is primed on the front. Tack holes can be seen all along the unprimed selvedge from a previous use of the canvas on a larger stretcher. Remains of the fold fixed by the priming can even be seen on the left edge. The frame is bevelled inwards along the canvas side, and the corners have butt joints. In each corner there are two keys, and there is also a key in each corner of the horizontal central stretcher bar. The canvas is firmly keyed out, as a result of which the corners at the top and bottom on the front side right no longer meet properly. This is particularly visible in raking light (ills 01; p.78; 01.A, 01.B).

Framing
Traces of bronze-coloured paint can be seen along all front edges, indicating that the painting originally had a frame whose visible side was parallel and flush with the surface of the painting. The current frame is a 1994 reconstruction.

Date
Until now it had been assumed that Mondrian completed the painting in the run-up to the exhibition at Kunsthandel Walrecht in April 1914, after it had been returned from the Salon des Indépendants, where he had exhibited it previously. The customs stamp on the back indicates, however, that the painting was previously shown in Germany. This could have been at the Neue Kunst – Hans Goltz Gallery, Munich in June 1913, and the painting might have been one of those with 'blue tiles' referred to in a review in a Munich newspaper. However, it might have been shown elsewhere in Germany. All this might indicate that Mondrian originally finished the painting in spring 1913 and that he revised it in April 1914. Given the previous use of the stretcher and canvas – primed on another stretcher – it could certainly be possible that Mondrian had already experimented on this canvas as early as autumn 1912.

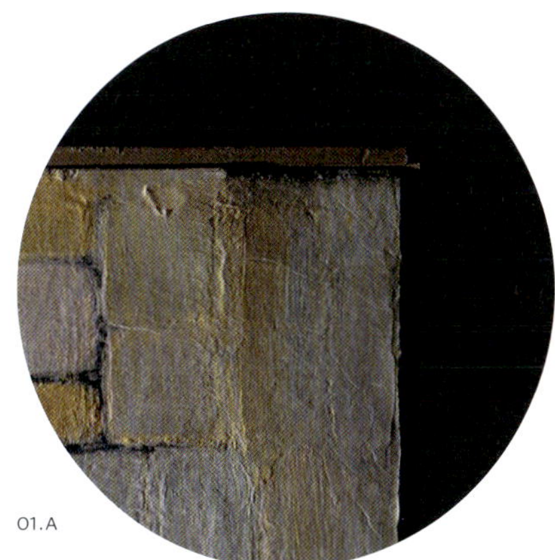
01.A

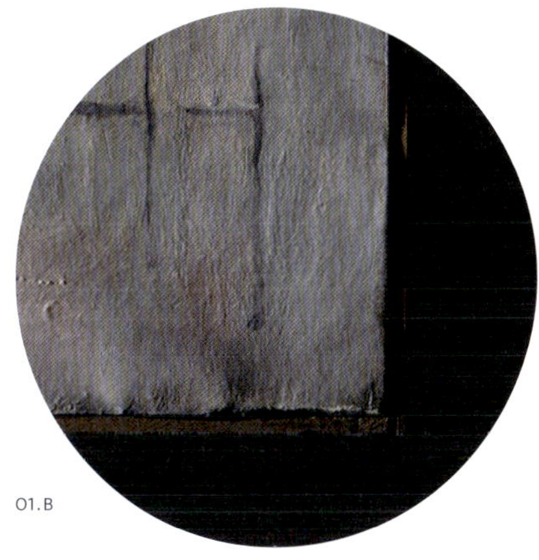
01.B

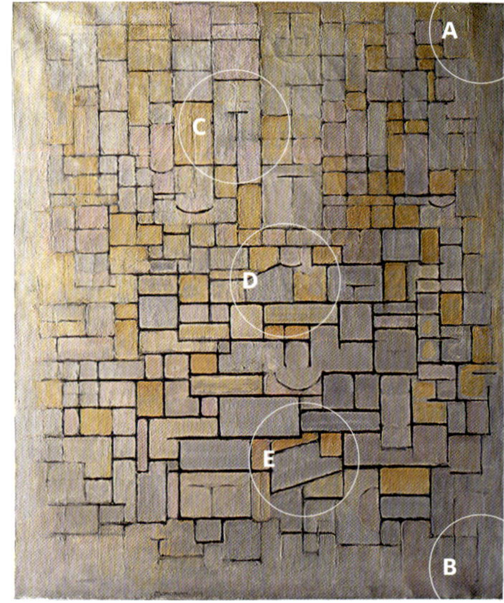

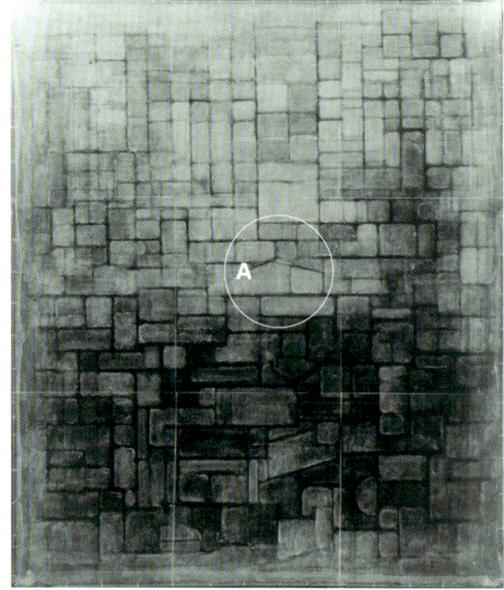

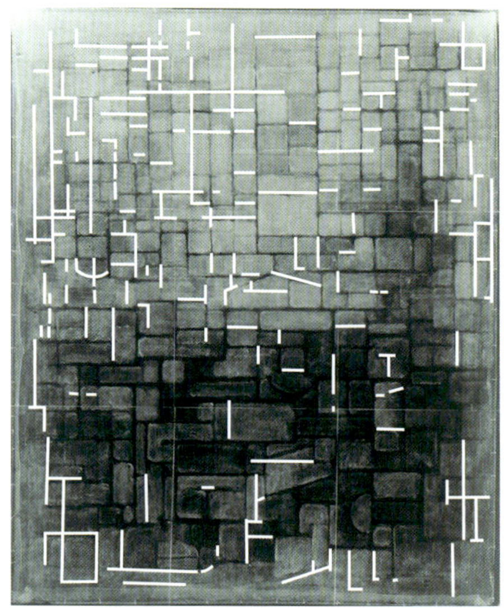

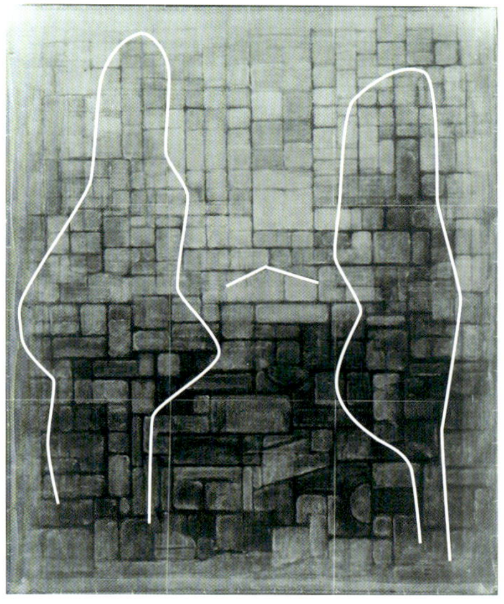

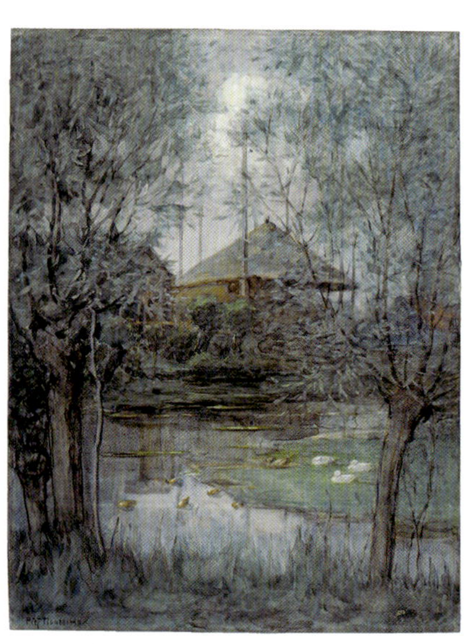

01 Raking light photograph with indications of details

02 x-ray photograph with indication of a detail

04 x-ray photograph

03 x-ray photograph with indicated marks of removed lines

05 *Hooischelf* (Hay Barn), 1897–98
Watercolour and gouache on paper, 64 x 47 cm
Gemeentemuseum Den Haag, The Hague

Provenance
The painting may have been purchased by Katinka Hannaert in Laren after 1915. It appeared on the Dutch art market after 1949. In 1983 it was bought by the Kimbell Art Museum, through The Anne Burnett and Charles Tandy Foundation of Fort Worth.

Painted surface
The first thing one notices about this painting is the many shades of grey, which are almost impossible to reproduce in photograph or print. Blue-grey, yellow-grey, green-grey and pink-grey are positioned so close together, and there is so little contrast and difference in clarity between them, that the variation becomes apparent only in bright light or after lengthy study. In the bottom half of the composition some strictly delineated rectangles have been painted in more or less even grey and ochre. From a third of the way up the canvas, where a bowl-like open section of a circle can be seen in the middle of the picture, the handling of paint becomes more diffuse and also more relaxed, and the black lines are partly covered by the colours of the planes, or have been played down as they were superficially passed over with grey or ochre (ill. 01.C). Further towards the top a diagonal line sloping down to the left can be seen. To the right is another sloping line, but this is partly concealed by a subsequent paint passage. The x-ray shows that the sloping lines originally suggested a roof-like shape (ills 02.A, 01.D).

The x-ray also reveals that the surface of the upper part of the picture, in particular, had far more vertical lines and that gradually Mondrian simplified the composition considerably. This might mean that Mondrian initially – possibly in autumn 1912 – set out a strictly regular grid as a basis for a cubist composition. He did not then choose an organic motif – a tree, a river view, a portrait – which he would subsequently geometricise while building the image. Instead, he began at the other end of the spectrum, as it were, with a strictly organised grid, into which he incorporated an image. In 1994 Michael Gallagher, then conservator at the Kimbell Art Museum, marked the positions of the lines that had been removed by Mondrian while painting (ill. 03). He observed that, under raking light, it can clearly be seen that the lines are deeper and only partially covered by paint. We can conclude from this that Mondrian simplified the composition at a relatively late stage in its genesis. The x-ray also clearly shows that the top half of the picture has thicker layers of paint, often bulked out with paint that is fairly impermeable to x-rays, such as lead white, which appears on the x-ray image as a white haze, indicating a more opaque layer (ill. 02). The top half of the picture also has more drying cracks because of the many layers of paint applied before previous layers were dry (ill. 01).

According to Joop M Joosten, the composition is based on the back of some residential buildings that Mondrian drew in his sketchbook sometime in 1913.[1] He is unable, however, to identify any clear example. The x-ray image shows something else that Gallagher refers to in his report, though he does not go into it in any depth. He observes that the division between black and opaque (white) passages is not strictly horizontal, but that a zone of opaque paint projects vertically into the upper half on the right-hand side. He concludes that this suggests the presence of a distinctly different composition underlying the present one. On the left, too, the x-ray shows a less white zone. Only in the centre, projecting upward from the 'small roof', has the paint surface been bulked out with a relatively large amount of white, in less resolved brushstrokes. This is far removed from the city roofscape that Joosten suggests as a basis. But it is daring to assume instead that Mondrian based this painting on a composition like *Hay Barn*, produced in 1897–98 (ill. 05). He might have taken a version of this composition on paper with him to Paris. The small willow trees on either side can be vaguely discerned, or read into the darker areas on the x-ray image, where more impermeable paints like lead white, used in creating sky for example, are missing (ill. 04). The water in the foreground with the resting ducks has therefore been transformed into the two parallel fragments of line running vertically – which in themselves serve to guide the eye into the pictorial world of the painting (ill. 01.E). If this is the case, Mondrian chose one of the oldest works on paper he had taken with him to Paris, a counterpoint to the strictly defined grid that must have formed the initial basis of this very daring composition.

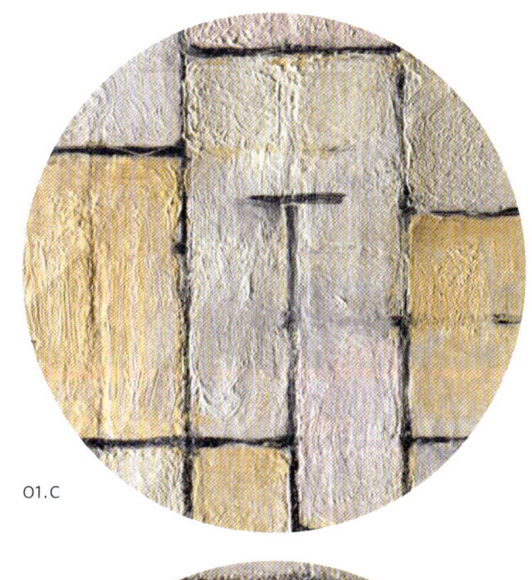
01.C

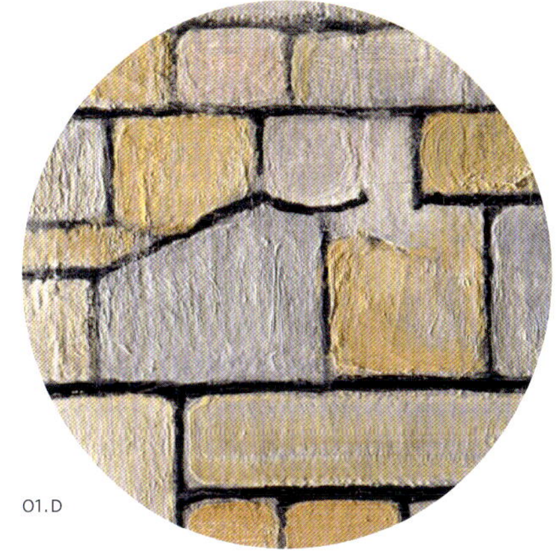
01.D

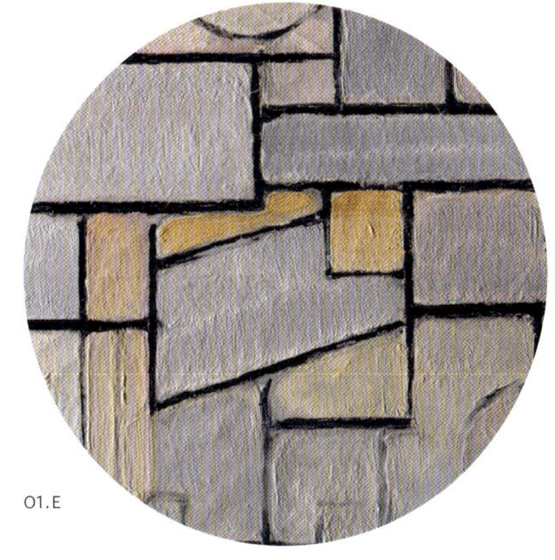
01.E

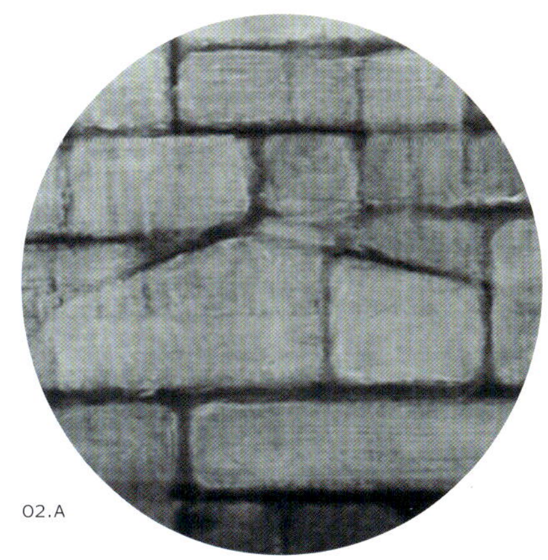
02.A

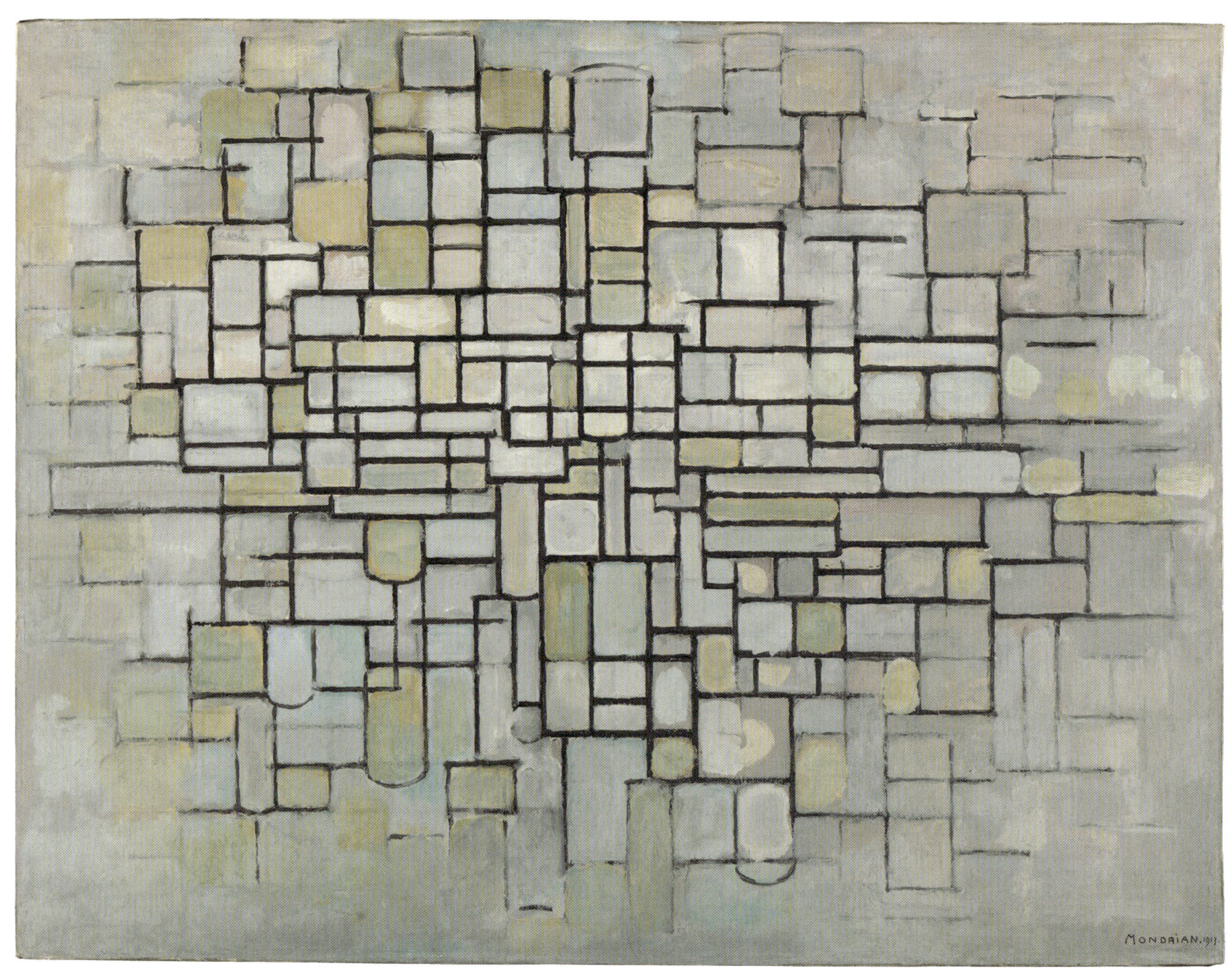

Composition No. 11 1913
(B42)
Oil on canvas, 88 x 115 cm
Kröller-Müller Museum, Otterlo

As this painting was not subjected to technical analysis, the technical information presented here is based mainly on that supplied by Joop M Joosten and Robert P Welsh, *Piet Mondrian: Catalogue Raisonné of the Work of 1911–1944*, vol.2, Prestel, Munich, 1998; as well as the other sources quoted.

Inscriptions
Front: signed in the lower right in black paint: MONDRiAN. 1913. [painted over an earlier signature; the date was added in the same paint as the more recent signature].

Back: on the left stretcher bar is a plain label with the inscription, in black ink: *no. 2 titel Molen | Piet Mondriaan | Amsterdam*. (This is probably a reference to the use of the stretcher for the painting *Mill in Sunlight* (1908), now in the Gemeentemuseum Den Haag's collection. Mondrian submitted this painting, as the second in a series of four pieces, to an exhibition of the association Doe stil voort, Brussels in 1909.) To the left, on the wood, in pencil, in cursive script: *3 Dans la forêt*; and to the right of the label: *Mondrian* [over the name is an Amsterdam customs stamp]. (This is a reference to the use of the stretcher for the painting that Mondrian intended to enter to the Salon des Indépendants of March 1912. It could be that this painting was later exhibited on another stretcher and in another form.) On the middle stretcher bar is a plain label with the inscription, in black ink: *nom: Mondrian. Titre:* [illegible because the rest of the label has been torn off]. In addition, on the middle stretcher bar, from top to bottom, in blue chalk: obraz 90 v [price of the piece at an exhibition in Prague in 1914] and K73. Both references have been crossed out with blue paint, using a broad brush. On the top stretcher bar, in blue paint, with a broad brush: COMPOSITION. – N: II. [the title at the Kunsthandel Walrecht exhibition]; beside this, in blue paint with a broad brush: MONDRiAN; next to this, in blue paint with a broad brush: HAUT.

Stretcher
The pine stretcher is original. The stretcher is simple with butt joints. The canvas has been keyed out, as a result of which the painting no longer meets properly in the bottom right corner. There are two keys in each corner, and one in each corner of the vertical central stretcher bar. The canvas has a white ground of unknown composition. The stretching is probably original, although tacks have been replaced here and there, as documented in a report by Tom Egelund in 1994, in the archive of the Kröller-Müller Museum's conservation department. The ground is thin and fairly regular: the structure of the canvas has not been completely filled so the weave is clearly visible. It is a plain weave canvas with threads of varying thickness. The vertical threads are more prominent, while the horizontal threads recede more. There is a selvedge along the left which was attached on the back using tacks, one of which is still in place. Along all other tacking margins the canvas has a narrow, roughly cut overlap. Mondrian probably trimmed (or cut) off the overlap himself, given the proximity of the inscriptions he made on the stretcher. In the centre of the tacking margins there are holes made by thin tacks that may have affixed the frame.

Framing
On the surface, along all front edges, beneath the last layer of paint, approximately 4–10 mm from the edge, there are traces of a rebated frame that must have been the painting's first framing. The raking light photograph clearly shows these traces (ill. 06; p.82), though bronze paint also shows through in the top right. In 1993 Joosten concluded that Mondrian later decided to replace the rebated frame by a strip frame with a flat surface that sat flush with the surface of the painting. The current frame is a 1994 reconstruction.

Date
It is assumed that Mondrian must have applied the overpainting, the new signature, the date and the new frame just before sending the painting to The Hague before 24 May 1914 (the date when the consignment arrived in The Hague; according to Mondrian in his letter to critic HP Bremmer of 5 May 1914 he had apparently enquired with the shipping agent as to when it would be delivered), but well after 29 March, the date on which the Prague exhibition ended. Allowing approximately two weeks for transport and delivery, we might assume a completion date somewhere in mid-April 1914. The works that were at the Salon des Indépendants – *Composition NO. I* (1913; p.76) and *Composition NO. V* (1914; p.94) – were returned later, after that exhibition closed on 30 April. It is not likely however that Mondrian would have dated the painting 1913 if he had dramatically reworked it. It would be wiser to assume that the painting was reworked before it was sent to Prague (around mid-February 1914) and that the revision, and thus completion of the painting, probably took place in the final months of 1913, allowing time for the paint to dry and causing the drying cracks on the earlier paint layers that were not yet dry when the last layer was applied.

Provenance
The painting was purchased by Helene Kröller-Müller at the Kunsthandel Walrecht exhibition in 1914. It was transferred to the collection of the Kröller-Müller Museum, Otterlo in 1938.

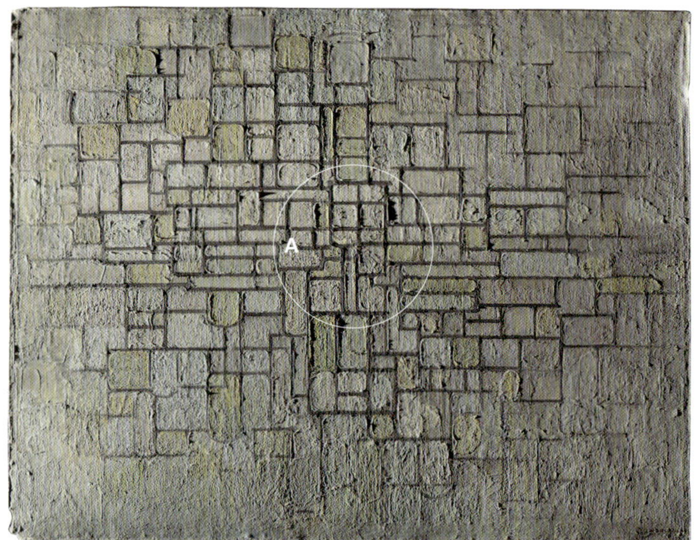

06 Raking light photograph with indication of a detail

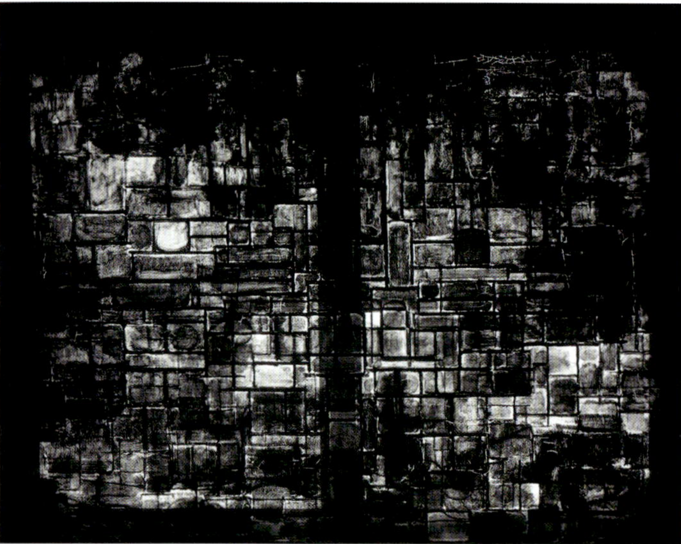

08 Transmitted infrared photograph

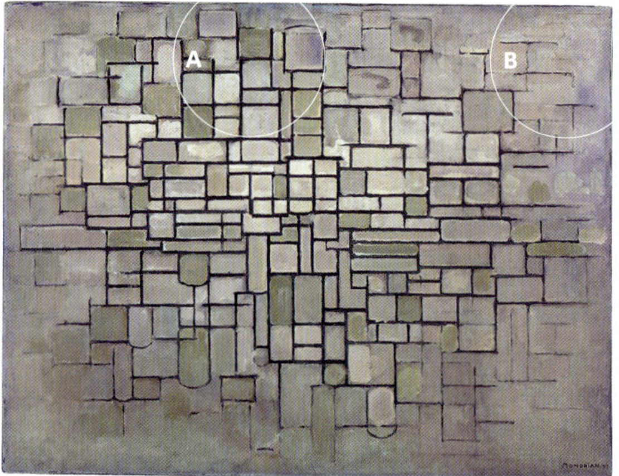

07 Ultraviolet light photograph with indications of details

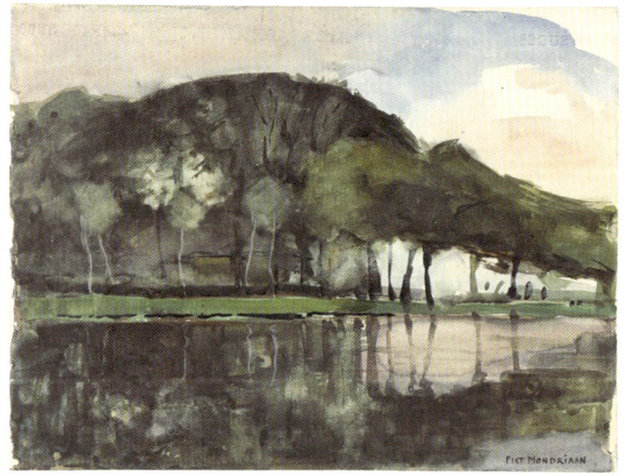

09 *Boerderij Geinrust* (Geinrust Farm), 1907
Watercolour, 31 x 41 cm
Gemeentemuseum Den Haag, The Hague

Painted surface
The canvas is almost entirely covered with colour and lines. There are no traces of visible ground, with the exception of the heart of the composition, where the prepared canvas can still be seen here and there. The raking light photograph shows that the lines between the planes also lie lower there, while around them the lines are painted on top of the paint layers (ill. 06.A). The painting extends to the tacking edges, but not beyond them. The top layers are generally more fluid than the underlying layers. The black lines were fluidly painted, with a certain liveliness and haste. Here and there the black has been applied over a surface that was smooth and probably just dry, as a result of which the black paint has beaded slightly. In the centre of the composition the black lines are firm and shiny, while towards the edges they become more faded and merge into the surrounding colours. It could easily be that Mondrian made a deliberate attempt to juxtapose matt and more fluid, shining layers of paint to create visual differentiation on another level besides that of colour or contrast.

In 1995, conservators Petria Noble of the Kröller-Müller Museum and Karin Groen of the Centraal Laboratorium, Amsterdam investigated the difference between the matt and more glossy passages in the painting, assuming that Mondrian deliberately sought such a contrast by mixing additives into the paint. The study provided no evidence that Mondrian added substances to his paint to alter the glossiness of the surface. The surface shows drying cracks that were most probably caused because earlier layers of paint had not sufficiently hardened before the final layer was applied.

In 1996, Joosten linked the composition to *Geinrust Farm* (1907), a watercoulour view of the Gein river in the Gemeentemuseum Den Haag collection (ill. 09). Just as the row of trees above the water descends into a bottle-neck shape towards the right, the thicker lines in *Composition No. II* also fit the same bottle-neck-like shape. In a personal interview with one of the authors in autumn 1996, Joosten also pointed out the fact that the arched fragments of line in the composition are almost all below the centre, and correspond exactly to water plants that break the reflection in the water in views of the Gein by Mondrian. The relatively denser positioning of the horizontal lines just above the halfway point might be related to the riverbank opposite, and the dividing line between water and land. However, this theory is not substantiated by the transmitted infrared photograph (ill. 08). Many more lines are visible, both horizontal and vertical, which were removed or shifted during the composition process but appear through the top layers of paint in the final result. There are also vertical bands and, at the top of the picture, lots of individual lines that run diagonally and crookedly through the field, but there are barely any lines that tie in with the view of the Gein that has been proposed as the basis for the composition. The arched line fragments may have originated in details in the work that served as a basis, but in *Composition No. II* they have become autonomous details in the composition, elements that attract and hold the viewer's attention.

Mondrian probably first laid out thin black lines over the entire plane. He then faded them out along the edges by painting them over with grey, though he did retain the division of the plane. The lines accentuated and traced later (in a more prominent black) lie within an oval extending across the entire painting. There is also a clear mix of colours, which might suggest a mirroring effect: light greenish-blue becomes pink when a lot of grey is added, light greenish-yellow becomes blue when white is added, and light purple becomes ochre when blue and sometimes white is added. Furthermore, passages with abundant creamy white have been applied locally over the whole painting. The bottom half is darker, where the colours are more mixed. Along the top edge the colours appear more separate.

At a certain point Mondrian applied extra paint along the edges of the painting to adapt the outer edge to the new frame (ill. 07.A). This adjustment was not made with a single colour, but in various shades of green, yellow and red, all mixed with grey in such a way that the colours are all very similar in terms of brightness and contrast, as on the rest of the painting's surface (ill. 07.B). This suggests that the adaptation to the frame was not a last-minute addition but that it should be seen more as the last phase of an ongoing process that eventually led to the final result.

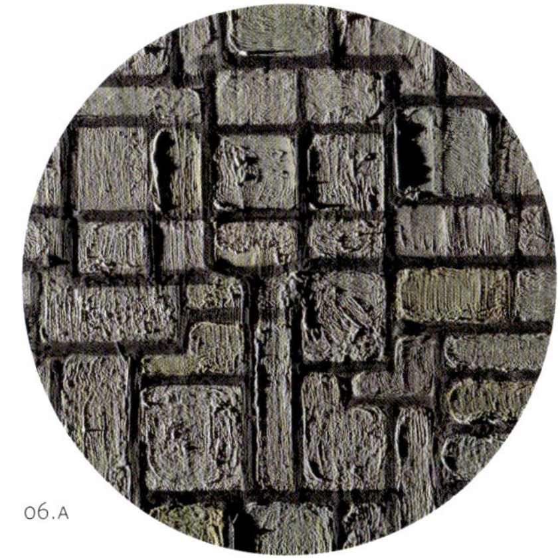
06.A

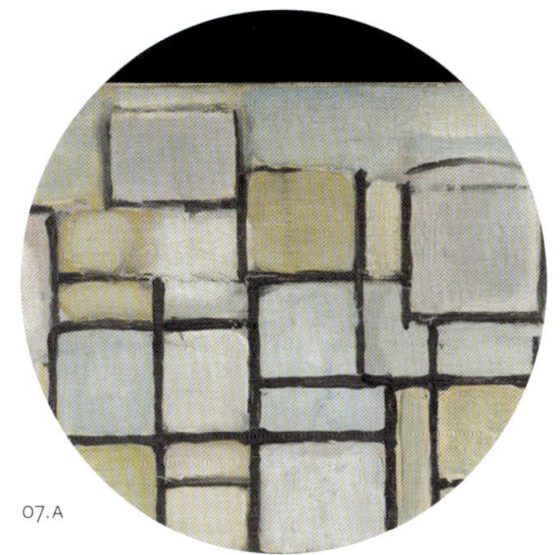
07.A

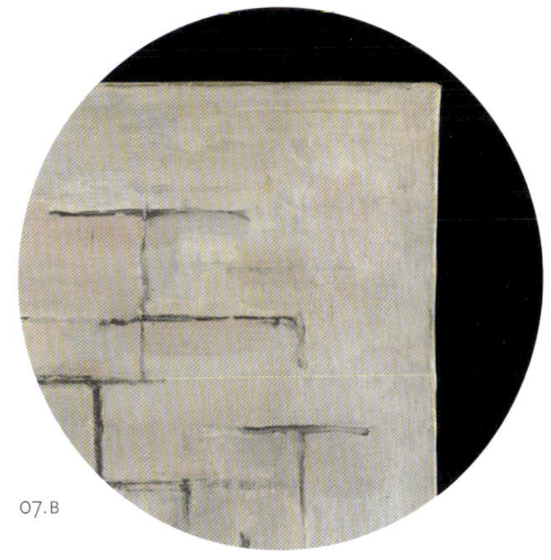
07.B

1914 Composition No. III

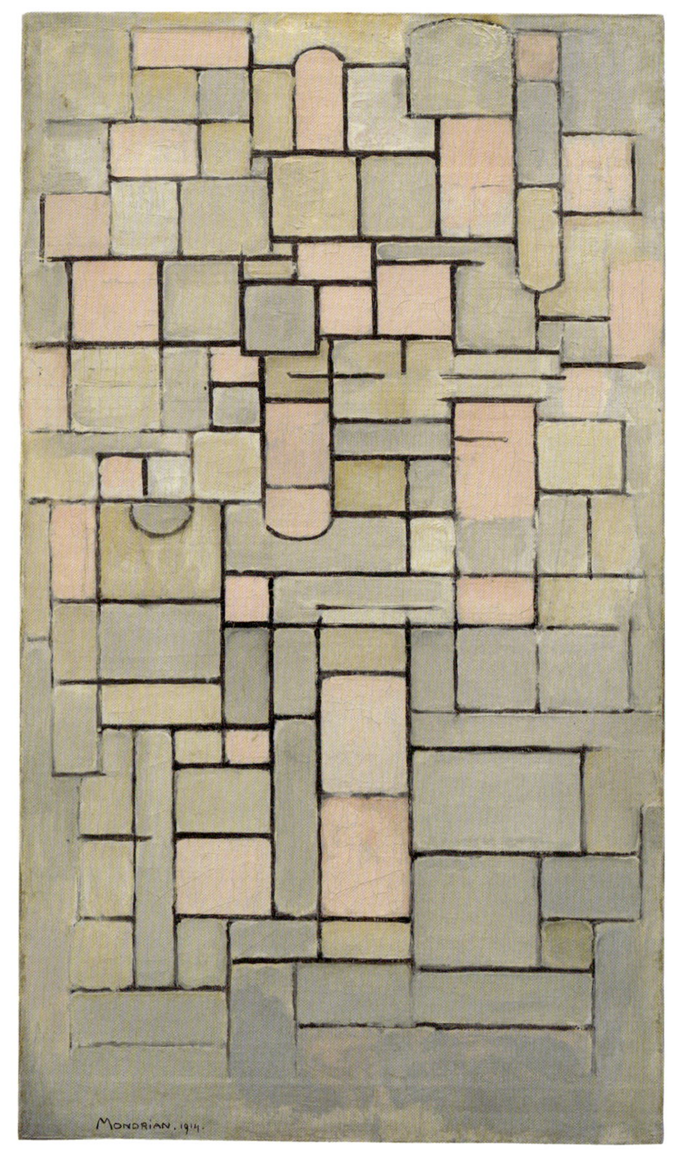

Composition No. III 1914
(B47 – Compositie No. III / Compositie 8)
Oil on canvas, 94.4 x 55.5 cm
Solomon R. Guggenheim Museum, New York

Inscriptions
Front: bottom left, in black paint: MONDRİAN. 1914.

Back: above the centre of the canvas a stamp of Blanchet, 38 rue Bonaparte, Paris; along the top in black paint with a narrow brush and thin paint: Compositie | 8 | P. Mondriaan [the surname flamboyantly underlined; this is a reference to the title Mondrian gave the painting at the exhibition with Schelfhout and others at the Stedelijk Museum, Amsterdam in 1915]. As the painting was given a new stretcher in 1953 no reference to the title *Composition No. III* is now present. It is possible that it was situated on the top stretcher bar, as was the case with most of the other paintings exhibited at Kunsthandel Walrecht.

Canvas
The canvas has an off-white ground of unknown composition. The entire surface of the canvas appears to have been reworked at an early stage with a layer of white paint, after which the surface was washed with solvent or scraped with a palette knife. Scraping marks can also be seen here and there. As a result, the texture of the canvas is barely visible on the surface and the weave no longer has any relief. The canvas has a plain weave, with threads of variable thickness. The canvas has a weave count of 18 threads vertically and 18 threads horizontally (c.14 cm from the left side, 9 cm from the top: 18h/19v; c.12 cm from the left side, 9 cm from the top: 18h/18v; c.14 cm from the right side, 9 cm from the top: 18h/18v and c.26 cm from the right side and 9 cm from the top: 19h/18v). There is no selvedge. The tacking edges were trimmed in line with the back of the stretcher at a later stage.

Framing
Along the turnover edge a strip of bronze paint can be seen, suggesting that the painting originally had a bronze-coloured strip frame running parallel to the paint surface (ill. 11.A). The frame was likely affixed to the painting using small nails.

Date
Mondrian began working on this canvas in March 1914. It must have been completed by mid-May 1914.

Provenance
The painting remained unsold at Kunsthandel Walrecht and was acquired by the artist Vilmos Huszár after an exhibition of work by Mondrian, Schelfhout and others in October 1915 at the Stedelijk Museum in Amsterdam. It appeared on the American market after 1947. The painting was purchased by the Solomon R. Guggenheim Museum, New York in 1949.

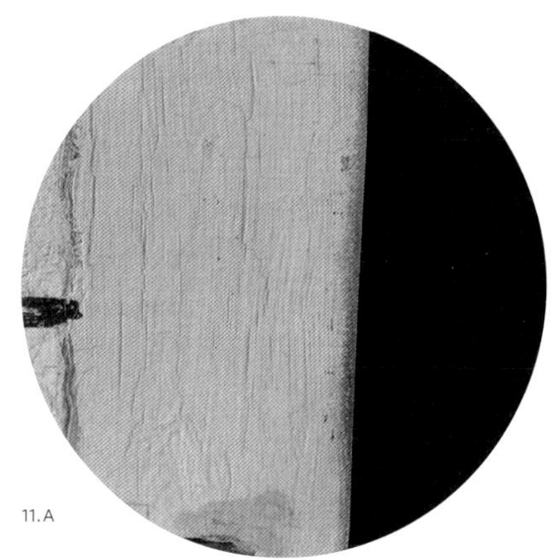
11.A

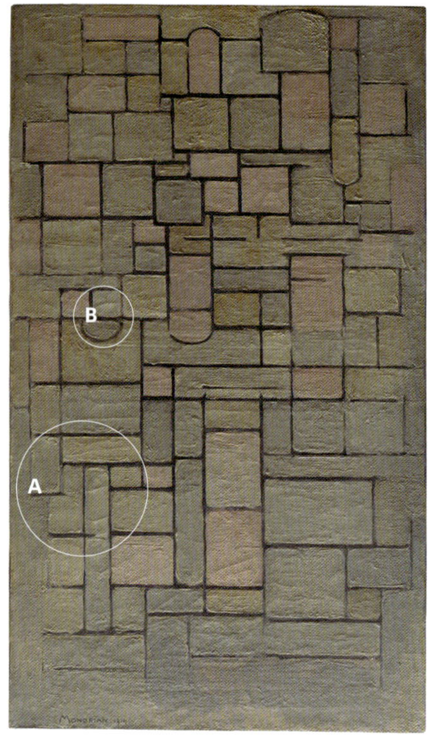

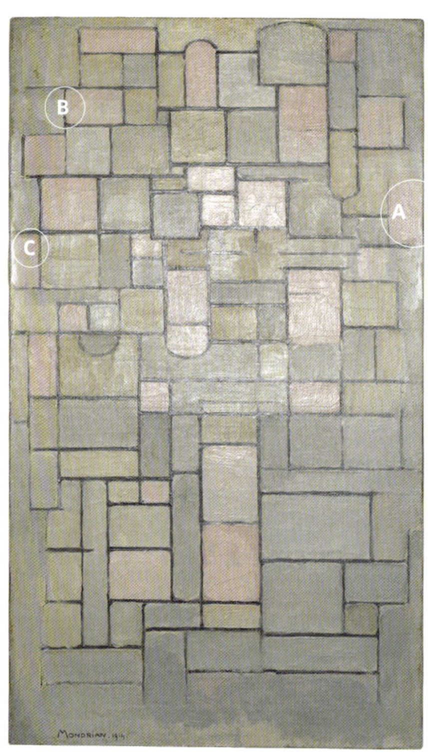

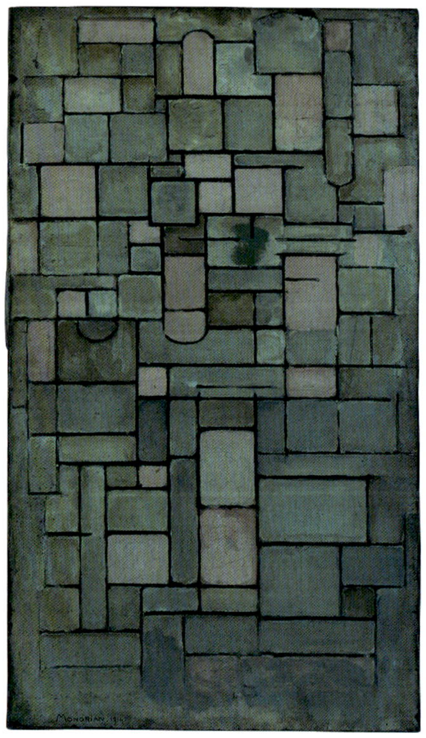

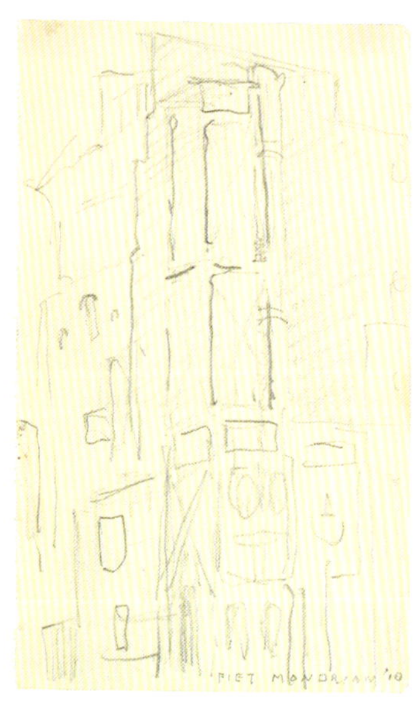

10 Raking light photograph with indications of details

11 Reflective light photograph with indications of details

12 Ultraviolet light photograph

13 *Scaffolding 1* (Sketchbook III, Folio 12), 1914
Pencil on paper, 17.2 x 10.5 cm
Gemeentemuseum Den Haag, The Hague

Painted surface

This painting gives the impression that Mondrian was very self-assured and certain of what he wanted to make when he embarked on this work. He appears to have worked on the basis of sketches like *Scaffolding 1* (1914) in the Gemeentemuseum Den Haag's collection (ill. 13). The raking light image does not reveal any changes under the paint surface (ill. 10). Generally speaking, the pink planes stand out, along with the darker grey-green planes. Along the top the picture is brighter and the juxtaposed planes contrast. Along the bottom of the composition there is less contrast between the planes and the colours are brighter and closer together. It appears very likely that the grey at the bottom was added at a much later stage, when the underlying paint layers had thoroughly dried; at any rate no drying cracks are visible in this area of the composition that might indicate insufficient hardening of underlying layers. This is confirmed by the condition report, written in September 1973 and published in the collection catalogue of the Guggenheim Museum by Angelica Rudenstine, which observes that the grey in the lower section of the composition was added just before the painting could be regarded as complete. The UV image of the painting also shows very little notable colour differences that might indicate use of paint with a substantially different composition (ill. 12).

Moving downwards, the paintwork billows with loose brushwork, as a result of which the sharp delineation of the black lines between the planes have suffered in places. Further upwards the brushstroke becomes firmer and more vertically arranged (ill. 10.A), a method abandoned again at the very top where there is relatively relaxed brushwork, and an application of thick, glossy areas of paint, as revealed in the reflective light photograph (ill. 11).

All planes are divided by prominent black lines between the adjacent colours except in one instance: two red-brown lines that break with the regimented pattern (arrows in ill. 10.B). These line fragments have been applied directly on the primed canvas, which might suggest a 'beginning' to the work or an initial version of the composition. All lines in *Composition No. III* are firmly positioned either horizontally or vertically. Along the left and right edges four diagonal lines can still be seen under the topmost layer of paint.

Nevertheless, we must assume – based on the black lines in which the white of the ground on the tips of the weave can be seen – that the painting was first laid out in thinly painted black lines, possibly partially scraped or rubbed off with a palette knife (ill. 11.B). Between the lines many planes were first filled in with a light blue-grey reminiscent of cool, no-nonsense industrial colours. Other planes were left white. Using this as a basis Mondrian then went through a process of weighing up and balancing colours. He applied, in three passages, grey on white on pink; ochre on greenish-white on white; grey on white on grey; ochre on white on grey; grey on greenish-white on grey; pink on greenish-white on grey; and grey on greenish-white on grey. Towards the bottom, the grey-green assumes a more prominent role in this reshuffling process. In a deeper shade, it starts to relate more clearly to the pink that is also applied more firmly here. Notably, pink played an increasingly prominent role as the painting neared completion. These later passages display a lot of drying cracks related to insufficient hardening of underlying paint layers: a sign that Mondrian executed the painting rather quickly. Along the left side and just below the centre there are planes that were first painted white and were finally treated with a thin 'wash' of highly diluted pink paint (ill. 11.C).

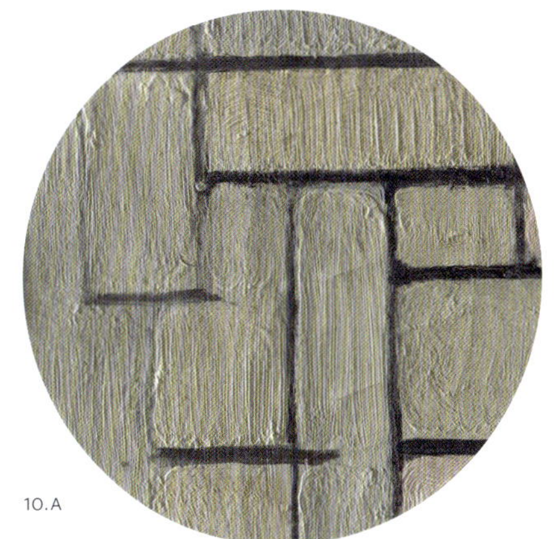
10.A

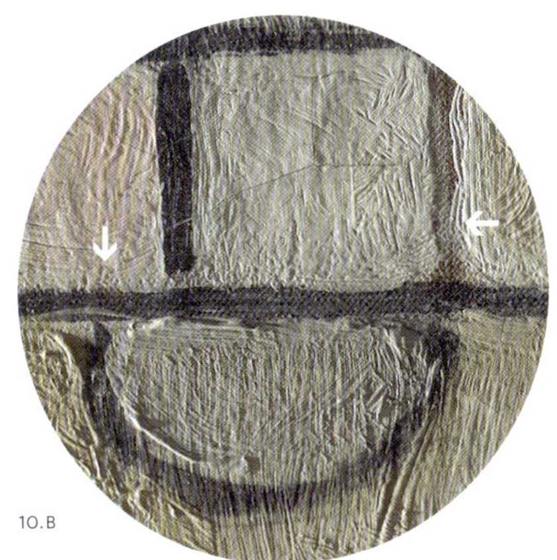
10.B

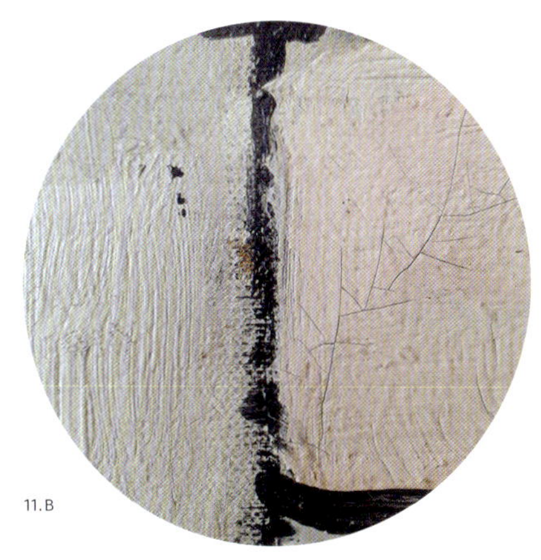
11.B

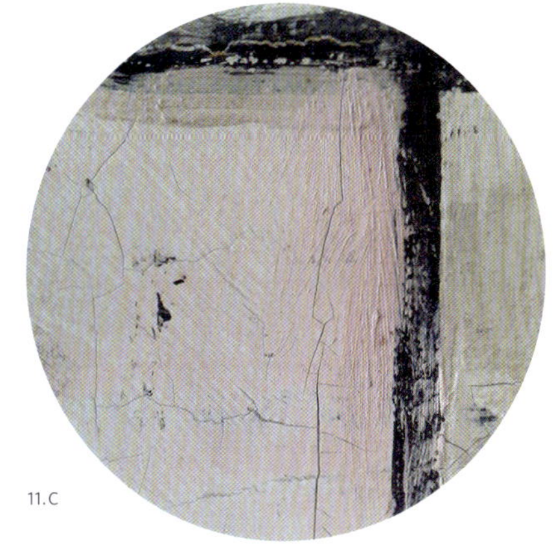
11.C

Composition NO. IV

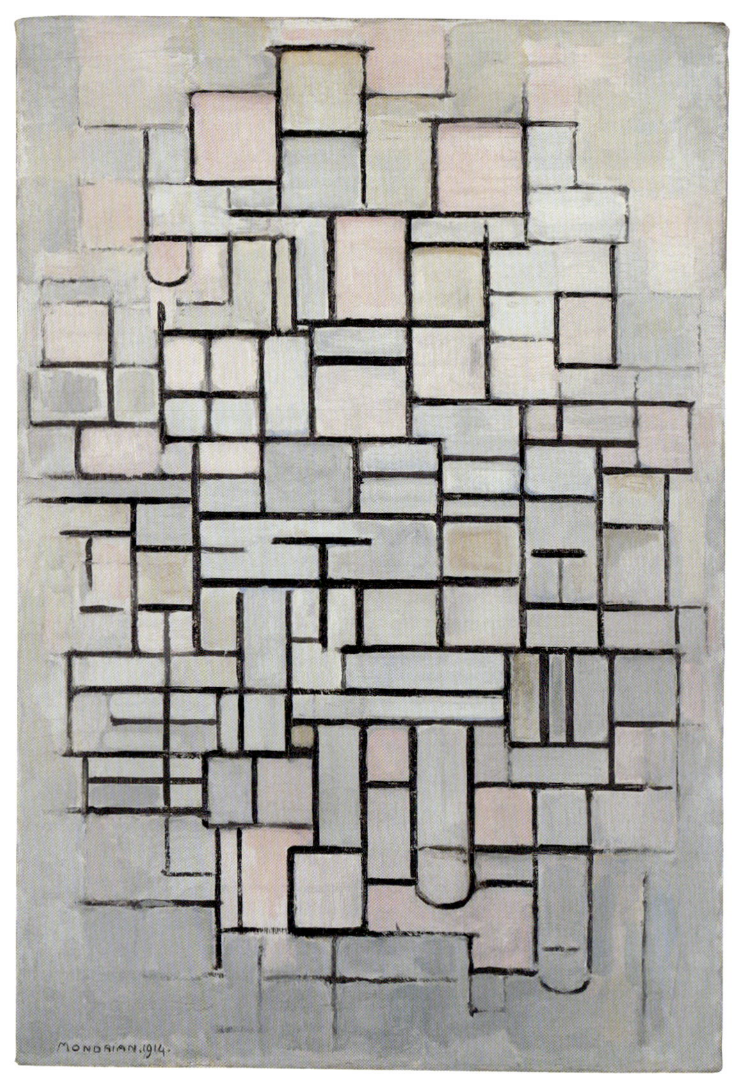

Composition NO. IV 1914
(B46 – Compositie NO. IV / Compositie 6)
Oil on canvas, 88 x 61 cm
Gemeentemuseum Den Haag, The Hague

Inscriptions
Front: signed and dated in bottom left in black paint: MONDRiAN. 1914. Signature and date have been applied over a grey paint layer, under which an identical signature is present. The probable reason for the double signature is that Mondrian wanted to change the original pink background to grey. It could also be that he was unhappy with the line he had drawn immediately below the first inscription.

Back: in the centre of the top half of the canvas, a stamp of Blanchet, 38 rue Bonaparte, Paris; in the top left, on the canvas, a customs stamp (illegible – in the centre probably: Paris); in the top half of the canvas in thinly painted black paint: Compositie 6 | P. Mondriaan [reference to the title at the exhibition at the Stedelijk Museum, Amsterdam in 1915]; on the top stretcher bar, almost entirely obscured by the remains of labels from the Gemeente-museum, in blue paint applied with a broad brush: COMPOSITION N:IV. (and slightly to the right) HAUT; this older title has been partly scored out with black paint because of the new title the work was given for the exhibition at the Stedelijk Museum in 1915; on the horizontal stretcher bar a blue-edged label with a handwritten inscription in black ink in Mondrian's hand, again rendered partly illegible with black paint and also damaged: 62. Compositie I | P. M [illegible] | terug [illegible] | Mevr. H [illegible; these are address details for the return shipment from the exhibition at the Rotterdamsche Kunstkring in 1915]; on the crossbar of the stretcher an inscription in pencil rendered illegible with blue paint applied with a broad brush; next to this, in blue paint with a broad brush and thus associated with the inscription on the top bar: MONDRiAN.

Stretcher
The pine stretcher is original. The bars are 4.8–5 cm wide and 1.5 cm thick. The stretcher has no bead on the canvas side, but does have a bevelled edge sloping towards the centre of the picture. The corners of the stretcher have been butt joined. In each corner two keys are present, plus one in each corner of the horizontal crossbar. The canvas has been firmly keyed out, as a result of which the top corners no longer meet properly. This must have been done after the inscription 'HAUT' was applied to the back, given that the 'T' is now split in two (ill. 14.A).

The canvas has a white ground of unknown composition, and was probably commercially primed. The ground is fairly regular and thin and does not entirely fill the structure of the canvas. The canvas has a plain weave, with threads of varying thickness. The vertical threads protrude slightly; the horizontal threads lie deeper in the weave. The thread density is c.20 horizontally and 17 vertically (14.5 cm from the right and 6 cm from the top: 20h/17v; 17.5 cm from the left and 15 cm from the top: 20h/17v; 17 cm from the right and 40 cm from the bottom: 21h/17v; 30 cm from the left and 37 cm from the bottom: 20h/17v; 8 cm from the left and 25 cm from the bottom: 20h/18v. This makes the average number of vertical threads per cm 17.2 with a min/max range of 17 to 18 threads/cm and the average number of horizontal threads per cm 20.2 with a min/max range of 20 to 21 threads/cm). There is no selvedge. The canvas has a narrow, roughly cut tacking edge on all sides. Mondrian probably trimmed the edge himself, given the proximity of the inscriptions on the stretcher applied by Mondrian. On the top edge a pencil line was drawn before the tacking edge was trimmed. The ground extends to the edge of the canvas on all sides. Along the left and right edges of the canvas heavy cusping is visible, apparently caused by the current stretching. The stretching is original as there is no row of extra tack holes in the tacking edge and some tacks are covered with the original bronze paint. Several tacks have rusted slightly.

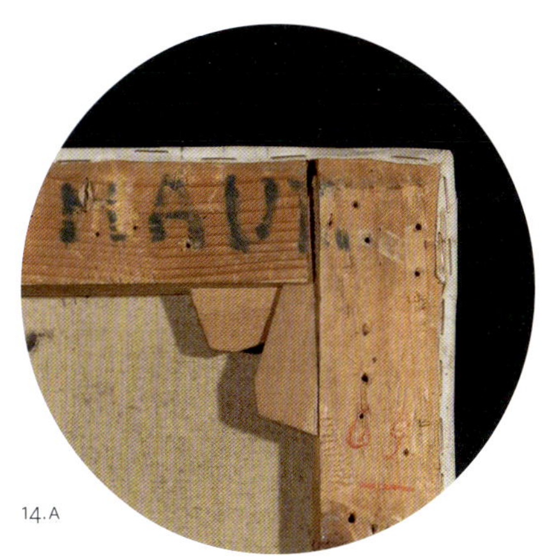

14.A

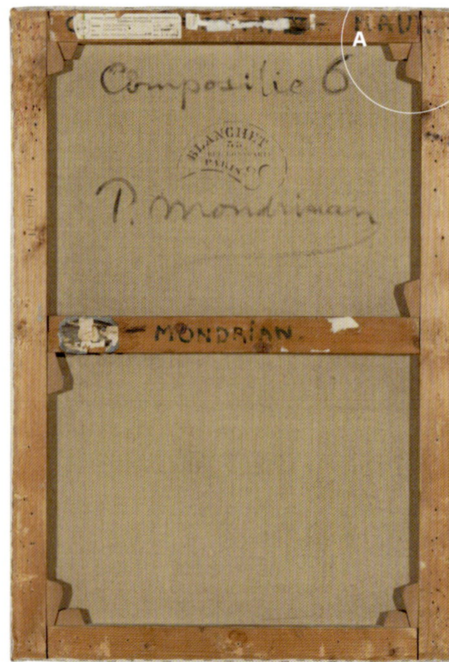

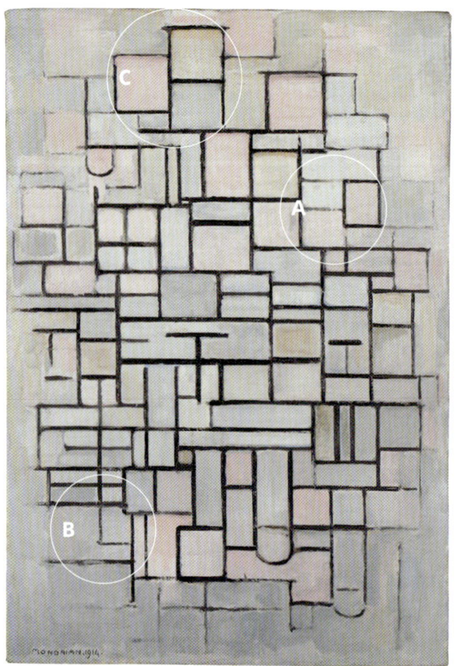

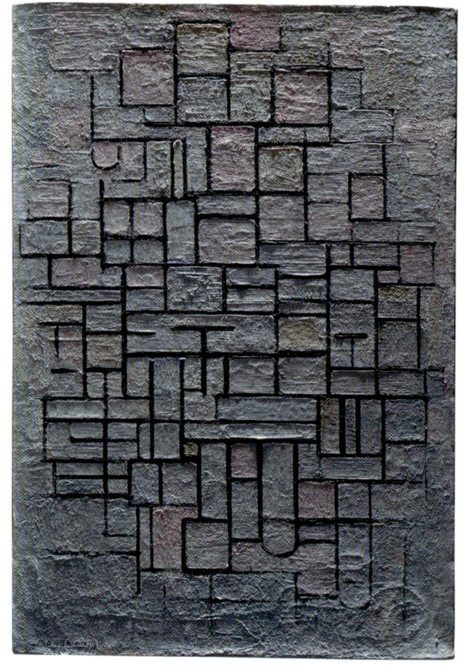

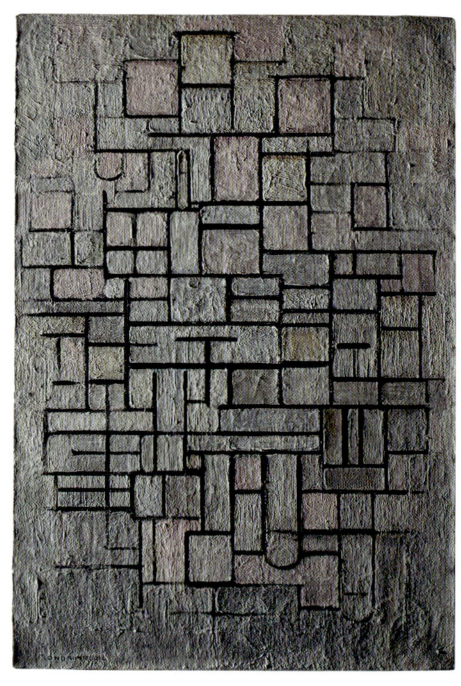

14 Back of the painting with indication of a detail

15 Normal light photograph with indications of details

16 Raking light photograph from above

17 Raking light photograph from the left side

Framing
On the tacking edges of the canvas a line of bronze paint can be seen close to the painted side (ill. 18). This suggests that the painting originally had a recessed strip frame that was affixed to the painting using thin tacks. Mondrian deliberately applied the bronze paint to the edges as a continuation of the frame. The present frame is a 1976 reconstruction with strips measuring c.7 x 7 mm.

Date
The historical reconstruction shows that Mondrian worked on the painting in the early spring of 1914, and that he probably thoroughly reworked it in early May. The painting is dated 1914 on the front and is one of the works, along with *Composition Nos. I* (1913), *II* (1913), *III* (1914) and *V* (1914), at the Kunsthandel Walrecht exhibition to have been dated.

Provenance
When the painting was exhibited in Rotterdam in January 1915 it still belonged to Mondrian, as suggested by a letter he sent to Albert Reballio, secretary of the Rotterdamsche Kunstkring, on 16 February 1915, in which he indicates which addresses the various works should be returned to. A label on the back of the stretcher that was affixed during this exhibition states that the work should be returned to a Mrs H [the rest is illegible], which probably refers to Katinka Hannaert. At that time, Mondrian was staying at her boarding house 'De Linden' in Laren. The catalogue of the Stedelijk Museum exhibition states that the painting is in private ownership; by then it was owned by Hannaert. Had Mondrian perhaps used it to pay for his board and lodging? Salomon Slijper purchased the painting for his collection in 1922, and in 1971 the painting was acquired by the Gemeentemuseum Den Haag as part of the Slijper bequest.

Painted surface
The painting is built up of shades of grey and pink. The lines are sharpest in the centre and diffuse towards the edges. The contrast in colour also decreases towards the edges, the outer edge being mainly grey, which gives the illusion that the form floats in the picture plane. In 1952 Harry Verburg, education officer at the Gemeentemuseum, was the first to conclude that Mondrian used this approach to realise a spatial effect that he would not realise in full until later compositions. The sharp black lines in the centre, along with the colours, draw the eye to the middle of the picture. The slightly more open colour planes in the centre of the composition make this area come forward optically, giving the impression of a slightly convex plane.[2] Most of the lines are short and irregularly positioned, focusing the attention more on the angular forms they delineate than on the lines themselves. Mondrian was aware of this. In a letter to Theo van Doesburg of November or December 1915 he characterised his own work as a 'construction of squares (previous period)'.

Mondrian used an opaque paint that almost entirely covers the ground, which is therefore only visible along the edges of the planes and of the painting. In other places paint from earlier stages is visible. This is due to the fact that the work is not painted very precisely; few of the lines and planes meet exactly and the lines were painted freehand and are very irregular (ills 16, 17). Given the fact that the fields of colour do not extend all the way to the black lines, it is easy to fathom the process by which the painting was created. The final painting appears to be the result of a quest with several phases, which are all still traceable beneath the current paint surface.

Mondrian appears to have made many changes to the colours of the planes and positions of the lines, giving the paint the chance to dry in the meantime. In the deeper layers the colours are brighter than in the final painting, and besides grey and pink, he also used light blue. Here and there the colour build-up of a plane is easy to trace (ill. 15.A): in the single field, shown in this illustration, whitish-pink has been applied over grey, under which both bright light-blue and pale pink can be seen. Some black lines were dispensed with and covered by a colour plane.

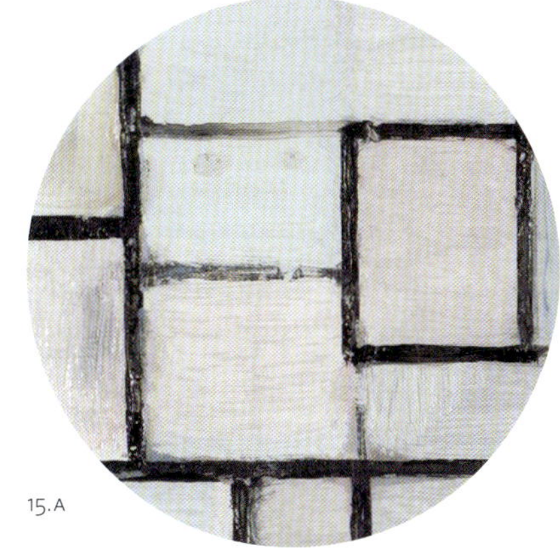
15.A

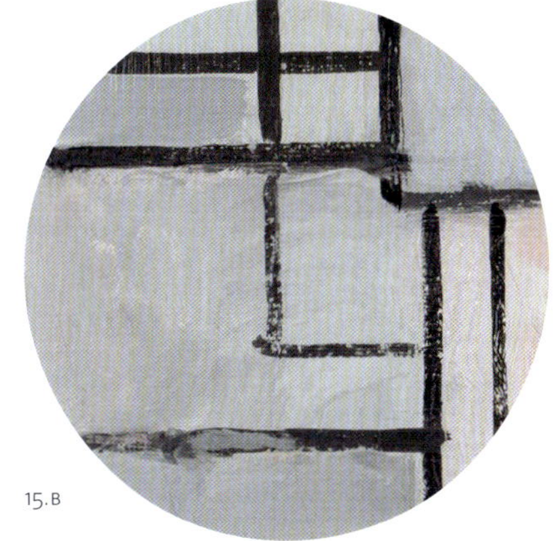
15.B

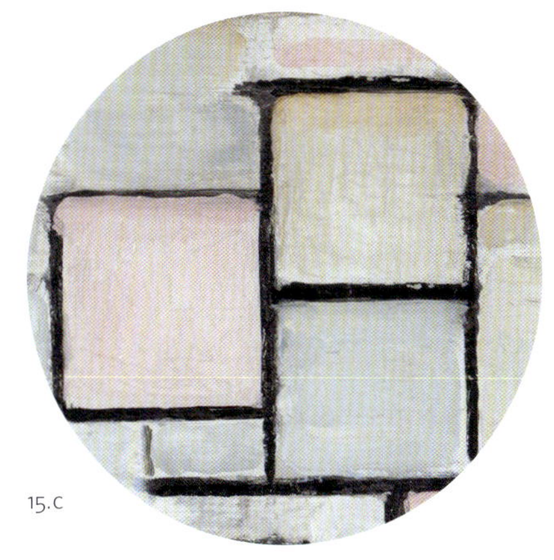
15.C

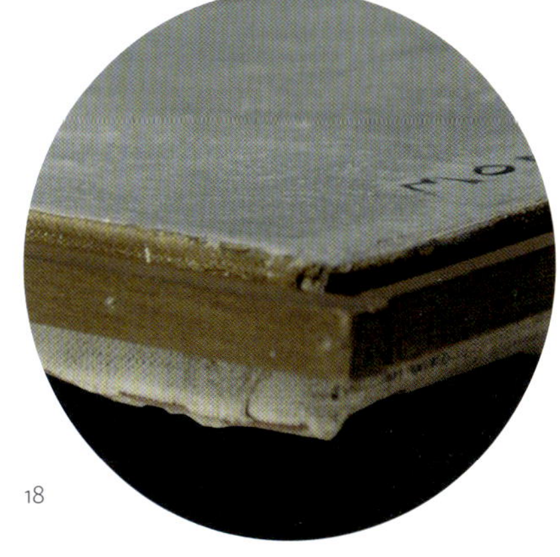
18

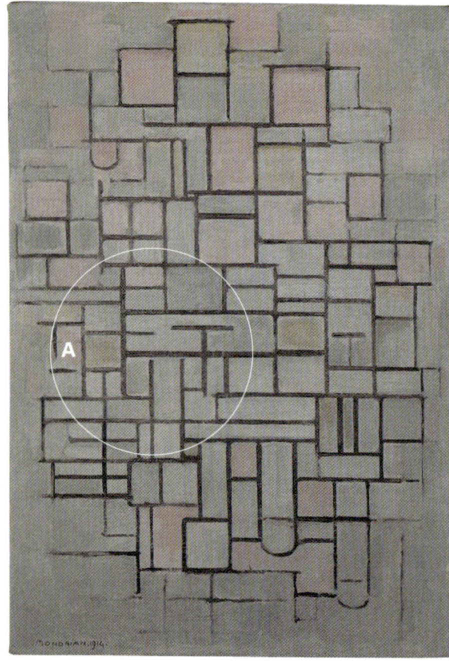

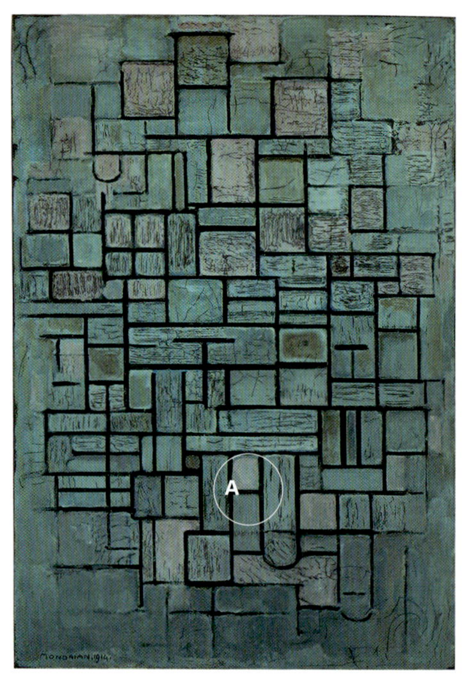

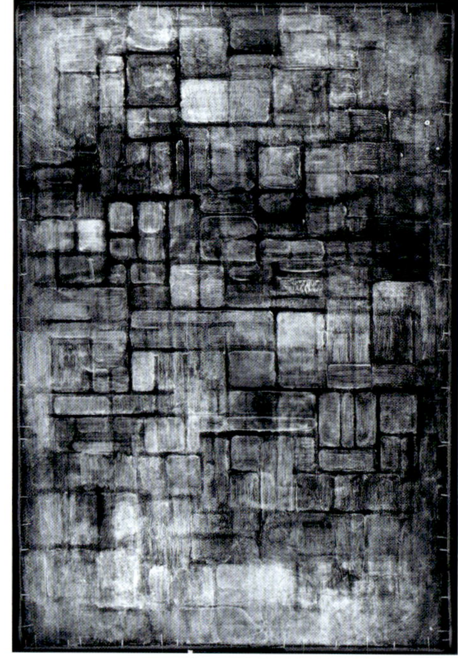

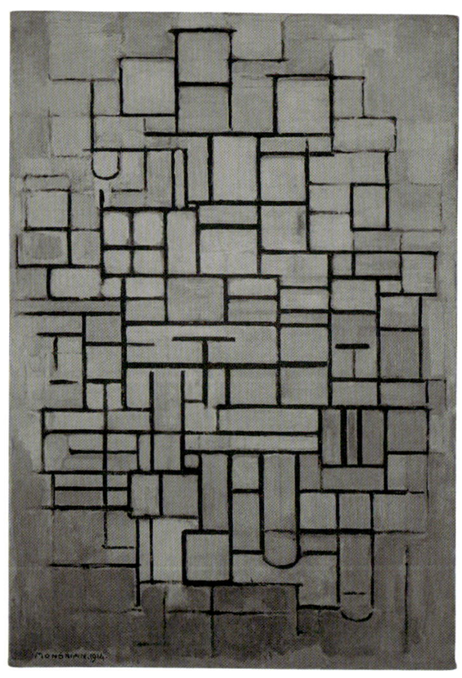

19 Reflective light photograph

20 x-ray photograph

21 Ultraviolet light photograph with indication of a detail

22 Reflective infrared photograph

At a late stage, conversely, new lines were added over colour planes. The shift from blue-grey to pink-grey made the work decidedly less cool in appearance, and the addition of ochre also made it warmer. The subduing of the colours also softened the contrasts in the picture.

Thus the painting was created in several phases and it appears that some time may have elapsed between the final two stages. The interval cannot have lasted too long though, because in UV light it is clearly visible that tiny drying cracks are present over the entire surface, particularly in the top half, which have now been retouched (ills 20, 20.A). Such cracks in the paint surface occur when paint layers have not hardened properly before being painted over.

The lines are not always black – many of them are in fact grey. Since these grey lines are partially covered by black lines, they appear to be from an earlier stage. The greyish lines are now found mainly at the edges of the composition. Hence, it would seem that late in the process the lines in the centre were accentuated with glossy black paint to enhance the contrast with the fields of colour. Some black lines graze over the texture of underlying layers and in many places they have beaded, which means that the paint has gathered into drops as it had little grip on the smooth (already dry) surface beneath (ill. 15.B; p.91). In an even later stage, some of the beaded lines have been painted again with a more liquid black paint. The surface was not varnished. However, under UV light a green fluorescence can be seen along a few edges of the black lines, or at the end of a stroke, with a gradual tapering. This suggests that a binder-rich skin has formed locally on the paint. Whether this binder contained varnish (or a siccative) as well as oil is not known (ills 19, 19.A, 20.A).

At a very late stage (probably after the signature was added for the second time because this area was left in reserve) Mondrian used dark grey, mainly to apply the curved end at the bottom of the composition. At the same time he applied the ochre, as both colours were mixed wet-on-wet here and there. The darker paint was used to cover colours along the edges, thereby shifting the focus towards the centre, enhancing the contrasts and creating the illusion of a floating image. Mondrian used a buttery paint, not exactly thin or smooth, nor really pastose. The shine is not even: here and there the paint is very matt, while elsewhere the finish is mainly silky, producing a subtle surface. In particular the pink and ochre fields of colour in the centre of the image, which had been applied last, have a matt appearance (ill. 19.A). These colours are all mixed with grey but not thoroughly. They were applied quickly and in haste, though not in a wild manner. This gives these fields a certain sense of movement that is apparent to the attentive viewer. The ochre, in particular, was applied very locally and with it Mondrian appears to have wanted to create the illusion of depth in the colour planes. The colours are so whitish and irregular that they suggest the paint has chemically degraded and discoloured (ill. 15.C; p.91). This can be seen in particular when this painting is compared with *Composition No. V* at the Museum of Modern Art (MOMA), New York, for example (p.94). However, during research and conservation treatment in 2010 no need was found to investigate this any further.

The movement in the painting was first noted by Aleid Loosjes-Terpstra who, in 1958, observed that this painting (and its counterparts *Composition Nos. I, II* and *III*) showed Mondrian's renewed interest in Impressionism. Later authors, such as EH Carmean, also noted this. Carmean contradicts Robert Welsh – who defines Mondrian's attitude in these paintings as a methodical notation of facades – and William Rubin, who reduces his perception of the painting to dematerialisation and constricted fragmentation, entirely in line with Clement Greenberg's Modernist views. In 1994 Carel Blotkamp also ignored any atmospheric effect of colour and line.

Investigation using infrared and X-ray has confirmed the many changes in the lines and planes, revealing a multitude of mainly horizontal, hastily obscured lines that are no longer visible to the naked eye (ills 21, 22). Two curved lines to the left of the centre above the two 'T's and slightly higher to the right, which meet at a point resembling a roof, are particularly interesting. It is known that Mondrian drew inspiration for this work from gable ends (ill. 64; p.126). In a letter to Augusta de Meester-Obreen of August 1915 he says, 'The one with squares is inspired by buildings'.[3] Comparison with his sketchbook shows that Mondrian did not choose a specific gable end or roofscape as the basis for the composition. *Composition IV* is a good example of a working method whereby any reference to reality was abandoned at a very early stage, to focus on what could be done using only lines and coloured planes. Mondrian described this in a letter to Theo van Doesburg in November 1915 as a 'construction of four squares'.[4]

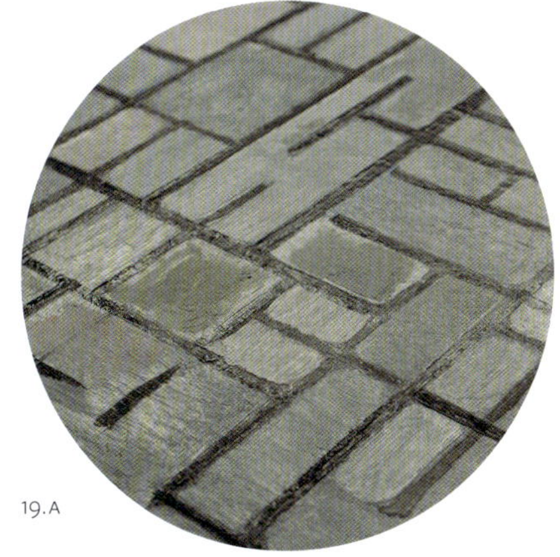
19.A

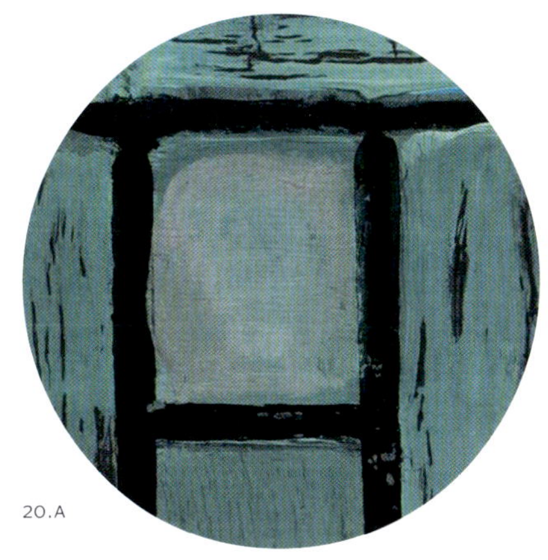
20.A

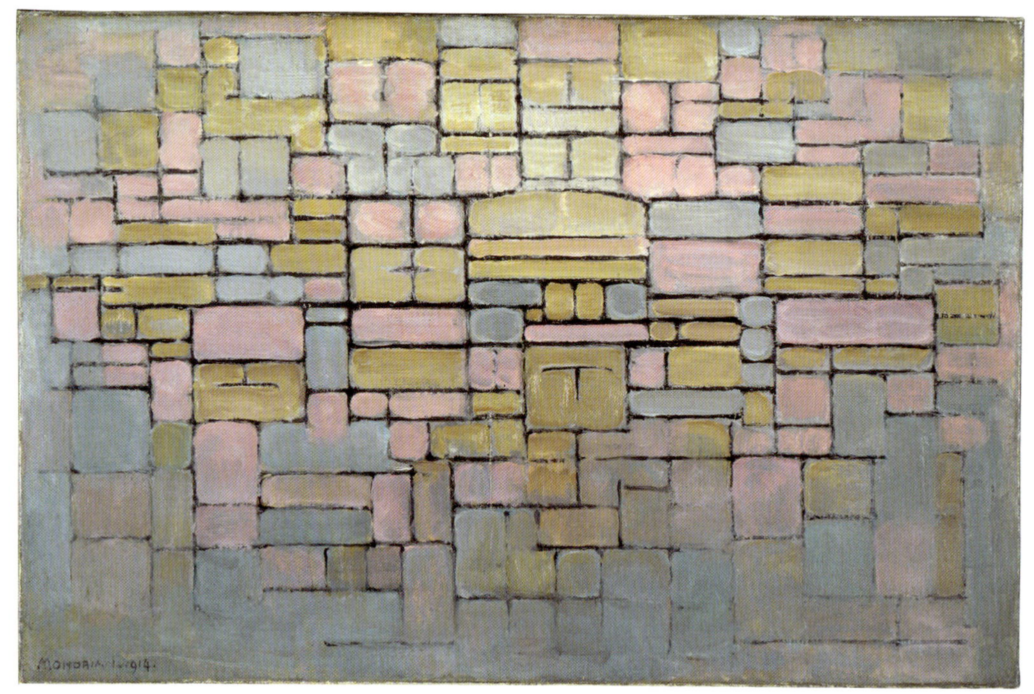

Composition no. v 1914
(B45 – Tableau no. 2 / Compositie no. v)
Oil on canvas, 54.8 x 85.3 cm
Museum of Modern Art, New York

Inscriptions

Front: signed in lower left corner in black: MONDRİAN. 1914.

Back: in the upper left quadrant, diagonally from bottom to top, in thin black paint with a medium flat brush: P. MONDRİAN., underlined with a black line; just beneath that and to the left centre is a canvas stamp of Blanchet, 38 rue Bonaparte, Paris, oriented vertically. To the upper right there may have been something that is now illegible, surrounded by moisture stains. The area has been struck through with a fine flat brush with horizontal strokes in blue paint that has become greenish due to the wax treatment (rubbed or wiped away); on the right side through the centre, diagonally in black paint with a medium flat brush: titre, [crossed out with a blue-green coloured line]; beneath that in black paint, again with a medium flat brush: TABLEAU N:2, [crossed out with a blue-green coloured line]; on the upper bar of the original stretcher [now lost, but indicated in MOMA archival records] in blue oil: COMPOSITION – N. V, and: HAUT; written in pencil on the original stretcher: Monsier [sic] Mondrian.

Stretcher

The original stretcher was removed during conservation treatment in 1968. The primary canvas was wax-resin lined to a thick linen canvas and then re-stretched on a Lebron-style stretcher. During scientific investigation and cleaning treatment in 2010 the full lining was determined to be unnecessary. The lining canvas was gently rolled away mechanically, revealing the rest of the inscriptions (ill. 23; p.96). The canvas support was strip lined and then re-stretched over a new thinner stretcher. Mondrian's *Composition No. IV* (1914), at the Gemeentemuseum and on its original stretcher, was used for reference during this treatment. The re-stretching brought the earlier bronze frame paint on the face of the picture just slightly closer (c.1.6 mm) to the turnover edge on all four sides (ill. 27; p.97).

The original canvas support has an average of 20 threads horizontally for the warp and 18 threads vertically for the weft. The canvas has split along the tacking margins in several areas. Aside from the splits, the tacking margins are intact save for some metal corrosion products surrounding tack holes or sites of earlier tacks. There are at least two sets of older tack holes. The original tack holes could be seen and are closer to the edge of the picture plane than the 1968 tacks were, as the original stretcher was much thinner. During the 2010 treatment the original tack holes were reused during stretching.

The off-white ground is moderately thick and evenly painted. It is visible along all of the tacking margins and in some instances along more thinly or openly painted passages on the face of the painting, such as in the upper right corner where some of the tops of the canvas weave peek out. Dr Ana Martins, conservation scientist at MOMA, performed x-ray fluorescence analysis (XRF) that confirmed the presence of lead white along the tacking edges and within the picture plane. Barium was also present, indicating that it may be a filler within the ground and/or an extender present in the paint layer. The canvas is pre-primed with the ground extending all the way to the cut tacking edges. Two-thirds of the way down on all of the tacking edges, or 0.5 cm from the surface edge, there appears to be a second layer of grey-white paint with the canvas weave more filled in in these areas. These reinforced areas may be residual frame paint from an earlier framing iteration. On the proper right tacking margin there is a build-up of grey paint mimicking wood grain that may have been from a wet strip frame or a frame applied and then painted in place.

Framing

When the painting entered MOMA's collection, photographs show that it was framed with a thin strip frame with mitred corners that appears slightly set back from the edge of the picture plane, attached to the picture with a layer of tape in between. This frame was not original. In 2010, research showed a greenish-brown material on the face of the painting, about 0.3 cm from the four turnover edges. This material was thought to be bronze paint. Under low magnification it appeared as though a dark green imprimatura was peeking out from under the edge of the paint or ground along all the edges, as well as a dilute pink (ill. 28; p.97). It looked as though at one time a frame was attached to – or very near to flush with – the face of the picture plane and was then painted or touched up in place with bronze paint. Under high magnification these areas exhibited a green waxy material that appeared to be reacting differently with the paint from one area to the next (ill. 29; p.97). In different areas it appeared to be on top of the paint, within the paint, and under paint layers and ground, and was very easily mechanically disturbed when probed. It is unclear whether this is corrosion product or green paint such as verdigris (copper acetate) in a lower layer of the painting. The author, along with conservation scientist Chris McGlinchey, took a few minuscule samples and performed technical analysis, including Fourier transform infrared spectroscopy (FTIR) and ultimately scanning electron microscopy (SEM-EDX), eventually identifying copper palmitate and copper stearate, indicating that the material is likely the result of organometallic corrosion. This may be an interaction from the bronze paint (from framing) along the tacking edges at the picture plane. It is possible that the oleates and stearates in concert with lining heat and pressure may have softened the linseed oil in the paint layer, thus contributing to its breakdown at the tacking edges. Preliminary testing of corrosion removal showed that the material has degraded the paint to the ground in some areas and actually appears to be creeping beneath the surface of surrounding paint. While the corrosion products are visually distracting they are well integrated within the paint layer and are indeed inherent to Mondrian's framing technique and material choices. Reducing the material might leave slight gaps along portions of turnover edges and possibly impact or remove surrounding paint and ground. It was decided to isolate this material and to monitor it over time.

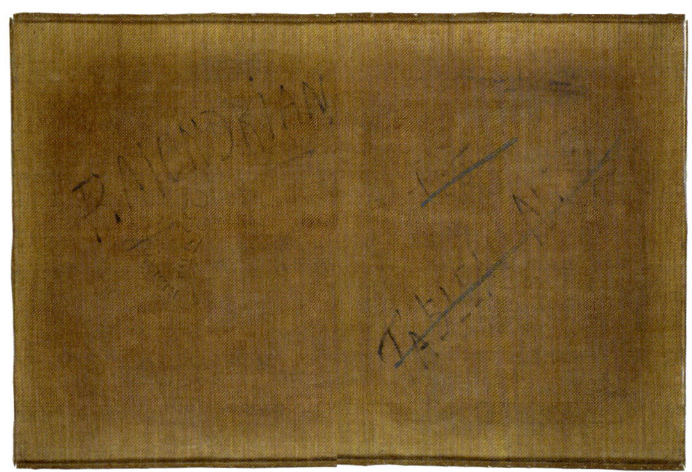

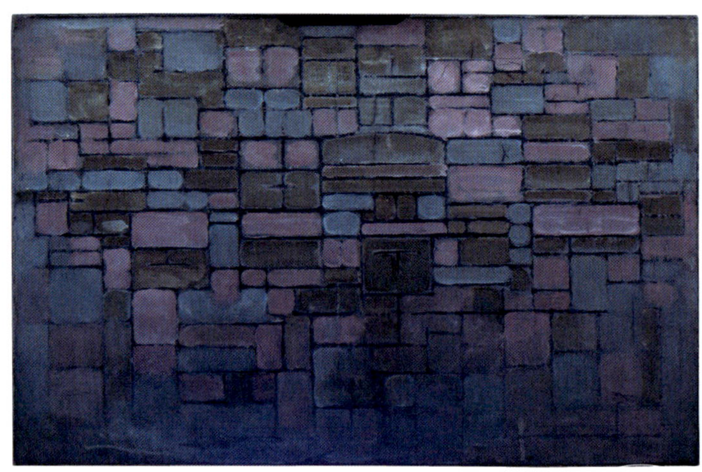

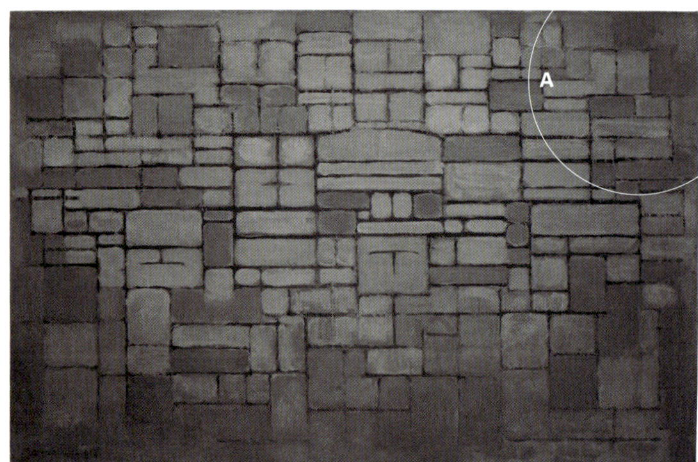

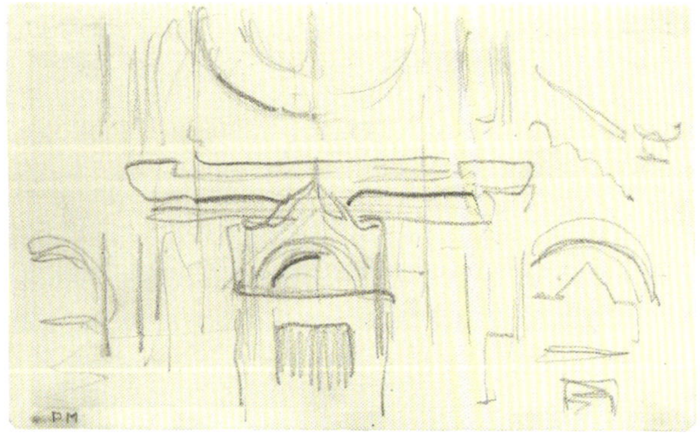

23 Back of the painting with visible inscriptions

24 Ultraviolet light photograph

25 Transmitted infrared photograph with indication of a detail

26 *Paris Church Facade* (Sketchbook III, Folio 9), 1914
Pencil on paper, 10.5 x 17.2 cm
Gemeentemuseum Den Haag, The Hague

Date
Mondrian regarded the painting as first completed in January or February of 1914, when he entered it for the Salon des Indépendants. In a review of the exhibition, Leo Faust discusses Mondrian's works as follows: 'On a grey ground, in dark green paint, the painter drew lots of horizontal and vertical lines along a ruler'.[5] *Composition V* could not currently be described as having 'dark green' paint. After the painting returned at the beginning of May, Mondrian might have taken it up again, partly under the influence of Fernand Léger's ideas about the use of pink in modern painting as expressed in his lecture given at the Académie Vassiliev. In a letter of 5 May 1914 to Bremmer, Mondrian asks to have until the end of the month of May to rework the pictures from the Salon.[6] In a letter to Schelfhout on 7 June Mondrian states that he was not happy with the Salon, but that he 'suddenly scored a good shot again'.[7] Mondrian may have revisited this picture between April and June of 1914, utilising a palette of pinks with white highlights to pull forms forward, and a pink, blue and grey mixture to push others backwards, visible under UV (ill. 24).

Provenance
The painting was acquired from the artist after the Walrecht Gallery exhibition by Gouda resident Reverend Hendrick van Assendelft. His heirs sold the painting, and in 1951 it appeared on the American market. In 1967 it was acquired by MOMA as part of the Sidney and Harriet Janis Collection.

Painted surface
Inspired by the urban landscape surrounding him, Mondrian's Parisian church facade drawings and roofscapes of 1913 and 1914 seem to have presented groundwork for the imagery in the painting. In January of 1914 he wrote to Bremmer explaining that 'the architecture of the ancients seems to me the greatest art ... brought to harmony and rhythm ... with the use of horizontal and vertical lines ... supplemented where necessary by lines in other directions or by curved lines'. He looked to the church of Notre-Dame-des-Champs on the boulevard du Montparnasse for cruciform shapes, ellipses, verticals and strong reinforced horizontal lines (ill. 26). (Mondrian considered the horizontal line to be a feminine characteristic.) In *Composition V* he ultimately maintains three cruciform shapes, curved downward, a single large ellipse to the right of the centre, and strong reinforced horizontal lines.

The painted surface is heavy-bodied oil with a high pigment concentration. Under magnification, for example, the blues appear to be mostly white paint bulked with blue pigments. During FTIR analysis of the aforementioned green material near the turnover edges, spectra presented linseed oil and/or cotton seed oil as possible binders. Using XRF, the pigments were identified on the basis of the distribution of the elements aluminium (Al), silicon (Si), sulphur (S), phosphorus (P), potassium (K), calcium (Ca), iron (Fe), chromium (Cr), cobalt (Co), zinc (Zn), strontium (Sr), cadmium (Cd), barium (Ba) and lead (Pb). Based on the location of detection coupled with visual analysis, Mondrian's palette consisted of pure paints or mixtures of white (zinc white, lead white), black (bone black), yellow (yellow ochre, cadmium yellow, chrome yellow), orange (earth pigments, orange earth), blues (small amount of cobalt in lower layer), pinks and blues comprising organic pigments and barium sulphate. Ba, Sr, S and Zn suggest lithopone as a filler.

While there is no pencil drawing visible on the face of the painting, throughout Mondrian's working and reworking process he lays very thin to medium lines, no wider than 0.5 cm, nearest to the ground using a fine brush. Here he draws a somewhat regular grid or scaffold of horizontal and vertical lines in black that goes on to reinforce and bring to the forefront in some areas or push completely to the background in others. XRF detected calcium and phosphorus in many tested areas of the black paint, indicating bone black paint. With reflected infrared light, one can see many more black grid lines from an earlier state, near the corners that he painted out, particularly in the top and bottom right corners (ills 25, 25.A). They can just be seen in normal light, but they are more clearly defined in the infrared. There is a dark black band throughout the bottom that is part of the underpainting, clearly seen in the infrared and x-ray, which seems to mimic the bottom stretcher (ill. 30; p.98).

Mondrian then paints a second layer of a slightly yellow blue-grey paint over nearly the entire surface. He reinforces the lines in some areas by filling in the negative space around them. He begins to fill in rectangles, enlarging them by painting through the dark verticals and horizontals with this yellow blue-grey in this first state. In some areas there are instances of a second pass of bone black on top of this grey, where he breaks the shapes back down again into smaller rectangles and squares, with slightly curved tops and ends.

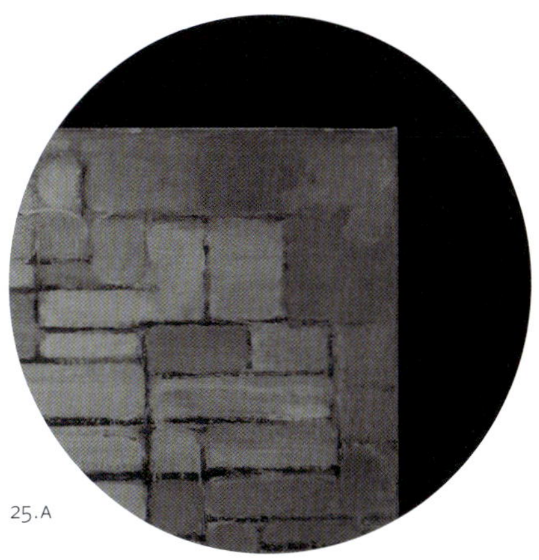
25.A

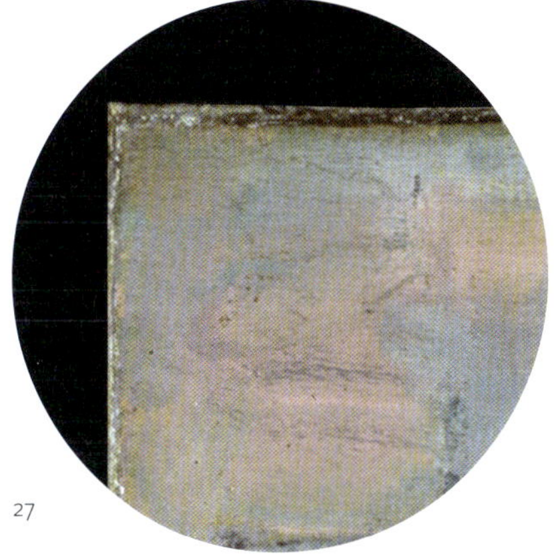
27

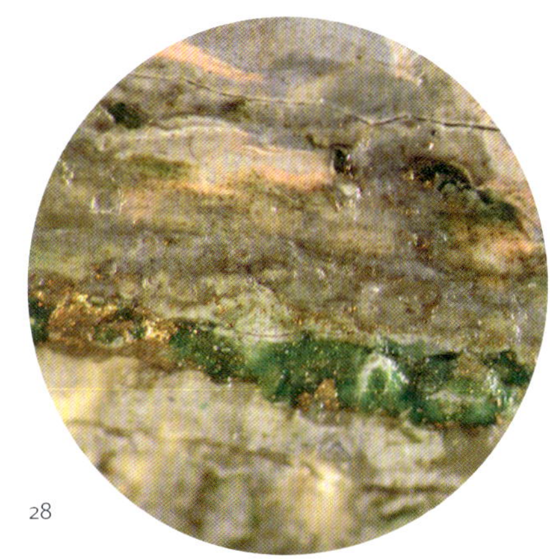
28

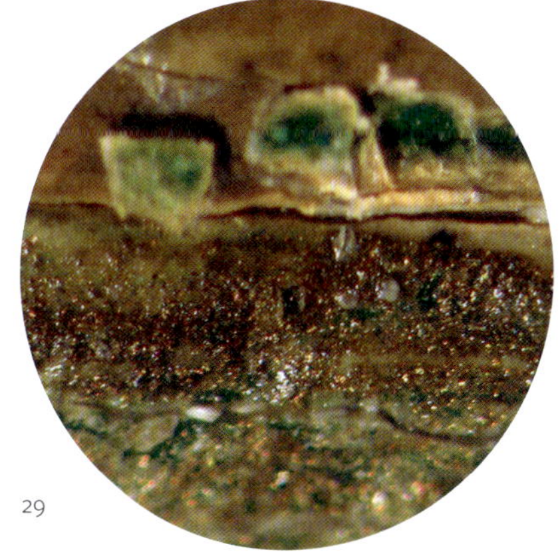
29

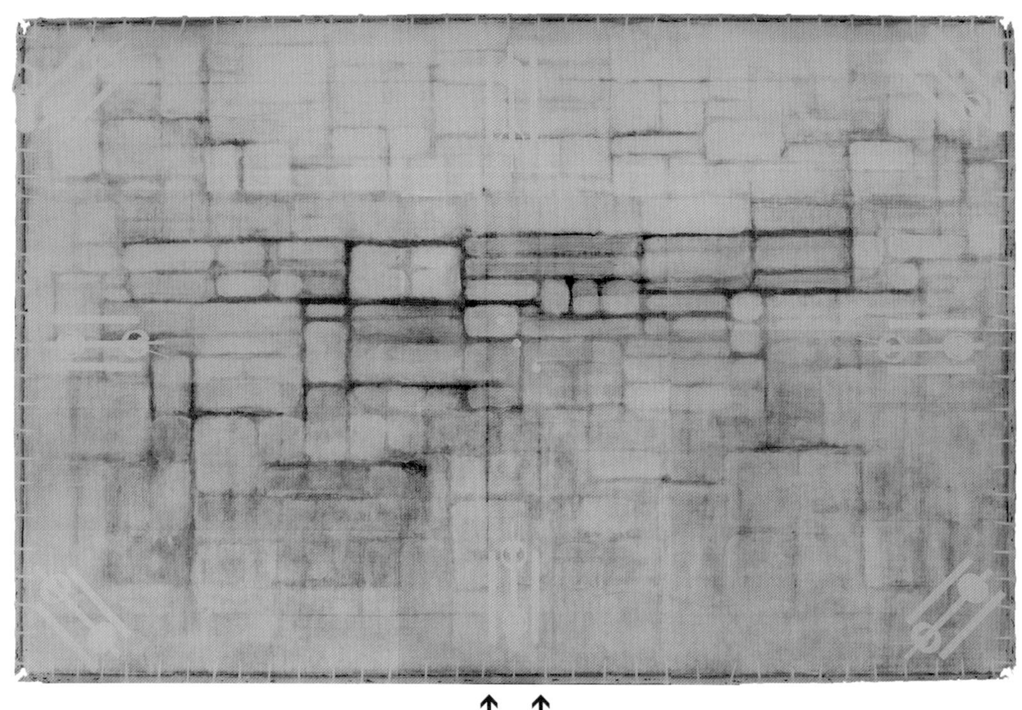

30 x-ray photograph

These passages may have been done quickly while the grey was still wet, resulting in drying cracks in some instances. Some lines in the centre left look as though they were sanded or rubbed down after the initial grey pass. These areas appear very fluid but also compressed as though the paint was diluted with solvent and manipulated before drying completely.

Mondrian then returns to the canvas with touches of yellow along the tops of the blue-grey. In the central blue forms this was likely wet on wet, where yellow mixed with blue creating small sporadic patches of yellow-green layers. In these same blue passages he then applies a darker, more purple blue-grey, almost as a lowlight, covering the yellow-green completely. This remains the final state for these blue squares.

In other areas he passes over the original blue-grey while dry with a yellow bulked with white. In many areas this layer becomes the final state, as in the square containing the central cross shape. In others, he glazes back over this upper yellow with a variety of pink washes. In some cases pink is bulked with white, leaving white highlights, while in others it serves as a dilute blue-pink glaze. Almost all of the upper pink forms flow slightly over the top of adjacent forms. In some cases there is an earlier cooler pink that rests under or within the lower layer of blue-grey. This indicates that there was some pink in this picture before the final upper layers, but the thick bold upper pink layer was very likely Mondrian's last state. This can best be seen in the lower left corner. Under magnification it is obvious that he painted out at least a portion of his signature and repainted it in black paint, as slight wisps of pink glaze the surface (ills 31, 32).

The brushstrokes are applied mostly horizontally in the upper layers, although in the lower right and lower left he edits with vertical brushstrokes, crossing over lines and almost pushing these forms entirely to the background. These lower sections of blue, pink and ochre-pink rectangles appear atmospheric and seem to float weightlessly. There are highlights bulked with white paint on some of the upper pink, blue and yellow brushstrokes that are more gestural, done quickly and occasionally with circling or zigzagging motions.

An x-ray from 2010 shows an image inclusive of the cracking in the upper paint layer along with gridwork and artist's changes (ill. 30). The gridwork along the bottom is more clearly seen in the infrared image than in the x-ray, due to the density of the non-original Lebron stretcher bar. A thin line of losses all around the turnover edge can be seen with additional losses slightly into the edges of the picture plane. The top corners and the whole bottom edge seem the most dense (suggesting thicker paint) in the x-ray, while in normal light these areas appear to have the most brushwork with overlapping and reworking. Through the centre of the x-ray there is evidence of where Mondrian painted on the canvas while over the original stretcher bar with slight impressions in the paint approximately 5 cm apart (as indicated by the arrows in ill. 30). The canvas pressed into the stretcher bars while he worked and it appears as though the paint did not get absorbed or built up in this area in the same way as it did in the rest of the picture.

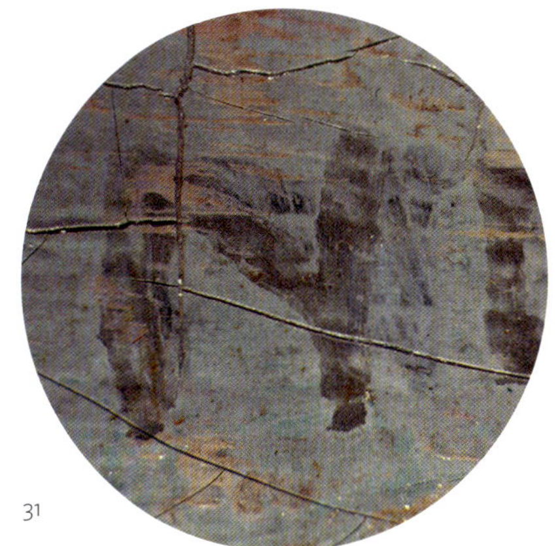

31

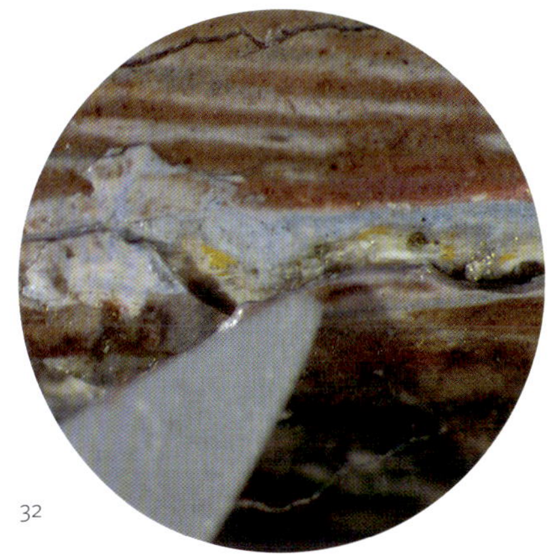

32

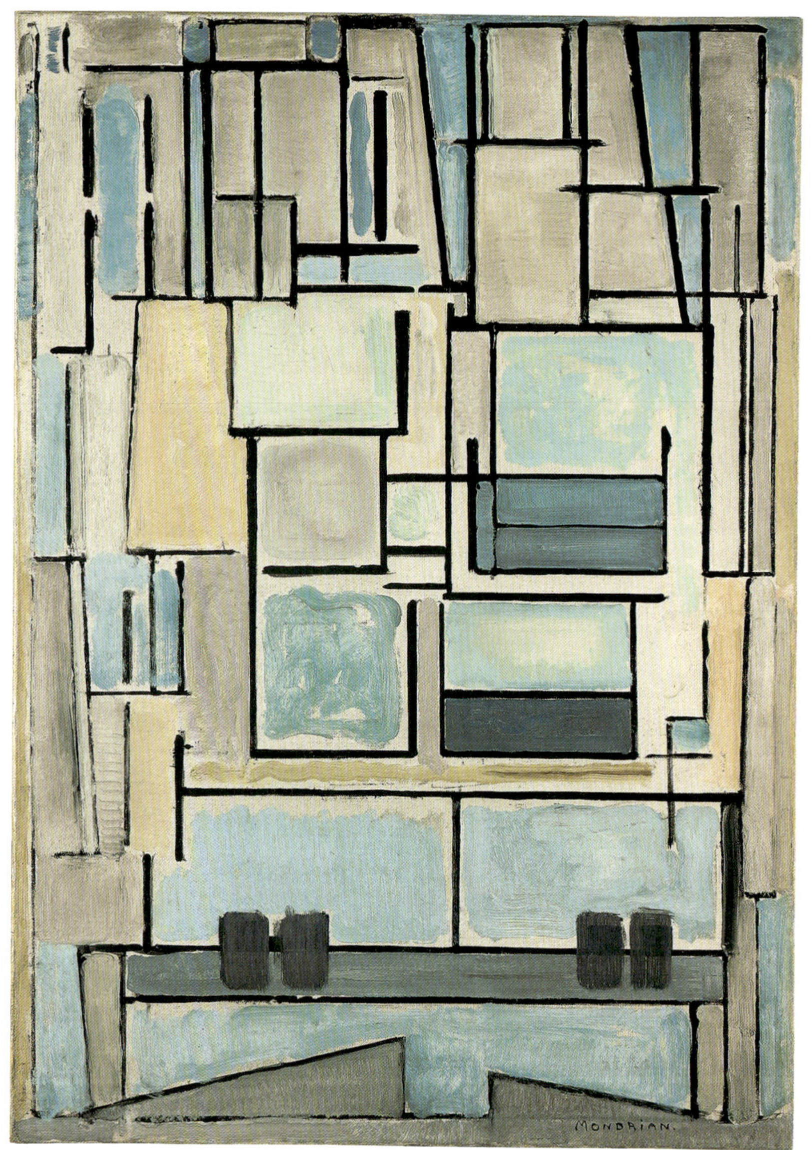

Composition NO. VI 1914
(B50 – Compositie NO. VI / Compositie 9)
Oil on canvas, 95.2 x 67.6 cm
Fondation Beyeler, Riehen/Basel

Since this painting was not subjected to technical analysis, the information presented here is based mainly on that supplied by Joop M Joosten and Robert P Welsh, *Piet Mondrian: Catalogue Raisonné of the Work of 1911–1944*, vol.2, Prestel, Munich, 1998; as well as the other sources quoted.

Inscriptions

Front: signed bottom right in black paint: MONDRiAN.

Back: on the top tacking edge, in blue paint |with a broad brush: COMPOSiTION NO. VI. MONDRiAN. [scored through with black paint, because of the new title the painting was given for the exhibition at the Stedelijk Museum in 1915, indicated on the back of the canvas in black paint: Compositie 9 | P. Mondriaan]. On the top half of the canvas, in blue paint: HAUT.

Stretcher

After 1971 the painting was lined and mounted on a Masonite panel. This procedure was reversed in 1994 and the painting was given a new stretcher. The canvas has a white ground of unknown composition and is probably factory pre-primed. The ground is thin and fairly regular; the canvas structure is not completely filled, so the weave is clearly visible.

Framing

Halfway across the tacking edges there are traces of bronze paint. This indicates that the painting originally had a receding bronze-coloured strip frame. The present strip frame is a reconstruction based on pre-1971 photographs of the painting. The vertical strips are longer than the horizontal strips and have butt joints.

Date

The painting was probably completed in May 1914, just before Mondrian sent his work to The Hague on 24 or 25 May 1914.

Provenance

In around 1950 the painting appeared on the American market, but it is not clear who owned it before this time. It was donated to MOMA in 1957. Gallery owner and collector Ernst Beyeler bought the work at an auction in 1989 for the Fondation Beyeler, Riehen/Basel.

Painted surface

The contours of a composition were applied with a thin brush using thin paint that sometimes barely touches the canvas. These lines appear to have been drawn with the aid of a ruler (ill. 33.A). There are no visible traces of pencil, chalk or charcoal. The composition is derived almost directly from a group of sketches that Mondrian made in spring 1914. These were sketches of situations where the normal order of the built environment had been disrupted, revealing strange, blank gable ends with interior walls and strangely coloured wallpaper, chimney flues, doors, panelling and remnants of hallways. Mondrian's attention was drawn to the patterns this produced, the ascending lines and the rhythm of the whole scene. In the final sketches he even made colour notes, placing letters in the squares: 'B' or 'D.G.' and, in another sketch 'W', 'G' and 'Gr' (ill. 35; p.102). Based on the colours eventually used in the fields, these must have signified blue, dark grey, white, yellow and grey. In 1926 Mondrian would still wax lyrical when he talked about the culture of the huge advertising boards and blank facades that

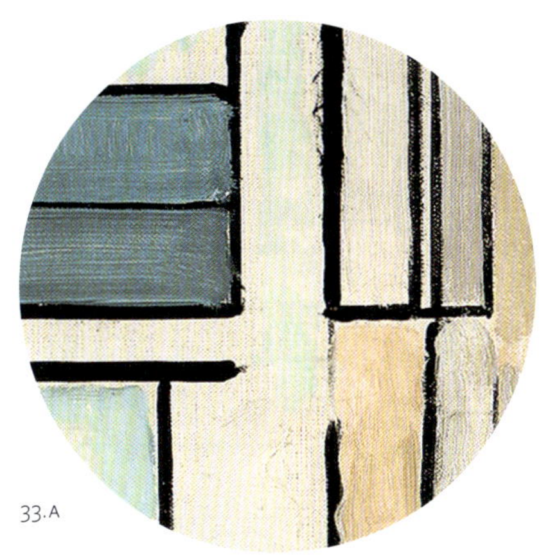

33.A

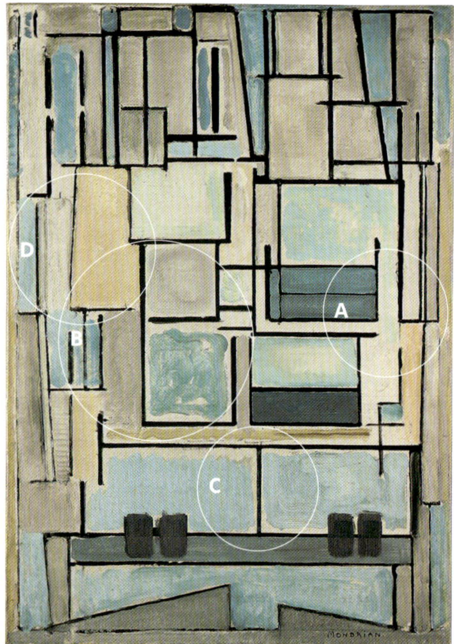

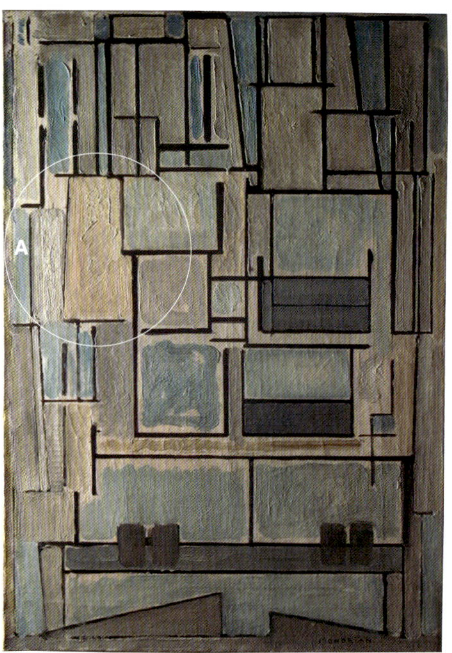

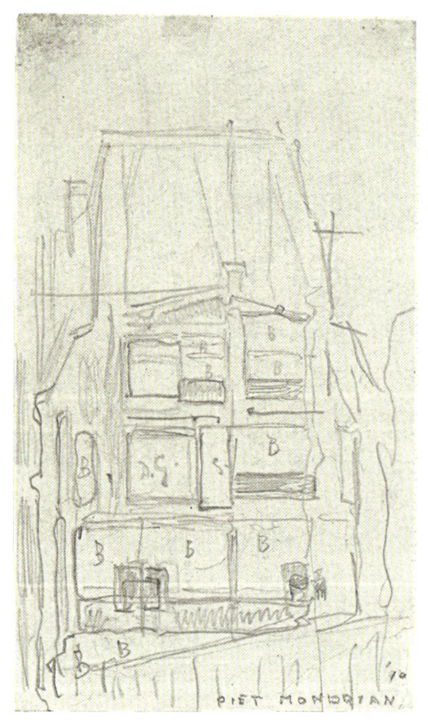

33 Nomal light photograph with indications of details

34 Raking light photograph with indication of a detail

35 *Demolished Building* (Sketchbook II, Folio 21), 1914
Pencil on paper, 17.2 x 10.5 cm
Gemeentemuseum Den Haag, The Hague

inspired artists like himself to work with large planes of colour.

The initial composition was then accentuated with fluid black paint applied with a narrow brush. In this process several mainly vertical lines were almost doubled in thickness. Some line fragments were not revisited at all, so a vivid contrast emerges between lines at various stages of development (ill. 33.B). Mondrian then filled the planes, opting to fill the edges of the picture mainly with various shades of grey. He filled the planes in a flat, comprehensive manner with parallel brushstrokes that continue with minute precision to the edges of the planes (ill. 34.A). Towards the centre of the picture the filling of the planes is less focused. Blue is reduced to a soft dab, and ochre is merely suggested. The grey-blue, on the other hand, is painted in a strict and orderly fashion in the planes. As a result, transience and completeness, process and result, the searching quality and the execution, all compete for our attention. Viewing remains unresolved. The eye completes, picks up intentions, follows the suggestion of possibilities (ill. 33.C).

It is as if in *Composition No. VI* Mondrian had taken what was 'mixed up' in the earlier compositions, with their many corrections, and the lines and planes that were part of one and the same process, and transformed it into something that was 'aligned' or 'set up', for line and colour do not mix anywhere and each has an autonomous function. Only at the edges of the composition and along the top are a number of lines obscured from view and pushed back by fields of colour. Vertical lines are shifted slightly to the left or right (ill. 33.D). At the last moment Mondrian tempered several black lines slightly by partly painting over them with colour.

The American painter Carl Holty heard during a stay in Paris in the early 1930s that Mondrian had found inspiration for this, and other compositions of around 1914–16, in blank gable ends revealed after a building in Paris had been demolished. Pieces of wallpaper, chimney flues, panelling and plasterwork produced an abstract interplay of square and rectangular planes of colour that closely resemble what Mondrian created in compositions like *Composition No. VI*. In an article in which he described recollections of Mondrian in the journal *Arts* of September 1957, Holty wrote that when he asked Mondrian about it he answered that he had often been inspired by the appearance of such gable ends, but went on to say 'when you have found your problem, many accidental things stimulate you, and if you have nothing in you a spot on a wall is just a spot on a wall'.[8]

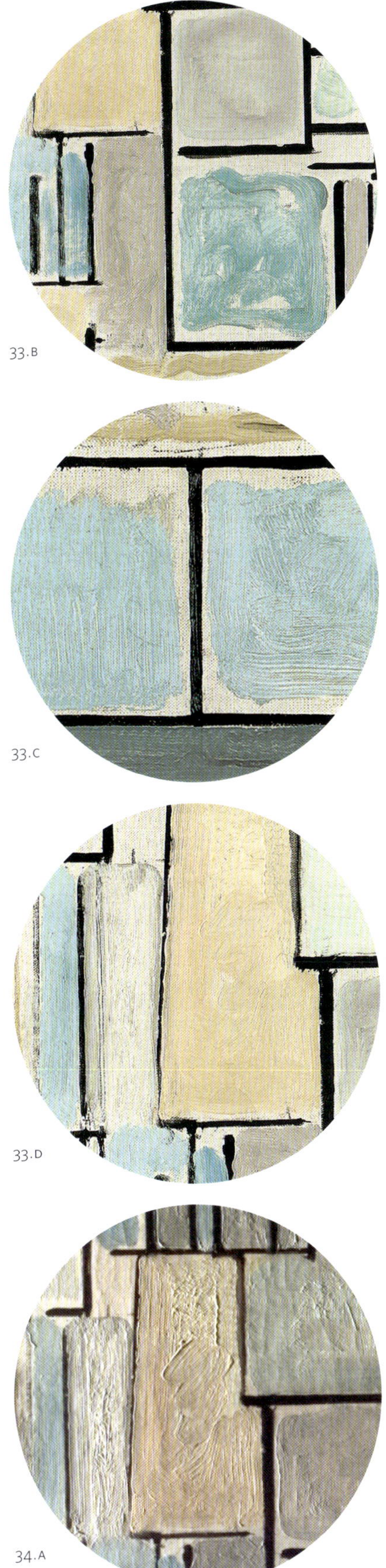

33.B

33.C

33.D

34.A

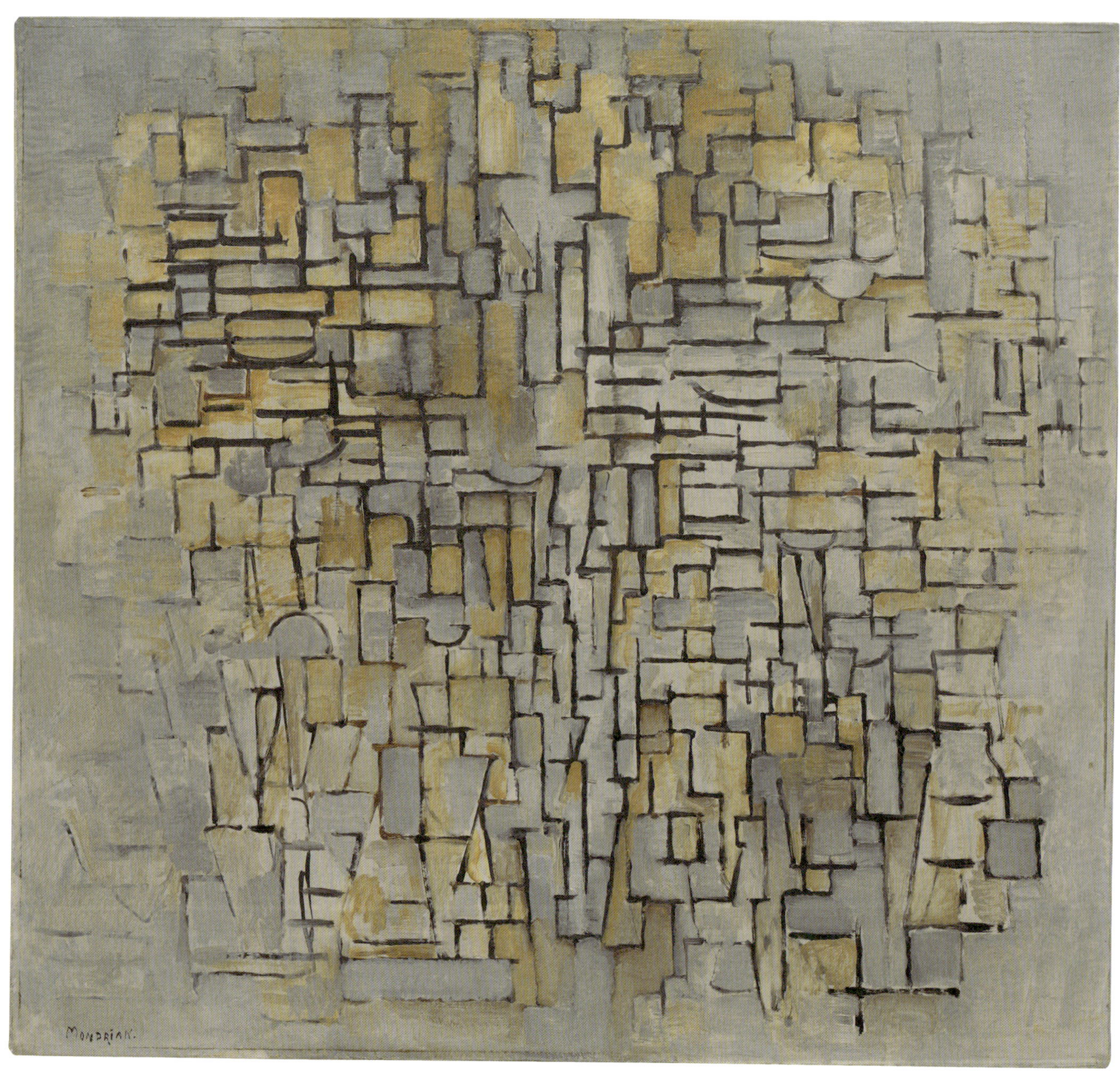

Composition NO. VII 1913
(B35 – Tableau NO. 2 / Compositie NO. VII)
Oil on canvas, 104.4 x 113.6 cm
Solomon R. Guggenheim Museum, New York

Inscriptions
Front: signed bottom left in black paint: MONDRiAN.

Back: top left, on the canvas, in black paint: MONDRIAN.; top right, on the canvas, in black paint: TABLEAU | LO: 2 [a reference to the Moderne Kunst Kring exhibition in Amsterdam in December 1913, where the painting was first shown; the title was later crossed out with black paint and partially covered with greyish-white paint, when Mondrian wrote the new title on the top stretcher bar in preparation for the Kunsthandel Walrecht exhibition]; on the top stretcher bar, in blue paint with a broad brush: COMPOSITION. NO: VII. MONDRIAN.; slightly to the right: HAUT [over a previous inscription: Oben, in black paint, partially covered with greyish-white paint]. It seems very likely that Mondrian here was indicating the top of a painting for the first time, on the back; apparently he believed this to be necessary because the picture was so non-representational. On the vertical bar through the centre of the stretcher, partially covered with labels, a note in blue chalk: 950 [a reference to the price of the painting in Prague, see p.52], the inscription CK74 in black chalk and the number 64 in blue chalk, all crossed out with blue paint, using a broad brush.

Stretcher
The pine stretcher is original and although the ground on the tacking edges has been damaged by successive applications of adhesive tape, it would appear that the canvas has been removed from the stretcher only once and that when it was remounted the same tacks and tack holes were used, in a slightly different position and combination (ill. 36). The bars are 5 cm wide and 1.8 cm thick. The outer frame is bevelled towards the centre along the canvas side. The stretcher is very similar to the type that Mondrian used during his Amsterdam period. He may have taken it with him from Amsterdam. The canvas is probably factory pre-primed, using a ground of unknown composition. The entire surface of the canvas seems to have been reworked at an early stage with a layer of white paint, after which it was washed with solvent or scraped with a palette knife. Traces of scraping can also be seen here and there. As a result, the canvas structure is barely visible in the surface and the weave no longer has a pronounced texture (ill. 38.A). The canvas is plain weave with threads of varying thickness. The vertical and horizontal threads have a density of 18 threads vertically and 18 horizontally (c.14 cm from the left edge, 9 cm from the top: 18h/19v; c.12 cm from the left edge, 9 cm from the top: 18h/18v; c.14 cm from the right edge, 9 cm from the top: 18h/18v; and c.26 cm from the right edge and 9 cm from the top: 19h/18v). There is no selvedge. The tacking edges were trimmed on the back at a later stage.

Framing
It is likely that when Mondrian framed this painting, for the Hollandse Kunst Kring exhibition at the Stedelijk Museum, Amsterdam in December 1913, he used a frame with a rebate. Traces of bronze paint can be seen along all sides, c.7–12 mm from the edge. A photograph in *Art d'Aujourdhui* from October 1950 shows the painting with what is probably the original frame, with a rebate that covers the edges of the paint surface, and with a facet rising away from the canvas and dipping away sharply to the back after c.1.5 cm (ills 39, 39.A; p.106–07). This frame must have been mounted when the final application of grey paint along the edges was still wet. Pieces of wood have been pressed into the paint, partially covered with bronze paint. And there are also traces of sawdust covered in bronze paint that has been scraped out of the paint in the direction of the corner edge, probably using a palette knife, leaving traces in the paint surface (ill. 37).

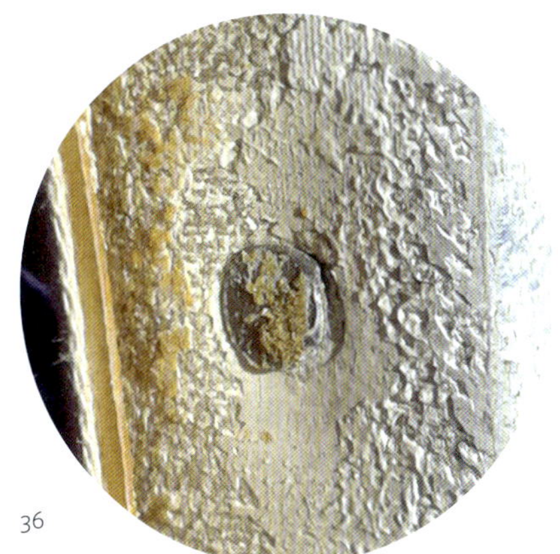
36

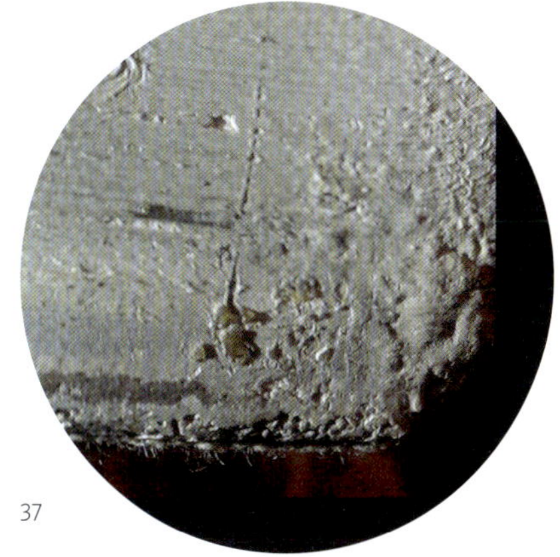
37

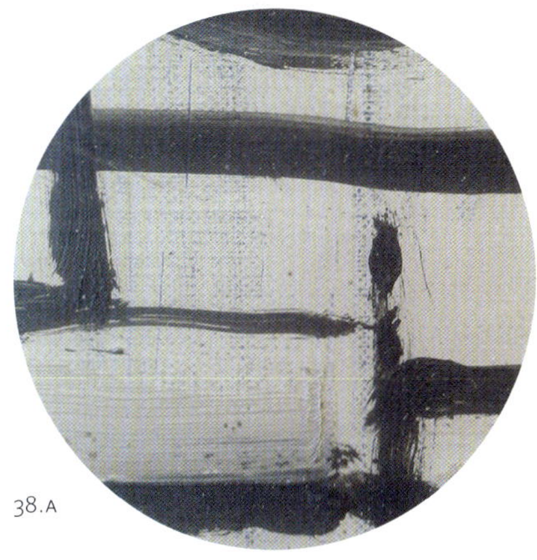
38.A

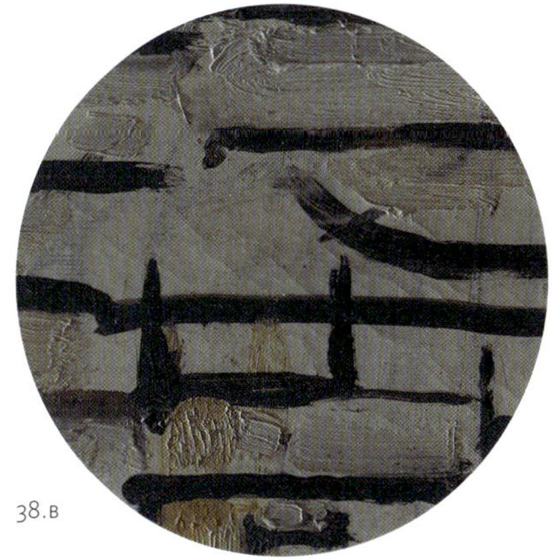
38.B

1913 Composition no. vii

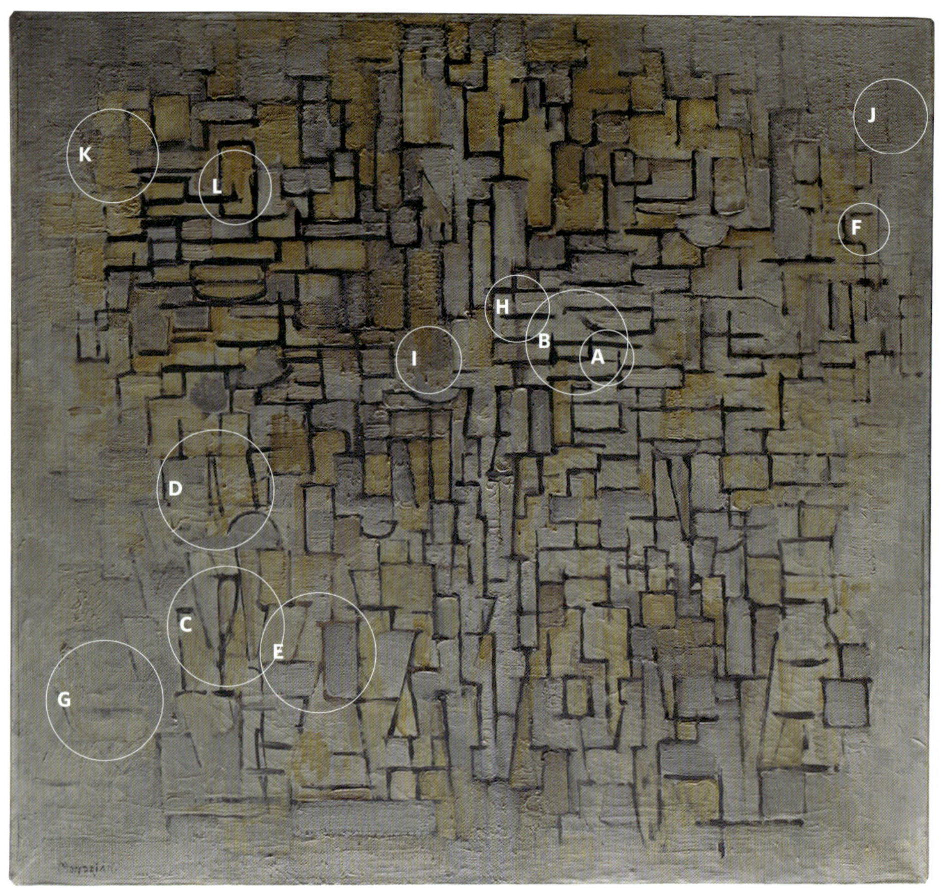

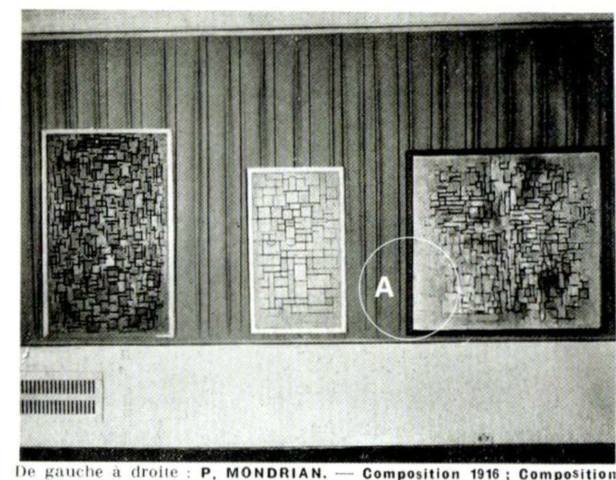

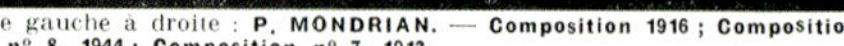

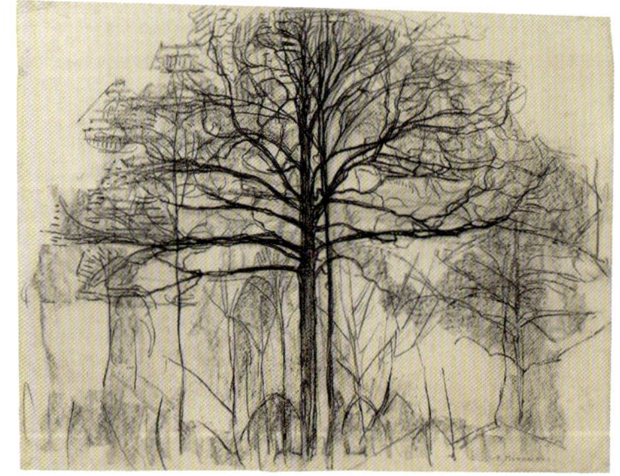

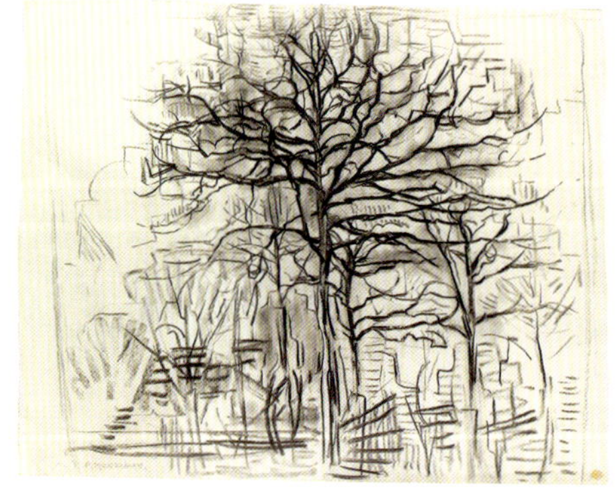

38 Raking light photograph with indications of details

39 Installation view of the 10th anniversary exhibition at the Museum of Non-Objective Painting, New York, June 1949

40 *Study of Trees 1 (Study for Tableau no. 2 / Composition no. vii)*, 1912
Black chalk on paper, 68 x 88.5 cm
Gemeentemuseum Den Haag, The Hague

41 *Study of Trees 2 (Study for Tableau no. 2 / Composition no. vii)*, 1913
Charcoal on paper, 65.7 x 82 cm
Gemeentemuseum Den Haag, The Hague

Date
We can deduce from the order of events that Mondrian started working on the composition in the winter of 1911–12 and that he must have completed the painting in late summer 1913. After it had returned from an exhibition in Prague he revised the edges of the paint surface and the framing in spring 1914, in the run-up to the Kunsthandel Walrecht exhibition.

Provenance
The painting was bought at the Kunsthandel Walrecht exhibition by Reverend Hendrick van Assendelft of Gouda. His family offered it for sale on the American market in 1947 and it was bought by the Solomon R. Guggenheim Museum, New York in 1949.

Painted surface
Mondrian sketched in very thin blueish paint at an early stage; this was then largely rubbed out and/or scraped off. Vague traces remain over the entire surface (ills 38.A, 38.B; p.105). It is unclear what the purpose of the drawing was. After this Mondrian hastily made an angular drawing in black paint, in glancing strokes made with a flexible brush (ill. 38.C). This was based on a large drawing of a tree that Mondrian made in Paris in summer 1913, on the basis of another large drawing he had produced a year earlier in the wooded landscape around Domburg (ills 40, 41).

The trunk of the tree is central to the image, represented by many short, partly stepped vertical lines projecting upwards, interposed mainly with light grey and white. The crown of the tree has been transformed into a palisade of mainly horizontal lines and planes in the top half of the picture. The reference to the charcoal drawing in the collection of the Gemeentemuseum Den Haag is a loose one, though the undergrowth to the left and right of the main central motif has been translated into sets of similar vertical lines projecting upwards, dissolving into smaller palisades.

Mondrian then partially filled the spaces between the lines with highly diluted layers, this time in light grey and ochre (ills 38.B; p.105; 38.C, 38.D). The paint is applied fluidly in places. Here and there, black lines have been obscured in this process, and planes have been joined to create new ones.

Mondrian then applied thick layers, sometimes augmenting the grey or ochre of the underlying layer, sometimes replacing the grey with ochre, or the ochre with grey. Some parts of the composition were left open, while others were very thickly painted, as clearly seen in raking light (ill. 38.E). Mondrian's search thus becomes clear to the viewer, and makes the resulting painting appear layered (ill. 38.F; p.109). This is also something that Mondrian must have discussed when asked about the work. Critic NH Wolf wrote a review in 1915 that demonstrates he must have exchanged ideas with Mondrian on precisely this painting.[9] Mondrian indicates that subjects are of no interest to him, serving only to awaken in him an interest in the relationship between line and colour. This allowed him to let himself go during the creative process. This is clearly visible in the result. Along the edges, in particular, there are areas where the brushstrokes are exceptionally fluid and expressive (ill. 38.G; p.109).

Belgian art critic Wilmon-Vervaert, invited to write a review for *De Kunst*, described Mondrian's motives in detail: 'His art cannot be reasoned, or compiled; he dreams in abstraction. With devotion, careless, he shares with charming conviviality the waves of feeling in harmonies of grey and yellow...His art is far removed from depiction, instead evoking sensations in the field of visual art equivalent to those evoked by music.'[10] The language used gives a good impression of the astonishment with which Wilmon-Vervaert regarded this oddity in the cubist stable, and has been used more recently to describe Mondrian's effort as 'dreaming in the abstract' in contrast to painters like Bracque and Picasso.[11]

Another big difference between Mondrian and Picasso at that time was highlighted by Aleid Loosjes-Terpstra in 1956: 'There is however – and this is closely related to the difference in starting point just outlined [the motif of the tree] – in Mondrian no trace of a *battle* between the object depicted and the painter's will to shape it which is so typical of the style of Picasso referred to here.'[12]

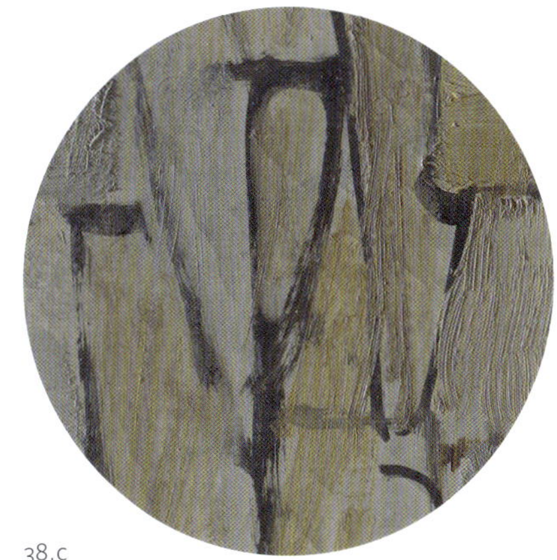
38.C

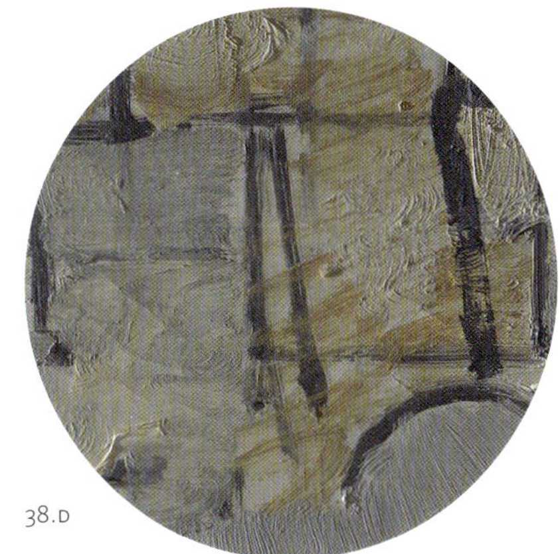
38.D

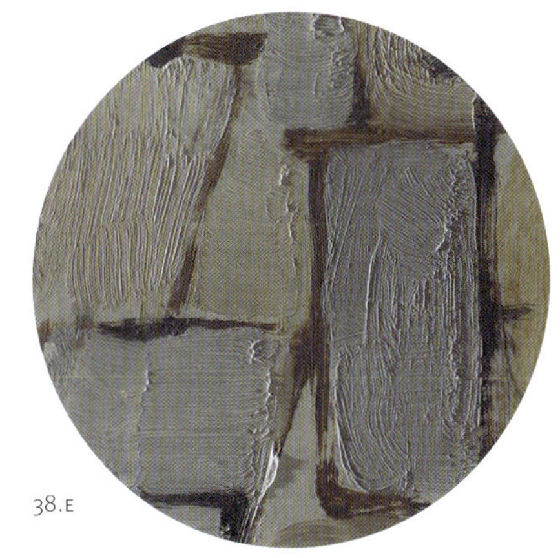
38.E

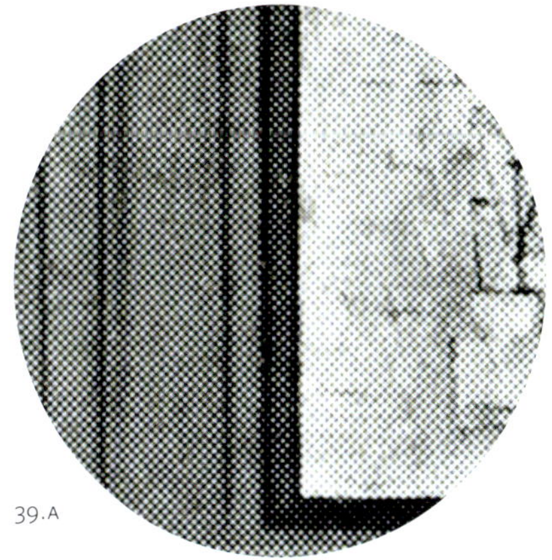
39.A

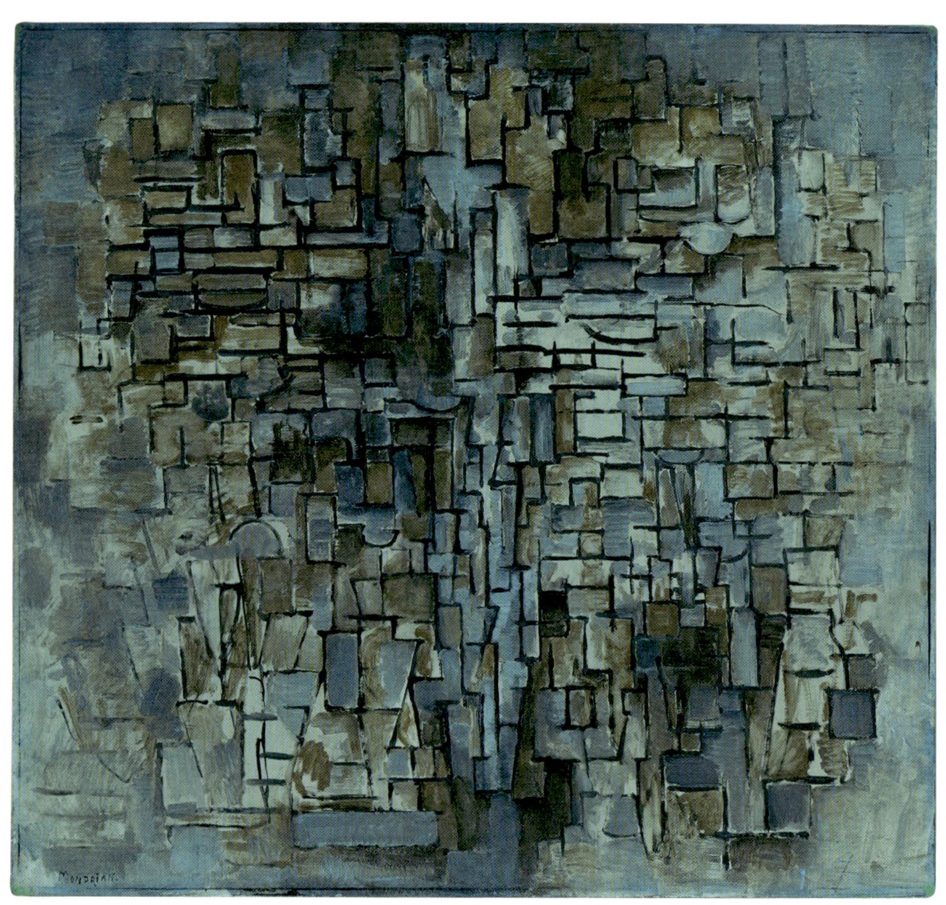

42 Ultraviolet light photograph

In the meantime, Mondrian emphasised the black lines here and there and reinforced some overpainted black lines by simply repeating them over the overpainting (ill. 38.H). Finally, using a very fluid ochre which occasionally produced some real drips, he reworked parts of the surface (ill. 38.I). This paint is matt and displays some meshed drying cracks, which might suggest that, particularly in this final phase, Mondrian used a drying agent. He revisited the painting, probably much later, when it returned from Prague to Paris, applying a layer of grey along the edges, which appears grey-blue in UV light (ill. 42). This procedure would be labelled later by art historian Yve-Alain Bois, discussing the work of Jackson Pollock as 'folding back'. More impressionistically it could also be described as 'fading away' or 'fading out': the artist does not allow the play of line and colour to spill over the edges of the painting, but brings it to a halt before it reaches the edges. This has a double effect: concentrating the attention on the picture and stressing that the composition is meant as a world in itself, and is not intended to interact with the surrounding space.

While applying the layers of grey, Mondrian scraped an area in the bottom right using a palette knife in order to create a more open structure. In the top right he painted around black lines, yet he wanted to achieve a considerable density of paint (ill. 38.J). This makes the remnants of black line appear slightly ghostly. In the top left Mondrian heightened certain lines using dark grey over the grey (ill. 38.K). And in the bottom left, the grey was applied thinly and with loose brushstrokes, as a result of which the underlying lines and colours still have a role in the final product. The chaotic conditions in the studio in the run-up to the exhibition are demonstrated clearly in the top left of the painting, where a thin grey horizontal stripe is visible. This can only be interpreted as an imprint of another painting (treated with the same grey along the edges!) that must have leaned against *Composition No. VII* (ill. 38.L).

The final result is highly experimental. Mondrian worked in a gradually more intuitive and relaxed manner. This is also the earliest painting in which he decided to state on the back, for clarity's sake, which edge was the top, from which we can conclude that he was only too aware that he had entered unknown – abstract – territory.

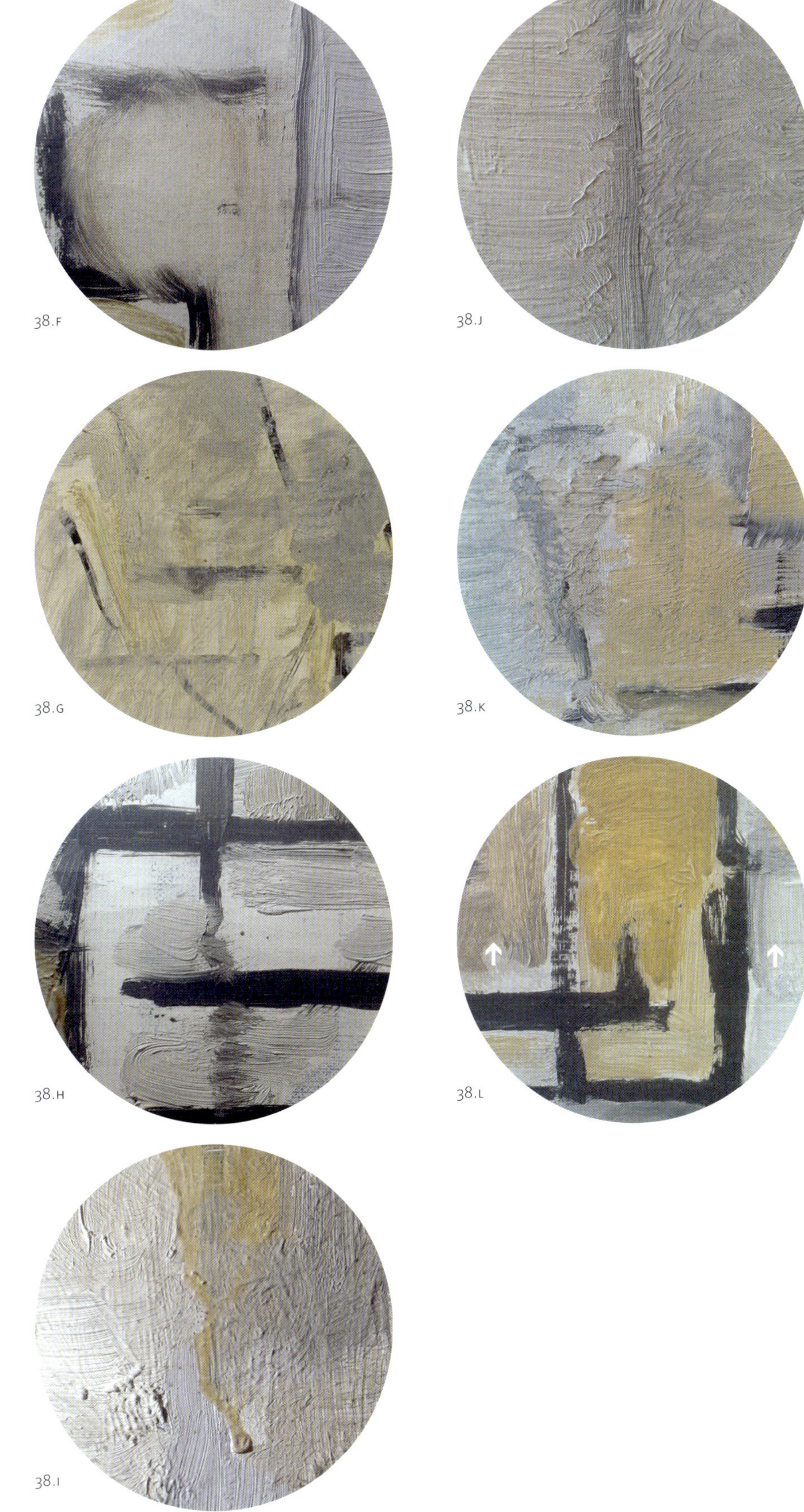

38.F

38.J

38.G

38.K

38.H

38.L

38.I

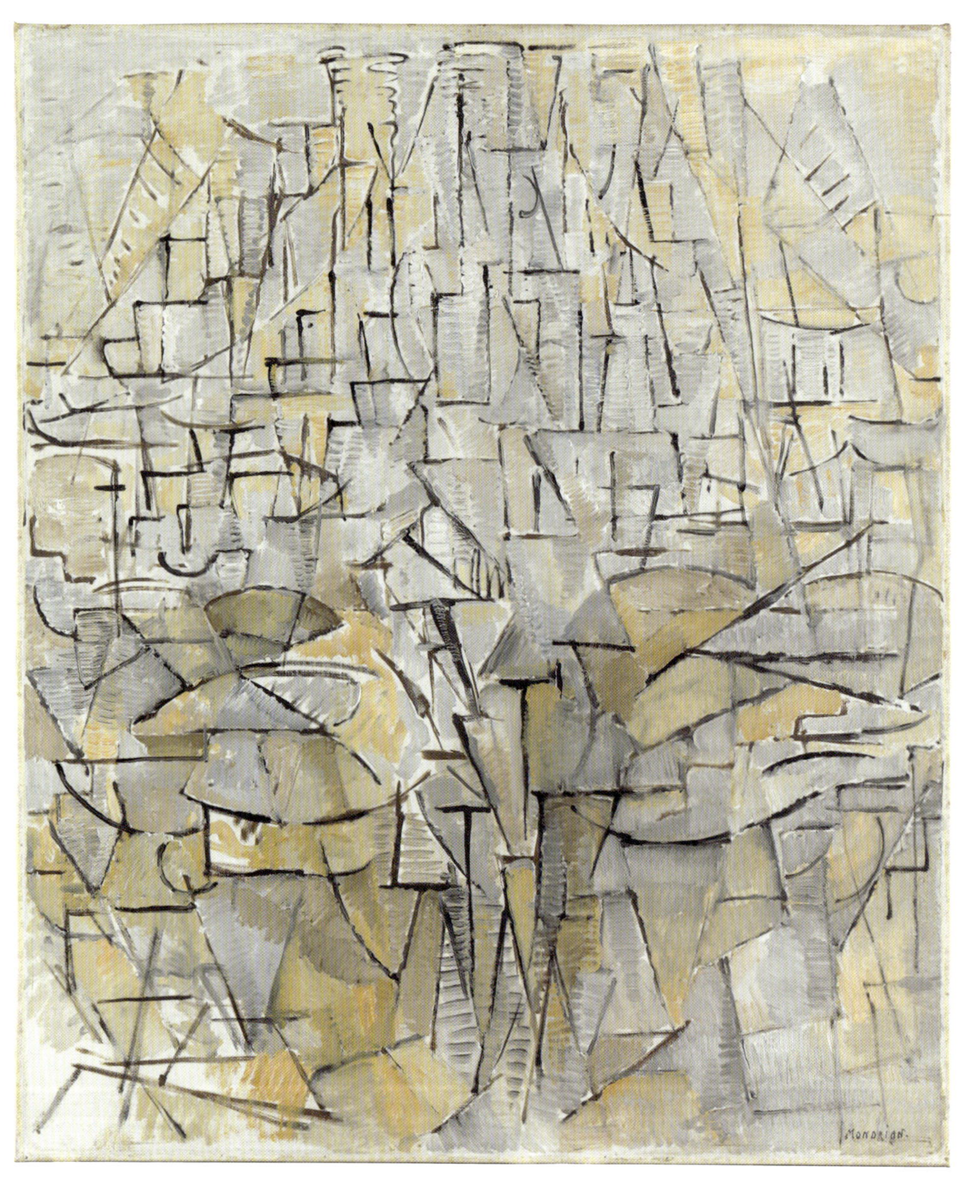

Composition no. viii 1913
(B27 – Tableau no. 4 / Compositie no. viii / Compositie 3)
Oil on canvas, 95 x 80 cm
Gemeentemuseum Den Haag, The Hague

Inscriptions
Front: signed bottom right in black paint: MONDRİAN.

Back: on the turnover edge, along the top, in thinly applied black paint, the remains of a title [crossed out in black paint] (ill. 43.A; p.113); on the left side of the top half of the canvas, in thinly applied black paint: MONDRİAN.; on the right side of the top half of the canvas, in thinly applied black paint: TABLEAU Nº 4C [crossed out in black paint (title and artist's name refer to the Moderne Kunst Kring exhibition of November–December 1913 at the Stedelijk Museum Amsterdam)]; on the bottom left half of the canvas, in thinly applied black paint: compositie 3 | P. Mondriaan [title and artist's name refer to the exhibition with Schelfhout, Sluyters, Gestel, Le Fauconnier, Toorop and JC Van Epen at the Stedelijk Museum, Amsterdam, in October 1915]. On the central stretcher bar, in blue paint applied with a broader brush: COMPOSITION N:VIII.; further to the right, in blue paint applied with a broad brush: MONDRİAAN [title and artist's name refer to the exhibition at Kunsthandel Walrecht in 1914].

Stretcher
Mondrian painted this composition on a linen canvas that is mounted on a wooden stretcher. The canvas has a commercially applied white ground that has discoloured to a creamy colour along the edges of the painting, where the canvas was covered by the frame. The thin ground does not show any traces of a palette knife or other tool being used for preparation. There are pushpin holes visible along the top edge of the canvas. This could be an indication that Mondrian had prepared the composition on the un-stretched canvas and did not mount the support until later, after he had finished the painting. The tacking holes from the original stretching can still be seen along the edges of the canvas.

The irregularly trimmed tacking edges are completely covered by the ground layer. Only a strip of canvas along the upper edge, approximately 3–3.5 cm wide, shows no priming. On the left edge the turnover edge is 1–2.3 cm wide, on the right 0–2.3 cm, and along the bottom edge, the width varies from 1–1.9 cm. The canvas has a plain weave with an average thread count of 17 horizontal and 21 vertical threads (top left, 7 cm from the left edge and 7 cm from the top edge: 17h/21v; bottom left 7 cm from the bottom edge and 7 cm from the left side: 17h/20v; top right, 7 cm from the right edge and 7 cm from the top edge: 17h/21v; bottom right, 7 cm from the right edge and 7 cm from the bottom edge: 18h/20v; 35 cm from the right and 43 cm from the top: 17h/21v. This gives an average of 17 weft threads per cm, with a min/max range of 17 to 18 threads/cm, and an average of 21 warp threads per cm, with a min/max range of 20 to 21 threads/cm).

There are no traces of a palette knife or other tool. The current stretching of the canvas was carried out at the conservation department of the Gemeentemuseum Den Haag after 1954. On that occasion the dimensions of the painting were made larger on all sides by attaching c.1 cm wide strips of wood to the outer edges of the stretcher. This was probably done when the painting was placed in a new frame, in order to prevent the painted areas of the picture plane along the edges from being covered by the frame rabbet. The original stretcher bars are 4.3 cm wide with bevelled edges, and the thickness of the bars varies between 1.3 and 2 cm thick along the outer edges and 1.3 cm along the inner edges. The stretcher has a horizontal and a vertical crossbar, both the same width as the outer bars and 1.3 cm thick. The corners have butt joints, presumably tongue and groove, and each corner is fixed with four tacks.

Framing
The current frame is a reconstruction that was made after 1971, with the frame profile based on the original frame on *Flowering Apple Tree* (1912), which can be seen in a photograph, taken before 1934, showing the painting in the sitting room of Conrad Kickert's house (ill. 47; p.112). Traces of bronze colour that are visible along the left and bottom edges of *Composition No. VIII*, c.1.8 cm from the edge, suggest that the original frame was painted in a bronze colour. Because the original dimensions of the stretcher were changed these traces are now situated c.8–10 mm from the edge. Approximately 8–10 mm of the primed tacking edges is visible all along the edges of the picture plane. When the painting is framed, this part is covered by the frame rebate.

Date
Mondrian sent the painting to the Salon des Indépendants in early March 1913, where it was displayed as number 2136 with the title *Tree in Flower*. This means that Mondrian must have completed the painting in the winter of 1912–13, and then probably revised it in the summer of 1913.

Provenance
The painting was acquired by PM Broekmans of Amsterdam after October 1915. On 24 January 1922 Salomon Slijper bought it at auction at A. Mak in Amsterdam, and gave the work to the Gemeentemuseum Den Haag in 1954 as a long-term loan. Since 1971 the painting has been owned by the Gemeentemuseum as part of the Slijper bequest.

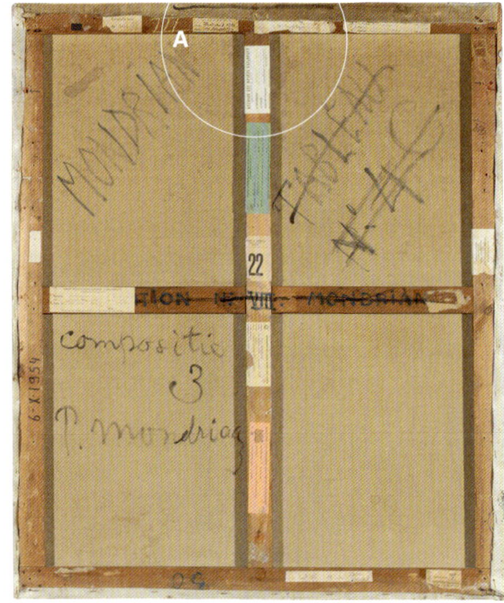

43 Back of the painting with indication of a detail

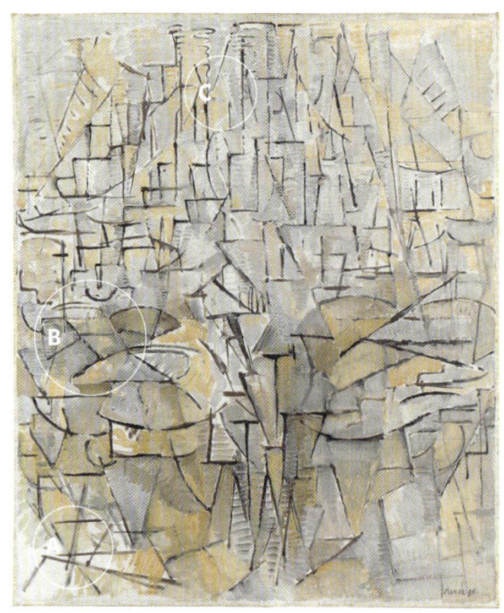

44 Normal light photograph with indications of details

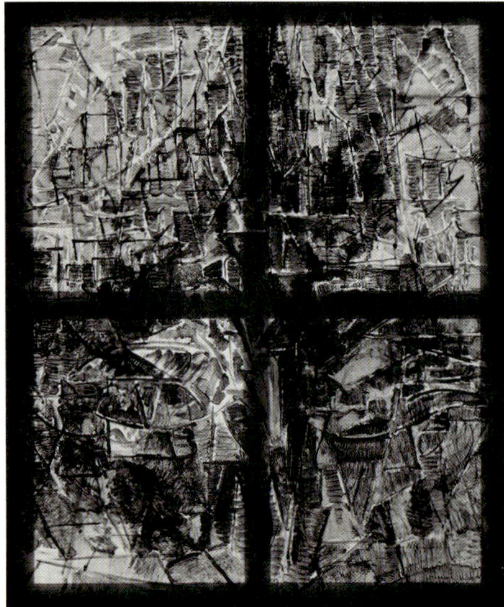

45 Transmitted infrared photograph

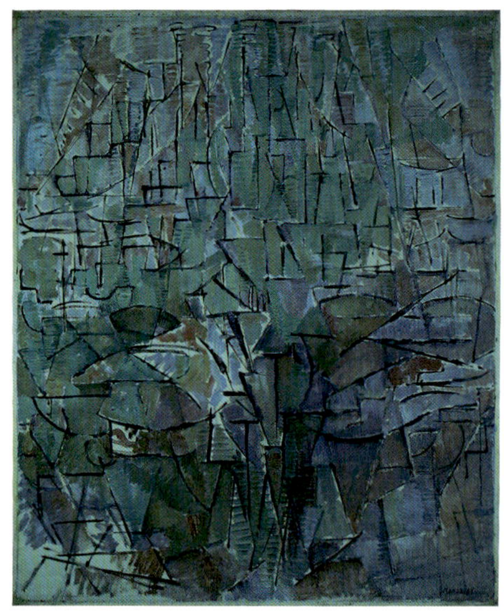

46 Ultraviolet light photograph

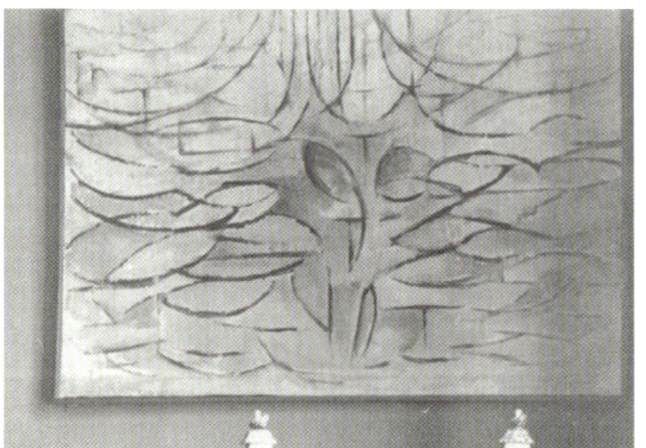

47 *Flowering Apple Tree*, 1912
Oil on canvas, 78,5 x 107,5 cm
Gemeentemuseum Den Haag, The Hague

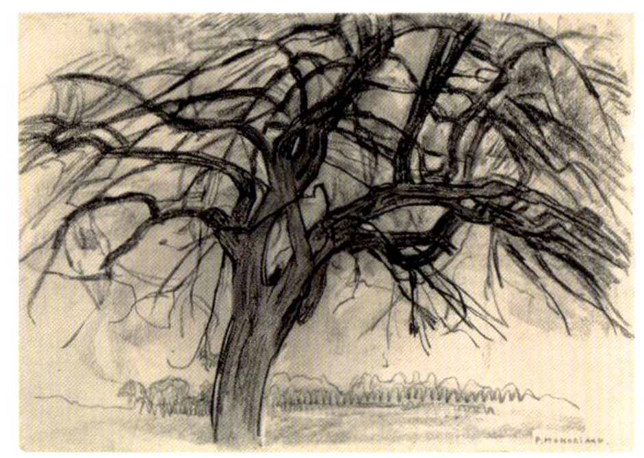

48 *Study for Evening: The Red Tree*, 1908
Black chalk and charcoal on paper, 31 x 44 cm
Gemeentemuseum Den Haag, The Hague

Painted surface

There is no underdrawing present. There is a linear sketch painted directly on the ground in brown paint with a narrow brush. The sketch comprises thin, short, fragmented lines that overlay each other like sticks in a Mikado game (ill. 44.A). Some of the lines were applied with fairly lean paint, the brush barely touching the canvas. It appears that those lines formed the first phase in the painting process. Some of the lines were later enhanced with black paint and a broader, more saturated brush. Towards the edges of the composition the lines appear sketchy, whereas in the centre of the picture they are more deliberately arranged in a structure of stepped and zigzagging shapes that tower upwards.

Straight and curved lines cross one another in the lower part of the composition, whereas the upper half comprises predominantly straight lines, alternating short, horizontal lines, and long, diagonal lines that reach upwards. This creates a rising upward movement, suggesting a tree trunk with its crown. HP Bremmer told Aleid Loosjes-Terpstra how Mondrian had enthusiastically pointed out a certain tree in the Jardin du Luxembourg that had been the starting point for this painting and others in a series. However, it would seem more likely that drawings from Mondrian's portfolio provided the initial direction for these compositions (ill. 48).

Halfway up the right part of the composition there is a horizontal line fragment, accentuated in black, which is echoed in two line fragments that are placed slightly higher. These are partially obscured by curved lines and vertically rising planes. On the left the lines are obscured by curved coloured planes that are painted more thickly, and by small, hooked and arched shapes that criss cross and swirl over the lines (ill. 44.B). There is little harmonisation of line and colour here. In the upper part, however, colour seems to be more adjusted to the lines, and the lines correspond with the colour, although even here, lines are hidden under fields of colour, and colour fields are divided by black lines painted wet-on-wet as visible in the transmitted infrared light photograph (ill. 45). This gives the composition a searching, pondering air. In the top part of the composition the spaces between the lines are loosely filled in with ochre and grey and a little white. In the lower half the grey and ochre tones are either mixed or applied on top of each other, thus creating a darker tonality and a more compact paint built-up in this part of the painting. The colour shades are also blended wet-on-wet using white, grey and ochre in different proportions, which creates a rich and lively image (ill. 44.C).

In the year before his death, Mondrian used to tell visitors who came to his studio in New York that in *Victory Boogie Woogie* (1944) he had rediscovered his fascination with the extremely potential effect of white, grey and yellow, which had first gripped him in 1912–13. Despite the painting's intricate structure, the ground is visible here and there in between the lines and colour planes – evidence of the caution with which the artist set about his work.

The composition was painted in several phases, allowing underlying layers to dry before new ones were applied. This supports the hypothesis that Mondrian revised the painting after the Salon des Indépendants of 1913. He reworked the lower part of the composition by adding dark shades of ochre and grey, which resulted in a more subdued tonality in this area (ill. 46) that contrasts with the top part of the composition. By mixing the grey and yellow with heavy-bodied white paint and working with short, separate brushstrokes, this effect was further enhanced, bringing a certain sparkle to the composition which suggests dappled light shining through the leaves of a tree. In this sense, it is interesting to link this work to that of Picasso and Braque, such as Picasso's *Mandolin Player* (1911; p.33), now in the Fondation Beyeler, which was displayed at the Moderne Kunst Kring exhibition in October 1912, and Braque's *Bottle of Bass* (c.1911–12; p.26), now in the Triton Collection Foundation . The main difference is that Mondrian continued to make a clear distinction between colour and line.

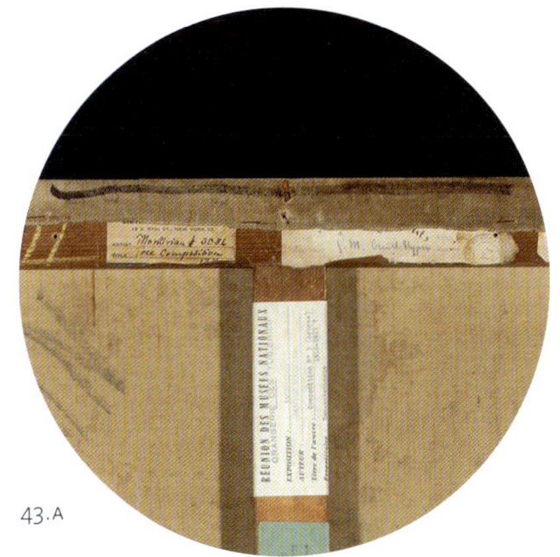
43.A

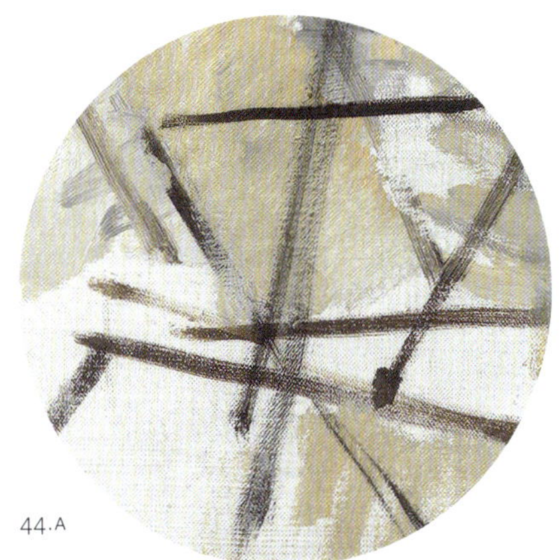
44.A

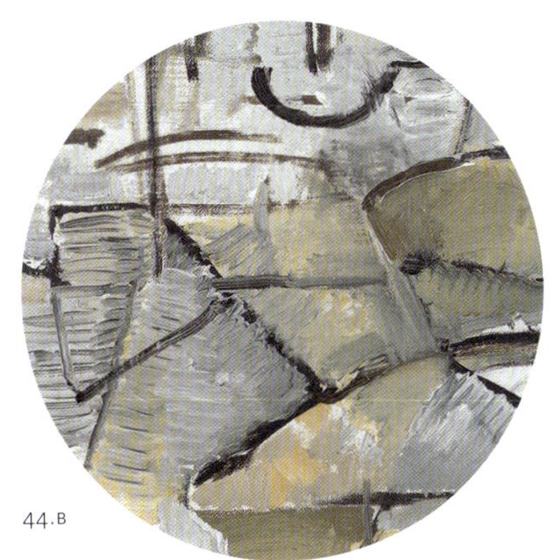
44.B

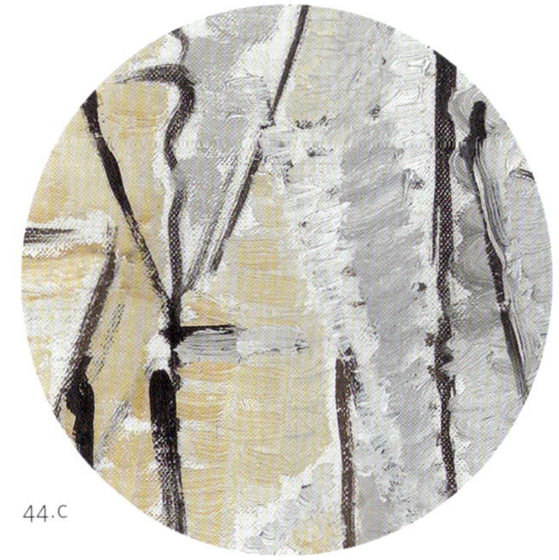
44.C

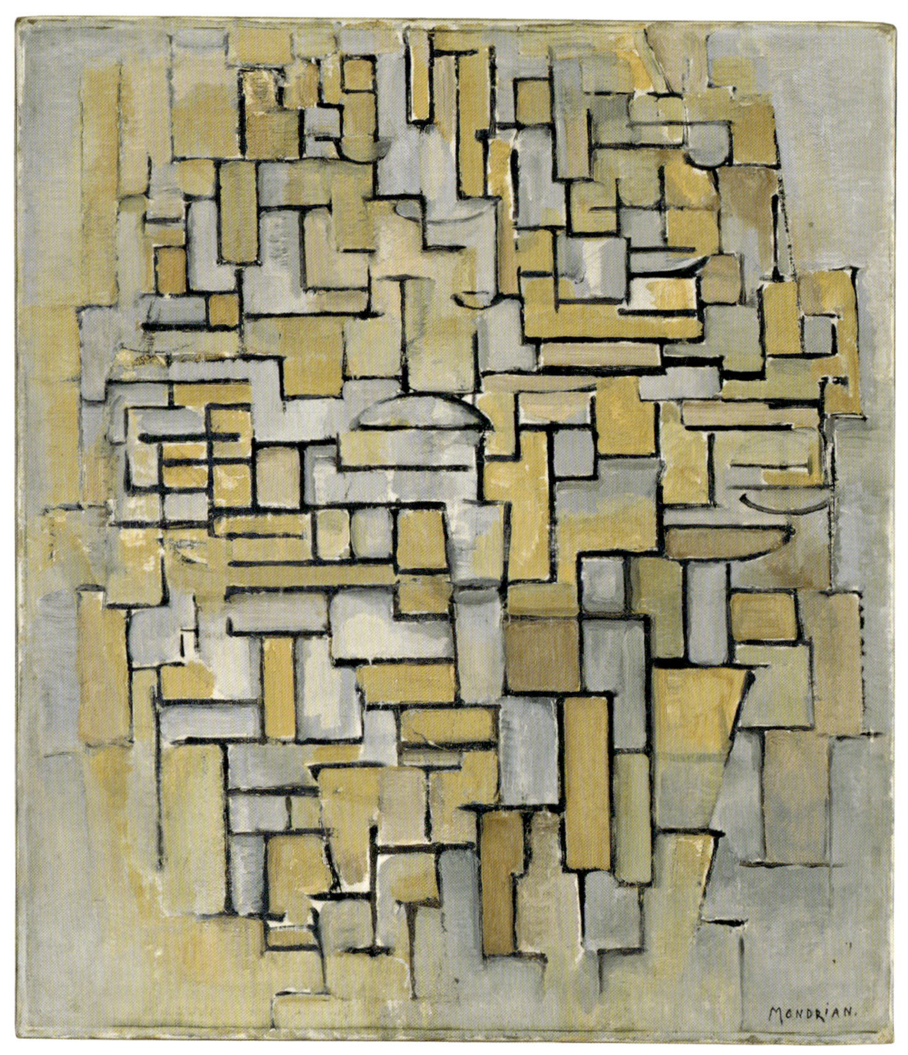

Composition NO. IX 1913
(B36 – Gemälde NO. II / Compositie NO. IX / Compositie 5)
Oil on canvas, 85.7 x 75.6 cm
Museum of Modern Art, New York

Inscriptions

Front: signed in the lower right: MONDRiAN

Back: on the upper half in dilute black ink or paint: titel: | Gemälde N. II [rubbed over with greyish-white paint] HAUT. In black written over greyish white | nom: *P. Mondrian* [in cursive letters, large black letters in thin ink or dilute paint applied with a medium round brush]; beneath that, in black paint: Compositie 5 [crossed out with a broad, bold black brushstroke] in large black thin ink or dilute paint applied with a medium round brush; on the lower half of the canvas, upside down to the composition, is a stamp of Blanchet, 38 rue Bonaparte, Paris; on the upper bar of the stretcher from left to right, in a broad blue paint stroke applied with a medium flat brush, COMPOSiTiON NO: IX MONDRiAN [crossed out with a thin black line]. Beneath NO: IX there is white paint obscuring the word OBEN/OUT.

Framing

The picture entered the Museum of Modern Art's collection in 1950. In July 1950 conservators Sheldon and Caroline Keck made no mention of the frame, yet a 1958 survey checklist by MOMA conservator Jean Volkmer lists the frame as in good condition. During recent examination it was noted that remnants of greenish-brown paint appear sporadically along the face of the picture plane on all four sides, about 1.3 cm inward from the edge. Under magnification, this material appears very green and in some instances is located on top of the paint layer, while in other areas it appears within or beneath the paint passages (ill. 49.A; p.117). Based on investigations of green-brown paint on *Composition NO. V*, also in MOMA's collection, it is assumed that this is also organometallic corrosion product from old bronze paint. X-ray fluorescence (XRF) spectroscopy performed by Ana Martins confirmed the presence of copper at the edge of the picture plane. This indicates that the painting may have originally been framed with a rebated bronze-coloured frame that was touched up while the painting was in it.

The picture is on its original French-style back bevelled stretcher. There are four outer members, measuring 5.7 cm wide with one 5 cm wide horizontal cross bar, and two keys at all corners secured with picture wire and one key at the middle bar. Hand-tooled or chisel marks can be seen in a few areas where the central members were reshaped. Despite having a small patch just below centre, the painting appears not to have been taken off the stretcher. The tacks show appropriate age and there are no extraneous tack holes. If it came off the stretcher, pains were taken to reuse tacks and the original holes.

The painting is on a fine plain-weave linen canvas with an average of 19.5 threads per cm in the vertical warp direction and 17 threads per cm in the horizontal weft direction. There is a great deal of staining on the back of the canvas from medium absorption into and through the canvas fibres. The tacking edges are all cut, exhibiting no selvedge. They are intact and in very good condition. They were tacked on the sides of the stretcher bar and then stapled onto the reverse of the stretcher where necessary. There are pencil marks on the upper left and right tacking edge that might be associated with the cutting of the tacking edges by the artist.

Prior to 1950 a patch had been placed on the reverse with wax resin to repair a surface puncture. The painting does not appear to have been removed from the stretcher. The ground on the tacking edges surrounding the tacks appears completely undisturbed. Although the picture was at times singled out for thorough treatment, it is unlined and on an original stretcher.

The canvas is factory pre-primed, the ground extending all the way to the edge of the tacking margins. It is moderately thick and evenly applied. X-ray fluorescence presented lead (Pb) throughout the painting and on the tacking margins, indicating that it is a lead white ground.

Date

In early spring of 1913 Mondrian bought several canvases at Blanchet. In late September this painting was exhibited in Germany. This means that he must have finished the painting in August 1913. He may have reworked the corners after its return from Germany in January 1914.

Provenance

The painting was acquired from the artist by Jakob and Maaike van Domselaer-Middelkoop, Amsterdam/Bergen. It was purchased by MOMA in 1950 through Miss H Imbach from S van Deventer, Wassenaar.

Painted surface

The picture was painted very quickly with a sense of immediacy. Mondrian clearly drew directly on the ground with a thin wash-like matt black paint, skipping across the tops of the canvas threads. Using XRF, conservation scientist Ana Martins helped the author determine that there are two blacks present: one comprising calcium and phosphorus, indicative of bone black, while the other contains silicon (Si), potassium (K), manganese (Mn) and iron (Fe), which points to Mars black.

Using these paints, Mondrian ultimately formed a perimeter of irregularly shaped trapezoids, with squares, rectangles and ellipses interlaced in the interior. In transmitted light it is evident that there is an underlayer of at least six black lines drawn to the lower edge of the painting, originally extending beneath the lowermost forms. Joosten was the first to suggest, in 1998, that this image originated from tree sketches (ills 53, 54; p.116). Indeed trunks and branches start to appear when the initial lines are followed off the page and back up through the centre of the picture.

After laying in the tree-like lattice forms, Mondrian began to colour in the spaces with dilute and almost transparent washes of ochres, raw sienna, umbers and a cool blue

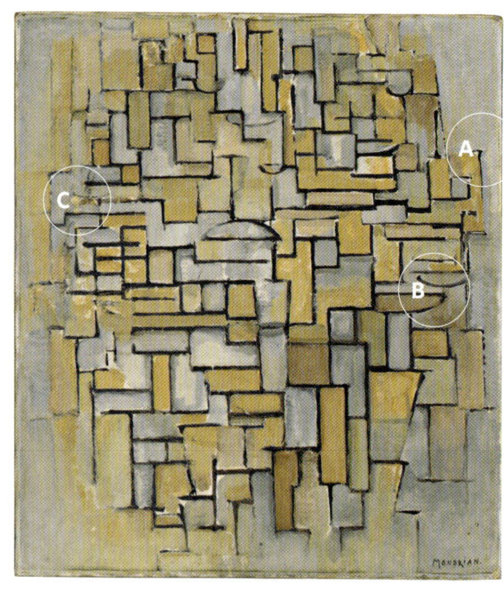

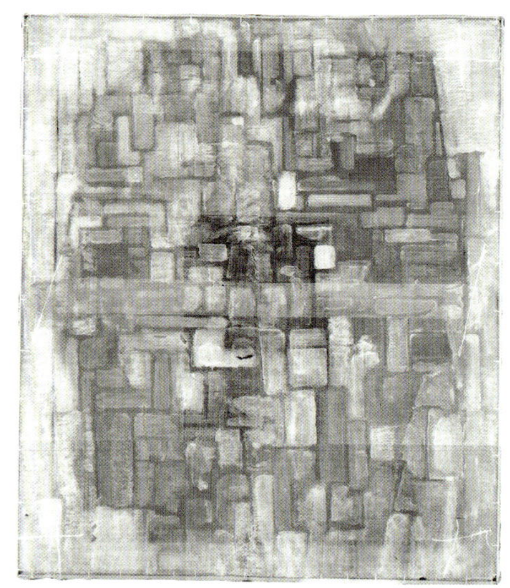

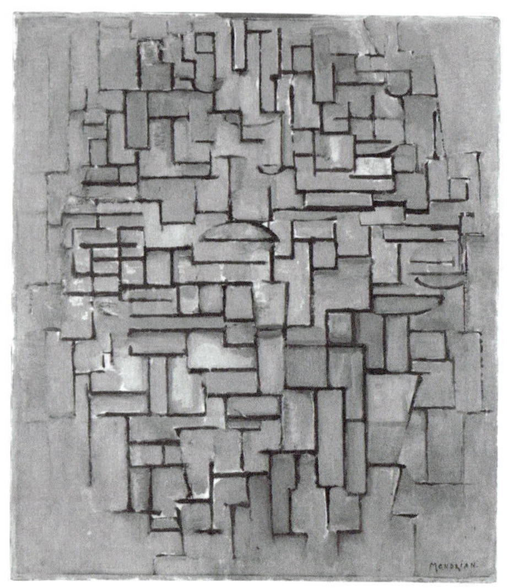

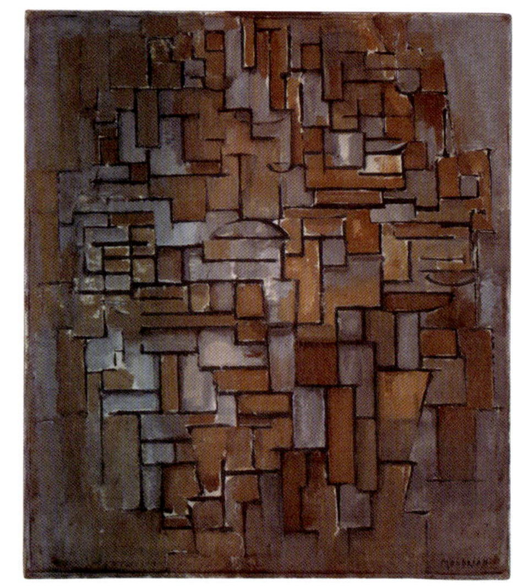

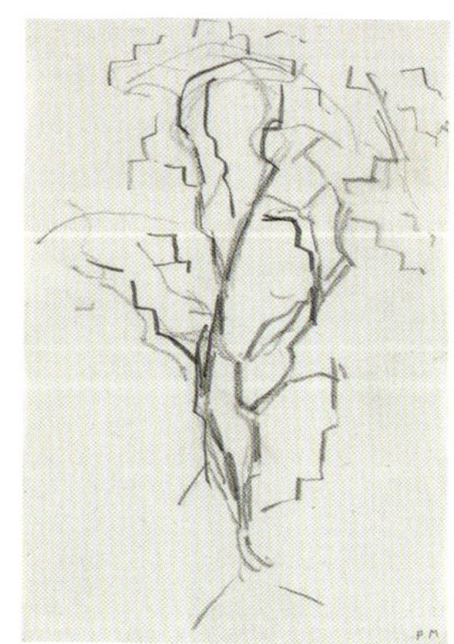

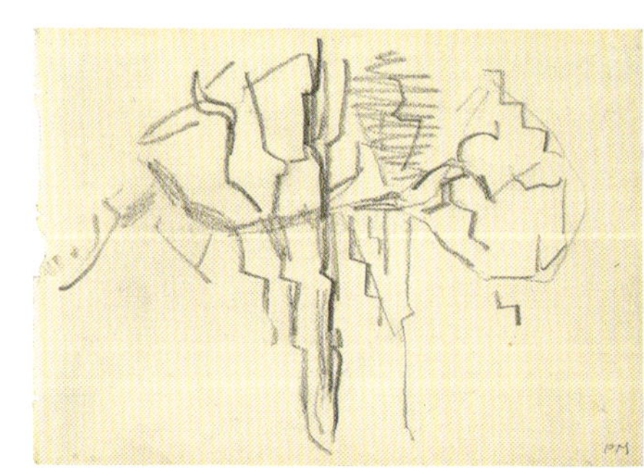

49 Normal light photograph with indications of details

50 x-ray photograph

51 Reflected infrared photograph

52 Ultraviolet photograph

53 *Tree* (Sketchbook IV, Folio 3), early 1913
Pencil on paper, 16.8 x 12.4 cm
Gemeentemuseum Den Haag, The Hague

54 *Tree* (Sketchbook IV, Folio 5), early 1913
Pencil on paper, 12.4 x 16.8 cm
Gemeentemuseum Den Haag, The Hague

grey, leaving the ground exposed in many areas. XRF detected the elements aluminium (Al), silicon (Si), sulphur (S), phosphorus (P), potassium (K), calcium (Ca), iron (Fe), zinc (Zn), strontium (Sr), barium (Ba), lead (Pb), titanium, (Ti), manganese (Mn) and arsenic (As). XRF of the ochres presented earth pigments with barium, strontium, zinc and sulphur possibly present as a lithopone filler. The browns appear to be burnt umber, as evidenced by the presence of manganese and iron.

Often the blue grey is used to fill in around the perimeter of the picture and reaches to the turnover edges on all sides except the upper left corner. The surface here looks worn, perhaps from slight frame abrasion. The x-ray shows much self-editing, particularly along the outside atmospheric border (ill. 50). These areas appear whiter or denser, and are indicative of lead white mixed in with ochres and umbers to reinforce or eliminate a shape. Near the centre of the painting and the radiograph, a darker contrast is presented. These areas are made up of less dense paint or less lead white mixed in the ochres, umbers and blacks.

There remain instances of ground showing throughout the centre. This gives an idea of the first state: some of these forms and lines became final, while Mondrian would revisit others once if not twice. In a second round of application, Mondrian applied a layer of bold glossy black lines with a broader brush, particularly visible in the centre of the image (ill. 49.B). At the same time he may have scraped back or wiped back areas with a rag soaked in solvent (ill. 49.C). There is evidence of scraping and rubbing as well as some drying cracks in the upper layer where the bottom layer was not yet dry. Simultaneously he began to reinforce some of the forms with a thicker application of paint using brushes and a palette knife in both vertical and horizontal motions. These upper layers are more robust, more forceful and heavy bodied, using broad brush-strokes without hesitation.

There is evidence that he later returned to this picture between exhibitions. It appears to have been reworked while already in its frame. There is obvious paint build-up 1.5 cm in from the turnover edge in the lower left corner and up along the left side. Here Mondrian was butting up against the edge of a rebated bronze frame that was already in place. He scraped back the paint to the ground and original black lines in some areas. Using a palette knife he then reapplied, smearing over black lines and blurring forms at all four corners, both smoothing and ripping the paint surface with an upper layer of blue grey and ochre grey. In the upper left, paint has built up in a serrated tooth-like pattern. There are two areas on the centre left side where it appears as though something stuck to the surface and pulled the paint away. This may have been Mondrian trying to manipulate the surface when it was a bit too dry. On the other hand, the wet-on-wet technique can clearly be seen and in some areas he worked back down into a lower layer blending one colour with another in a single stroke. In the lower right, he seems to have at least partially painted out his signature and then repainted it at completion.

Mondrian continued to paint nearer to the centre using thick, heavy-bodied yellow ochres in some areas, perhaps inadvertently pulling the underlying texture to the surface, leaving some areas thick and texturally disturbed, while others still show evidence of the original dilute wash-like state. An occasional third application of black lines is evident at the surface and mix with the upper most layer wet-on-wet. This last layer – the highlights in the work – consists of raw umbers with white. Here Mondrain plays with the textures and paints in zigzag and swirling motions to create a shimmering appearance. The brushstroke direction is deliberate and immediate with a sense of urgency, like he is trying to capture a moment. At first glance the overall effect appears sloppy, but closer examination reveals that he was extremely restrained.

With one to three applications of black, the paint does not generally appear cracked. With two thin layers, drying cracks can often be seen as Mondrian worked very quickly and possibly with a drying oil or siccative. Where the black picks up yellow ochre, the stroke begins to crack immediately. There are also drying cracks throughout the picture in the upper layers of thin-wash yellow paint. There are mechanical cracks down the left side of the picture, and cracks radiating out from the lower left and upper right corners. There is also a large radial crack in the upper centre that may be the result of a tap to the reverse of the canvas. Reflected infrared shows that Mondrian cancelled as many circle segments as he maintained. Diagonal, horizontal and vertical lines pass freely through objects (ill. 51). Under ultraviolet-induced visible fluorescence the ground on the tacking margins looks very yellow green (ill. 52). The x-ray confirms this, showing a multitude of adjustments that are now concealed by top layers, that appear red-brown and grey-violet under ultraviolet light (ill. 50).

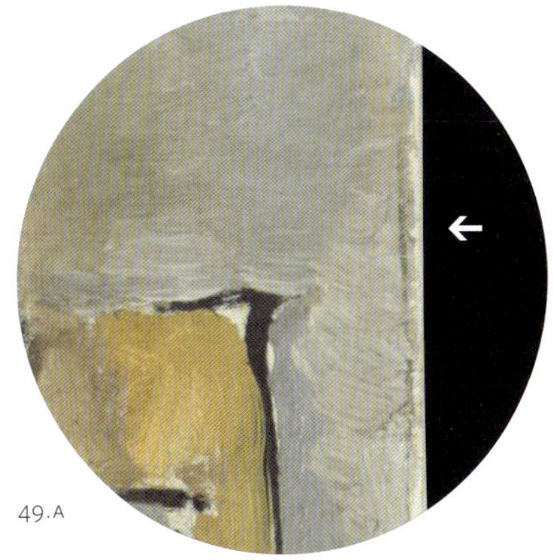
49.A

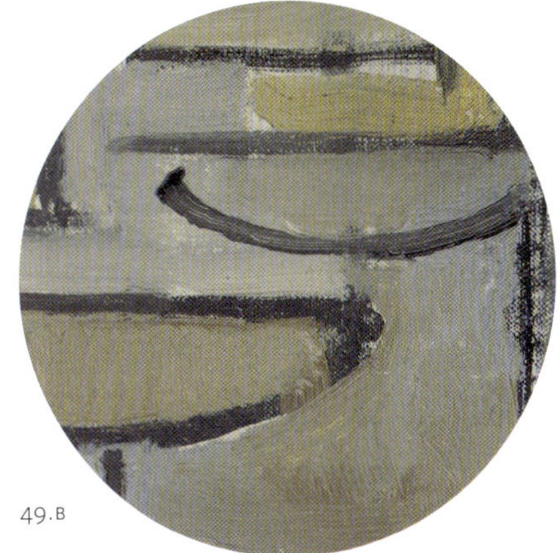
49.B

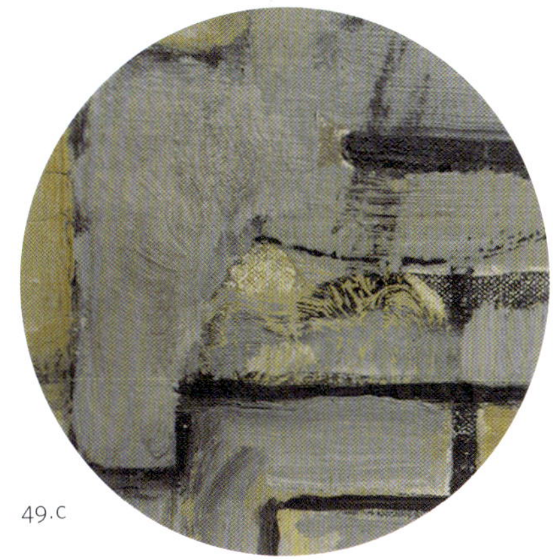
49.C

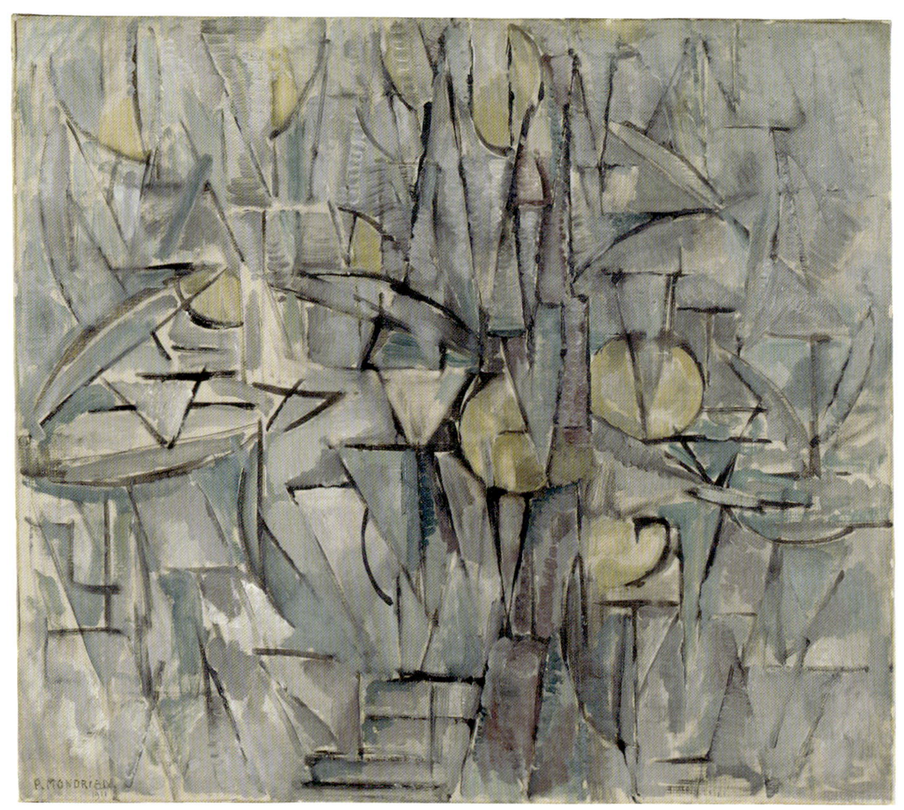

Composition No. X 1912–13
(B25)
Oil on canvas, 65.5 x 75.7 cm
Museum Folkwang, Essen

Since this painting could not be subjected to technical analysis, the information presented here is based mainly on that supplied by Joop M Joosten and Robert P Welsh, *Piet Mondrian: Catalogue Raisonné of the Work of 1911–1944*, vol.2, Prestel, Munich, 1998; as well as the other sources quoted.

Inscriptions
Front: signed lower left in black paint: MONDRiAN.

Back: on the canvas, in pencil: P. MONDRiAN. On the upper stretcher bar, in blue paint with a broad brush, over a previous notation in thinly applied black paint: COMPOSiTION NO. X.

Relevant markings by others
Below the signature on the front, written in pencil: 1911 [probably by HP Bremmer after he bought the painting at the Walrecht exhibition in 1914].

Framing
We may assume that Mondrian framed this painting when it was exhibited at Kunsthandel Walrecht. Since no traces of bronze paint have been found along the edges of the painting, it can be assumed that it was framed with an unpainted, bare wooden frame.

Date
We cannot rule out the possibility that Mondrian was already working on this composition in November 1911 and that he continued to work on this, and other compositions, until spring 1913 before arriving at his 'own way of expressing' himself, as he called it.

It would seem logical that after meeting HP Bremmer at the opening of the Moderne Kunst Kring exhibition in November 1913, and Bremmer's purchase of *Composition NO. X* at Kunsthandel Walrecht, Mondrian spoke to him at length at some point. Mondrian may have indicated then or later that he had been working on this composition from the late autumn of 1911. This may have prompted Bremmer to date the work accordingly. Mondrian must have regarded the painting as finished in spring 1913.

Provenance
HP Bremmer bought the painting at the Kunsthandel Walrecht exhibition in 1914. It was acquired by the Eugen und Agnes von Waldthausen-Platzhoff Museums-Stiftung in 1957 for Museum Folkwang, Essen.

Painted surface
The striking building blocks of this composition are narrow, vertically oriented triangles, as artist and critic Cor Blok remarked in 1972. But small sections of circle can also be seen, particularly towards the edges, bringing direction, rhythm and movement to the composition, as well as a spatial quality, as in an exuberant bunch of overblown tulips. The colours are predominantly bluish-green and bluish-purple. Towards the outer edges the relationship between colour planes and lines becomes more relaxed and open. The brushstrokes go in all directions and partially blur the lines. This blurring makes the composition appear to recede from the edges slightly.

Towards the centre the composition becomes more dense, forming a compact and cohesive area of thickened black lines and shapes. The colour is also deepest here, and the horizontal brushstrokes are neatly organised. This gives the composition a layered appearance that also suggests depth. Only towards the top is the paint bulked with white, wet-on-wet, adding a touch of incident light to the suggestion of depth. Here and there round forms in bright, light yellow are strikingly present. Joosten pointed out that the composition was not based on a flowering apple tree, but that it was more likely to be based on a drawing like *Rhododendrons* (1910) or the painting of the same theme – now lost – that Mondrian executed in 1910.

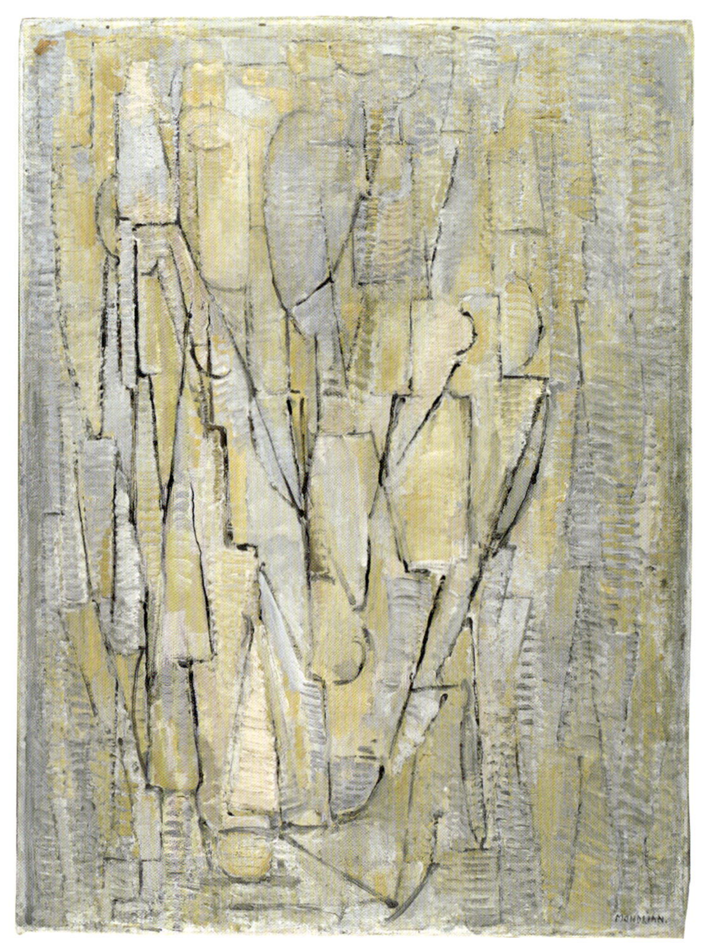

Composition NO. XI 1913
(B31)
Oil on canvas, 76 x 57.5 cm
Kröller-Müller Museum, Otterlo

Since this painting could not be removed from its frame during research, the information presented here is based partly on that provided by Joop M Joosten and Robert P Welsh, *Piet Mondrian: Catalogue Raisonné of the Work of 1911–1944*, vol.2, Prestel, Munich, 1998, and on condition reports from the Kröller-Müller Museum, Otterlo, consulted on 21 October 2013.

Inscriptions
Front: signed bottom right in black paint: MONDRiAN

Back: on the top half of the canvas in blue paint, with a broad brush: MONDRiAN.; on the stretcher, top bar, in blue paint with a broad brush over an earlier inscription, partially covered with grey-white paint: COMPOSiTiON N:XI. On the stretcher, along the top of the right bar, a partially torn off label, with a printed inscription inside an angular, decorative edging: Ku[nsthandel] W. Walrecht | [Smid]splein | ['s-Gra]venhage. Written on the label in black ink: [P.] Mond[riaan] | [Co]mposition No. [partly torn away] | 75 x [57] | *f* 100,- (ill. 60; p.123).

Stretcher
The stretcher is original, in view of the inscriptions and the label from Kunsthandel Walrecht. It has been firmly keyed out, so the joints between the bars no longer form a complete right angle. Extra bars c.3 mm wide have been added along the top and bottom of the stretcher. Tacks are missing along the sides at the top and bottom. The canvas here is also relatively deformed. Raking light photographs show that the canvas was not evenly stretched along the right-hand side at the time of painting (ill. 56; p.122). There is no evidence on the tacking margins that the painting was removed from the stretcher and then re-stretched using new tack holes. However, the tacking margins do have small holes from thin wire nails that were probably used to attach a frame to the stretcher. On the left there are five such holes, at the top there are two, to the right there are five and on the bottom there are four, as revealed in a report of August 2000 in the archives of the Kröller-Müller Museum. The tacking margin in one corner was attached on the back using a drawing pin. This was removed during a treatment in 2004 and replaced by regular and proper tacks.

The canvas has a white ground of unknown composition, and was probably commercially primed. The ground is thin and fairly regular, and the canvas structure has not been entirely filled, so the weave of the linen is still clearly visible. The canvas has a plain weave. The average thread density of the weave is 21 horizontal threads and 21 vertical threads per cm, as revealed in a January 2004 study by conservator Devi Ormond, consulted in the archives of the Kröller-Müller Museum. The ground extends to the very edges of the canvas, except along the bottom, where a selvedge can be seen. There, primary cusping (the result of sizing and/or priming that was done on an earlier occasion and on another – presumably much bigger – stretcher than the present one) extend deep into the weave of the canvas (c.35 cm). The presence of the selvedge and of the primary cusping suggests that the canvas was commercially primed.

Framing
The current rebated frame with a c.8 mm rebate is new. There are traces of bronze paint on the paint surface that can be linked to this new frame. Notably, the paint surface along the edges – reworked by Mondrian at a late stage of the painting's genesis – displays no paint edging, nor any flattened layers of paint that might be associated with a rebated frame. Given the holes that suggest the use of thin wire nails along the tacking margins, the painting could have been framed in an unpainted wooden strip frame that lay flush with the painted surface.

Date
The painting is said to have been exhibited at the Salon des Indépendants in March 1913 under the title *Femme*, and it would make sense to assume that it must have been completed in the early months of 1913. HP Bremmer dated the painting to 1911 in the Kröller-Müller catalogue of 1917. It may be assumed that Mondrian gave him this date. We can therefore conclude that Mondrian was working on this composition for at least a considerable part of, if not all of, 1912.

Provenance
Helene Kröller-Müller purchased the painting from Willem Walrecht in 1916. This suggests that Walrecht bought it during or after the exhibition at his gallery. In 1937 it was incorporated into the collection of the Kröller-Müller Museum in Otterlo.

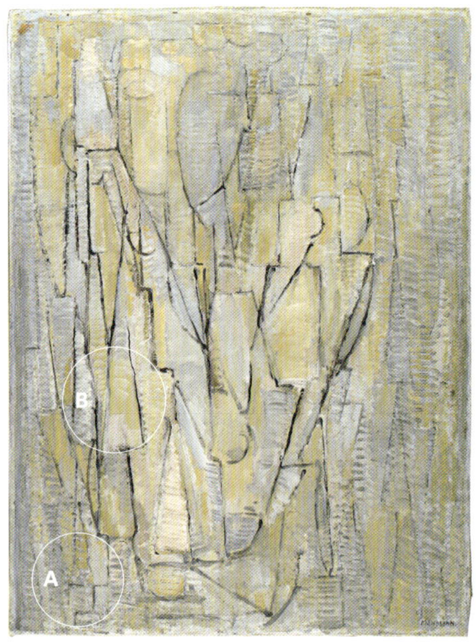

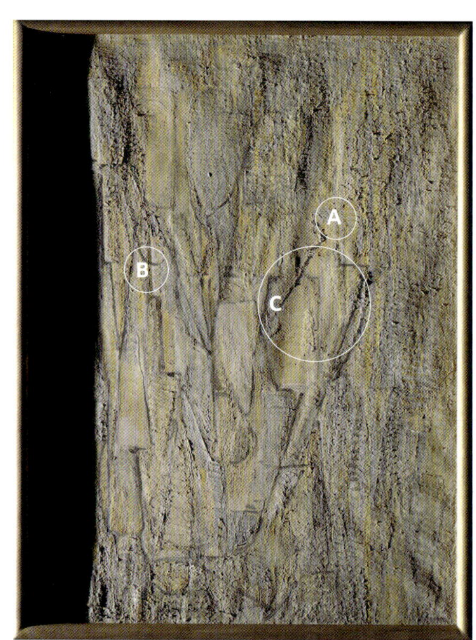

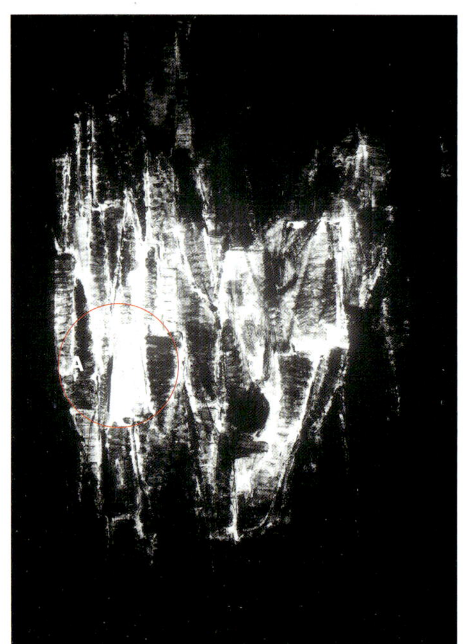

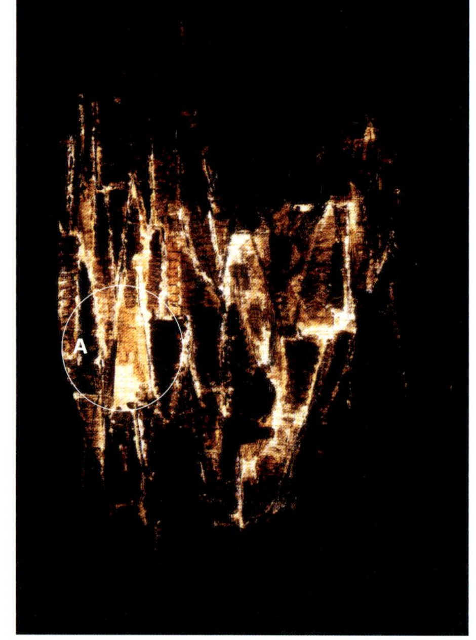

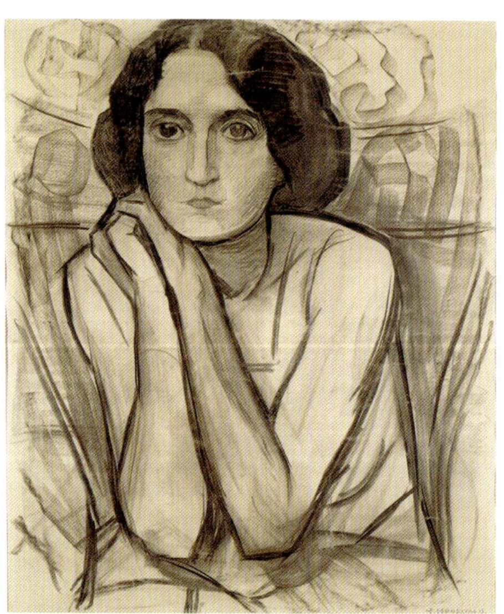

55 Normal light photograph with indications of details

56 Raking light photograph with indications of details

57 Transmitted infrared photograph with indication of a detail

58 Transmitted light photograph with indication of a detail

59 *Vrouw op haar ellebogen leunend* (Woman Leaning on her Elbows), 1908-09
Charcoal on paper, 75 x 63 cm
Gemeentemuseum Den Haag, The Hague

Painted surface

The paint is thick and shows impasto (ill. 56.A). The layers applied last display many drying cracks, which might indicate that the layers below were not fully hardened when they were applied. Along the side and bottom edges the picture ends with separate horizontal brush-strokes in dark grey and white (ill. 55.A). In this process, the strip of unpainted canvas along the bottom that was created when the stretcher was extended by 3 mm along the bottom was covered with paint. It could be that the late addition of the grey was associated with the expansion of the stretcher along the top and bottom. Along the top, the picture was extended with touches of ochre and light grey after the 3 mm strip was added. The composition was initially built up with black lines applied with a thin brush. Mondrian worked on the basis of a drawing that is currently known as *Woman Leaning on her Elbows*, demonstrated by art historian Marco Entrop in 2003 to be a portrait of Eva de Beneditty (ill. 59). The hesitant black lines follow the contour of the shoulders, the hands and the head, and these elements are echoed in the adjacent individual line fragments, curves and ovals. The raking light photograph shows that most of the black lines lie significantly lower than the thick paint with which the planes have been filled. (ills 56, 56.B).

It is difficult to see how the composition was built up, but the planes between the lines must have been filled with light grey and off-white (ill. 55.B). The transmitted light image shows that the centre of the composition is thinly painted and includes few repeated passages (ills 58, 58.A). This is confirmed by the image taken in transmitted infrared light (ills 57, 57.A). Over this, Mondrian applied thicker white, ochre and grey, with no systematic regard for the underlying colour. Some black lines were sacrificed in this process. Afterwards, certain lines were applied over the paint that was still partly wet. Mondrian then set to work in detail, harmonising the different planes using ochre, grey and dark grey. In this passage, he used many mixtures of white and grey, grey and ochre, and ochre and white (ill. 56.C). Bright yellow ochre was added at a very late stage.

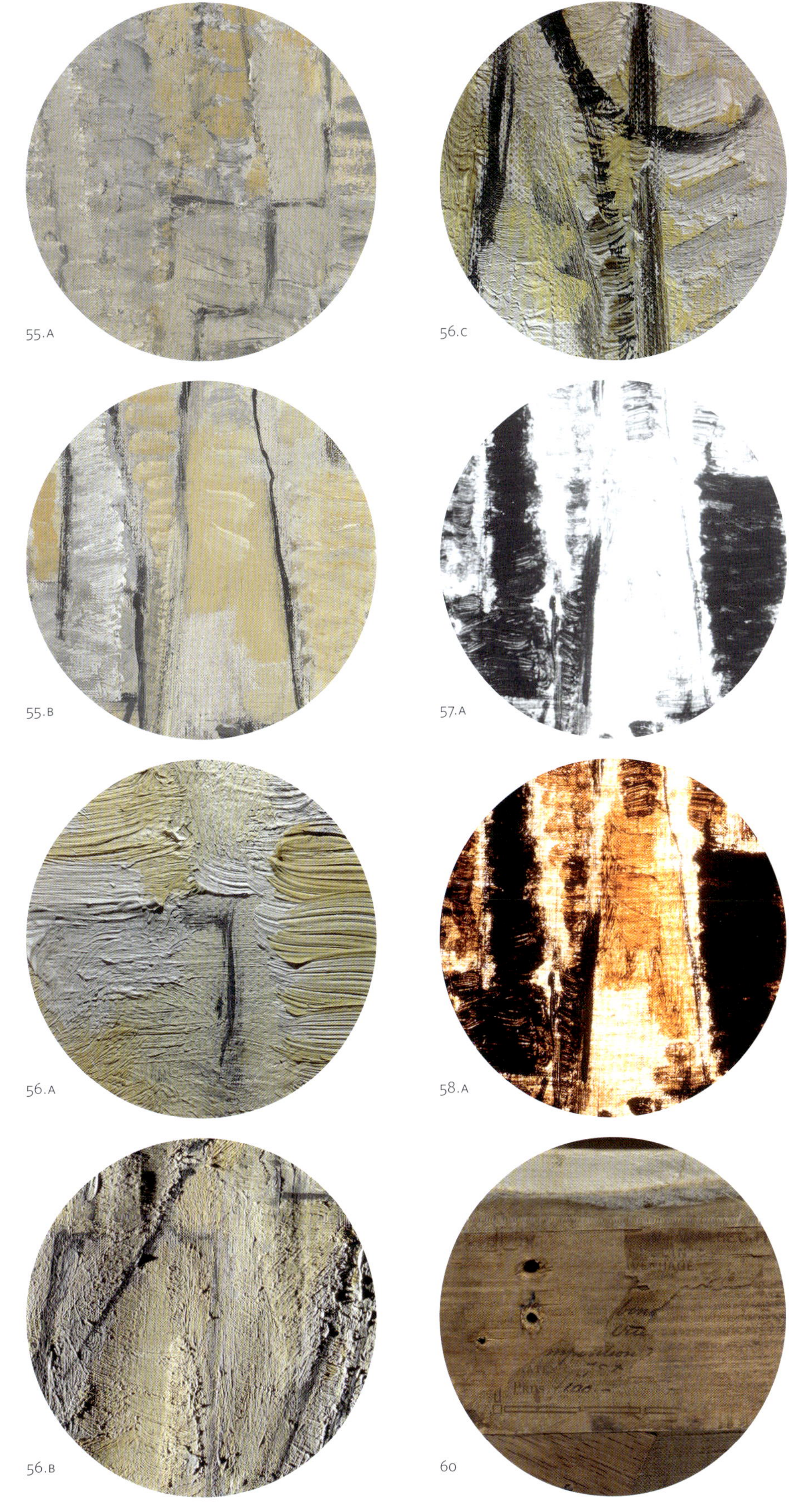

55.A

56.C

55.B

57.A

56.A

58.A

56.B

60

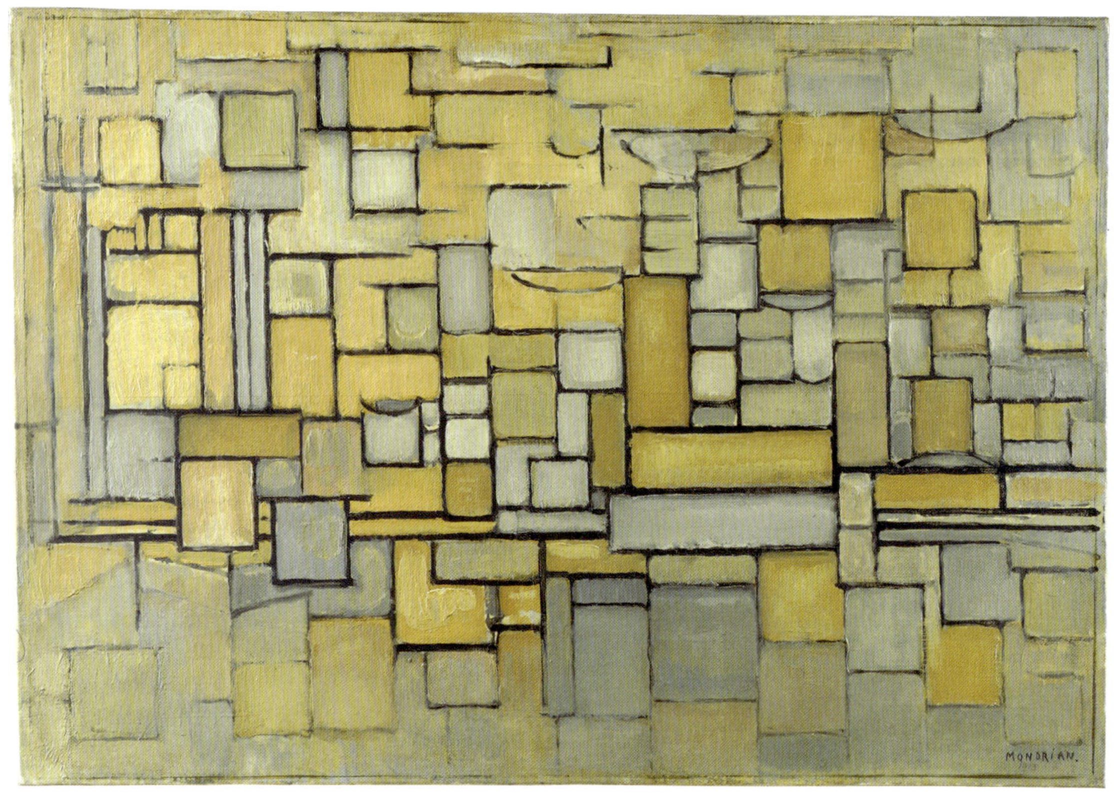

Composition NO. XII 1913
(B40 – Gemälde NO. I / Compositie NO. XII)
Oil on canvas, 64 x 94 cm
Private collection, New York

Inscriptions

Front: signed bottom right in black paint: MONDRİAN.

Back: left, on the canvas: nom | P. Mondrian, with a narrow brush, in thinly painted black paint; in the same manner, right, on the canvas: titre | Gemälde NO. I [struck through with black paint using a narrow brush]; on the top stretcher bar, in blue paint with a broad brush: COMPOSITION NO. XII and, more to the right: - HAUT [in blue paint with a broad brush over an earlier inscription in black paint obscured with grey-white paint: Oben]. Next to this, in blue paint, with a broad brush: MONDRIAN. On the left stretcher bar a partially torn off printed label: KUN [torn away] and beneath that, surrounded by an edging, in typeface: Künstler: ...| Titel: ... | Besitzer: ... | Katalog-Nr.: ... [torn away]. It is not clear when this label was applied and it is also unclear to which exhibition or relocation it refers. An illegible customs stamp is also visible on the left bar.

Relevant markings made by others

Beneath the signature, in pencil, someone has written: 1913 - this was probably HP Bremmer in preparation for the Kunsthandel Walrecht exhibition in 1914. Joosten suggests that the date might have been applied in reference to the catalogue of the Kröller-Müller collection published by Bremmer in 1921, in which *Composition NO. X* is also listed and dated as 1911. *Composition NO. XII*, like *Composition NO. X* and *Composition NO. XVI*, has a date written in pencil just beneath the signature on the front. This suggestion is based on a letter to Joosten from 20 September 1973, in which Floris Bremmer gives an account of sales of Mondrian's paintings brokered by his father.

Stretcher

The pine stretcher is original and the canvas does not appear to have been removed from the stretcher (ill. 61). The bars are 5.3 cm wide; the vertical central bar is 5 cm wide. The bars are not bevelled on their inward edge. The stretcher has been keyed out evenly on all sides over a distance of about 3 mm in a vertical direction. A pencil line on the left side shows where the tacking edge was trimmed.

Framing

We may assume that Mondrian framed this painting when it was exhibited at Kunsthandel Walrecht. Since traces of bronze paint have been found c.8 cm from the edges of the painted surface, we can assume that the painting was in a frame painted in a bronze colour with a rebated edge that overlapped the painting's surface. It appears that Mondrian treated the frame twice, with differently coloured bronze paint (ill. 62).

Date

The reconstruction of events shows that Mondrian worked on the painting from spring 1913. He must have completed it before it went to Berlin in summer 1913 for an exhibition that ran there from September to December. In January 1914 it returned from Berlin or Munich. After its return, in May 1914, Mondrian will have made some alterations to the painting before sending it to The Hague for the exhibition at Kunsthandel Walrecht.

Provenance

HP Bremmer bought the painting at the Kunsthandel Walrecht exhibition. He kept it until 1950, when it appeared on the New York art market. It was bought by a private collector at an auction at Sotheby's in 1989.

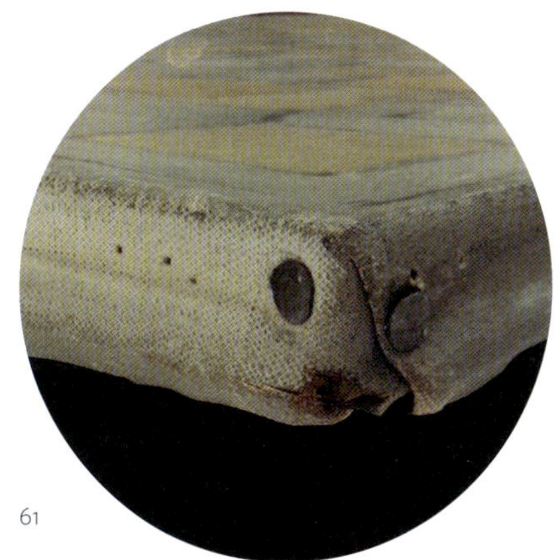

61

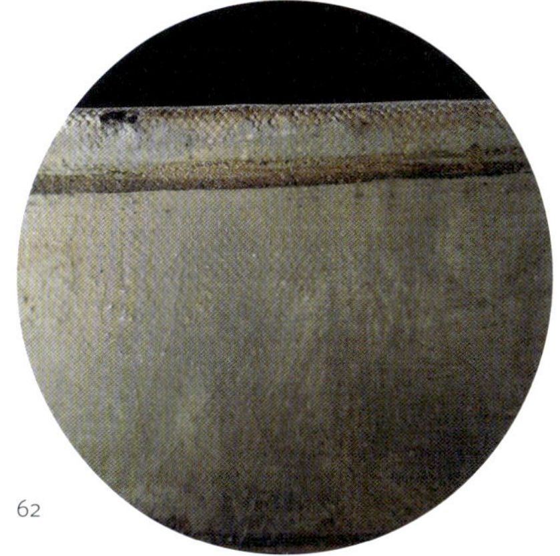

62

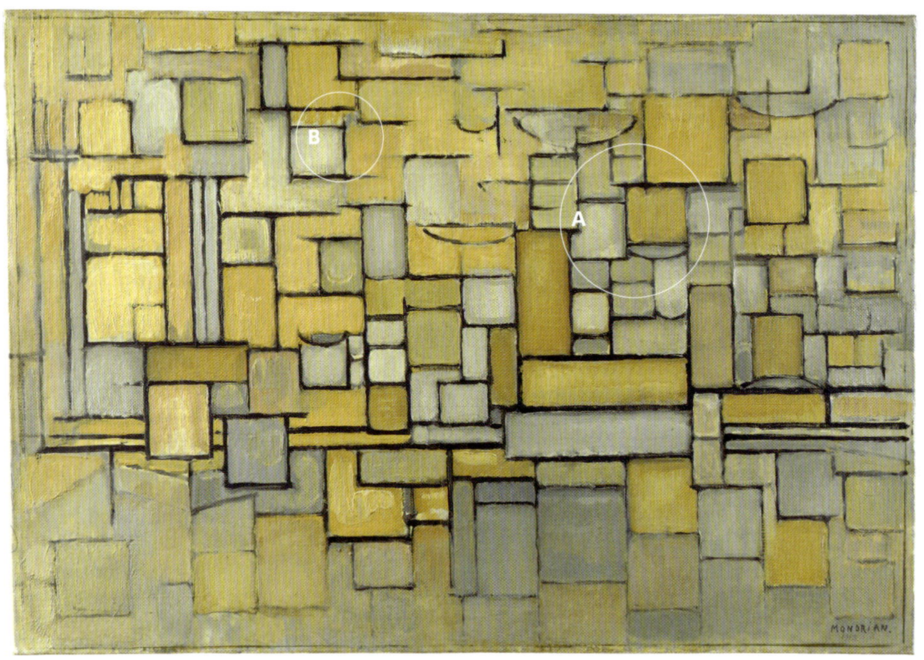

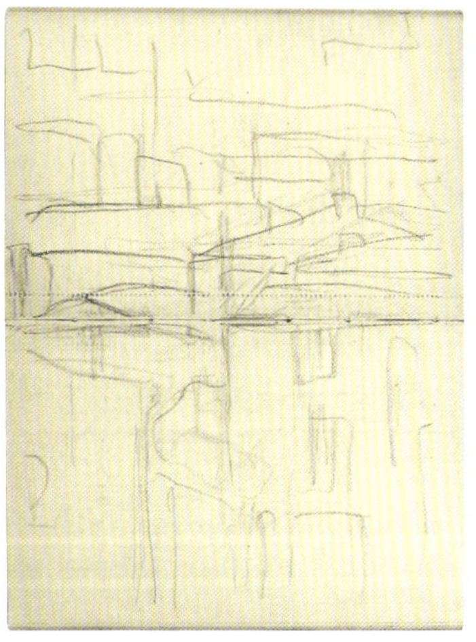

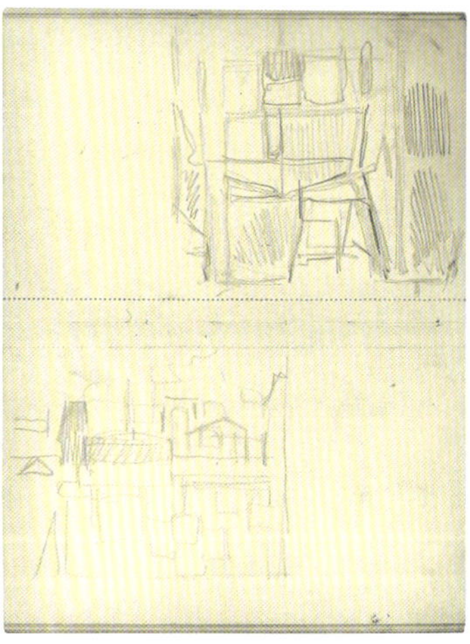

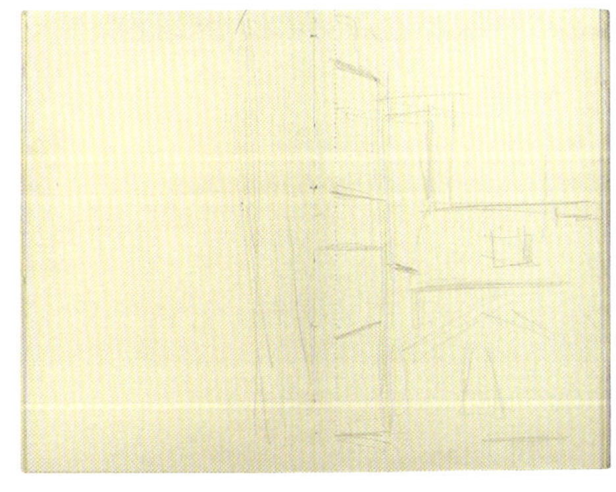

63 Normal light with indications of details

64 *Demolished Building* (Sketchbook II, Folio 26), early 1914
Pencil on paper, 10,5 x 17,2 cm
The Solomon R. Guggenheim Museum, New York,
Gift of David Finn and Maurice Kaplan

65 *Paris Roofs* (Sketchbook II, Folio 25), early 1914
Pencil on paper, 10,5 x 17,2 cm
The Solomon R. Guggenheim Museum, New York,
Gift of David Finn and Maurice Kaplan

66 *Paris Roofs* (Sketchbook II, Folio 17a/b), early 1914
Pencil on paper, 21,0 x 17,2 cm
The Solomon R. Guggenheim Museum, New York,
Gift of David Finn and Maurice Kaplan

Painted surface

The bottom half of the painting is fairly dark, with lines and forms much more blurred and less sharply defined in relation to each other in comparison to those in the top of the painting. The colours are also less articulated and fade to grey. Along the top, by contrast, the composition has a clear structure in terms of colour and line, with firmly applied and tightly outlined squares in strong ochres that provide restful interludes in a field of fragmentary, loosely linked visual elements (ill. 63.A). The brushstrokes at the top are mainly vertical, while towards the bottom the brushwork is bristly and velvety, and also diffuse in tone, with ochres that shine through gradations of grey. The grey and ochre appear to be harmonised in such a way that the ochre passages seem to come forward through the grey, though the picture could be read the other way round, with the ochre planes as 'gaps' and the grey planes having a more material presence.

It would appear that Mondrian first began by applying thin black lines with a thin brush, and there are occasional indications that the lines were lightly scoured away, exposing the white of the tips of the weave (ill. 63.B). Mondrian then filled the planes with bright, light grey and light ochre. He then began to shift and adjust, mostly effecting changes in colour across the centre: from almost red ochre to dark grey to light grey, from dark grey to red ochre to grey ochre, and from grey to yellow ochre or vice versa. In this process lines were also painted over fields of colour (ill. 67). In the top half of the composition, several gradations of one or more colours were used to fill some fields, creating an illusionary 'shadow effect'. For instance, a lick of yellow ochre has been placed along the bottom of a grey plane, and dark grey along a light grey plane, light beige over dark grey or light ochre over grey ochre. This produces a lively spatial image. Strictly defined monochrome squares and rectangles were placed throughout the composition between the planes of colour with this shadow effect.

The curves also appear as autonomous visual elements formulated in an isolated fashion. They have the air of notation, like a note in a musical composition. It seems that here, for the first time, Mondrian is exchanging the connection between line and form – what Cézanne and Picasso called '*passage*', the intermingling of lines and forms to create illusionary worlds – for the sovereign form of the strictly defined visual element. From that moment on, one no longer perceives a world when looking at a painting, one perceives a structure. Interestingly, in 1917 HP Bremmer described the painting as an 'abstract composition in rectangles of various sizes and shapes, in yellow and grey'. It seems likely that this wording echoed conversations he had about the painting with Mondrian, in 1913 or 1914.

Just below the centre, where the horizontal line fragments grow more dense at the surface, a few diagonal lines show through the paint surface to the left and right. These are remains of rooflines as can be seen in sketches that Mondrian made from spring 1913 onwards from the window of his studio, as he observed the view of haphazard buildings adjacent to Gare Montparnasse (ills 64, 65, 66). WFA Roëll, correspondent of *Het Vaderland*, described a visit to Mondrian's studio in 1924: 'Amidst a Paris fading into autumn it seems here always to be a happy Whit weekend. Modern life blows in through two windows: trains thunder by, sirens wail, immensely high, brutally interrupted multi-storied blocks of housing alternate with higgledy-piggledy sawtooth roofs.' The diagonal lines are only discernible still; they are not part of the fabric of the composition. In the part where they are visible the black lines are actually thickest at the surface. Above that the lines are more open, fading towards the bottom.

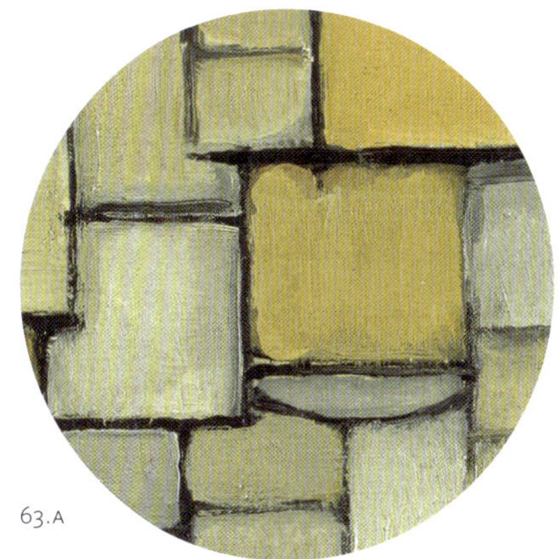

63.A

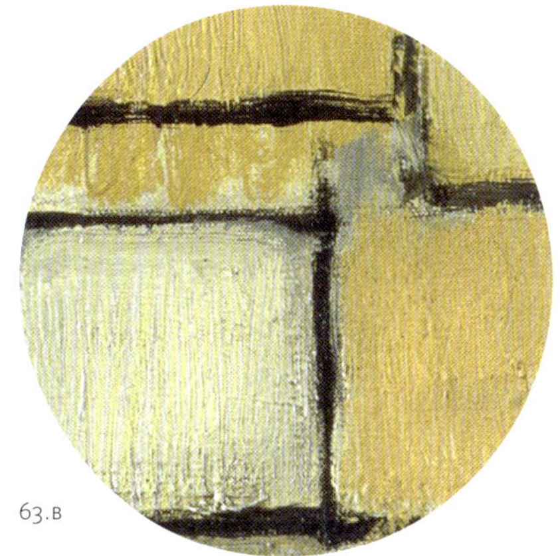

63.B

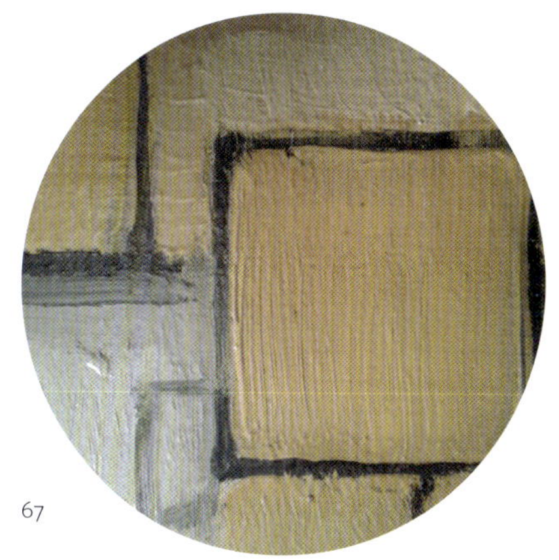

67

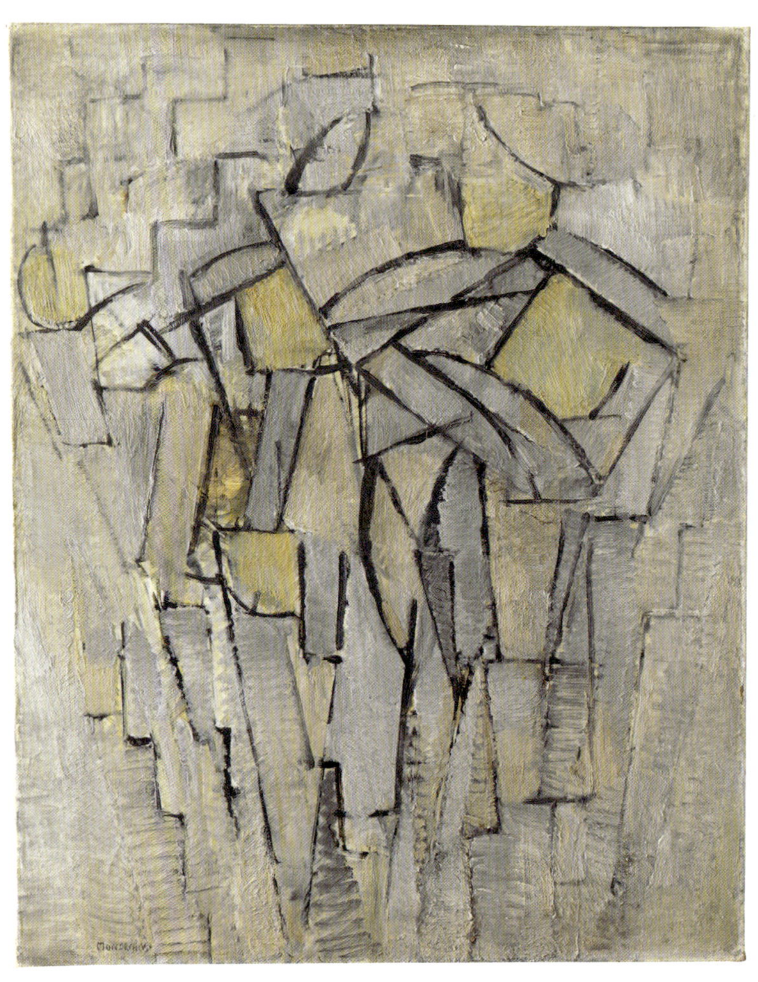

Composition NO. XIII 1913
(B28 – Compositie NO. XIII / Compositie 2)
Oil on canvas, 79.5 x 63.5 cm
Museo Thyssen-Bornemisza, Madrid

Since this painting could not be subjected to technical analysis, the information presented here is based mainly on that supplied by Joop M Joosten and Robert P Welsh, *Piet Mondrian: Catalogue Raisonné of the Work of 1911–1944*, vol.2, Prestel, Munich, 1998; as well as other sources quoted.

Inscriptions
Front: signed bottom left in black paint: MONDRİAN.

Back: on the canvas, in thinly painted black paint: compositie 2 [struck out with black paint] | P. Mondriaan. On the new stretcher, with the same dimensions as the original stretcher – judging by the painted surface – a partially removed sticker with black ink: Mondrian.

Framing
The bronze-coloured traces on the left and bottom edges of the paint surface indicate that the original frame was painted a bronze colour and had a rebated edge that partially covered the edge of the painting (ill. 68.A).

Date
We cannot rule out the possibility that Mondrian was already working on this composition in November 1911 and that he continued to work on this and other compositions before arriving at his 'own way of expressing' himself. On the back of a photograph of this painting that Mondrian sent to Ben Nicholson in 1937 is a handwritten inscription in Mondrian's hand: 'Eucaliptus / 1911'. It seems likely that Mondrian regarded the painting as complete in spring 1913. It is possible, however, that he revisited it at the point when he framed it in preparation for the Kunsthandel Walrecht exhibition in 1914.

Provenance
The painting was not sold at Kunsthandel Walrecht. After October 1915 it was acquired by Marie Tak van Poortvliet. After it passed through several private collections, it was acquired in 1992 by Baron Hans Heinrich Thyssen-Bornemisza of Lugano, whose collection is housed at the Museo Thyssen-Bornemisza, Madrid.

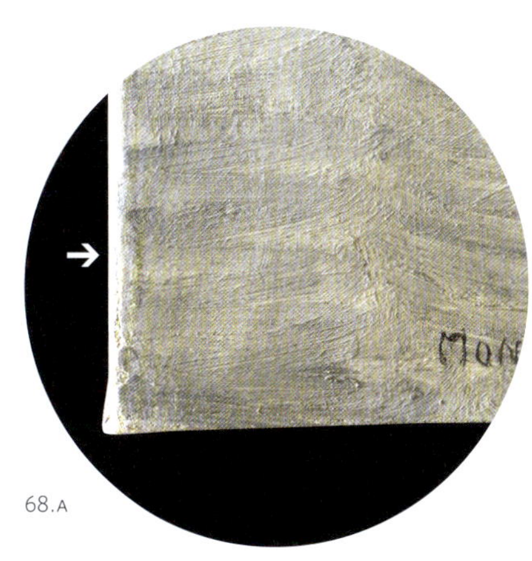

68.A

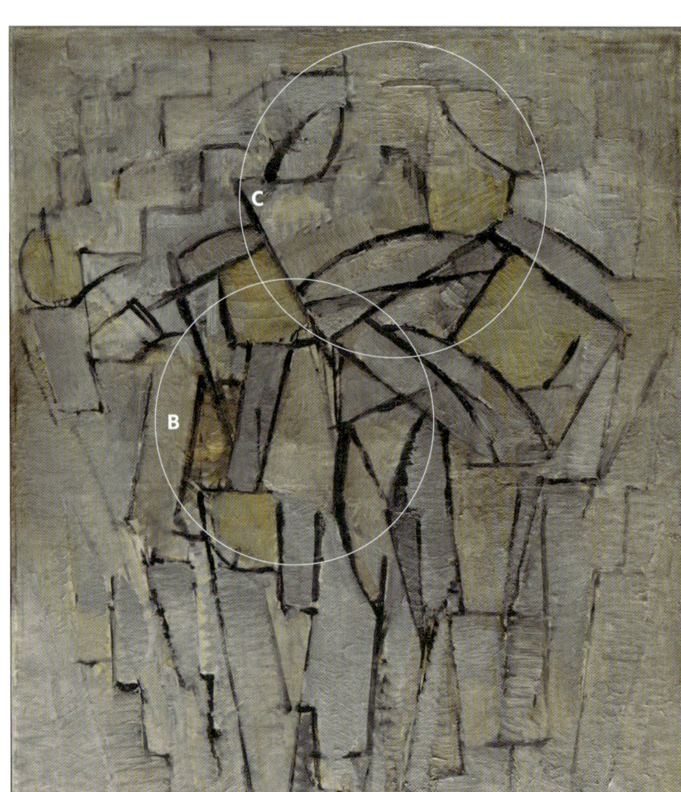

68 Raking light photograph with indications of details

Painted surface

The painting has been worked and reworked, which makes it almost impossible to reconstruct the build-up of the underlying drawing and layers (ill. 68.B). German critic Friedrich Markus Huebner wrote an article in 1921 on Marie Tak van Poortvliet's collection, which included a thorough description of this painting. The colours 'gypsum grey and clay yellow' are captured in a fine weave of short brushstrokes, curvatures, delineated forms and shrouding. Huebner concludes that Mondrian densified his starting point, using the word *versachlicht* with which the Germans are able to indicate so nicely that something is 'objectified' through being turned into an autonomous composition (ill. 68.C).

Mondrian himself indicated that the basis of *Composition XIII* was a drawing of a eucalyptus which he had taken to Paris. However, this has been literally buried under the many base layers and components of elements of the composition from spring 1912, which can be seen, such as the stair-like structure in the top left. Elements from spring 1914 are also visible, including the hasty colouring of irregular yet autonomous planes of yellow. In a strangely geometrical drawing that Mondrian gave as a gift to artist Adriaan Lubbers around 1932, he characteristically highlighted those planes as autonomous entities in the picture. The shadow effect that Mondrian applied in spring 1914 – by placing darker shades of a colour along two or three edges of a plane – can also be seen. It would seem that after the painting had been framed in a bronze frame, Mondrian revisited the edge of the painting, applying ochre along the top and the right edge to create a suggestion of depth (ill. 68.D).

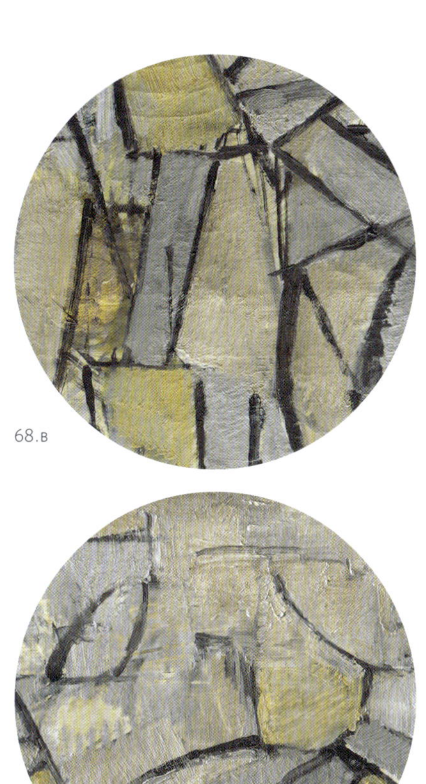

68.B

68.C

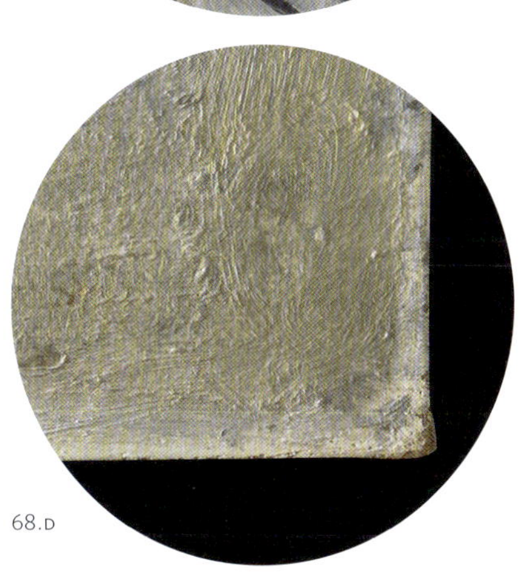

68.D

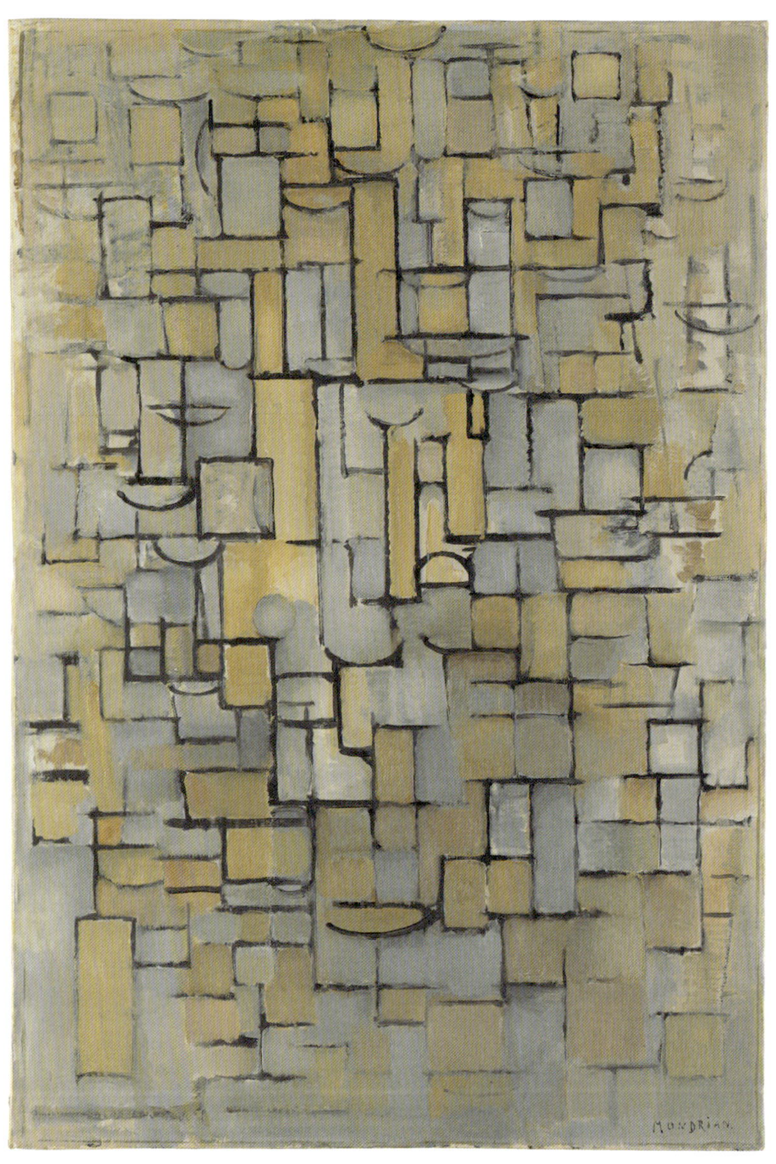

Composition NO. XIV 1913
(B38 – Gemälde NO. I / Compositie NO. XIV)
Oil on canvas, 94 x 65 cm
Van Abbemuseum, Eindhoven

Inscriptions

Front: signed bottom right in black paint: MONDRiAN.

Back: in the centre of the bottom half of the canvas a stamp of Blanchet, 38 rue Bonaparte, Paris; along the bottom in the right half a customs stamp: Douane Bruxelles; along the bottom of the stretcher a Kingdom of the Netherlands customs stamp; on the top half of the canvas, in thinly painted black paint: nom: P. [partially painted out with white paint] MONDRiAN. [picked out in blue paint, using a broad brush]/title: [crossed out in black paint with a broader brush]/Gemälde N:I. [struck through with black paint, using a broad brush]. On the top stretcher bar, in blue paint with a broad brush over an earlier inscription covered with grey-white paint: COMPOSITION N:XIV. Further to the right, in blue ink: SCHIJVEN-ASSENDELFT/ A.M. V. SOLMSLAAN/30/ZEIST. On the central stretcher bar a handwritten inscription on a label [in Mondrian's hand], partially obscured with white paint: P.Mondrian./ titre:/[illegible]. Further to the right, on the left stretcher bar, a Kingdom of the Netherlands customs stamp. On the bottom stretcher bar, in blue paint using a broad brush: 39 [struck out in blue paint using a broad brush]. On the left stretcher bar, in blue chalk: obraz 550 Kor [crossed out in blue paint using a broad brush].

Stretcher

The canvas has a white ground of unknown composition and was probably factory pre-primed. The ground is thin and fairly regular; the canvas structure has not been completely filled so the tips of the threads are clearly visible. The canvas has a plain weave with an average of 21 threads horizontally and 18 threads vertically. (Top right, 3 cm from the top and 4 cm from the right edge: 22h/19v; 21 cm from the top and 22 cm from the right edge: 20h/18v. Bottom left: 12 cm from the left edge and 16 cm from the bottom: 21h/17v; 30 cm from the left edge and 15 cm from the bottom: 20h/17v. This gives an average number of warp threads per cm of 17 with a min/max range of 17 to 18 threads/cm. Average number of weft threads per cm: 20.2 with a min/max range of 20 to 21 threads/cm.) No traces of a palette knife or other tools are visible. The ground extends all the way round the tacking edges. Cusping is visible on the back, along the left edge. The canvas was cut or trimmed in a highly irregular way close to the back of the frame. Tack holes from an earlier stretching are visible along the edges of the canvas. This suggests that the canvas was removed from the stretcher and re-stretched at least once. The stretcher is original and still completely intact. It does not appear to have been enlarged or reduced along the sides.

Framing

Traces of bronze paint can be seen along the edges of the canvas, except for the left edge. This suggests that the painting originally had an overhanging frame painted in a bronze colour. The current frame was probably mounted when the painting was purchased by the Van Abbemuseum, Eindhoven in 1955.

Date

The open, spindly structure of the painting is reminiscent of *Tableau NO. 1*, a painting that must have been completed before the Moderne Kunst Kring exhibition of November–December 1913, and was purchased by HP Bremmer for Helene Kröller-Müller. Bremmer's handwritten catalogue from 1917 of Kröller-Müller's collection gives the year as 1913. It is therefore likely that Mondrian was working on *Composition NO. XIV* in autumn 1913.

Provenance

The painting was sold to Hendrick van Assendelft of Gouda during the Kunsthandel Walrecht exhibition. Since 1955 it has been part of the collection of the Van Abbemuseum.

Painted surface

No clear underdrawing is visible with the naked eye. However, in transmitted infrared light all kinds of loosely organised short fragments of line show up as black lines that absorb infrared (ill. 70; p.134). Some of them can still be discerned on the surface as the black lines bordering the planes. Other fragments are no longer visible on the surface. They cross planes that are still fully or partially visible (ill. 70.A; p.135). Four remnants of long lines projecting upwards from the bottom of the composition are also visible in the transmitted infrared image (ill. 71; p.134). The same image also shows a multitude of curves at the top of the picture, which in the final work have been reduced mainly to horizontal sections of circle with occasional vertical circular sections. Similar curves can also be seen in other places within the final composition. Because of these curves, some connection with the large drawing *Pine Woods* (1906; ill. 72; p.134) may be assumed. In this work, the tall trunks rising to the left have a crown of compact foliage that causes the twinkling of the light seen in the sections of circle. Those in the bottom of the picture could be interpreted as dappled light on the ground.

The strange grey circle shape halfway up *Composition NO. XIV* might suggest a light source, such as the sun or the moon. In this context it is interesting to note a remark made by a reporter from the 24 July 1913 edition of a Munich newspaper, the *Münchener Neueste Nachrichten*, after seeing this painting exhibited with the title *Painting NO. I*. The reviewer wrote that the artist 'draws thick and thin lines, a little like frost flowers across the plane', and wrote *Trees* beneath it. Once again it seems that Mondrian was constantly searching for ways to clarify his aims by informing journalists about his procedures.

Using *Pine Woods* as a starting point, Mondrian might have sketched an initial drawing using thin black paint and a narrow brush. He later partially scraped off or otherwise removed this drawing, as a result of which weave shows through on the more protruding parts of the canvas, and the pigment remains only in the more recessed parts of the weave (ill. 69.A; p.135). It appears that the beginning of the composition was applied to the white ground using black paint that dried with a matt finish, not visible in transmitted infrared (ill. 70; p.134). The planes were then filled. During this process some lines were lost, planes were joined with other planes and new demarcation lines were added between adjacent planes.

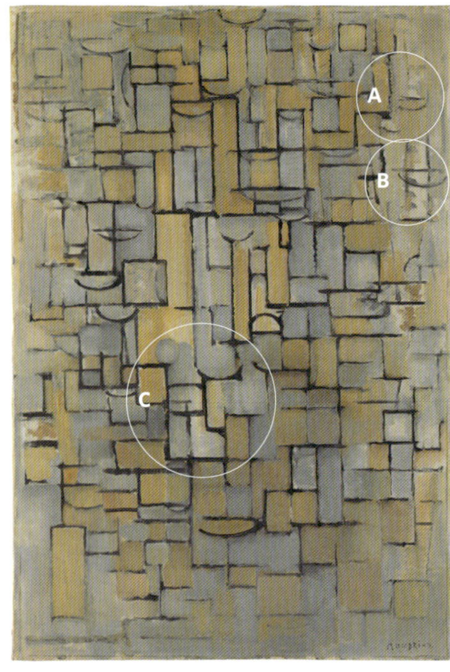

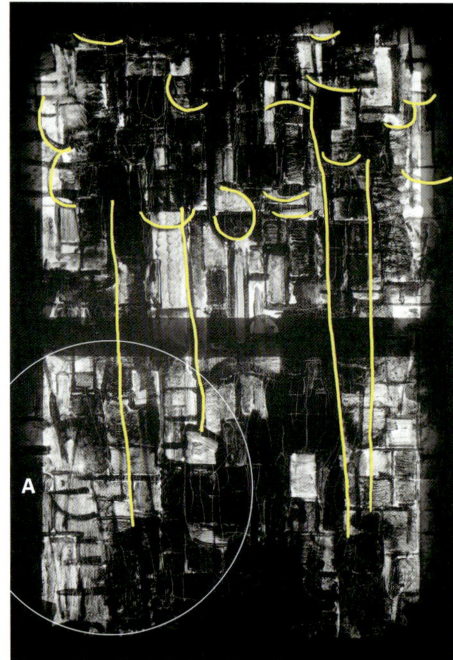

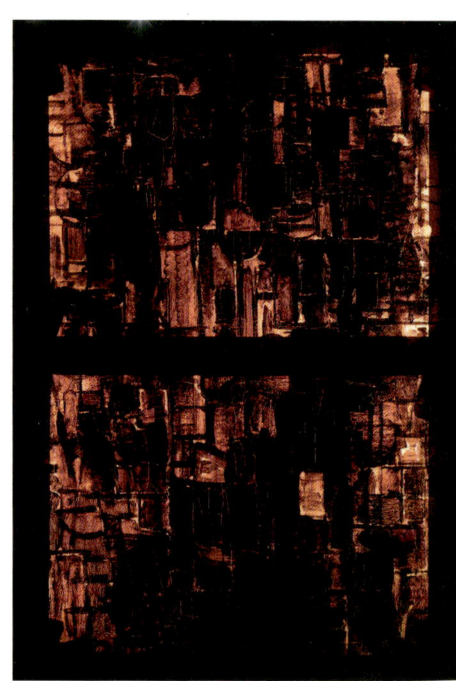

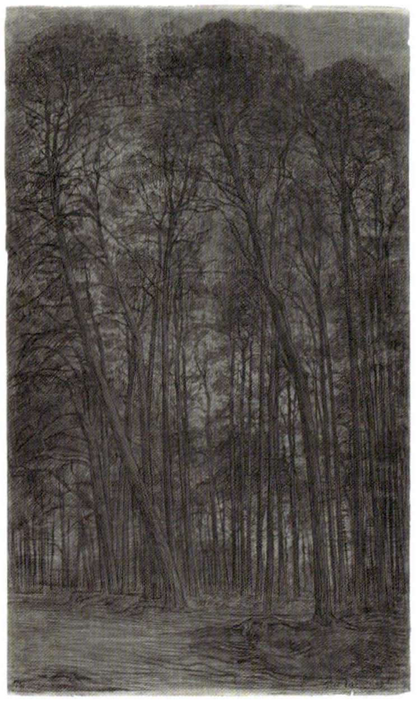

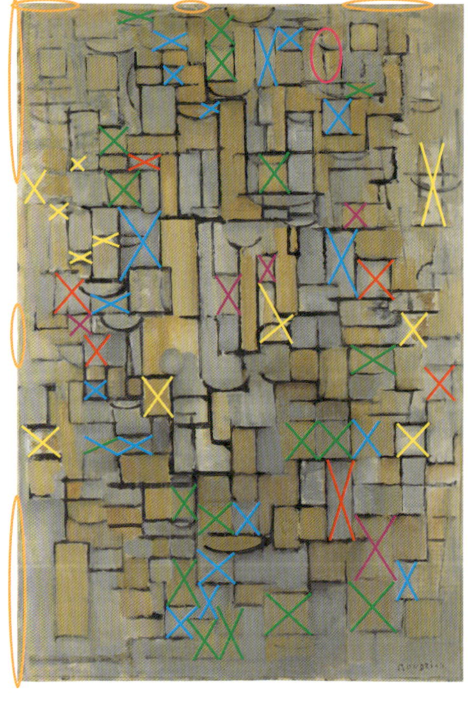

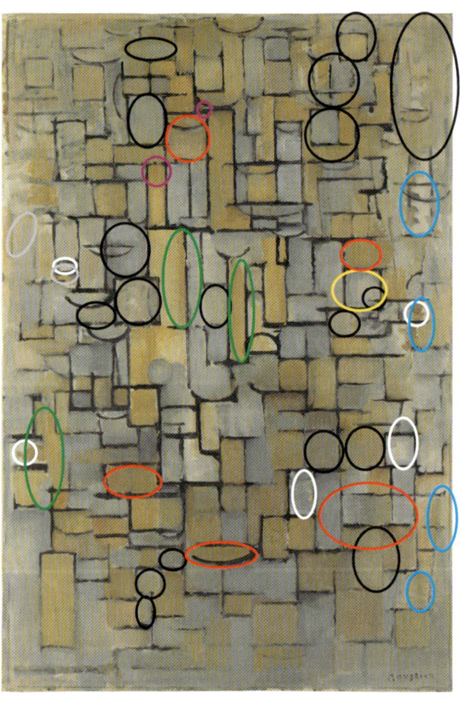

69 Normal light photograph with indications of details

70 Transmitted infrared photograph with indication of a detail

71 Transmitted light photograph

72 *Dennebosch* (Pine Woods), 1906
Black chalk on paper, 111 x 67 cm
Gemeentemuseum Den Haag, The Hague

73 Normal light photograph with indications of details and peculiarities:
- 'White' top layer over complex under layer
- Ochre over grey
- Grey over ochre
- Mixture of grey and ochre
- Light grey over dark grey
- 'Holes' in which there is no paint, or clearly a single layer
- Bronze colour from a protruding frame
- Spots that were probably scraped

74 Normal light photograph with indications of details and peculiarities:
- Intended horizontal brushstrokes
- Late adding of an admixture of ochre in grey
- Black lines still wet when planes where painted
- Hardly touched planes
- Rough touching up with ochre of initial drawing in black
- Fluently zigzagging brushstroke in ochre
- Underdrawing visible
- Grey over ochre touched up with ochre

Once these first layers were dry Mondrian emphasised the line pattern here and there, and also altered or shifted it in some places. The colours were then adjusted, painted over, emphasised and then, in some places - and particularly in the segment to the bottom left - the black lines were emphasised even more prominently. The colour was then adjusted again in places. It appears that Mondrian initially worked with a light grey and bright ochre, fairly drily, and that he attempted to bring the colours and contrasts gradually closer together, resulting in the gradation seen in the painting. In the top part of the composition, particularly in the gradual blend from grey to ochre, there are many drying cracks, which indicates that the changes were made before the underlying layer had properly hardened.

The inclination to the left in the original drawing was partially retained in this process, and can be seen in the eventual composition of lines. This element is further emphasised by the colour. There are 'gatherings' of white on the left, along the edge of the composition (ill. 69.B). This stimulates the leftward inclination of the composition, which for the rest is painted fairly densely, with strange open places here and there that more or less correspond to openings to the sky in the original drawing (ills 71, 72). Generally speaking, however, the densely packed gradations of grey, ochre and white create a closed feeling. In a piece about an exhibition in 1915 where this painting was on display, art critic NH Wolf commented that the grey produced a much finer sensation than in the other works in the exhibition.[13]

The final composition has narrow vertical planes stacked high, some of them ochre, some light, some dark, and others that are grey, again sometimes dark, sometimes light - sometimes so light that the grey and the yellow almost become white, for instance just above the lowest part of the painting, where dark grey and dark yellow planes dominate. Some of the yellow and grey planes in this bottom part are not separated by black lines. Here, the grey and yellow mingle, sometimes more abruptly divided, and sometimes flowing into each other. Along the bottom edge some planes are not outlined by black contours (ill. 73). Although some planes have been applied horizontally, the majority were applied vertically. Towards the top of the painting the colours become lighter and more contrasting, from creamy ochre to bright ochre and even orange ochre, or from light grey to bright metallic grey to grey white (ill. 74).

In certain places it is clear that the colour was filled in while the black lines were still wet, though these might also be places where the black line was augmented when the colour (often ochre) was applied (ill. 69.C). It would seem that a mixture of ochre and grey was applied at a very late stage. The same can be seen along the bottom of the painting, but there the blend is more towards ochre, creating a light brown colour.

Towards the top the composition is more open, with more light grey planes and white. The ochre has been painted in a swirling motion, whereas the grey-whites have been applied in a more staccato or zigzagging manner. This means that in all cases (swirling, staccato, zigzagging) the stroke was horizontal, but also tends slightly to the vertical. Everything is lighter in tone, particularly in the centre, where the contrast between yellow and grey is greatest and the black lines delineate the planes most sharply. Towards the edges (left and right) the grey and white dissolve into each other more and form a brownish yellow.

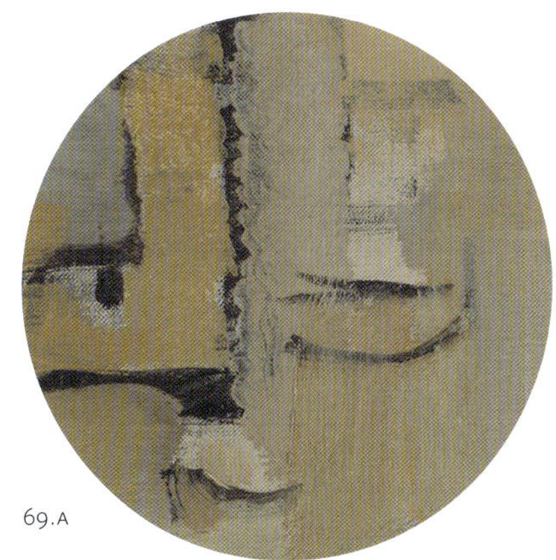
69.A

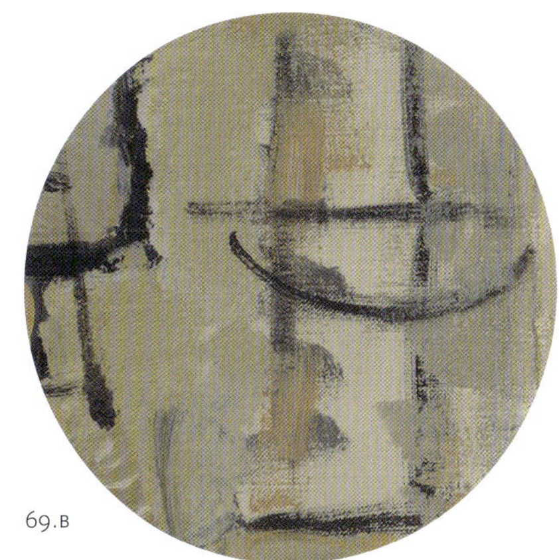
69.B

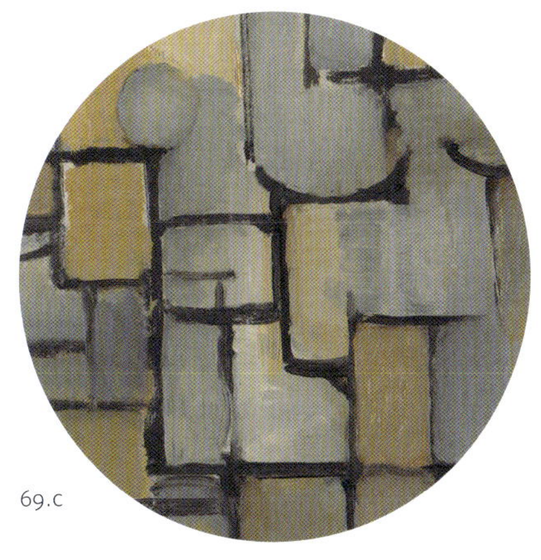
69.C

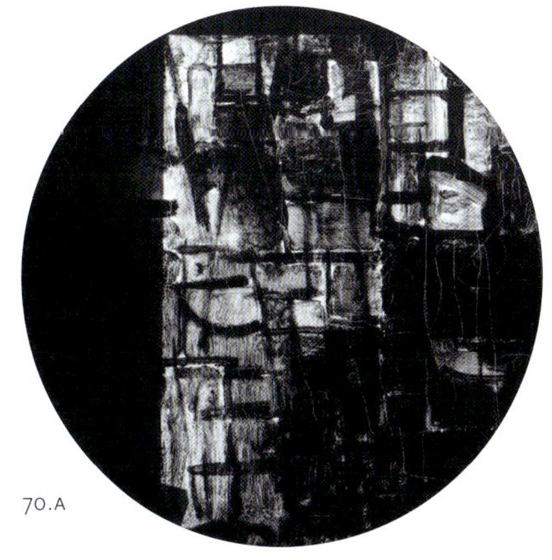
70.A

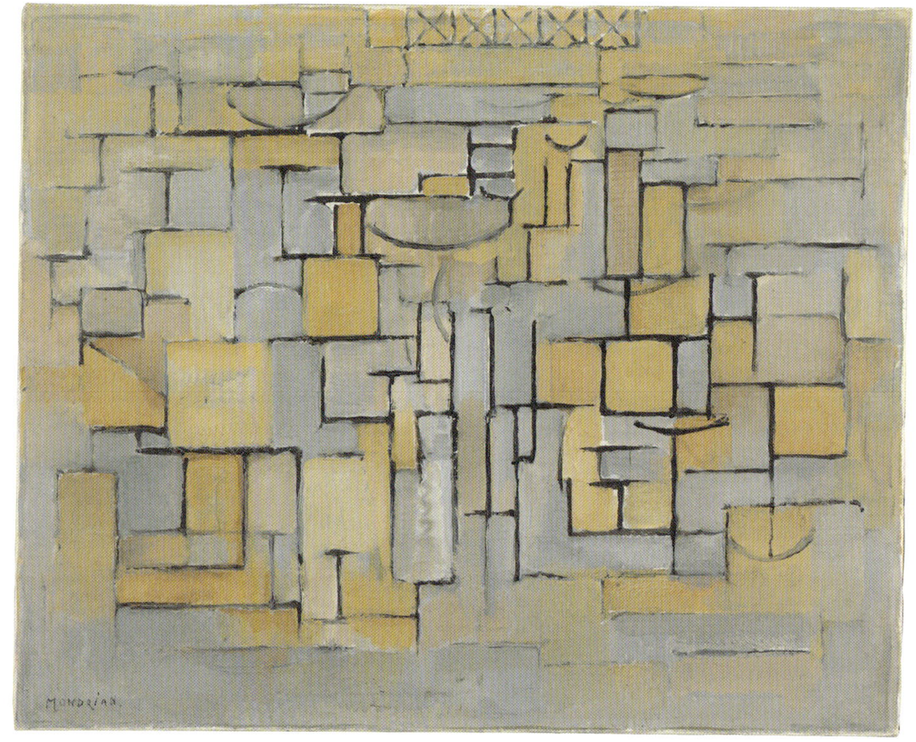

Composition NO. XV 1913
(B39 – Gemälde NO. II / Compositie NO. XV / Compositie 4)
Oil on canvas, 61.5 x 76.5 cm
Stedelijk Museum, Amsterdam

Inscriptions
Front: signed bottom left in black paint: MONDRiAN.

Back: in the centre of the right half of the canvas a stamp of Blanchet, 38 rue Bonaparte, Paris; on the left half of the canvas, along the top, in thinly painted black paint [for one of the exhibitions in Germany]: nom: P. [partly painted out in whitish-grey paint to bring uniformity to the references to the exhibition at Kunsthandel Walrecht] MONDRiAN. [augmented with blue paint using a broad brush, in preparation for the exhibition at Kunsthandel Walrecht]/titre: [scored out with black paint using a narrow brush, to bring uniformity to the references to the exhibition at Kunsthandel Walrecht]/ Gemälde N:II. [also scored out with black paint using a narrow brush, and partially painted out with grey-white paint]; on the right half of the canvas, along the top, in black paint, using a broad brush: Compositie 4 [scored out with black paint using a broad brush] and beneath this: P. Mondriaan. On the top stretcher bar, a partially torn off sticker with a handwritten inscription in black ink: nom: P. Mondrian. Along the bottom of the sticker, in printer's ink, the inscription in block letters: J.H. Gos[schalk]. Next to this, in blue paint applied with a broad brush: COMPOSITION N:XV. [the title at the Kunsthandel Walrecht exhibition, crossed out in black paint using a broad brush].

Stretcher
The canvas has a white ground and was probably factory pre-primed. The ground is thin and fairly regular; the canvas structure has not been filled so the tips of the threads are still clearly visible. The canvas has a plain weave, with an average of 22 threads horizontally and 23 vertically. (Top right, 13 cm from the top edge and 13 cm from the right edge: 21h/23v; 13 cm from the bottom edge and 13 cm from the right edge: 21h/24v. Bottom left: 13 cm from the left edge and 13 cm from the bottom edge: 23h/23v; 13 cm from the left edge and 13 cm from the top edge: 22h/23v; 30 cm from the top edge and 38 cm from the left edge: 22h/23v. As such, the average number of horizontal threads per cm is 21.8, with a min/max range of 21 to 23 threads/cm. The average number of vertical threads per cm is 23.2, with a min/max range of 23 to 24 threads/cm.) No traces of a palette knife or other tool are visible. The ground covers the canvas up to and including the tacking edges (ill. 75). On the back, cusping can be seen along the left and right edges. The canvas was irregularly trimmed close to the back of the frame (ill. 76). Tack holes are visible along the edges of the canvas from an earlier stretching iteration. This suggests that the canvas was removed and re-stretched at least once. The frame is original and still completely intact. It does not appear to have been enlarged or reduced along either side. The frame, however, is firmly keyed out, particularly in a vertical direction. This has deformed the rectangular shape of the canvas as a result of which the top right corner and, to a lesser extent, the bottom left corner, are no longer at right angles. The painted edges on the front suggest that the deformation occurred before the final layer of paint was applied to the canvas.

Framing
Traces of bronze paint can be seen along the edges of the canvas on the front, except on the left edge (ill. 77). This suggests that the painting originally had a frame painted in a bronze colour with a rebated edge protruding over the edge of the picture plane. The current frame was mounted after thorough research at the Stedelijk Museum around 1980.

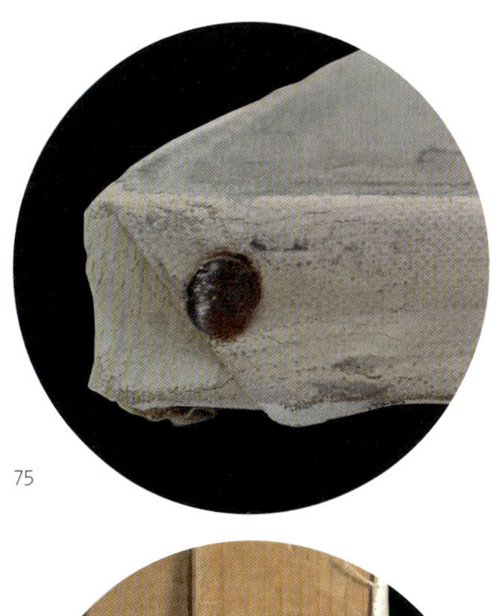
75

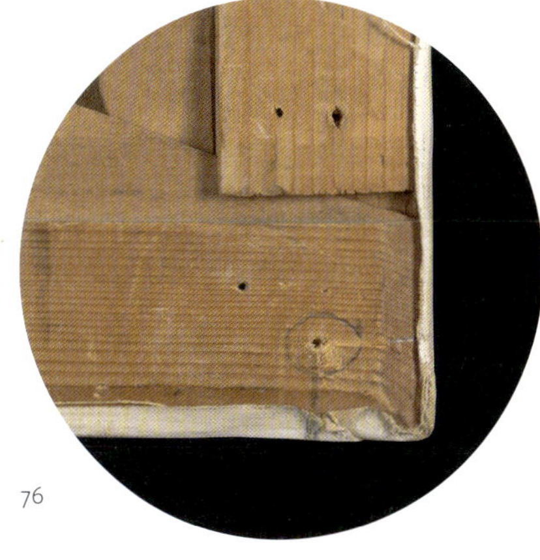
76

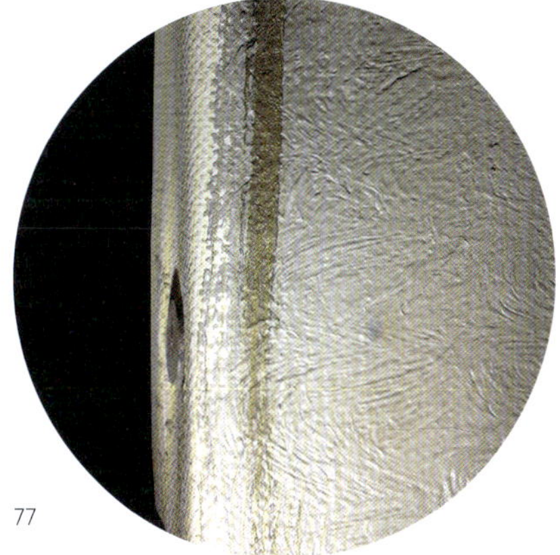
77

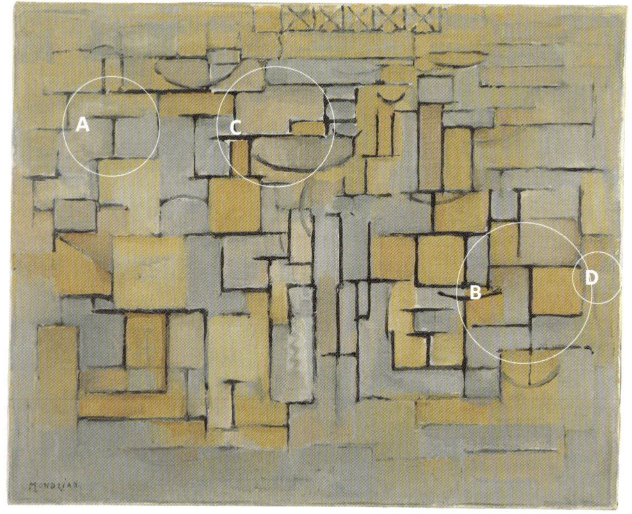

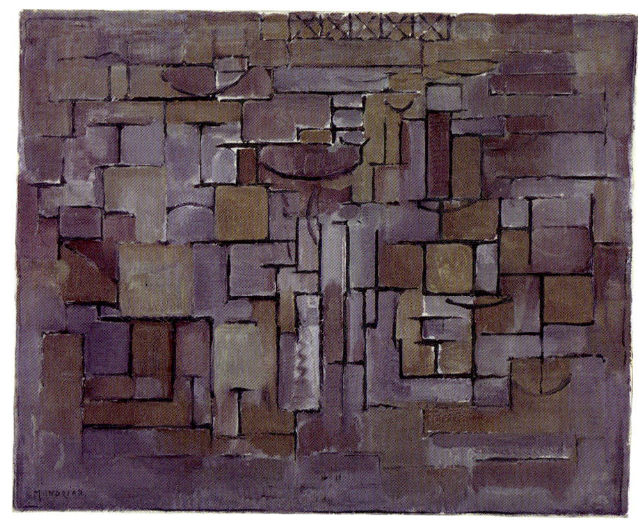

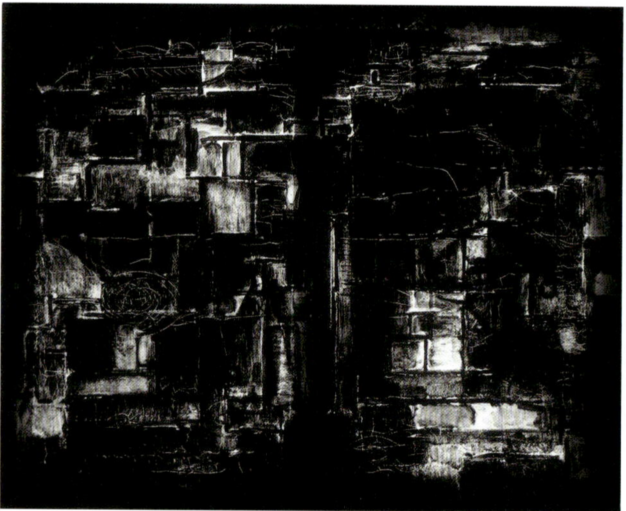

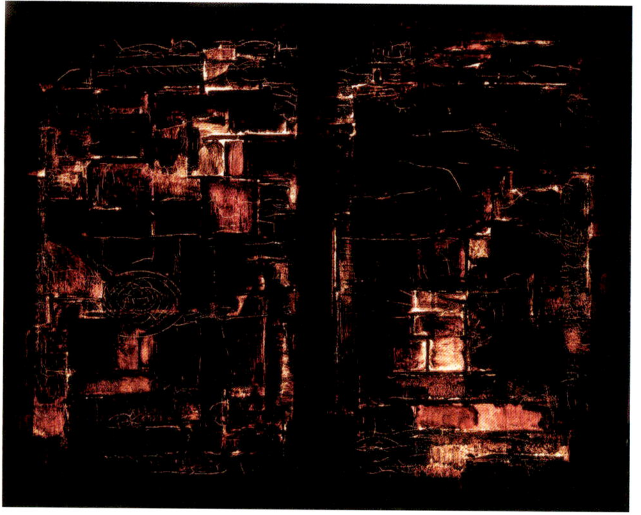

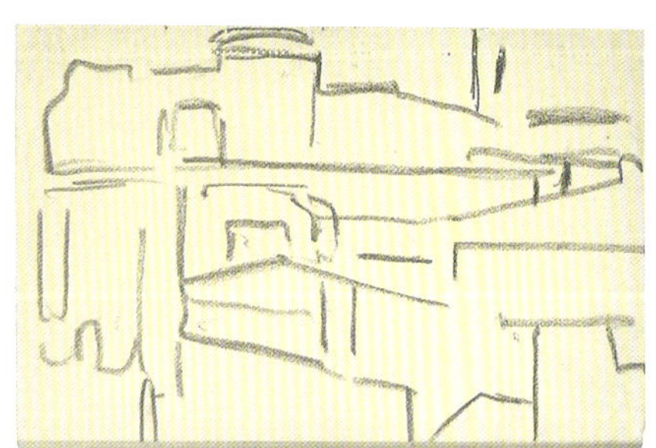

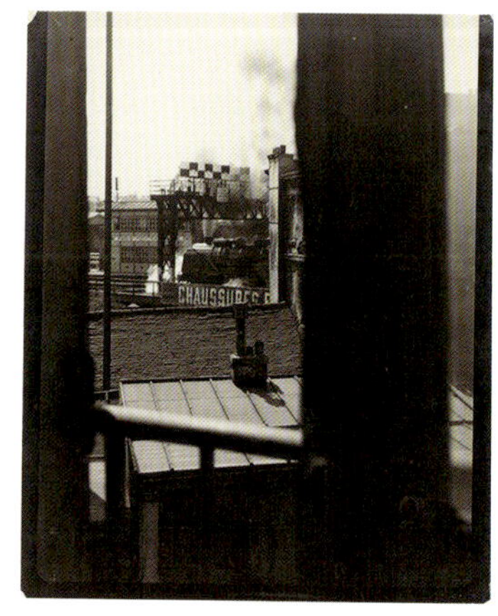

78 Normal light photograph with indications of details

79 Ultraviolet photograph

80 Transmitted infrared photograph

81 Transmitted light photograph

82 *Paris Roofs, Paris* (Sketchbook II, sketch 14), early 1914
Pencil on paper, 17.2 x 10.5 cm
Solomon R. Guggenheim Museum, New York
Gift of David Finn and Maurice Kaplan

83 László Moholy-Nagy
Gare Montparnasse from Mondrian's studio, 1926
Gelatine silver print, 30 x 24.1 cm
Gemeentemuseum Den Haag, The Hague

Date

This piece was created after Mondrian bought the canvas at Blanchet, probably in spring 1913. He completed the painting by the end of the summer.

Provenance

The painting was purchased after October 1915 by PM Broekmans of Amsterdam, who offered it for sale at an auction at A. Mak in Amsterdam, where it was bought by JH Gosschalk. The Stedelijk Museum, Amsterdam purchased the painting in 1949.

Painted surface

The painting is in landscape orientation. This was the first time since September 1912 that Mondrian had chosen this format. The majority of paintings he was working on were in portrait orientation, for compositions based on trees. All these compositions display a vertical densification of the line structure in the centre of the image, echoing the trunk of the tree. This is also true of *Composition* NO. XV. In addition, grey blocks and triangles fan out to the top left and right of the canvas, which could be seen as an echo or regression of a heavily elaborated organic motif like the crown of a tree. However, Mondrian builds up the composition almost entirely in horizontal and vertical lines that form squares, some with black contours. Some of the horizontal lines are truncated, balancing on vertical fragments of line that continue to function as contours (ill. 78.A). Curved sections of line have been incorporated here and there, interrupting the structure and creating space in the composition. No diagonal lines can be seen, with the exception of a large plane on the left edge that is transected almost diagonally.

The transmitted infrared image shows that the picture is laced throughout with a material containing carbon (ill. 80). The transmitted light photograph shows that the layers of paint were not very thick in the end (ill. 81). Although ochre and grey dominate, the grey is often mixed to a cool blue and the ochre to almost orange, or not quite yellow. The contrasts between grey and ochre are sharpest in the centre; towards the edges the contours fade and the grey and yellow blend together or are juxtaposed within the same plane (ill. 78.B). Along the bottom this results in largely grey fields, while ochre dominates along the top. The alternation of grey and ochre planes evokes a sense of front and back, with the two colours alternately functioning as front and back. The mixing of dark and light colours has created intermediate shades in places, which can be seen as shadows (ill. 78.C).

The genesis of the painting can be traced quite well using a combination of photographs taken in transmitted light and transmitted infrared, and x-ray images. It seems that Mondrian applied an initial composition using a thin brush. This composition featured line fragments inclined to the left and the right, possibly allusions to rooflines - like those in his sketchbooks of the period (ill. 82) - that Mondrian could see from his back window, with its view over the chaotic structures along the yard of Gare Montparnasse. A photograph taken by László Moholy-Nagy in 1926 shows the view with the signal gantry under which trains would pass as they left the station (ill. 83). The gantry returns in the final composition along the top edge of the painting, in the small planes linked with crosses. The initial reference to the rooflines was soon incorporated into the general pattern as the diagonal of a rectangle. It looks like Mondrian then filled the vacant fields with grey or bright ochre. In certain spots it is possible to see how thinly these planes have been applied, or perhaps he removed some paint using solvent (ill. 78.D). A process of harmonisation then began, in which the initially thinly applied lines were painted out, or else augmented, and planes were linked, truncated or expanded, and colours were also mixed. The tendency to keep the composition open persisted only in the top half (just above the 'little dish'), and halfway down on the right (ill. 79). The rest of the composition is very dense, with lots of closed layers and planes. Colour fields occasionally lie adjacent to one another without any dividing lines.

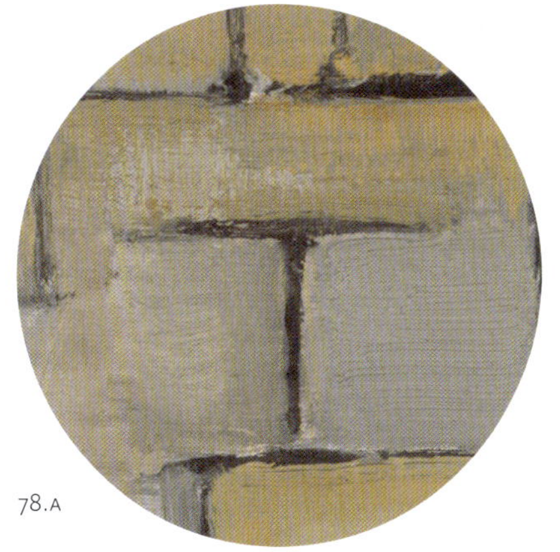

78.A

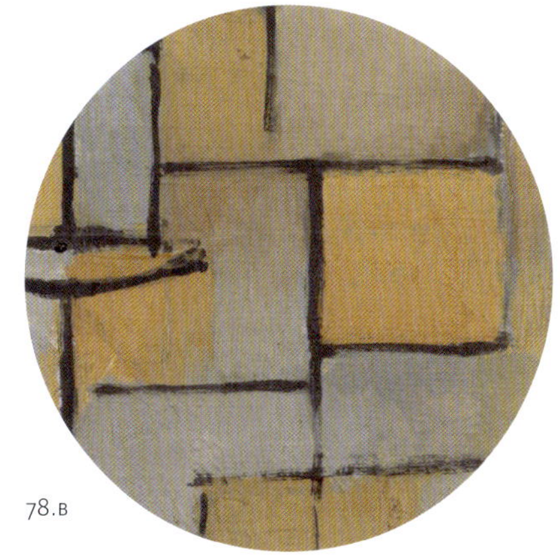

78.B

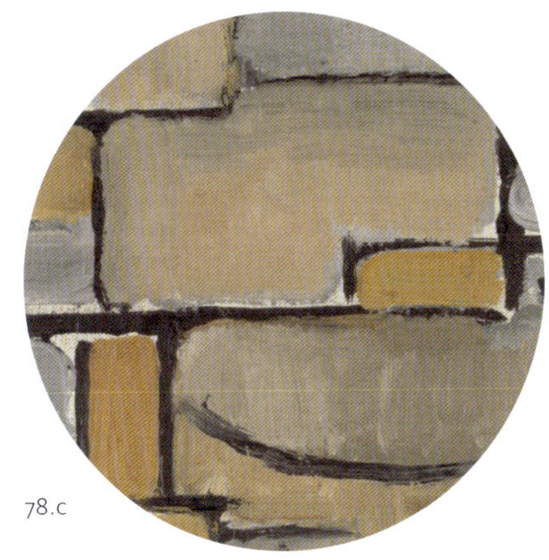

78.C

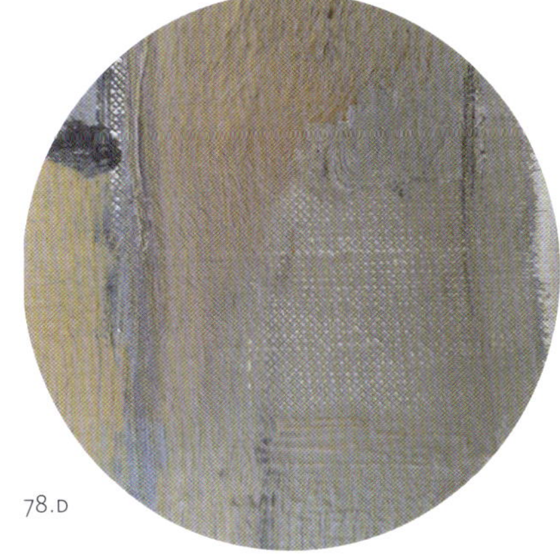

78.D

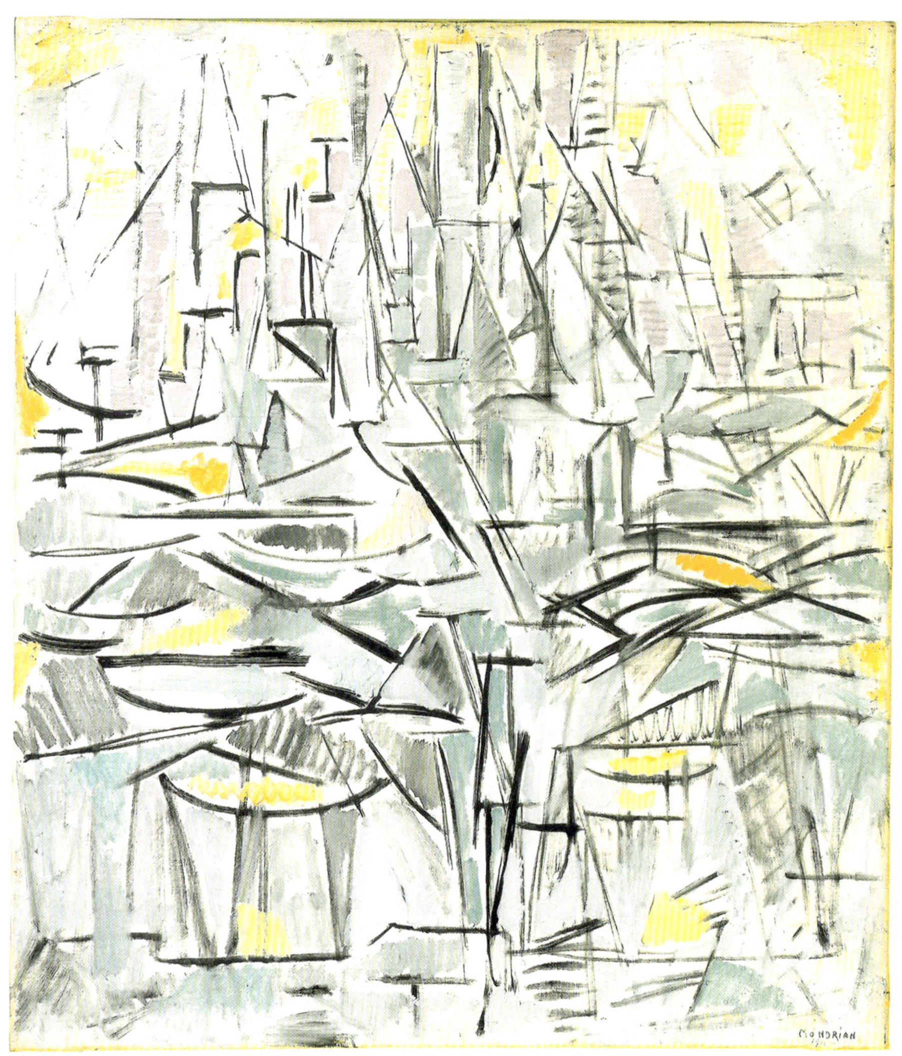

Composition NO. XVI 1912–13
(B26 – Compositie NO. XVI / Compositie 1)
Oil on canvas, 85.8 x 75 cm
Fondation Beyeler, Riehen/Basel

Since this painting was not subjected to technical analysis, the information presented here is based mainly on that supplied by Joop M Joosten and Robert P Welsh, *Piet Mondrian: Catalogue Raisonné of the Work of 1911–1944*, vol.2, Prestel, Munich, 1998; as well as the other sources quoted.

Inscriptions

Front: signed bottom right in black paint: MONDRiAN

Back: on the canvas, in thinly painted black paint: Compositie I/P. Mondriaan; on the upper bar of the stretcher, in blue paint with a broad brush: COMPOSiTION N:XVI

Relevant marks made by others

Beneath the signature, in pencil, someone has written: 1911 – this was probably HP Bremmer in preparation for the Kunsthandel Walrecht exhibition in 1914. Joosten suggests that the date might have been applied in reference to the catalogue of the Kröller-Müller collection published by Bremmer in 1921, in which *Composition No. XVI* is listed with the date 1911. Like *Composition No. X* and *Composition No. XII*, *Composition No. XVI* also has a date written in pencil just beneath the signature on the front. This suggestion is based on a letter to Joosten from 20 September 1973, in which Floris Bremmer gives an account of sales of Mondrian's paintings brokered by his father.

Framing

We may assume that Mondrian framed this painting when it was shown at Kunsthandel Walrecht in 1914. Since no traces of bronze paint have been found along the edges of the painted surface, we can assume that it had an unpainted, bare wooden frame, such as the frame in the photograph of this painting at the *Cubism and Abstract Art* exhibition at the Museum of Modern Art, New York in 1936.

Date

As with *Composition No. X* (see p.118), the inscription '1911' on the front, probably applied by Bremmer, may be the result of Mondrian's report to Bremmer of the difficulty he had had in arriving at his 'own way of expressing' himself from late autumn 1911.

Provenance

The painting was acquired by Helene Kröller-Müller in 1917. Her family sold it after 1945. Gallery owner and collector Ernst Beyeler bought the work in 1975 for the Fondation Beyeler, Riehen/Basel.

Painted surface

The paint has been exceptionally thinly applied, with the white ground visible in many places between the lines and the colour patches. In the 1921 catalogue of the Kröller-Müller collection, Bremmer describes the composition as 'lines partially radiating from the centre and partially horizontal and vertical, with patches of violet, grey, green and yellow'. The line armature is painted thinly in black paint and distributed over the surface in such a way that along the bottom there is no direction, only isolated, fairly disordered, taut fragments of line and curved lines. Upwards of this the taut line fragments appear to be directed – as if by magnetism – towards a single point in the centre of the upper edge of the painting. On the dividing line between the two areas, taut horizontal lines can be seen to the left and right, like a horizon. The lines that Bremmer describes as 'partially horizontal and vertical' appear to lie one level lower because they are partly obscured by the lines and colour planes at the surface, and also because they are painted very thinly, with a very fine brush. This produces a sensation of layering and of searching for the elimination of opposites. The planes between the fragments of lines are filled with light grey, dark grey, blue-green and yellow paint. These are in fact more like superficial colour references than carefully applied planes of colour. This appears as slightly jittery and ephemeral. Only occasionally is the colour applied to cover a line fragment. In addition, black lines have been positioned over the colour fields in some places. Joosten is convinced that *Composition No. XVI* is based on the painting *Flowering Apple Tree* of 1912 (ill. 47; p.112). But a more obvious starting point might be the radiant Divisionist painting *Apple Tree, Pointillist Version* (1908–09) in the collection of the Dallas Museum of Art. In *Apple Tree, Pointillist Version*, the same apparently magnetic effect is seen in the top of the tree. In the spring of 1912 Mondrian gave this work as a gift to Adriaan van de Vijsel, who had written a horoscope for him. This would mean that the initial design for the painting must have been set up early in 1912 and that *Composition No. XVI* could have been completed before the summer of 1912.

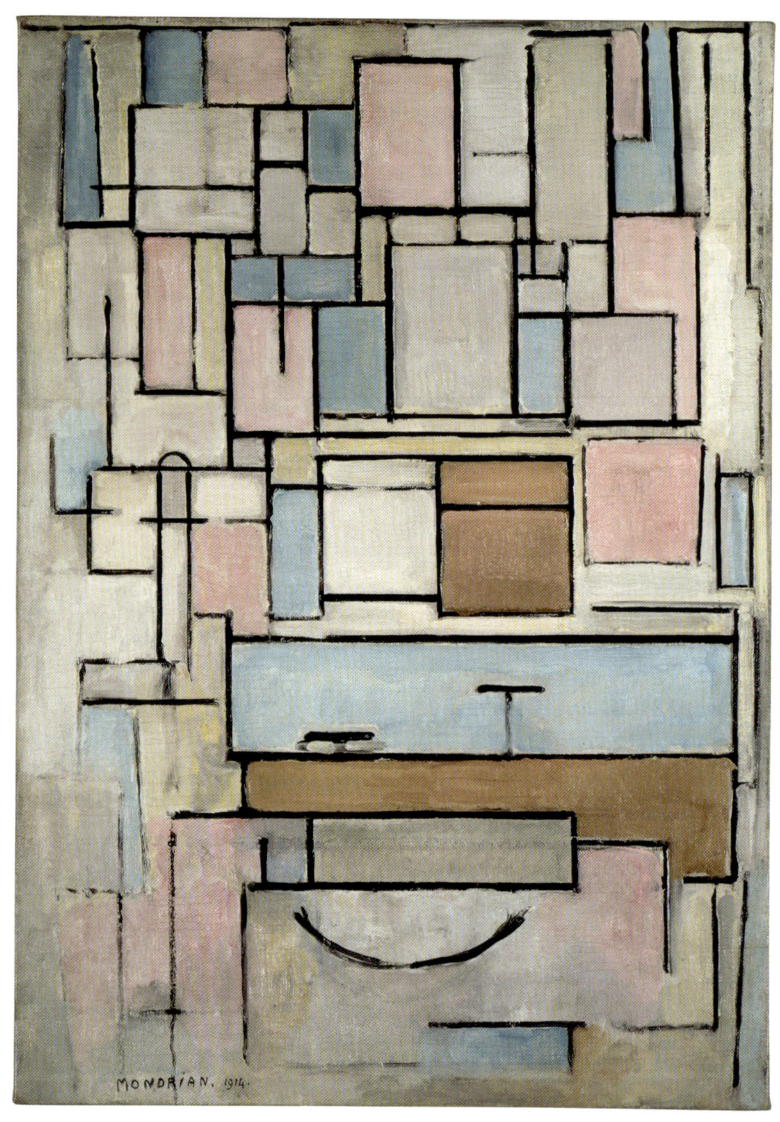

Composition with Colour Planes: Facade 1914
(B51)
Oil on canvas, 91.7 x 65.2 cm
Kunsthaus, Zurich

Since this painting was not subjected to technical analysis, the information presented here is based mainly on that supplied by Joop M Joosten and Robert P Welsh, *Piet Mondrian: Catalogue Raisonné of the Work of 1911–1944*, vol.2, Prestel, Munich, 1998; as well as the other sources quoted.

Inscriptions

Front: signed bottom left in black paint: MONDRiAN

Back: there are no inscriptions by Mondrian.

Stretcher

The canvas has a white ground of unknown composition and was probably factory pre-primed, although the ground does appear to be thin and irregular in places; the canvas structure has not been filled, so the tips of the threads are clearly visible. Here and there the upper parts of the weave has worn away down to the fibres (ill. 85.A; p. 145). It could be that Mondrian applied an extra layer of ground himself, which he then scoured smooth. Under a microscope the traces of scouring can be seen to continue beneath the paint layers, which suggests that the scouring occurred before painting. The canvas is of plain-weave linen, with an average of 20 threads horizontally and 20 threads vertically (measured on the front in places where the ground is visible). (Top left: 20 cm from the left edge and 19 cm from the top: 21h/20v; halfway down the left side 40 cm from the top and 14 cm from the left edge: 20h/20v. Top right: 11.5 cm from the right edge and 34.5 cm from the top: 19h/20v. Bottom right: 0.5 cm from the right edge and 28.5 cm from the bottom: 21h/21v; 6.5 cm from the left edge and 36.5 cm from the bottom: 19h/20v. This gives an average number of weft threads per cm of 20, with a min/max range of 19 to 21 threads/cm. Average number of warp threads per cm is 20, with a min/max range of 20 to 21 threads/cm.) There are no traces of a palette knife or other tool. The ground extends over the tacking edges. The painting has been wax-resin lined. The original canvas shows no tears or holes. It was probably lined to improve the surface adhesion of the paint. The canvas has been trimmed in a highly irregular manner close to the back of the stretcher.

Older tack holes can be seen along the edges of the canvas from an earlier stretching. This suggests that the canvas has been removed from the stretcher and re-stretched at least once. The stretcher was probably replaced when the painting was lined. The outer bars of the current stretcher are c.6.9 cm wide and 2.5 cm thick (with a bevelled edge, so the tacking edge actually measures 2 cm). This is almost 2 cm wider than the stretcher on other paintings from the group exhibited at Kunsthandel Walrecht, some of which came from paint and canvas supplier Blanchet.

Framing

Traces of bronze paint can be seen in the middle of the tacking edge. This suggests that the painting originally had a receding bronze-coloured frame (ill. 87; p. 145). The current strip frame is painted white. The vertical strips are longer than the horizontal strips, which are butt-jointed.

Date

The painting was probably completed after Mondrian sent his work to The Hague on 24 or 25 May 1914. A dating in June or early July 1914 would therefore seem likely.

Provenance

The painting remained unsold at Kunsthandel Walrecht, Mondrian having probably added it to the exhibition after his arrival in the Netherlands on 25 July. In late September 1914 it was bought by Griettie Smith-Van Stolk of Rotterdam, a student of HP Bremmer's. After the Second World War the painting appeared on the American market via the Sidney Janis Gallery in New York. It was purchased in 1969 by Ernst Beyeler of Basel who then sold it to the Sammlung Steegmann, which gave it on permanent loan to the Staatsgalerie Stuttgart in 1998.

1914 Composition with Colour Planes: Facade

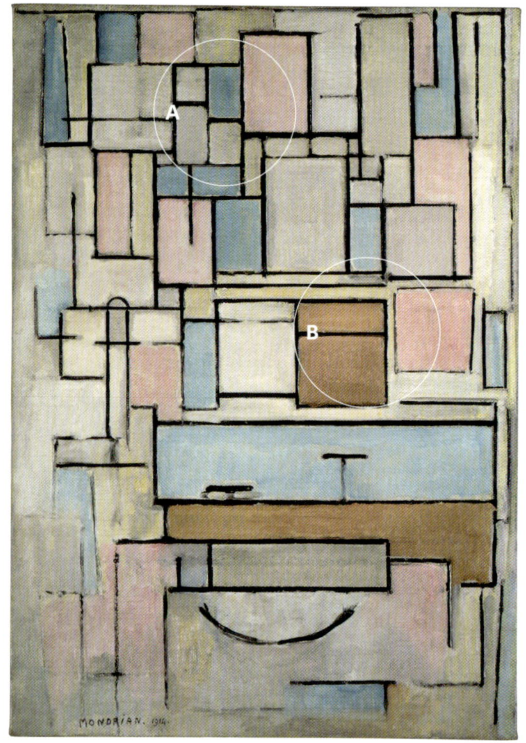

84 Normal light photograph with indications of details

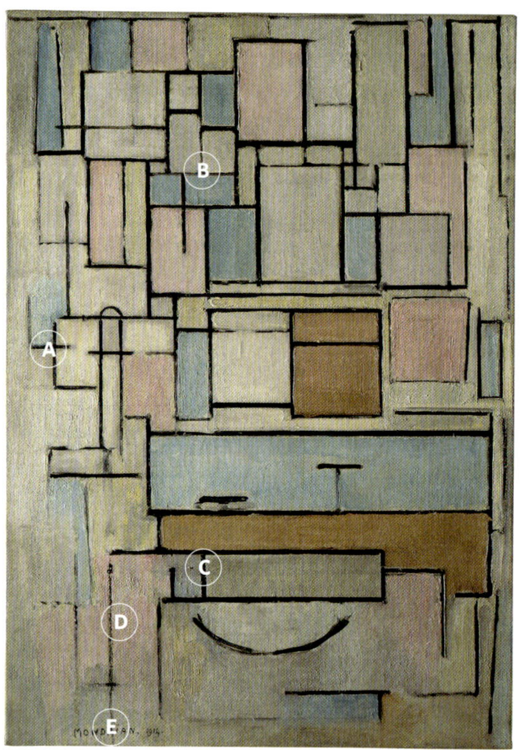

85 Raking light photograph with indications of details

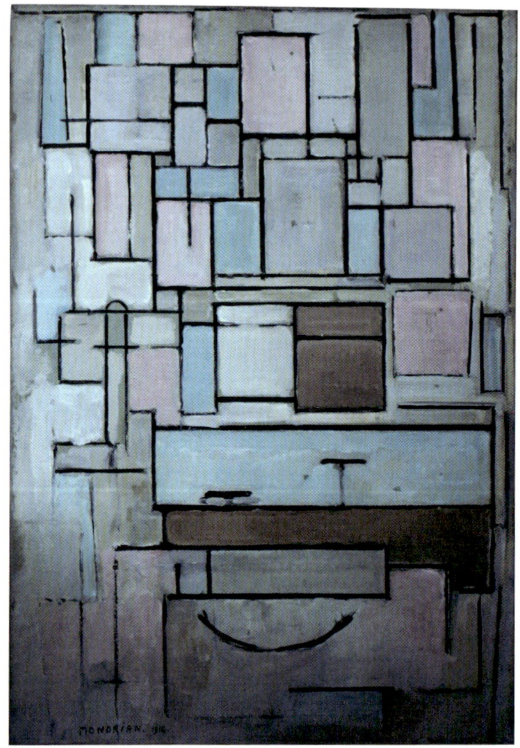

86 Ultraviolet photograph

Painted surface

No traces of an underdrawing are visible, though there are indications that an initial composition was applied using a thin brush and thin paint, sometimes barely touching the canvas. Mondrian tried out many things, as a result of which some higher parts of the weave show many traces of black (ill. 85.B). The eventual lines were partly applied with fluid black paint. Prior to this the planes were filled with white, light grey, pink, bright blue, yellow and light ochre. The brushstrokes are visible in the colour and it would appear that a brush c.1.2 cm wide was used. In some places black lines have been painted over the colour, some unexpectedly sharp – in a manner similar to the craftsmanship Mondrian showed after 1920 – using a brush that cannot have been any wider than 4 mm (ill. 84.A). After that, the colour of several planes was changed: from off-white to blue, from grey to white, from yellow to pink, from pink to yellow, from grey to blue, often working wet-on-wet. This obscured some black lines, generally horizontal ones in the bottom half of the picture and vertical ones in the top half (ill. 85.C). Some black lines were also hastily covered with a bit of white, grey or yellow, or narrowed by covering them partially using the colour of the adjacent fields (ill. 86). The paint used in these final layers is very cracked, partly because the underlying layers had not properly hardened when the new layer was applied, and partly because Mondrian may have used a drying oil as a siccative, as he was known to do in his later years (ill. 84.B). Here, again, the black paint of the lines has beaded in places, and has even run into the white and over the signature (ills 85.D, 85.E). This suggests that the ground was very oily when the line was drawn. The colour planes are applied casually in some places and do not extend to the edges of the planes. At the bottom of the painting the tone is darker and the colours are more diffuse and less sharply delineated. At the top the colours are much brighter and sharply distinguished. Mondrian must have regarded the painting as a 'sketch', like *Composition NO. VI*. The signature was written in the white paint when it was still wet (ill. 85.E).

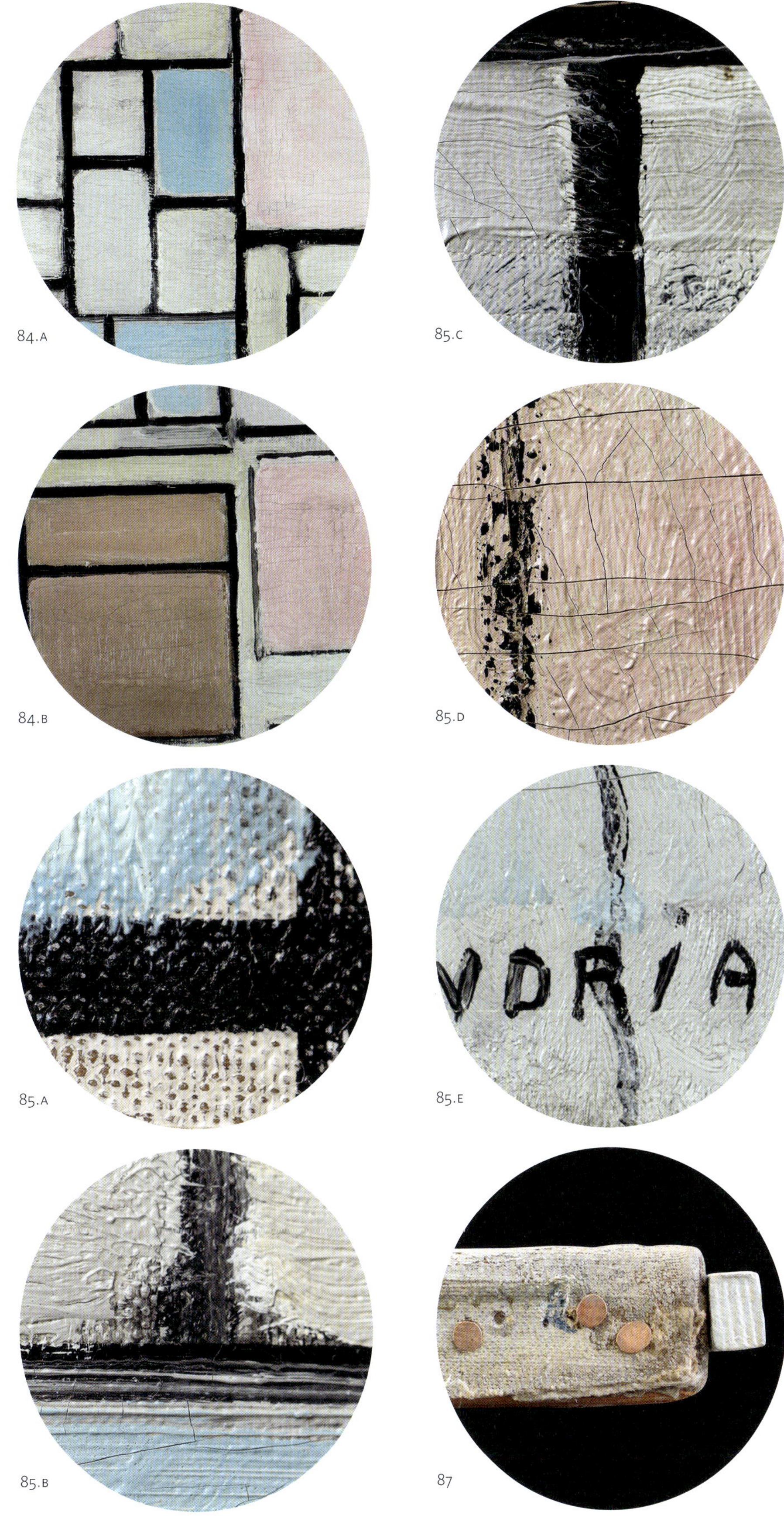

84.A

85.C

84.B

85.D

85.A

85.E

85.B

87

Endnotes

Chronolgy 1911-1914

1 Postcard Piet Mondrian sent from Paris to Simon Maris in Amsterdam on 19 May 1911. Simon Maris archive, RKD (Netherlands Institute for Art History), The Hague.

2 Kickert changed his name from Kikkert - barely recognisable, let alone pronouncable, to the French - in around 1910.

3 Peter Brooke, 'Chronologie de sa Vie, 1881-1953', in Christian Briend, Peter Brooke, et al., *Le Cubisme en Majesté. Albert Gleizes*, Musée des Beaux-Arts, Lyon, 2001, p.23.

4 Anon. [GH Marius], *Nieuws van den Dag*, first section, 2 May 1911, p.2.

5 James Johnson Sweeney, 'Piet Mondrian', Joop M Joosten archive, RKD (Netherlands Institute for Art History), The Hague, p.3.

6 John Richardson, *A Life of Picasso, Volume II, 1907-1917: The Painter of Modern Life*, Jonathan Cape, London, 1996, p.213.

7 David Cottington, *Cubism in the Shadow of War: The Avant-Garde and Politics in Paris 1905-1914*, Yale University Press, New Haven and London, 1998, p.45.

8 Anon., 'Rond den Moderne Kunst Kring I', *De Tijd*, section 2, 7 October 1911.

9 *De Stijl*, vol.1, no.11, September 1918, pp.127-31.

10 Dee Reynolds, *Symbolist Aesthetics and Early Abstract Art: Sites of Imaginary Space*, Cambridge University Press, Cambridge, 2005, passim.

11 Gino Severini, *The Life of a Painter: The Autobiography of Gino Severini*, Jennifer Franchina (trans), Princeton University Press, Princeton, NJ, 1995, p.58.

12 Guillaume Apollinaire, *Chroniques d'art (1902-1918)*, Gallimard, Paris, 1960, p.200.

13 Anon. [GH Marius], 'Wetenschap en kunst. Het Neo-Impressionisme en de Ultra-Moderne Tentoonstelling', *Nieuws van den Dag*, section 3, 5 October 1911, p.10.

14 Undated letter in the archive of the Kröller-Müller Museum, Otterlo. The name of Aletta de Jongh has previously been spelled 'Iongh' because in her handwriting the 'J' appears as an 'I'. In Dutch newspapers of the time, however, the violinist is advertised and reviewed as 'Jongh' and therefore this spelling has been favoured. See for example 'Letteren en Kunst', in the *Middelburgsche Courant* from 3 September 1910.

15 Mondrian gives a precise account of the work he took with him in a letter of 21 July 1919 to Salomon Slijper. Salomon Slijper archive, RKD (Netherlands Institute for Art History), The Hague.

16 See p.38, November-February 1912-13: B25, B26, B27 and B28.

17 Christoph Charle, *Naissance des 'intellectuels' 1880-1900*, Éditions de Minuit, Paris 1990, passim.

18 Anon., 'De Moderne Kunst Kring', *De Telegraaf*, evening edition, section 2, 6 November 1911.

19 Jan van Adrichem, *De ontvangst van de moderne kunst in Nederland 1910-2000. Picasso als pars pro toto*, Prometheus, Amsterdam, 2001, pp.54-55.

20 Reported to Carel Blotkamp by N van der Schoot, published in Carel Blotkamp, *Mondrian: The Art of Destruction*, Reaktion, London, 1994, p.59; p.243, fn.62. It is not known whether the Société Théosophique had a headquarters in the French capital in 1912.

21 Cottington, *op.cit.*, pp.42-43.

22 The last surviving letter from Mondrian to Aletta de Jongh, written from 33 avenue du Maine, Paris. The letter is not dated, but must have been written before the end of January 1912. Archive of the Kröller-Müller Museum, Otterlo.

23 James Johnson Sweeney, 'Piet Mondrian', *The Museum of Modern Art Bulletin*, vol.12, no.4, spring 1945, p.3.

24 Ardengo Soffici, '36 lettere inedite di G. Apollinaire', *Rete Mediterranea*, September 1920, p. 230.

25 Joan Ungersma Halperin, *Félix Fénéon, Aesthete & Anarchist in Fin-de-Siècle Paris*, Yale University Press, New Haven and London, 1988, pp.359-61.

26 Richardson, *op.cit.*, p.301.

27 NH Wolf, 'Moderne Kunstkring', *De Kunst*, vol.5, 12 October 1912.

28 Jacqueline de Raad, *Jan Sluijters: Schilder met verve*, Singer Museum, Laren/Zwolle, 1999, p.89.

29 B5, B6 and B7.

30 Louis Vauxcelles, 'Au Salon des Indépendants', *Gil Blas*, vol.34, no.12817, 13 March 1913, p.2.

31 André Salmon, 'Le Salon des Indépendants', *Paris-Journal*, 19-20 March 1912: '[Mondrian] fait du cubisme à l'aveuglette, dans l'ignorance complète de la loi des volumes, et son inspiration vient de Van Dongen'.

32 A.v.V., 'Kunst. Kunstzaal Meylink. Jan Sluijters', *Algemeen Handelsblad*, morning edition, section 1, 24 April 1912.

33 A672, A695, A705 and A710 as opposed to B11, B14, B15, B16.

34 This is B18.

35 P.v.d.M.d.W. [Pieter van der Meer de Walcheren], 'Buitenland. Uit Parijs II', *De Tijd*, third section, 28 December 1912.

36 Aleid Loosjes-Terpstra, *Moderne Kunst in Nederland 1900-1914*, Haentjens Dekker & Gumbert, Utrecht, 1959 (1988), p.200.

37 Robert P Welsh and Joop M Joosten, *Two Mondrian Sketchbooks: 1912-1914*, Meulenhoff, Amsterdam, 1969, p.24.

38 GH Marius, 'Wetenschap en kunst in Kunstzaal Biesing - Den Haag', *Het Nieuws van den Dag*, section 1, 12 January 1912, p.2.

39 Loosjes-Terpstra, *op.cit.*, p.123; p.273, fn.1; p.274, fn.7.

40 Jacqueline van Paaschen-Louwerse, Arend Huussen, *Jacoba van Heemskerck 1876-1923. Schilderes uit roeping*, Waanders, Zwolle, 2005, p.43.

41 Joop M Joosten, 'Documentatie over Mondriaan (1)', *Museumjournaal*, vol.13, no.4, 1968, p.210. Letter from Mondrian to Lodewijk Schelfhout, dated 25 May 1913: 'I think I will go and stay in Domburg for a few weeks this summer, as I did last year'. The other letters to Schelfhout referred to in this section are also taken from this source.

42 Apollinaire, *op.cit.*, p.399. Apollinaire wrote this in an article in the *Soirées de Paris*, 23 June 1914.

43 Richardson, *op.cit.*, p.259.

44 For further arguments in favour of this identification, see Hans Janssen, *Mondriaan in Amsterdam 1892-1912*, Thoth, Bussum, 2013, p.118.

45 Jan van Deene, 'Rechtvaardiging', *Centraal Museum Utrecht Mededelingen*, vol.16/17, 1977, p.79.

46 Joosten, 'Documentatie over Mondriaan (1)', *op. cit.*, p.210. Letter from Mondrian to Lodewijk Schelfhout, dated 7 June 1914: 'So you understand that I have nothing to do with Kikkert and he is not paying for my studio. I do however still owe him 100 francs because he no longer wanted any work from me.' See also Lucien Gard, *Conrad Kickert: Le peintre hollandais de Montparnasse*, A et L Gard, Marsat-Riom, 2006, p.47. Gard reports that Lodewijk Schelfhout 'lodged' with Kickert; in other words 'lodged at Kickert's expense', from autumn 1911 at least, first at 33 avenue du Maine and then at 26 rue du Départ. The same was true of Rudolf Lévy. Gard, p.59, suggests that Schelfhout 'borrowed' the studio at 26 rue du Départ from Conrad Kickert, and that he received 100 francs a month to live on in exchange for one painting a year, and the first copy of any drypoint etching he made. It therefore appears very likely that Kickert provided accommodation for all his artist friends. See also p.38, November 1912.

47 Loosjes-Terpstra, *op.cit.*, p.157. Loosjes-Terpstra was the first to point out that in 1912 Mondrian's views were still an extension of those of the Impressionists.

48 Sweeney, *op.cit.*, p. 4.

49 *De Telegraaf*, morning edition, section 2, 22 May 1912.

50 *Ibid.*

51 Joosten, 'Documentatie over Mondriaan (1)', *op. cit.*, p.210. In a letter from Mondrian to Lodewijk Schelfhout, dated 12 June 1914, Mondrian says that he is referring to the situation two years earlier, the summer of 1912.

52 This might be B25, B28, B31, B35, B38 and B42.

53 Joop M Joosten, 'Documentatie over Mondriaan (4)', *Museumjournaal*, vol.18, no.4, 1973, p.178. Letter from Mondrian to Van Assendelft dated 29 September 1914 that Mondrian ends by saying 'I have not yet heard anything from our Bles', suggesting that Van Assendelft and Bles knew each other well. The other letters to Van Assendelft referred to in this chapter are also taken from this source.

54 For this characterisation of Bles, see: Joosten, 'Documentatie over Mondriaan (4)', *op.cit.*, p.174; and Christie's Book Sale, London, 2 June 1999, no.178, which included a postcard from Piet Mondrian to Dop Bles of 21 June 1912 and three letters from Gino Severini to Dop Bles written in 1913 on Movimenta Futurista writing paper. Bles gave a lecture on 'Theatre and its Future' in 1916, in which he aired his ideas, see: *De Telegraaf* and *Algemeen Dagblad* of 8 February 1916, and the report in the *Nieuwe Rotterdamsche Courant* of 25 March 1916. Bles was often seen at cultural events in the cities he visited, including Paris, Rotterdam and The Hague.

55 Vosmaer, 'Brieven uit Amsterdam', *Het Nieuws van den Dag voor Nederlandsch-Indië*, no.132, 8 June 1912.

56 Jan van Deene, 'Rechtvaardiging', *Centraal Museum Utrecht Mededelingen*, no.10–17, March 1977, p.79.

57 This could be B4.

58 Judith Cousins, 'Documentary Chronology', in William Rubin, *Picasso and Braque: Pioneering Cubism*, Museum of Modern Art, New York, NY, 1989, p.398.

59 J Kalff, 'Kunst. Kunst in Nijmegen', *Algemeen Handelsblad*, evening edition, section 2, 31 July 1912.

60 Elina Taselaar, *Jacob Bendien 1890–1933*, Fries Museum and Centraal Museum, Leeuwarden and Utrecht, 1985, p.15.

61 Joop M Joosten, 'Documentary Chronicle', *Piet Mondrian: Catalogue Raisonné of the Work of 1911–1944*, Prestel, Munich, 1998, p.101.

62 Anon., 'Kunst in Den Haag. De Futuristen bij Biesing', *Algemeen Handelsblad*, evening edition, section 2, 7 August 1912.

63 The exhibition ran from 28 July to 19 August 1912.

64 This painting, B23, known until now as *Tree Composition 1*, has always been regarded as incomplete. It is, however, a finished composition in two stages: one initial stage in thinner black paint, and a second reworked stage in thicker black paint. The initial version was signed, not because Mondrian did not wish to take the painting further, but because he liked the initial result of the sketch. He decided to submit this version to the Moderne Kunst Kring in October, evidenced by the fact that his signature, MONDRIAN, can also be found on the other work he submitted to Amsterdam. No. 162 is included in the catalogue under the title *Trees, Sketch*.

65 U5=B17 and U6=B16. Van Paaschen-Louwerse, *op.cit.*, pp.47–49.

66 On 25 August Mondrian writes to Conrad Kickert that Bine de Sitter 'has bought that tree of mine: after much reflection she decided she would rather have it than the sea – which argues in favour of the sea – n'est ce pas? For only a little money she could have had a good thing.' This means that *Seascape*, was already complete then. The tree that De Sitter bought was a drawing made in 1911 (B3).

67 Two of the three paintings have new stretchers so no information can be derived about how and when they were transported. B16 has a sticker like B19 with the inscription '*paysage*' and the designation M III. This might suggest that the painting was part of a group comprising (at least) three pieces.

68 Welsh and Joosten, *op.cit.*, p. 61.

69 Cousins, *op.cit.*, p.404.

70 Anon., 'Kunst. Domburg', *Algemeen Handelsblad*, evening edition, section 2, 20 July 1912, pp.6–7.

71 NH Wolf, 'Naar Domburg! Kunsttentoonstelling', *De Kunst*, 16 August 1912.

72 These are B18, B19, B20 and B21.

73 Letter from Mondrian to Conrad Kickert marked 'Sunday' and with a postmark for Monday 26 August 1912. The picture he refers to is B18.

74 Letter from Piet Mondrian to Mies Elout Drabbe, dated 20 September 1912, RKD (Netherlands Institute for Art History), The Hague.

75 Guillaume Apollinaire, 'Demain a lieu le vernissage du salon d'automne', *L'Intransigeant-Journal de Paris*, 30 September 1912.

76 Cottington, *op.cit.*, p.13.

77 Anon., 'Kunstnieuws. De Futuristen-Tentoonstelling in Den Haag', *Rotterdamsch Nieuwsblad*, 26 August 1912, p.2. The writer was probably Henri Dekking, who was the paper's art reporter and reviewer at the time.

78 *Nieuws van den Dag*, 5 October 1912, p.21, where Mondrian is mentioned as 'P. Mondrian (formerly Piet Mondriaan)'. Dake used this same ironic tone in *De Telegraaf* of 15 October 1912: 'What one is to call Piet Mondriaan, or, as he is now called, Mondrian, no mere mortal knows'.

79 Postcard from Piet Mondrian in Paris to Willem Steenhoff, sent 30 September 1912, on which Mondrian wrote that he could not meet up until Thursday because he would be busy with the selection for the exhibition on Wednesday. See Joop M Joosten, 'Documentary Chronicle', *op.cit.*

80 The works he entered were B18, B21, B19, B20, B17, B16 and B23.

81 Dorothy Kosinski and Katharina Schmidt (eds), *Fernand Léger 1911–1924: Der Rhythmus des modernen Lebens*, Prestel, Munich, 1994, p.66.

82 Carel Dake, 'Beeldende Kunsten. De Moderne Kunst Kring', *De Telegraaf*, evening edition, section 2, 15 October 1912. Given the use of the word 'rhythmic', perhaps Dake spoke to Mondrian directly about the work.

83 Willem Beffie bought B21, Marie Tak van Poortvliet bought B16, and Fritz Meyer-Fierz bought B19. For the sale to Marie Tak van Poortvliet, see Hans Janssen, *Mondriaan in het Gemeentemuseum Den Haag*, Gemeentemuseum Den Haag, The Hague and Zwolle, 2007, p.174. For the sale to Fritz Meyer-Fierz, see Anne Tabak and Hans Janssen, 'Konnte man nicht einmal grosse Franzosen einladen?', Mondrian, Hodler und der Einzug der Moderne in den Niederlanden', in Beat Wismer, *Ferdinand Hodler – Piet Mondrian, Eine Begegnung*, Aargauer Kunsthaus, Aarau, 1998, pp.91–120.

84 Guillaume Apollinaire, 'Art et Curiosité. Les Commencement du cubism', *Le Temps*, no.18730, 14 October 1912, p. 5.

85 Willem Steenhoff, 'De Modern Kunstkring II', *De Amsterdammer*, no.1843, 20 October 1912, p.6.

86 Richardson, *op.cit.*, p.245.

87 Henri Le Fauconnier, 'La sensibilité moderne et le tableau', in Moderne Kunst Kring catalogue, Amsterdam, 1912, pp.17–25, as reproduced in an appendix to Aleid Loosjes-Terpstra, *op.cit.*, pp.327–30.

88 Joosten, 'Documentatie over Mondriaan (1)', *op.cit.*, p.211. Letter from Mondrian to HP Bremmer dated 29 January 1914. Although this letter was written a year later, the articulate and self-assured way in which Mondrian expresses these ideas suggests he had already held them for some time. The other letters to Bremmer quoted are also taken from this source.

89 B24.

90 AvV, 'Kunsthandel Oldenzeel. Het expressionisme. W. Kandinsky. Rotterdam', *Algemeen Handelsblad*, evening edition, second section, 6 November 1912, p.7.

91 *Ibid.*

92 Maaike van Domselaer-Middelkoop, 'Herinneringen aan Piet Mondriaan', *Maatstaf. Maandblad voor Letteren*, vol.7, no.5, August 1959, pp.270–71.

93 Recollections of Toon de Jong of Blaricum, who frequently visited Hamdorff, where Mondrian and Van Domselaer would dance. RKD (Netherlands Institute for Art History), The Hague, Joop M Joosten archive.

94 *Journal officiel de la République française: Débats parlementaires. Chambre des députés*, 3 December 1912, pp.2924–29.

95 Anon., 'Kunst in Den Haag. Naar aanleiding van L. Gestel's werk', *Algemeen Handelsblad*, evening edition, section 2, 25 March 1913.

96 Anon., 'Kunst. Expressionisten', *Algemeen Handelsblad*, evening edition, section 2, 24 December 1912, p.7.

97 Loosjes-Terpstra, *op.cit.*, pp.200–01.

98 B30, B27 and B31 respectively.

99 Letter from Jacoba van Heemskerck to Lodewijk Schelfhout, dated 9 March 1913.

100 Guillaume Apollinaire, 'Au Quai d'Orsay. Le Salon des Indépendants', *L'Intransigeant-Journal de Paris*, 18 March 1913, p.2.

101 Guillaume Apollinaire, 'A travers le Salon des Indépendants', *Montjoie!*, 18 March 1913.

102 Letter from Mondrian to Salomon Slijper, dated 21 July 1919, RKD (Netherlands Institute for Art History), The Hague, Slijper archive.

103 Apollinaire, *Montjoie!*, *op.cit.* From what Apollinaire wrote about Mondrian, it would appear he was very well informed about Mondrian's ideas and intentions. Previous Dutch reviews also suggest that Mondrian kept critics, like Steenhoff, Wolf and Kalff, well informed.

104 Anon., 'Kunst. Subjectieve en objectieve schilderkunst', *Algemeen Handelsblad*, evening edition, second section, 22 April 1913.

105 Piet Mondrian, 'De nieuwe beelding in de schilderkunst. IV Beeldingsmiddel en compositie', *De Stijl*, vol.1, no. 4, February 1918, pp.44.

106 These are B36, B38, B39 and B40.

107 B25–B28.

108 Fernand Léger, 'Les Origines de la Peinture et sa Valeur Répresentative', *Fonctions de la Peinture*, Gonthier, Paris, 1965, pp.11–19.

109 Cottington, *op.cit.*, pp.191–93.

110 Severini, *op.cit.*, p.119; and Joosten, 'Documentatie over Mondriaan (4)', *op.cit.*, p.174.

111 Anon., 'Letteren en kunst. St. Lucas', *Nieuwe Rotterdamsche Courant*, morning edition C, 4 May 1913, p.2.

112 CL Dake, 'Aanteekeningen over beeldende kunst. St. Lucas I', *De Telegraaf*, morning edition, first section, 11 May 1913, p.2.
113 Ester L Wouthuyzen, 'Willem Beffie (1880–1950), onthechte verzamelaar, stille mecenas', in Hubert Schijf and Edward van Voolen (eds), *Gedurfd Verzamelen. Van Chagall tot Mondriaan. Moderne kunst en Joods mecenaat, 1885–1940*, Waanders, Amsterdam, 2010, pp.119–28.
114 Guillaume Apollinaire, 'Première exposition de sculpture futuriste du peintre et sculpteur futuriste Boccioni', *L'Intransigeant-Journal de Paris*, 21 June 1913, in *Chroniques d'art, op.cit.*, pp.333–34.
115 Letter from Mondrian to Lodewijk Schelfhout, dated 25 July 1913.
116 B27, B33, B35 and B37.
117 Van Paaschen-Louwerse, *op.cit.*, p.54.
118 Cottington, *op.cit.*, pp.179–88.
119 Anon., 'Letteren en kunst. De Protector. L. Schelfhout', *Nieuwe Rotterdamsche Courant*, evening edition B, 7 June 1913, p.1.
120 Piet Mondrian, 'The New Plastic in Painting', *De Stijl*, vol.1, no.7, May 1918, pp.73–77.
121 Piet Mondrian, 'The New Plastic in Painting', *De Stijl*, vol.1, no.11, September 1918, pp.130–31.
122 Richardson, *op.cit.*, pp.281–83, 299.
123 Cousins, *op.cit.*, p.420.
124 *Ibid.*, p.421.
125 Cornelis Veth, 'Moderne Kunst Kring', *Elsevier's Geïllustreerd Maandschrift*, vol.23, part 46, July–December 1913.
126 A591 and B410 and 411, eventually resulting in B38 and B39.
127 B30 and B40.
128 Letter from Mondrian to Lodewijk Schelfhout, dated 12 June 1914. The paintings are B36 and B40.
129 This would have been B38 and B39.
130 In, for example, Anon., 'Kunst. De futuristen te Rome. Rome. 22 March', evening edition, section 2, *Algemeen Handelsblad*, 27 March 1913.
131 Edward Venn, 'Rethinking Russolo', *Tempo* 64, no.251, 2010, pp.8–16.
132 Anon., 'Kunst en Wetenschappen. De Domburgsche Tentoonstelling (Slot)', *Middelburgsche Courant*, 6 August 1913.
133 See Van Paaschen-Louwerse, *op.cit.*, p.61.
134 Letter from Mondrian to Lodewijk Schelfhout, dated 7 June 1914.
135 These were thus B21, just back from Munich, B27 and B30, which, like B21, had only been shown previously at the Salon des Indépendants of 1912; B33, B35 and B37, see letter from Conrad Kickert to Jan Toorop, undated, National Library of the Netherlands, The Hague, Jan Toorop archive.
136 B33, B35 and B37. These pieces are numbered in reverse chronological order: B37, the most recent painting, is titled *Tableau No. I* and B21, the oldest, from spring 1912, is titled *Tableau No. VI*.
137 B33 and B37.
138 Giovanni [J. Kalff], 'Moderne Kunst Kring', *Algemeen Handelsblad*, evening edition, section 2, 14 November 1913, p.7.
139 Guillaume Apollinaire, 'Le vernissage du Salon d'Automne', *L'Intransigeant-Journal de Paris*, 29 November 1913.
140 Anon., 'Letteren en Kunst. De Moderne Kunstkring', *Nieuwe Rotterdamsche Courant*, evening edition B, 8 November 1913, p.1.
141 Letter from Mondrian to Lodewijk Schelfhout, dated 7 June 1914.
142 Richardson, *op.cit.*, p. 262.
143 HP Bremmer, 'De Nood', *Beeldende Kunst*, vol.1, 1913, pp.9–10.
144 B21, B27, B30 and B35. This last painting goes to Prague, however, along with B38 and B42, a painting that is only just finished and therefore came from Paris. B38 had been returned to Paris with B40.
145 He will then have exhibited B21, B27, B30 and B40 in Berlin, and B35, B38 and B42 in Prague.
146 The rationale behind this reconstruction includes the fact that, though the invitation to exhibit in Zurich came from Jan Verhoeven, a good friend of Mondrian's, it would not benefit him artistically, whereas the Prague exhibition was being organised by a well-known critic. It was more important for Mondrian to 'prove' himself in Prague than in Zurich.
147 Alexandre Mercereau, *Modern Art: 45th Exhibition S.V.U. Manes in Prague*, February–March 1914.
148 Cottington, *op.cit.*, p.195.
149 Loosjes-Terpstra, *op.cit.*, p.120.
150 These are B44 and B45.
151 André Salmon, 'Le Salon', *Montjoie!*, vol.2, no.3, 18 March 1914, p.14; Guillaume Apollinaire, 'Le Salon des Indépendants', *L'Intransigeant-Journal de Paris*, 3 March 1914.
152 Leo Faust, 'Kunst te Parijs II', *De Kunst*, 28 March 1914, p.403.
153 Richardson, *op.cit.*, p. 287.
154 HP Bremmer, 'Beeldende kunst', *Beeldende Kunst*, vol.1, no. 4, 1914, pp.47–48.
155 Letter from Mondrian to HP Bremmer, dated 21 March 1914.
156 B46, B47 and B50.
157 Michael C FitzGerald, *Making Modernism: Picasso and the Creation of the Market for Twentieth-Century Art*, FSG, New York, 1995, pp.15–46.
158 Cottington, *op.cit.*, p.195.
159 Letter from Mondrian to HP Bremmer, dated 8 April 1914.
160 B42, B44.
161 Letter from Mondrian to HP Bremmer, dated 5 May 1914.
162 Georges Roque drew my attention to this very important lecture in terms of the development of Mondrian's use of colour, in his lecture 'Chromatisme et achromatisme' at the Centre Pompidou in Paris in 2011.
163 Letter to the editors of *Algemeen Dagblad* from Erich Wichman, published in the 18 May 1914 issue, section 2, p.7.
164 Letter from Mondrian to Lodewijk Schelfhout, dated 25 May 1913.
165 Letter from Mondrian to Lodewijk Schelfhout, dated 7 June 1914.
166 Letter from Mondrian to Reverend Hendrik van Assendelft, dated 28 August 1914.
167 Cousins, *op.cit.*, p.426.
168 Rudi Oxenaar, *Bart van der Leck tot 1920: Een primitief van de nieuwe tijd*, Dissertation, Library of the Gemeentemuseum, The Hague, p.76.
169 Letter from Mondrian to Lodewijk Schelfhout, dated 7 June 1914.
170 In a matter of a few weeks he most certainly completely reworked B45, B44 and B38, and possibly B47.
171 B46, B42 and B35.
172 B47?, B40 and B50.
173 Letter from Jacoba van Heemskerck to Herwarth Walden, dated 1 June 1914, in Van Paaschen-Louwerse, *op.cit.*, p. 70.

Finding Balance in Art and Music

1 Maaike van Domselaer-Middelkoop, 'Herinneringen aan Piet Mondriaan', *Maatstaf. Maandblad voor letteren*, vol.7, no.5, August 1959, pp.269–93.
2 Anon., 'Jakob van Domselaer', *Algemeen Handelsblad*, evening edition, section 2, 19 April 1916.

The Exhibition at Kunsthandel Wahlrecht, The Hague

1 Joop M Joosten and Robert P Welsh, *Piet Mondrian: Catalogue Raisonné of the Work of 1911–1914*, vol.2, Prestel, Munich, 1998, p.29.
2 Harry Verburg, 'Piet Mondriaan. Beschouwingen bij een belangrijk bruikleen', *Mededelingen van de Dienst voor Schone Kunsten* 7, 1952, no. 1–2, pp.22-25; pp.64–67; p.74.
3 See WHK van Dam, 'Een onbekende brief van Piet Mondriaan', *Oud Holland*, vol.104, no.3–4, 1990, pp.341–43.
4 Unnumbered letter from Piet Mondrian to Theo van Doesburg, undated (but after 20 November 1915), Van Doesburg Archive, RKD (Netherlands Institute for Art History), The Hague.
5 Leo Faust, 'Kunst te Parijs II', *De Kunst*, 28 March 1914.
6 Letter from Mondrian to HP Bremmer, 5 May 1914, Bremmer Archive, Municipal Archive of The Hague.
7 Joop M Joosten, 'Documentatie over Mondriaan (1)', *op.cit.*, p.210. Letter from Mondrian to Lodewijk Schelfhout, dated 7 June 1914.
8 Carl Holty, 'Mondrian in New York: A Memoir', *Arts*, vol.31, no.10, September 1957, pp.17–21.
9 NH Wolf, 'Modernen', *De Kunst*, vol.8, no.403, October 1916, p.30.
10 Wilmon-Vervaert, 'Exposition Internationale du Cercle de l'Art Moderne, Musée Municipal, Amsterdam, Nov-Dec, 1913', *De Kunst*, vol.6, no. 302, 8 November 1913, p.86.
11 Michael White, 'Dreaming in the Abstract: Mondrian psychoanalysis and abstract art in the Netherlands', *Burlington Magazine*, vol.148, no.1235, February 2006, pp.98–106.
12 Loosjes-Terpstra, *op.cit.*, p.160.
13 NH Wolf, 'Rotterdamsche Kunstkring: Petrus Alma, Le Fauconnier, Piet Mondriaan', *De Kunst*, vol.7, 1914-15, no.369, 20 February 1915, pp.251–52.

Image credits

Collection RKD – Netherlands Institute for Art History: pp.4, 17 (left), 21 (right), 24 (left), 28 (middle)

© Succession, Picasso/DACS, London 2015: pp.12 (left), 16 (right), 21 (left), 22, 28 (right), 33 (right), 37 (right), 38 (middle), 41 (middle), 48 (right), 56 (right)

© Estate of Henri Le Fauconnier: pp.12 (middle), 19, 29 (right), 37 (middle), 45 (left)

© ADAGP, Paris and DACS, London 2015: pp.13 (left), 14, 16 (middle), 23, 26, 33 (left), 35, 44 (middle), 50 (right), 51 (left; right), 57 (middle)

Photo © RMN-Grand Palais (Musée Picasso de Paris)/Franck Raux: p.13 (right)

Bibliothèque nationale de France: pp.16 (left), 20 (left; right), 25 (left), 29 (left), 41 (right), 43, 44 (left)

Photo © RMN-Grand Palais (Musée Picasso de Paris)/Droits réservés: pp.16 (right), 38 (middle), 48 (right), 59 (middle)

Photo © RMN-Grand Palais (Musée Picasso de Paris)/Michèle Bellot: p.21 (left)

© 2015 Museo Thyssen-Bornemisza/Scala, Florence: p.22

Courtesy Mme. Camille Bondy, Paris: p.24 (right)

© Estate of Chris Lanooy: p.42

© Nationaal Archief/Collection Spaarnestad: pp.45 (middle), 59 (right)

© DACS 2015: pp.47, 49 (right), 52 (left), 58 (right)

Foundation Dina Vierny – Musée Maillol, Paris: p.51 (middle)

Gemeentearchief, Den Haag: pp.54–55, 56 (left; middle)

© Estate of Emil Filla: p.58 (left)

© Archives Laurens, Paris: p.59 (left)

Collections

Folkwang Museum, Essen
Fondation Beyeler, Riehen/Basel
Gemeentemuseum Den Haag, The Hague
Kimbell Art Museum, Fort Worth
Kröller-Müller Museum, Otterlo
Kunsthaus, Zurich
Museum of Modern Art, New York
Museo Thyssen-Bornemisza, Madrid
Solomon R. Guggenheim Museum, New York
Stedelijk Museum, Amsterdam
Stedlijk Van Abbemuseum, Eindhoven

Great care has been taken to identify all image copyright holders correctly. In cases of errors or omissions please contact the publishers so that we can make corrections in future editions.

Expanded English edition published in 2016 by
Ridinghouse and Gemeentemuseum Den Haag

First published in Dutch by Uitgeverij THOTH Bussum and Gemeentemuseum Den Haag on the occasion of *Mondrian en het kubisme, Parijs 1912–1914*
25 January – 11 May 2014

Gemeentemuseum Den Haag
Stadhouderslaan 41
2517 HV Den Haag
The Netherlands
gemeentemuseum.nl

Director: Benno Tempel
Curator at Large for Modern Art: Hans Janssen

Ridinghouse
46 Lexington Street
London W1F 0LP
United Kingdom
ridinghouse.co.uk

Publisher: Doro Globus
Publishing Manager: Louisa Green
Publishing Associate: Daniel Griffiths
Publishing Assistant: Jay Drinkall

Distributed in the UK and Europe only:
Cornerhouse Publications
c/o Home
2 Tony Wilson Place
Manchester M15 4FN
United Kingdom
cornerhousepublications.org

Images courtesy Gemeentemuseum Den Haag unless noted on p.150

Edited by Hans Janssen
Project-managed by Diana Perry Schnelle
Picture research by Sophie Kullmann
Proofread by Eileen Daly
Designed by Typography Interiority & Other Serious Matters, The Hague
Set in Whitney (Tobias Frere-Jones)
Printed in Belgium by Die Keure

ISBN 978 1 909932 14 2

British Library Cataloguing-in-Publication Data:
A full catalogue record of this book is available from the British Library

Cover
Piet Mondrian
Composition NO. VIII (detail), 1913
(B27 – Tableau NO. 4 / Compositie NO. VIII / Compositie 3)
Oil on canvas, 95 x 80 cm
Gemeentemuseum Den Haag, The Hague